healthy cooking

Taste of Home

annual recipes

Taste of Home
RDA ENTHUSIAST BRANDS, LLC • MILWAUKEE, WI

healthy Taste of Home cooking annual recipes

19

23

136

1610 N. 2ND ST., SUITE 102, MILWAUKEE WI 53212-3906

INTERNATIONAL STANDARD BOOK NUMBER: 978-1-61765-642-2

INTERNATIONAL STANDARD SERIAL NUMBER: 1944-7736

COMPONENT NUMBER: 117900046H

PRINTED IN U.S.A.
1 3 5 7 9 10 8 6 4 2

PICTURED ON FRONT COVER: Fantastic Fish Tacos (p. 182).
PICTURED ON TITLE PAGE: Cheesy Spinach-Stuffed Shells (p. 187).
PICTURED ON BACK COVER: Garlic Spaghetti Squash with Meat Sauce (p. 102), Bacon & Swiss Chicken Sandwiches (p. 112), Reese's Chocolate Snack Cake (p. 218) and Fresh Corn & Potato Chowder (p. 34).

Contents

Eat great and feel great the whole year through with 390+ amazing heart-smart dishes. Discover the comforting soups, slow cooker classics and fiery grilled specialties that are just pages away. You'll also find savory dinner breads, eye-opening breakfasts and showstopping sweets. Make it your best year yet!

220

For Good Health, Challenge Yourself to Cut Added Sugar

With *Healthy Cooking Annual Recipes*, it's easy to make smart choices!

I'm a firm believer that all foods can fit into a healthy diet—including sweets. But over the last several decades, we have been eating more and more sugar in foods other than dessert.

Sugar is added to processed foods in so many forms it almost becomes unidentifiable as sugar:

- Sucrose
- Maltose
- Malt Syrup
- Honey
- Corn syrup
- Molasses
- Fructose
- Dextrose
- Raw sugar
- High-fructose corn syrup
- Juice concentrates
- Invert sugar

These added sugars have little to no redeeming nutritional value. They are different from sugars that exist naturally in fruits, milk, vegetables and some grains. Those aren't the sugars to be concerned about; it's the ones that are added to our foods that can increase blood pressure, bad cholesterol and the risk of obesity, diabetes and heart disease.

Added sugar is common in cereals, snacks, sauces, mixes and dressings. Breakfast meals are particularly challenging, because of traditionally sweet choices like pancakes, waffles and cereal.

Find new, sugar-free ways to start the day—such as **CALICO SCRAMBLED EGGS (P. 68).** It's an easy, nutrition-packed alternative to a sugary breakfast, but just as fast to make.

This year, challenge yourself to find new recipes with less or no sugar. Read food labels on packaged foods to spot added sugar in the ingredient list, then compare brands to find the best choice. And most of all, make more foods from scratch, using home cooks' favorite dishes and test kitchen-approved recipes like those in *Healthy Cooking Annual Recipes,* of course!

Happy Cooking,

Peggy

Peggy Woodward, RDN
Food Editor

About Our Nutrition Facts

The *Healthy Cooking Annual Recipes* cookbook provides a variety of recipes that fit into a healthy lifestyle.

- Whenever a choice of ingredients is given (such as ½ cup sour cream or plain yogurt), the first ingredient is used in our calculations.
- When a range is given for an ingredient, we calculate using the first amount.
- Only the amount of a marinade absorbed is calculated.
- Optional ingredients are not included in our calculations.

NEW! We've added total sugars to our Nutrition Facts: 294 cal., 12g fat (2g sat. fat), 64mg chol., 218mg sodium, 20g carb. (13g sugars, 3g fiber), 24g pro.
Note: This represents added sugars plus naturally occurring sugars, like what you see in the Nutrition Facts label on packaged foods.

SPECIAL INDICATORS

To help those on restricted diets easily find dishes to suit their needs, we clearly mark recipes that are especially low in fat, sodium or carbohydrates, as well as those that contain no meat. You will find these icons, plus quick-to-fix recipes and healthy insights throughout the book:

HEALTH TIP New this year, Peggy shares her best secrets to help you make healthy eating choices.

F One serving contains 3 grams fat or less.

S One serving contains 140 milligrams sodium or less.

C One serving contains 15 grams carbohydrates or less.

M Recipe contains no gelatin, Worcestershire or other meat products.

FAST FIX Dish is table-ready in 30 minutes or less.

Favorite Dishes with Little or No Added Sugar

Bottled and even homemade salad dressings usually have added sugar, but ***Deborah Loop's*** **ITALIAN SALAD WITH LEMON VINAIGRETTE** skips it altogether. The dressing is easy to make and versatile enough to complement a wide range of salads. **P. 51**

For your next potluck, swap sugary-sweet baked beans for **SIMPLE VEGETARIAN SLOW-COOKED BEANS** from Maine home cook ***Jennifer Reid.*** The slow cooker means easy prep, and the fresh flavors will make this dish a new party favorite. **P. 92**

Milwaukee's ***Melissa Hansen*** uses the natural sweetness of raspberries and ripe bananas in **RASPBERRY-BANANA SOFT SERVE.** Her recipe uses less than 1 teaspoon of maple syrup per serving, compared to the 4-6 teaspoons of sugar you'd find in traditional ice cream. **P. 234**

Drink Smart

The USDA recommends limiting added sugar to no more than 10% of calories. For a 2,000-calorie diet, that's about 12 teaspoons. The American Heart Association suggests even less—about 9 teaspoons a day for men and 6 for women.

Sweetened drinks are a major source of added sugar.	Teaspoons of added sugar*
12 oz. cola	10
8 oz. lemonade	8
8.4 oz. energy drink	7
12 oz. chai latte	6
12 oz. sports drink	5
12 oz. sweet tea	5
12 oz. cafe mocha	4.5
8 oz. fruit punch drink	4
8 oz. chocolate milk	3.5
20 oz. vitamin-infused water	3

**4g sugar is equivalent to 1 teaspoon granulated sugar*

Smart sugar-free, calorie-free choices:

- Plain water
- Sparkling water
- Fruit-infused water
- Unsweetened tea
- Unsweetened coffee

Perk up regular water with citrus fruit, herbs or even cucumber. This makes the flavor more interesting without unwanted calories or added sugar.

10

14

18

Starters & Snacks

"We moved into a house with a garden that needed tending. Using the herbs we found, we made these freshtastic wraps for our first dinner there."

—CHRIS BUGHER ASHEVILLE, NC
about her recipe, Fresh from the Garden Wraps, on page 19

CHEESY SNACK MIX M

Our love for Mexican food inspired me to add taco seasoning to my party mix. The flavor is mild enough to make it kid-friendly.

—**ELIZABETH WYNNE** AZTEC, NM

PREP: 10 MIN. • **COOK:** 5 MIN. + COOLING
MAKES: 2½ QUARTS

- **3 cups Corn Chex**
- **3 cups Rice Chex**
- **3 cups cheddar miniature pretzels**
- **¼ cup butter, melted**
- **1 envelope cheesy taco seasoning**
- **2 cups white cheddar popcorn**

1. In a large microwave-safe bowl, combine cereal and pretzels. In a small bowl, mix melted butter and taco seasoning; drizzle over cereal mixture and toss to coat.

2. Microwave, uncovered, on high for 3-3½ minutes or until heated through, stirring once every minute. Stir in popcorn. Transfer to a baking sheet to cool completely. Store in an airtight container.

NOTE *This recipe was tested in a 1,100-watt microwave.*

PER SERVING *¾ cup: 151 cal., 5g fat (3g sat. fat), 11mg chol., 362mg sodium, 23g carb. (2g sugars, 1g fiber), 3g pro.* ***Diabetic Exchanges:*** *1½ starch, 1 fat.*

CHEESY SNACK MIX

MANGO AVOCADO SPRING ROLLS

MANGO AVOCADO SPRING ROLLS S M

As a lover of both mangoes and avocados, I really like the flavor combo in these wraps. The fresh taste reminds me of spring. If rice paper wraps are hard to find, you can use tortillas. And if I don't have sprouts, I sub lettuce or spinach.

—**GENA STOUT** RAVENDEN, AR

PREP: 40 MIN. • **MAKES:** 8 SPRING ROLLS

- **4 ounces reduced-fat cream cheese**
- **2 tablespoons lime juice**
- **1 teaspoon Sriracha Asian hot chili sauce or ½ teaspoon hot pepper sauce**
- **1 medium sweet red pepper, finely chopped**
- **⅔ cup cubed avocado**
- **3 green onions, thinly sliced**
- **⅓ cup chopped fresh cilantro**
- **8 round rice paper wrappers (8 inches)**
- **1 medium mango, peeled and thinly sliced**
- **2 cups alfalfa sprouts**

1. Mix cream cheese, lime juice and chili sauce; gently stir in pepper, avocado, green onions and cilantro.

2. Fill a large shallow dish partway with water. Dip a rice paper wrapper into water just until pliable, about 45 seconds (do not soften completely). Allow excess water to drip off.

3. Place wrapper on a flat surface. Place cream cheese mixture, mango and sprouts across bottom third of wrapper. Fold in both ends of wrapper; fold bottom side over filling, then roll up tightly. Place on a serving plate, seam side down. Repeat with remaining ingredients. Serve immediately.

PER SERVING *1 spring roll: 117 cal., 5g fat (2g sat. fat), 10mg chol., 86mg sodium, 16g carb. (6g sugars, 2g fiber), 3g pro.* ***Diabetic Exchanges:*** *1 starch, 1 fat.*

TOP TIP

Ripe mangoes have green-yellow skin with a pronounced red blush; unripened ones are firm and green with just a hint of red. To ripen a mango, let it stand at room temperature and out of the sunlight. Then refrigerate the ripened mango until ready to use.

RAISIN & HUMMUS PITA WEDGES F M FAST FIX

The best part about this easy appetizer is you can make your own hummus, or if you don't have time, you can purchase some at the store. It's a year-round food that everyone enjoys.

—**HELENE STEWART-RAINVILLE**
SACKETS HARBOR, NY

START TO FINISH: 15 MIN.
MAKES: 8 SERVINGS

- **¼ cup golden raisins**
- **1 tablespoon chopped dates**
- **½ cup boiling water**
- **2 whole wheat pita breads (6 inches)**
- **⅔ cup hummus**
- **Snipped fresh dill or dill weed, optional**

1. Place raisins and dates in a small bowl. Cover with boiling water; let stand for 5 minutes. Drain well.
2. Cut each pita into four wedges. Spread with hummus; top with raisins, dates and, if desired, dill.

PER SERVING *1 wedge: 91 cal., 2g fat (0 sat. fat), 0 chol., 156mg sodium, 16g carb. (4g sugars, 3g fiber), 3g pro.* ***Diabetic Exchanges:*** *1 starch.*

PEANUT BUTTER & BANANA CHOCOLATE RICE CAKES S M FAST FIX

Here's a healthy snack that's easy to make and take on the go. It's tasty any time of year.

—**CONSTADINA VASILIADES** KAPOLEI, HI

START TO FINISH: 10 MIN.
MAKES: 2 SERVINGS

- **2 tablespoons peanut butter**
- **2 chocolate rice cakes**
- **1 medium banana, cut into slices**
- **1 teaspoon honey**
- **⅛ teaspoon ground cinnamon**

Spread peanut butter over rice cakes; top with banana. Drizzle with honey and sprinkle with cinnamon.

PER SERVING *220 cal., 9g fat (2g sat. fat), 0 chol., 110mg sodium, 32g carb. (16g sugars, 3g fiber), 6g pro.* ***Diabetic Exchanges:*** *1½ fat, 1 starch, 1 fruit.*

PICKLED SHRIMP WITH BASIL F S C

PREP: 15 MIN. + MARINATING
MAKES: 20 SERVINGS (½ CUP EACH)

- **½ cup red wine vinegar**
- **½ cup olive oil**
- **2 teaspoons seafood seasoning**
- **2 teaspoons stone-ground mustard**
- **1 garlic clove, minced**
- **2 pounds peeled and deveined cooked shrimp (31-40 per pound)**
- **1 medium lemon, thinly sliced**
- **1 medium lime, thinly sliced**
- **½ medium red onion, thinly sliced**
- **¼ cup thinly sliced fresh basil**
- **2 tablespoons capers, drained**
- **¼ cup minced fresh basil**
- **½ teaspoon kosher salt**
- **¼ teaspoon coarsely ground pepper**

1. In a large bowl, whisk the first five ingredients. Add shrimp, lemon, lime, onion, sliced basil and capers; toss gently to coat. Refrigerate, covered, up to 8 hours, stirring occasionally.
2. Just before serving, stir minced basil, salt and pepper into shrimp mixture. Serve with a slotted spoon.

PER SERVING *½ cup: 64 cal., 2g fat (0 sat. fat), 69mg chol., 111mg sodium, 1g carb. (0 sugars, 0 fiber), 9g pro.* ***Diabetic Exchanges:*** *1 lean meat, ½ fat.*

Red wine vinegar plus the freshness of citrus and basil perk up marinated shrimp with hardly any prep work. Serve over greens if you'd like a salad. —**JAMES SCHEND** PLEASANT PRAIRIE, WI

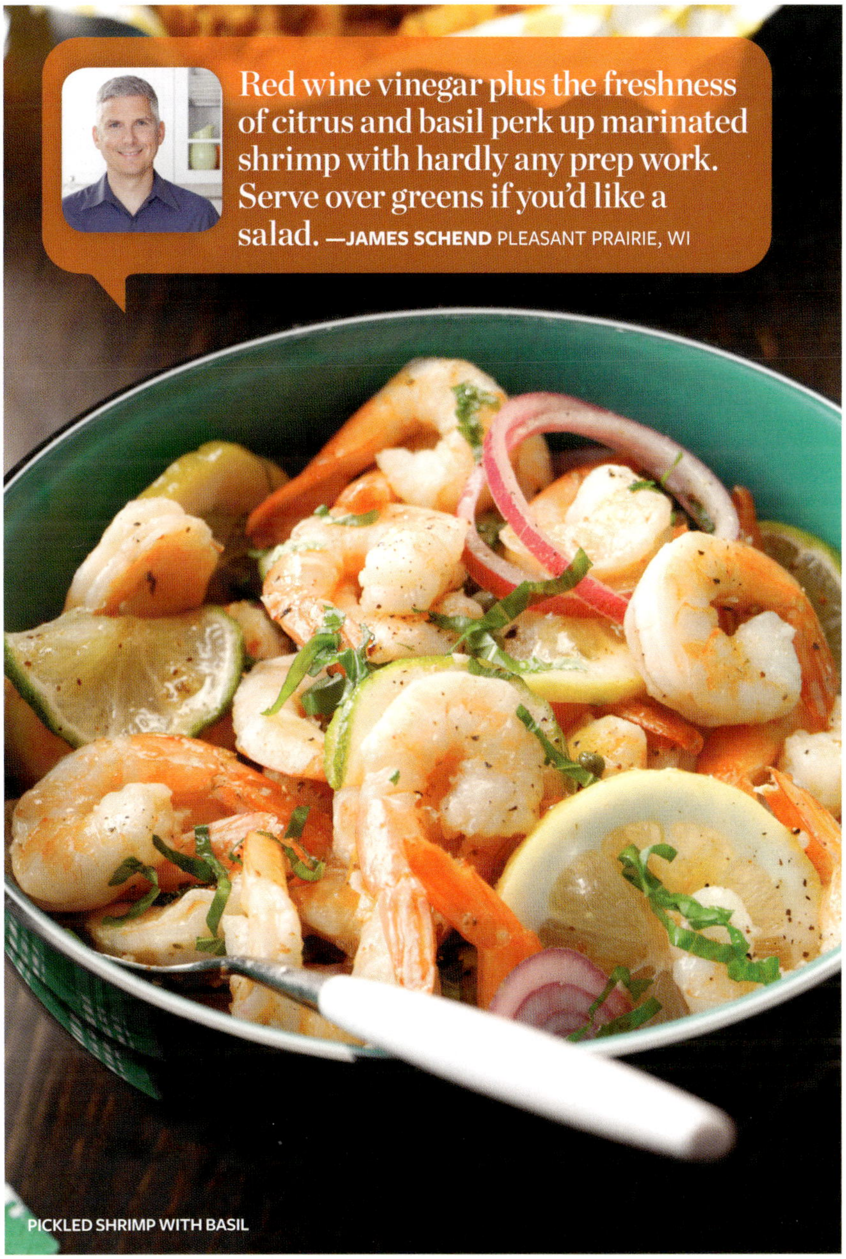

PICKLED SHRIMP WITH BASIL

ROASTED RED PEPPER TAPENADE C M

I turn to this bright recipe often since it takes just 15 minutes to whip up. Sometimes I'll swap out the almonds for walnuts or pecans.

—**DONNA MAGLIARO** DENVILLE, NJ

PREP: 15 MIN. + CHILLING • **MAKES:** 2 CUPS

- **3 garlic cloves, peeled**
- **2 cups roasted sweet red peppers, drained**
- **½ cup blanched almonds**
- **⅓ cup tomato paste**
- **2 tablespoons olive oil**
- **¼ teaspoon salt**
- **¼ teaspoon pepper**
- **Minced fresh basil**
- **Toasted French bread baguette slices or water crackers**

1. In a small saucepan, bring 2 cups water to a boil. Add garlic; cook, uncovered, 6-8 minutes or just until tender. Drain and pat dry. Place red peppers, almonds, tomato paste, oil, garlic, salt and pepper in a small food processor; process until blended. Transfer to a small bowl. Refrigerate at least 4 hours to allow flavors to blend.

2. Sprinkle with basil. Serve with baguette slices.

PER SERVING *2 tablespoons: 58 cal., 4g fat (0 sat. fat), 0 chol., 152mg sodium, 3g carb. (2g sugars, 1g fiber), 1g pro.* ***Diabetic Exchanges:*** *1 fat.*

ROASTED RED PEPPER TAPENADE

THREE-PEPPER GUACAMOLE

THREE-PEPPER GUACAMOLE S C M FAST FIX

START TO FINISH: 25 MIN.
MAKES: 4 CUPS

- **3 tablespoons plus ¼ cup minced fresh cilantro, divided**
- **4 tablespoons finely chopped onion, divided**
- **3 tablespoons minced seeded jalapeno pepper**
- **1 tablespoon minced seeded serrano pepper**
- **2 to 3 teaspoons chopped chipotle pepper in adobo sauce**
- **3 garlic cloves, minced**
- **½ teaspoon salt**
- **4 medium ripe avocados, peeled and cubed**
- **⅓ cup finely chopped tomatoes**
- **Tortilla chips**

In a large bowl, combine 3 tablespoons cilantro, 2 tablespoons onion, peppers, garlic and salt; mash together with a fork. Stir in avocados; fold in tomatoes and remaining cilantro and onion. Serve immediately with chips.

NOTE *Wear disposable gloves when cutting hot peppers; the oils can burn skin. Avoid touching your face.*

PER SERVING *¼ cup: 76 cal., 7g fat (1g sat. fat), 0 chol., 82mg sodium, 4g carb. (0 sugars, 3g fiber), 1g pro.* ***Diabetic Exchanges:*** *1½ fat.*

HEALTH TIP *Avocados are known for their healthy monounsaturated fat, but they are also a good source of vitamins C, K and E plus most B vitamins.*

DIJON-MARINATED COCKTAIL SHRIMP F S C

I like to prepare the shrimp for this recipe a day ahead and store it in an airtight container in the refrigerator. Then all you have to do is serve the dish when you're ready!

—SARAH CONAWAY LYNCHBURG, VA

PREP: 15 MIN. + MARINATING
MAKES: 3½ DOZEN

- **½ cup olive oil**
- **¼ cup tarragon vinegar**
- **¼ cup Dijon mustard**
- **1 teaspoon salt**
- **1 teaspoon crushed red pepper flakes**
- **¼ teaspoon pepper**
- **1½ pounds peeled and deveined cooked shrimp (26-30 per pound)**
- **2 green onions, chopped**
- **¼ cup minced fresh parsley**

1. In a small bowl, whisk together first six ingredients. In a large resealable plastic bag, combine shrimp, green onions, parsley and marinade; seal bag and turn to coat.

2. Refrigerate 2 hours or overnight. To serve, remove shrimp from marinade; discard marinade.

PER SERVING *1 shrimp: 32 cal., 2g fat (0 sat. fat), 25mg chol., 78mg sodium, 0 carb. (0 sugars, 0 fiber), 3g pro.*

RICOTTA SAUSAGE TRIANGLES F S C

Stuffed with cheese, sausage and seasonings, these pockets are hard to put down! They freeze well, so go ahead and make a big batch for future parties.

—VIRGINIA ANTHONY JACKSONVILLE, FL

PREP: 1 HOUR • **BAKE:** 15 MIN./BATCH
MAKES: 12 DOZEN

- **1 carton (15 ounces) part-skim ricotta cheese**
- **1 package (10 ounces) frozen chopped spinach, thawed and squeezed dry**
- **1 jar (8 ounces) roasted sweet red peppers, drained and chopped**
- **⅓ cup grated Parmesan cheese**
- **3 tablespoons chopped ripe olives**
- **1 large egg**
- **1 tablespoon minced fresh basil or 1 teaspoon dried basil**
- **1 teaspoon Italian seasoning**
- **¼ teaspoon salt**
- **¼ teaspoon pepper**
- **1 pound bulk Italian sausage**
- **1 medium onion, chopped**
- **96 sheets phyllo dough (14x9-inch size)**
- **Olive oil-flavored cooking spray**
- **Warm marinara sauce, optional**

1. In a large bowl, combine the first 10 ingredients. In a large skillet, cook sausage and onion over medium heat until meat is no longer pink; drain. Stir into cheese mixture.

2. Place one sheet of phyllo dough on a work surface with a short end facing you; spray with cooking spray. Top with a second sheet of phyllo; spray again with cooking spray. (Keep the remaining phyllo covered with plastic wrap and a damp towel to prevent it from drying out.) Cut layered sheets into three 14x3-in. strips.

3. Place a rounded teaspoonful of filling on lower corner of each strip. Fold dough over filling, forming a triangle. Fold triangle up, then fold triangle over, forming another triangle. Continue folding, like a flag, until you come to the end of the strip.

4. Spritz end of dough with spray and press onto triangle to seal. Turn triangle and spritz top with spray. Repeat with remaining phyllo and filling.

5. Place triangles on baking sheets coated with cooking spray. Bake at 375° for 15-20 minutes or until golden brown. Serve warm with marinara sauce if desired.

FREEZE OPTION *Freeze unbaked triangles in freezer containers, separating layers with waxed paper. To use, bake triangles as directed, increasing time as necessary until golden and heated through.*

PER SERVING *1 appetizer: 42 cal., 2g fat (0 sat. fat), 4mg chol., 64mg sodium, 5g carb. (0 sugars, 0 fiber), 2g pro.* ***Diabetic Exchanges:*** *½ starch.*

RICOTTA SAUSAGE TRIANGLES

TANGY TEXAS SALSA F S C M

I'm a transplant to Texas from Wisconsin, and even after some 20 years, I still can't get enough of our wonderful local citrus. This combination of tangy fruit, spicy jalapeno and distinctive cilantro is perfect with chips. We also serve it over meat, poultry or fish.

—LOIS KILDAHL MCALLEN, TX

PREP: 15 MIN. + CHILLING • **MAKES:** 12 SERVINGS (⅓ CUP EACH)

- **1 medium green pepper, chopped**
- **1 medium sweet red pepper, chopped**
- **1 medium sweet yellow pepper, chopped**
- **1 medium tomato, seeded and chopped**
- **1 jalapeno pepper, seeded and chopped**
- **3 tablespoons chopped red onion**
- **1 tablespoon minced fresh oregano**
- **1½ teaspoons sugar**
- **½ teaspoon salt**
- **1 medium red grapefruit**
- **1 large navel orange**

1. In a large bowl, combine first nine ingredients.
2. Cut a thin slice off top and bottom of grapefruit and orange; stand upright on a cutting board. With a knife, cut off peel and outer membrane of fruit. Cut along the membrane of each segment to remove fruit; add to pepper mixture.
3. Stir gently to combine. Refrigerate, covered, at least 2 hours.

NOTE *Wear disposable gloves when cutting hot peppers; the oils can burn skin. Avoid touching your face.*

PER SERVING *⅓ cup: 28 cal., 0 fat (0 sat. fat), 0 chol., 100mg sodium, 6g carb. (5g sugars, 1g fiber), 1g pro.*

TANGY TEXAS SALSA

GINGER PORK LETTUCE WRAPS

GINGER PORK LETTUCE WRAPS F S C FAST FIX

These snack wraps are so good. The first time we had them we ate so many, we were too full for supper. I've used ground chicken in them, too.

—MARY KISINGER MEDICINE HAT, AB

START TO FINISH: 30 MIN. • **MAKES:** 2 DOZEN

- **1 pound lean ground pork**
- **1 medium onion, chopped**
- **¼ cup hoisin sauce**
- **4 garlic cloves, minced**
- **1 tablespoon minced fresh gingerroot**
- **1 tablespoon red wine vinegar**
- **1 tablespoon reduced-sodium soy sauce**
- **2 teaspoons Thai chili sauce**
- **1 can (8 ounces) sliced water chestnuts, drained and finely chopped**
- **4 green onions, chopped**
- **1 tablespoon sesame oil**
- **24 Bibb or Boston lettuce leaves**

1. In a large skillet, cook pork and onion over medium heat 6-8 minutes or until pork is no longer pink and onion is tender, breaking up pork into crumbles.
2. Stir in hoisin sauce, garlic, ginger, vinegar, soy sauce and chili sauce until blended. Add water chestnuts, green onions and oil; heat through. To serve, place pork mixture in lettuce leaves; fold lettuce over filling.

FREEZE OPTION *Freeze cooled meat mixture in freezer containers. To use, partially thaw in refrigerator overnight. Heat through in a saucepan, stirring occasionally and adding a little water if necessary.*

PER SERVING *1 filled lettuce wrap: 54 cal., 3g fat (1g sat. fat), 11mg chol., 87mg sodium, 4g carb. (2g sugars, 1g fiber), 4g pro.*

STUFFED ASIAGO-BASIL MUSHROOMS F S C M

PREP: 25 MIN. • **BAKE:** 10 MIN. • **MAKES:** 2 DOZEN

- **24 baby portobello mushrooms (about 1 pound), stems removed**
- **½ cup reduced-fat mayonnaise**
- **¾ cup shredded Asiago cheese**
- **½ cup loosely packed basil leaves, stems removed**
- **¼ teaspoon white pepper**
- **12 cherry tomatoes, halved**
- **Grated Parmesan cheese, optional**

1. Preheat oven to 375°. Place mushroom caps in a greased 15x10x1-in. baking pan. Bake 10 minutes. Meanwhile, place mayonnaise, Asiago cheese, basil and pepper in a food processor; process until blended.

2. Drain juices from mushrooms. Fill each with 1 rounded teaspoon mayonnaise mixture; top each with a tomato half.

3. Bake 8-10 minutes or until lightly browned. If desired, top with Parmesan cheese.

PER SERVING *1 appetizer: 35 cal., 3g fat (1g sat. fat), 5mg chol., 50mg sodium, 2g carb. (1g sugars, 0 fiber), 2g pro.*

If you don't like mushrooms, you'll have to try them again with this recipe. These pretty appetizers taste divine. For a main dish, double the filling and use large portobellos. —**LORRAINE CALAND** SHUNIAH, ON

STUFFED ASIAGO-BASIL MUSHROOMS

THAI SHRIMP & CUCUMBER ON RYE F S C FAST FIX

This low-fat shrimp, veggie and cream cheese spread is versatile. You can serve it as a dip with fresh vegetables or crackers. It is cool and crisp—the perfect healthy starter for any party or outdoor barbecue.

—**MARY SHIVERS** ADA, OK

START TO FINISH: 20 MIN. • **MAKES:** 3 DOZEN

- **1 package (8 ounces) reduced-fat cream cheese**
- **¼ cup sweet chili sauce**
- **⅛ teaspoon salt**
- **⅛ teaspoon pepper**
- **½ pound peeled and deveined cooked shrimp (61-70 per pound), finely chopped**
- **⅓ cup chopped peeled cucumber**
- **2 tablespoons finely chopped celery**
- **1 green onion, thinly sliced**
- **2 tablespoons finely chopped walnuts**
- **36 slices snack rye bread**

In a small bowl, beat first four ingredients until blended. Stir in shrimp, vegetables and walnuts. Serve with rye bread.

PER SERVING *1 tablespoon shrimp mixture with 1 slice bread: 47 cal., 2g fat (1g sat. fat), 14mg chol., 115mg sodium, 5g carb. (1g sugars, 0 fiber), 3g pro.*

HEALTHY BLUE CHEESE WALNUT DIP C M

I couldn't get my family to even try tofu. So, I combined it with some blue cheese and walnuts and they never knew—at least until now! It has been my secret as they gobbled it up. This is best made a couple of hours ahead so the flavors can meld.

—**MARY MARLOWE LEVERETTE** COLUMBIA, SC

PREP: 15 MIN. + CHILLING • **MAKES:** 1⅓ CUPS

- **8 ounces silken firm tofu**
- **¼ cup finely chopped onion**
- **¼ cup fat-free sour cream**
- **3 tablespoons crumbled blue cheese**
- **¾ teaspoon salt**
- **3 tablespoons chopped walnuts, toasted**
- **Apple or pear wedges**
- **Baked pita chips or assorted crackers**

1. Process tofu and onion in a food processor until smooth, scraping down sides as needed. Transfer mixture to a small bowl.

2. Stir in sour cream, blue cheese and salt. Refrigerate, covered, at least 1 hour. Stir in walnuts just before serving. Serve with fruit and pita chips.

PER SERVING *¼ cup dip: 90 cal., 6g fat (1g sat. fat), 4mg chol., 439mg sodium, 3g carb. (2g sugars, 0 fiber), 6g pro.*

HEALTH TIP *Silken tofu adds a creamy texture to dips and spreads like mayonnaise or cream cheese would, but it's lower in fat and calories. It also adds 3g protein per serving in this dip!*

GARDEN-FRESH BLACK BEAN SALSA

F S C M FAST FIX

After taking an inventory of all the fresh produce from my mom's garden, we created this fresh salsa recipe. It's a hit each year when the harvest comes in.

—**ERIN DAVIS** GRAND RAPIDS, MN

START TO FINISH: 25 MIN.
MAKES: 32 SERVINGS (¼ CUP EACH)

- **6 plum tomatoes, seeded and chopped (about 4 cups)**
- **1 can (15 ounces) black beans, rinsed and drained**
- **1 medium cucumber, chopped**
- **1 medium green pepper, finely chopped**
- **1 small onion, finely chopped**
- **1 jalapeno pepper, seeded and minced**
- **3 tablespoons cider vinegar**
- **2 teaspoons sugar**
- **1 teaspoon salt**
- **1 teaspoon chili powder**
- **½ teaspoon ground cumin**
- **⅛ teaspoon pepper**

In a large bowl, combine the first six ingredients. Whisk the remaining ingredients; pour over salsa and toss to combine. Refrigerate until serving.

NOTE *Wear disposable gloves when cutting hot peppers; the oils can burn skin. Avoid touching your face.*

PER SERVING *1/4 cup: 17 cal., 0 fat (0 sat. fat), 0 chol., 101mg sodium, 3g carb. (1g sugars, 1g fiber), 1g pro.*

DID YOU KNOW?

Many grocery store cucumbers are coated with protective wax to prolong their shelf life. They should be peeled before eating. There's no need to peel English cucumbers that are wrapped in plastic. Ditto for cukes from the farmers market or your own garden. Whether or not to peel these is a matter of taste.

BAKED POT STICKERS WITH DIPPING SAUCE

BAKED POT STICKERS WITH DIPPING SAUCE

F S C

Twisting these wonton wrappers like little candies makes them fuss-free, and the dipping sauce is packed with sweet heat.

—**TAYLOR MARSH** ALGONA, IA

PREP: 30 MIN. • **BAKE:** 15 MIN./BATCH
MAKES: 4 DOZEN (¾ CUP SAUCE)

- **2 cups finely chopped cooked chicken breast**
- **1 can (8 ounces) water chestnuts, drained and chopped**
- **4 green onions, thinly sliced**
- **¼ cup shredded carrots**
- **¼ cup reduced-fat mayonnaise**
- **1 large egg white**
- **1 tablespoon reduced-sodium soy sauce**
- **1 garlic clove, minced**
- **1 teaspoon grated fresh gingerroot**
- **48 wonton wrappers**
- **Cooking spray**

SAUCE

- **½ cup jalapeno pepper jelly**
- **¼ cup rice vinegar**
- **2 tablespoons reduced-sodium soy sauce**

1. Preheat oven to 425°. In a large bowl, combine the first nine ingredients. Place 2 teaspoons of filling in center of each wonton wrapper. (Cover wrappers with a damp paper towel until ready to use.)

2. Moisten wrapper edges with water. Fold edge over filling and roll to form a log; twist ends to seal. Repeat with remaining wrappers and filling.

3. Place pot stickers on a baking sheet coated with cooking spray; spritz each with cooking spray. Bake 12-15 minutes or until edges are golden brown.

4. Meanwhile, place jelly in a small microwave-safe bowl; microwave, covered, on high until melted. Stir in vinegar and soy sauce. Serve sauce with pot stickers.

PER SERVING *1 pot sticker with 3/4 teaspoon sauce: 52 cal., 1g fat (0 sat. fat), 6mg chol., 101mg sodium, 8g carb. (2g sugars, 0 fiber), 3g pro.* ***Diabetic Exchanges:*** *1/2 starch.*

MINI FETA PIZZAS

M FAST FIX

We usually have an abundance of pesto from the basil in our garden, which we use in our feta-covered mini pizzas. My family loves this dish, and we often add a little extra feta.

—NICOLE FILIZETTI STEVENS POINT, WI

START TO FINISH: 20 MIN.
MAKES: 4 SERVINGS

- **2 whole wheat English muffins, split and toasted**
- **2 tablespoons reduced-fat cream cheese**
- **4 teaspoons prepared pesto**
- **½ cup thinly sliced red onion**
- **¼ cup crumbled feta cheese**

1. Preheat oven to 425°. Place muffins on a baking sheet.
2. Mix cream cheese and pesto; spread over muffins. Top with onion and feta cheese. Bake until lightly browned, 6-8 minutes.

PER SERVING *1 mini pizza: 136 cal., 6g fat (3g sat. fat), 11mg chol., 294mg sodium, 16g carb. (4g sugars, 3g fiber), 6g pro.* ***Diabetic Exchanges:*** *1 starch, 1 fat.*

MINI FETA PIZZAS

GORGONZOLA POLENTA BITES

GORGONZOLA POLENTA BITES

F C M FAST FIX

Here's a cozy appetizer for a cold day. The flavors blend so well, and prepared polenta makes the prep super fast.

—MARGEE BERRY WHITE SALMON, WA

START TO FINISH: 25 MIN.
MAKES: 16 APPETIZERS

- **⅓ cup balsamic vinegar**
- **1 tablespoon orange marmalade**
- **½ cup panko (Japanese) bread crumbs**
- **1 tube (18 ounces) polenta, cut into 16 slices**
- **2 tablespoons olive oil**
- **½ cup crumbled Gorgonzola cheese**
- **3 tablespoons dried currants, optional**

1. In a small saucepan, combine vinegar and marmalade. Bring to a boil; cook 5-7 minutes or until liquid is reduced to 2 tablespoons.
2. Meanwhile, place bread crumbs in a shallow bowl. Press both sides of polenta slices in bread crumbs. In a large skillet, heat oil over medium-high heat. Add polenta in batches; cook 2-4 minutes on each side or until golden brown.
3. Arrange polenta on a serving platter; spoon cheese over top. Sprinkle with currants if desired; drizzle with vinegar mixture. Serve warm or at room temperature.

PER SERVING *1 appetizer: 67 cal., 3g fat (1g sat. fat), 3mg chol., 161mg sodium, 9g carb. (3g sugars, 0 fiber), 1g pro.* ***Diabetic Exchanges:*** *½ starch, ½ fat.*

FRESH FRUIT SALSA WITH CINNAMON CHIPS

F S M

Lime and basil really brighten the flavors in this colorful salsa. It's best when scooped up on a homemade cinnamon chip.

—**NAVALEE HYLTON** LAUDERHILL, FL

PREP: 30 MIN. • **BAKE:** 10 MIN.
MAKES: 4½ CUPS SALSA (64 CHIPS)

SALSA

- **1 medium pear, peeled and finely chopped**
- **1 medium apple, peeled and finely chopped**
- **1 medium kiwifruit, peeled and finely chopped**
- **1 small peach, peeled and finely chopped**
- **½ cup fresh blueberries**
- **½ cup finely chopped fresh pineapple**
- **½ cup finely chopped fresh strawberries**
- **2 tablespoons honey**
- **1 tablespoon lime juice**
- **¾ teaspoon grated lime peel**
- **3 small fresh basil leaves, thinly sliced**
- **3 fresh mint leaves, thinly sliced**

CINNAMON CHIPS

- **8 flour tortillas (8 inches)**
- **Cooking spray**
- **½ cup sugar**
- **1 teaspoon ground cinnamon**

1. In a large bowl, combine the salsa ingredients; mix lightly. Refrigerate until serving.

2. Lightly spritz both sides of tortillas with cooking spray; cut each into eight wedges. In a large bowl, combine sugar and cinnamon. Add tortillas; toss to coat.

3. Arrange in a single layer on ungreased baking sheets. Bake at 350° for 10-12 minutes or until golden brown. Serve with salsa.

PER SERVING *1/4 cup salsa with 4 chips: 124 cal., 2g fat (0 sat. fat), 0 chol., 118mg sodium, 25g carb. (9g sugars, 2g fiber), 2g pro.* ***Diabetic Exchanges:*** *1½ starch.*

FRESH FRUIT SALSA WITH CINNAMON CHIPS

MUSHROOM BUNDLES

S C M

Guests always count on me to bring fun starters and drinks. I made these for a New Year's party. After trying these bundles, everyone was fed, happy and wanting to come back for more.

—**TINA COOPMAN** TORONTO, ON

PREP: 30 MIN. • **BAKE:** 15 MIN.
MAKES: 1 DOZEN

- **1 tablespoon olive oil**
- **1 cup chopped fresh mushrooms**
- **1 cup chopped baby portobello mushrooms**
- **¼ cup finely chopped red onion**
- **2 garlic cloves, minced**
- **¼ teaspoon dried rosemary, crushed**
- **⅛ teaspoon pepper**
- **4 sheets phyllo dough (14x9-inch size)**
- **3 tablespoons butter, melted**
- **2 tablespoons crumbled feta cheese**

1. Preheat oven to 375°. In a large skillet, heat oil over medium-high heat. Add mushrooms and onion; cook and stir 4-5 minutes or until tender. Add garlic, rosemary and pepper; cook 2 minutes longer. Remove from heat.

2. Place one sheet of phyllo dough on a work surface; brush with butter. (Keep remaining phyllo covered with plastic wrap and a damp towel to prevent it from drying out.) Layer with three additional phyllo sheets, brushing each layer. Using a sharp knife, cut the layered sheets into twelve 3-in. squares. Carefully press each stack into an ungreased mini-muffin cup.

3. Stir feta into mushroom mixture; spoon 1 tablespoon into each phyllo cup. Form into bundles by gathering edges of phyllo squares and twisting centers to close. Brush tops with remaining butter. Bake 12-15 minutes or until golden brown. Serve warm.

FREEZE OPTION *Freeze cooled bundles in resealable plastic freezer bags. To use, reheat the bundles on a greased baking sheet in a preheated 375° oven until they are crisp and heated through.*

PER SERVING *1 pastry: 53 cal., 4g fat (2g sat. fat), 8mg chol., 50mg sodium, 3g carb. (1g sugars, 0 fiber), 1g pro.*

MUSHROOM BUNDLES

BALSAMIC-GOAT CHEESE GRILLED PLUMS

BALSAMIC-GOAT CHEESE GRILLED PLUMS

F S C M FAST FIX

Make a real statement at your next summer dinner party with this simple and elegant treat. Ripe plums are grilled, then dressed with a balsamic reduction and sprinkled with tangy goat cheese.
—**ARIANA ABELOW** HOLLISTON, MA

START TO FINISH: 25 MIN.
MAKES: 8 SERVINGS

- **1 cup balsamic vinegar**
- **2 teaspoons grated lemon peel**
- **4 medium firm plums, halved and pitted**
- **½ cup crumbled goat cheese**

1. For glaze, in a small saucepan, combine vinegar and lemon peel; bring to a boil. Cook 10-12 minutes or until mixture is thickened and reduced to about ⅓ cup (do not overcook).
2. Grill plums, covered, over medium heat 2-3 minutes on each side or until tender. Drizzle with glaze; top with cheese.

PER SERVING *1 plum half with 1 tablespoon cheese and 2 teaspoons glaze: 58 cal., 2g fat (1g sat. fat), 9mg chol., 41mg sodium, 9g carb. (8g sugars, 1g fiber), 2g pro.*

TOASTED RAVIOLI PUFFS

F S C M FAST FIX

I call toasted ravioli a fan favorite because it disappears faster than I can make it. With just five ingredients, this is how you get the party started.
—**KATHY MORGAN** TEMECULA, CA

START TO FINISH: 30 MIN.
MAKES: 2 DOZEN

- **24 refrigerated cheese ravioli**
- **1 tablespoon reduced-fat Italian salad dressing**
- **1 tablespoon Italian-style panko (Japanese) bread crumbs**
- **1 tablespoon grated Parmesan cheese**
- **Warm marinara sauce**

1. Preheat oven to 400°. Cook ravioli according to package directions; drain. Transfer to a greased baking sheet. Brush with salad dressing. In a small bowl, mix bread crumbs and cheese; sprinkle over ravioli.
2. Bake 12-15 minutes or until golden brown. Serve with marinara sauce.

PER SERVING *1 ravioli: 21 cal., 1g fat (0 sat. fat), 3mg chol., 43mg sodium, 3g carb. (0 sugars, 0 fiber), 1g pro.*

CUCUMBER DIP

F S C FAST FIX

My family asks for this dip at least once a week in the summertime. I'm happy to make it for them because it's light—and a great way to use all of the cucumbers and onions from my garden.
—**LYNDSAY WILLIAMS** FARGO, ND

START TO FINISH: 10 MIN.
MAKES: 2½ CUPS

- **1 package (8 ounces) fat-free cream cheese**
- **¼ cup reduced-fat mayonnaise**
- **4 teaspoons Worcestershire sauce**
- **½ teaspoon garlic powder**
- **¼ teaspoon salt**
- **¼ teaspoon pepper**
- **2 cups chopped seeded cucumbers**
- **1 medium onion, finely chopped**
- **Assorted crackers or fresh vegetables**

In a small bowl, beat the first six ingredients. Stir in cucumbers and onion. Refrigerate until serving. Serve with crackers or vegetables.

PER SERVING *2 tablespoons: 26 cal., 1g fat (0 sat. fat), 2mg chol., 127mg sodium, 2g carb. (1g sugars, 0 fiber), 2g pro.*

TOASTED RAVIOLI PUFFS

FRESH FROM THE GARDEN WRAPS F C M

(PICTURED ON P. 6)

We moved into a house with a garden that needed tending. Using the herbs we found, we made these freshtastic wraps for our first dinner there.
—**CHRIS BUGHER** ASHEVILLE, NC

PREP: 20 MIN. + STANDING
MAKES: 8 SERVINGS

- **1 medium ear sweet corn**
- **1 medium cucumber, chopped**
- **1 cup shredded cabbage**
- **1 medium tomato, chopped**
- **1 small red onion, chopped**
- **1 jalapeno pepper, seeded and minced**
- **1 tablespoon minced fresh basil**
- **1 tablespoon minced fresh cilantro**
- **1 tablespoon minced fresh mint**
- **⅓ cup Thai chili sauce**
- **3 tablespoons rice vinegar**
- **2 teaspoons reduced-sodium soy sauce**
- **2 teaspoons creamy peanut butter**
- **8 Bibb or Boston lettuce leaves**

1. Cut corn from cob and place in a large bowl. Add cucumber, cabbage, tomato, onion, jalapeno and herbs.
2. Whisk together chili sauce, vinegar, soy sauce and peanut butter. Pour over vegetable mixture; toss to coat. Let stand 20 minutes.
3. Using a slotted spoon, place ½ cup salad in each lettuce leaf. Fold lettuce over filling.

NOTE *Wear disposable gloves when cutting hot peppers; the oils can burn skin. Avoid touching your face.*

PER SERVING *1 filled lettuce wrap: 64 cal., 1g fat (0 sat. fat), 0 chol., 319mg sodium, 13g carb. (10g sugars, 2g fiber), 2g pro.* ***Diabetic Exchanges:*** *1 vegetable, ½ starch.*

TOP TIP

With small, round, buttery leaves, Bibb lettuce is ideal for lettuce wraps. Tuna, chicken salad and taco meat all make tasty fillings.

GRILLED ZUCCHINI WITH PEANUT CHICKEN

GRILLED ZUCCHINI WITH PEANUT CHICKEN

F S C FAST FIX

Zucchini slices make perfect finger food. It's fun to come up with different toppings, and these are a good solution for a never-ending crop.
—**ELISABETH LARSEN** PLEASANT GROVE, UT

START TO FINISH: 30 MIN.
MAKES: ABOUT 16 APPETIZERS

- **2 medium zucchini, cut diagonally into ½-in. slices**
- **⅛ teaspoon salt**
- **⅛ teaspoon pepper**

TOPPING

- **¼ cup water**
- **3 tablespoons brown sugar**
- **2 tablespoons reduced-sodium soy sauce**
- **1 tablespoon creamy peanut butter**
- **1 teaspoon lime juice**
- **¼ teaspoon ground ginger**
- **¼ teaspoon cayenne pepper**
- **1 cup shredded cooked chicken**
- **2 tablespoons finely chopped red onion**
- **Julienned carrot and chopped fresh cilantro**

1. Place zucchini on an oiled grill rack over medium heat; grill, covered, until tender, 3-4 minutes per side. Sprinkle with salt and pepper.
2. In a small saucepan, whisk together the first seven topping ingredients; bring to a boil. Reduce heat; simmer, uncovered, until slightly thickened, 2-3 minutes, stirring occasionally. Stir in chicken and onion; heat through.
3. To serve, top zucchini slices with chicken mixture. Sprinkle with carrot and cilantro.

PER SERVING *1 appetizer: 38 cal., 1g fat (0 sat. fat), 8mg chol., 110mg sodium, 4g carb. (3g sugars, 0 fiber), 3g pro.*

24

30

32

Soups

"I like cozy comfort soups that taste creamy but without the cream. This one's full of good stuff like rutabagas, leeks, fresh herbs and almond milk."

—**MERRY GRAHAM** NEWHALL, CA
about her recipe, Autumn Bisque, on page 35

COLD-DAY CHICKEN NOODLE SOUP

COLD-DAY CHICKEN NOODLE SOUP

When I was sick, my mom would stir up a heartwarming chicken noodle soup. It's so soothing for colds and cold-weather days.

—ANTHONY GRAHAM OTTAWA, IL

PREP: 15 MIN. • **COOK:** 25 MIN.
MAKES: 8 SERVINGS (3 QUARTS)

- **1 tablespoon canola oil**
- **2 celery ribs, chopped**
- **2 medium carrots, chopped**
- **1 medium onion, chopped**
- **8 cups reduced-sodium chicken broth**
- **½ teaspoon dried basil**
- **¼ teaspoon pepper**
- **3 cups uncooked whole wheat egg noodles (about 4 ounces)**
- **3 cups coarsely chopped rotisserie chicken**
- **1 tablespoon minced fresh parsley**

1. In a 6-qt. stockpot, heat oil over medium-high heat. Add celery, carrots and onion; cook and stir 5-7 minutes or until tender.

2. Add broth, basil and pepper; bring to a boil. Stir in noodles; cook 12-14 minutes or until al dente. Stir in chicken and parsley; heat through.

PER SERVING *1½ cups: 195 cal., 6g fat (1g sat. fat), 47mg chol., 639mg sodium, 16g carb. (2g sugars, 3g fiber), 21g pro.* ***Diabetic Exchanges:*** *2 lean meat, 1 starch, ½ fat.*

HEALTH TIP *Stick with tradition. A number of scientific studies support the idea that chicken noodle soup can indeed help ease cold symptoms.*

GOLDEN SUMMER PEACH GAZPACHO F C

Since peaches and tomatoes are in season together, I like to blend them into a cool, delicious soup. Leftovers keep well in the fridge—but they rarely last long enough to get there.

—JULIE HESSION LAS VEGAS, NV

PREP: 20 MIN. + CHILLING
MAKES: 8 SERVINGS

- **3 cups sliced peeled fresh or frozen peaches, thawed**
- **3 medium yellow tomatoes, chopped**
- **1 medium sweet yellow pepper, chopped**
- **1 medium cucumber, peeled and chopped**
- **½ cup chopped sweet onion**
- **1 garlic clove, minced**
- **⅓ cup lime juice**
- **2 tablespoons rice vinegar**
- **1 tablespoon marinade for chicken**
- **1 teaspoon salt**
- **¼ teaspoon hot pepper sauce**
- **1 to 3 teaspoons sugar, optional**
- **Chopped peaches, cucumber and tomatoes**

1. Place the first six ingredients in a food processor; process until blended. Add lime juice, vinegar, marinade for chicken, salt and pepper sauce; process until smooth. If desired, stir in sugar.

2. Refrigerate, covered, at least 4 hours. Top servings with additional chopped peaches, cucumber and tomatoes.

PER SERVING *⅔ cup: 56 cal., 0 fat (0 sat. fat), 0 chol., 342mg sodium, 13g carb. (8g sugars, 2g fiber), 2g pro.* ***Diabetic Exchanges:*** *1 vegetable, ½ fruit.*

GOLDEN SUMMER PEACH GAZPACHO

ITALIAN VEGGIE BEEF SOUP C FAST FIX

My sweet father-in-law, Pop Pop, would bring this chunky soup to our house when we were under the weather. We like it so much, we take it to our own friends who need comfort. Always does the trick.

—SUE WEBB REISTERSTOWN, MD

START TO FINISH: 30 MIN.
MAKES: 12 SERVINGS (4 QUARTS)

- **1½ pounds lean ground beef (90% lean)**
- **2 medium onions, chopped**
- **4 cups chopped cabbage**
- **1 package (16 ounces) frozen mixed vegetables**
- **1 can (28 ounces) crushed tomatoes**
- **1 bay leaf**
- **3 teaspoons Italian seasoning**
- **1 teaspoon salt**
- **½ teaspoon pepper**
- **2 cartons (32 ounces each) reduced-sodium beef broth**

1. In a 6-qt. stockpot, cook ground beef and onions over medium-high heat 6-8 minutes or until beef is no longer pink, breaking up meat into crumbles; drain.
2. Add cabbage, mixed vegetables, tomatoes, seasonings and broth; bring to a boil. Reduce heat; simmer, uncovered, 10-15 minutes or until cabbage is crisp-tender. Remove bay leaf.

FREEZE OPTION *Freeze cooled soup in freezer containers. To use, partially thaw in refrigerator overnight. Heat soup through in a saucepan, stirring occasionally and adding a little broth if necessary.*

PER SERVING *1⅓ cups: 159 cal., 5g fat (2g sat. fat), 38mg chol., 646mg sodium, 14g carb. (6g sugars, 4g fiber), 15g pro.* ***Diabetic Exchanges:*** *2 lean meat, 1 vegetable, ½ starch.*

SALMON DILL SOUP

SALMON DILL SOUP FAST FIX

This is the best soup I have ever made, according to my husband who loves salmon so much that he could eat it every day. When I get salmon, I try to make it a very special dish because salmon is a treat for both of us.

—HIDEMI WALSH PLAINFIELD, IN

START TO FINISH: 30 MIN.
MAKES: 2 SERVINGS

- **1 large potato, peeled and cut into 1½-inch pieces**
- **1 large carrot, cut into ½-inch slices**
- **1½ cups water**
- **1 cup reduced-sodium chicken broth**
- **5 medium fresh mushrooms, halved**
- **1 tablespoon all-purpose flour**
- **¼ cup reduced-fat evaporated milk**
- **¼ cup shredded part-skim mozzarella cheese**
- **½ pound salmon fillet, cut into 1½-inch pieces**
- **¼ teaspoon pepper**
- **⅛ teaspoon salt**
- **1 tablespoon chopped fresh dill**

1. Place first four ingredients in a saucepan; bring to a boil. Reduce heat to medium; cook, uncovered, until vegetables are tender, 10-15 minutes.
2. Add mushrooms. In a small bowl, mix flour and milk until smooth; stir into soup. Return to a boil; cook and stir until mushrooms are tender. Reduce heat to medium; stir in cheese until melted.
3. Reduce heat to medium-low. Add salmon; cook, uncovered, until fish just begins to flake easily with a fork, 3-4 minutes. Stir in pepper and salt. Sprinkle with dill.

PER SERVING *2½ cups: 398 cal., 14g fat (4g sat. fat), 71mg chol., 647mg sodium, 37g carb. (7g sugars, 3g fiber), 30g pro.* ***Diabetic Exchanges:*** *3 lean meat, 2½ starch.*

COMFORTING BEEF BARLEY SOUP

When the weather outside is cool, we want a bowl of soup that's chock-full of beef, barley and veggies. It's the most delicious way to warm up.

—SUE JURACK MEQUON, WI

PREP: 10 MIN. • **COOK:** 35 MIN.
MAKES: 8 SERVINGS (3 QUARTS)

- **1 tablespoon butter**
- **1 medium carrot, chopped**
- **1 celery rib, chopped**
- **½ cup chopped onion**
- **4 cups beef broth**
- **4 cups water**
- **2 cups chopped cooked roast beef**
- **1 can (14½ ounces) diced tomatoes, undrained**
- **1 cup quick-cooking barley**
- **½ teaspoon dried basil**
- **½ teaspoon dried oregano**
- **½ teaspoon pepper**
- **¼ teaspoon salt**
- **½ cup frozen peas**

1. In a 6-qt. stockpot, heat butter over medium-high heat; saute carrot, celery and onion until tender, 4-5 minutes.

2. Add broth, water, beef, tomatoes, barley and seasonings; bring to a boil. Reduce heat; simmer, covered, for 20 minutes, stirring occasionally. Add peas; heat through, about 5 minutes.

PER SERVING *1½ cups: 198 cal., 4g fat (2g sat. fat), 36mg chol., 652mg sodium, 23g carb. (3g sugars, 6g fiber), 18g pro.* ***Diabetic Exchanges:*** *2 lean meat, 1½ starch, ½ fat.*

COMFORTING BEEF BARLEY SOUP

SOUTHWEST CHICKEN BARLEY CHOWDER

SOUTHWEST CHICKEN BARLEY CHOWDER

FAST FIX

Mashed squash helps make this chowder creamy but not heavy, and it's a favorite way to get barley on the table. My kids even ask for leftovers for lunch.

—PAMELA CLEGHORN CAMPBELLSBURG, IN

START TO FINISH: 30 MIN.
MAKES: 8 SERVINGS (2½ QUARTS)

- **2 tablespoons olive oil**
- **1 pound boneless skinless chicken breasts, cut into ¾-inch pieces**
- **1 small onion, finely chopped**
- **1 package (12 ounces) frozen mashed winter squash, thawed (about 1⅓ cups)**
- **¾ cup quick-cooking barley**
- **2 teaspoons reduced-sodium taco seasoning**
- **½ teaspoon salt**
- **¼ teaspoon pepper**
- **1 carton (32 ounces) reduced-sodium chicken broth**
- **1 can (15 ounces) black beans, rinsed and drained**
- **2 cups frozen corn**
- **1 cup half-and-half cream**
- **½ cup salsa**
- **½ cup chopped fresh cilantro**
- **Diced avocado and chopped tomatoes, optional**

1. In a 6-qt. stockpot, heat oil over medium-high heat. Add chicken and onion; cook and stir 2-3 minutes or just until onion is tender.

2. Stir in squash, barley, seasonings and broth; bring to a boil. Reduce heat; simmer, covered, 10-12 minutes or until barley is tender.

3. Add beans, corn, cream, salsa and cilantro; heat through, stirring occasionally. If desired, serve with avocado and tomatoes.

FREEZE OPTION *Freeze cooled soup in freezer containers. To use, partially thaw in refrigerator overnight. Heat soup through in a saucepan, stirring occasionally and adding a little broth or milk if necessary.*

PER SERVING *1¼ cups: 298 cal., 8g fat (3g sat. fat), 46mg chol., 681mg sodium, 35g carb. (4g sugars, 7g fiber), 20g pro.* ***Diabetic Exchanges:*** *2 starch, 2 lean meat, 1 fat.*

SIMPLE ASPARAGUS SOUP F C

My family and friends love this soup and think I spend hours making it, but the most time spent is on occasional stirring.

—KATHRYN LABAT RACELAND, LA

PREP: 20 MIN. • **COOK:** 55 MIN.
MAKES: 12 SERVINGS (ABOUT 2 QUARTS)

- **1 tablespoon butter**
- **1 tablespoon olive oil**
- **2 pounds fresh asparagus, trimmed and cut into 1-inch pieces**
- **1 medium onion, chopped**
- **1 medium carrot, thinly sliced**
- **½ teaspoon salt**
- **¼ teaspoon pepper**
- **¼ teaspoon dried thyme**
- **⅔ cup uncooked long grain brown rice**
- **6 cups reduced-sodium chicken broth**
- **Reduced-fat sour cream, optional**
- **Salad croutons, optional**

1. In a 6-qt. stockpot, heat butter and oil over medium heat. Stir in vegetables and seasonings; cook until vegetables are tender, 8-10 minutes, stirring occasionally.

2. Stir in rice and broth; bring to a boil. Reduce heat; simmer, covered, until rice is tender, 40-45 minutes, stirring occasionally.

3. Puree soup using an immersion blender. Or, cool slightly and puree soup in batches in a blender; return to pot and heat through. If desired, serve with sour cream and croutons.

FREEZE OPTION *Freeze cooled soup in freezer containers. To use, partially thaw in refrigerator overnight (soup may separate). In a saucepan, reheat to boiling, whisking until blended.*

PER SERVING *¾ cup: 79 cal., 3g fat (1g sat. fat), 3mg chol., 401mg sodium, 11g carb. (2g sugars, 2g fiber), 4g pro.* ***Diabetic Exchanges:*** *1 vegetable, ½ starch, ½ fat.*

CHICKEN BUTTERNUT CHILI

PREP: 20 MIN. • **COOK:** 35 MIN.
MAKES: 4 SERVINGS

- **1 tablespoon canola oil**
- **2 medium carrots, chopped**
- **2 celery ribs, chopped**
- **1 medium onion, chopped**
- **2 cups cubed peeled butternut squash**
- **1 medium tomato, chopped**
- **2 tablespoons tomato paste**
- **1 envelope reduced-sodium chili seasoning mix**
- **2 cups chicken stock**
- **1 cup cubed cooked chicken breast**
- **Chopped fresh cilantro**

1. In a large saucepan, heat oil over medium heat; saute carrots, celery and onion until tender, 6-8 minutes.

2. Stir in squash, tomato, tomato paste, seasoning mix and stock; bring to a boil. Reduce heat; simmer, covered, until squash is tender, 20-25 minutes. Stir in chicken; heat through. Sprinkle with cilantro.

FREEZE OPTION *Freeze cooled chili in freezer containers. To use, partially thaw in refrigerator overnight. Heat chili through in a saucepan, stirring occasionally.*

PER SERVING *1¼ cups: 201 cal., 5g fat (1g sat. fat), 27mg chol., 591mg sodium, 25g carb. (8g sugars, 4g fiber), 15g pro.* ***Diabetic Exchanges:*** *2 lean meat, 1 starch, 1 vegetable, ½ fat.*

At our house, we just love a comforting, hearty, tomato-based chili with a bold taste! This unique chili is loaded with veggies and flavor. You can also prepare the recipe in the slow cooker. Just add the ingredients to the crock and cook over high heat for about 4 hours. **—COURTNEY STULTZ** WEIR, KS

CHICKEN BUTTERNUT CHILI

ITALIAN SAUSAGE ZUCCHINI SOUP

ITALIAN SAUSAGE ZUCCHINI SOUP C

My mom used to make this recipe. Whenever I decide to make it, it reminds me of her, taking me back to days of my childhood.

—LOUISE KLINE FORT MYERS, FL

PREP: 20 MIN. • **COOK:** 45 MIN.
MAKES: 10 SERVINGS (3¼ QUARTS)

- **1 package (19½ ounces) hot or sweet Italian turkey sausage links, casings removed**
- **4 celery ribs, chopped**
- **1 medium onion, chopped**
- **2 teaspoons Italian seasoning**
- **1 teaspoon dried oregano**
- **½ teaspoon salt**
- **½ teaspoon garlic powder**
- **½ teaspoon dried basil**
- **2 medium zucchini, cut into ½-inch cubes**
- **2 medium green peppers, chopped**
- **4 cans (14½ ounces each) no-salt-added whole tomatoes, undrained, crushed**
- **1 can (14½ ounces) reduced-sodium chicken broth**
- **1 teaspoon sugar**

1. In a 6-qt. stockpot, cook and crumble sausage over medium-high heat until no longer pink, 5-7 minutes. Remove with a slotted spoon.
2. Add celery, onion and seasonings to same pot; cook and stir until onion is tender, 4-6 minutes. Stir in sausage and remaining ingredients; bring to a boil. Reduce heat; simmer, covered, until zucchini and peppers are tender, about 30 minutes.

FREEZE OPTION *Freeze cooled soup in freezer containers. To use, partially thaw in refrigerator overnight. Heat soup through in a saucepan, stirring occasionally.*

PER SERVING *1¼ cups: 104 cal., 4g fat (1g sat. fat), 20mg chol., 483mg sodium, 10g carb. (6g sugars, 4g fiber), 9g pro.* ***Diabetic Exchanges:*** *1 lean meat, 1 vegetable.*

EASY WHITE CHICKEN CHILI FAST FIX

Chili is one of our best cold-weather strategies. We use chicken and white beans for a twist on the regular bowl of red. It's such soothing comfort food.

—RACHEL LEWIS DANVILLE, VA

START TO FINISH: 30 MIN.
MAKES: 6 SERVINGS

- **1 pound lean ground chicken**
- **1 medium onion, chopped**
- **2 cans (15 ounces each) cannellini beans, rinsed and drained**
- **1 can (4 ounces) chopped green chilies**
- **1 teaspoon ground cumin**
- **½ teaspoon dried oregano**
- **¼ teaspoon pepper**
- **1 can (14½ ounces) reduced-sodium chicken broth**
- **Optional toppings: reduced-fat sour cream, shredded cheddar cheese and chopped fresh cilantro**

1. In a large saucepan, cook chicken and onion over medium-high heat 6-8 minutes or until chicken is no longer pink, breaking up chicken into crumbles.
2. Place one can of beans in a small bowl; mash slightly. Stir mashed beans, remaining can of beans, chilies, seasonings and broth into chicken mixture; bring to a boil. Reduce heat; simmer, covered, 12-15 minutes or until flavors are blended. Serve with toppings as desired.

FREEZE OPTION *Freeze cooled chili in freezer containers. To use, partially thaw in refrigerator overnight. Heat chili through in a saucepan, stirring occasionally and adding a little broth if necessary.*

PER SERVING *1 cup: 228 cal., 5g fat (1g sat. fat), 54mg chol., 504mg sodium, 23g carb. (1g sugars, 6g fiber), 22g pro.* ***Diabetic Exchanges:*** *3 lean meat, 1½ starch.*

READER RAVE

Wow—this was such a delicious, easy weeknight meal. I used leftover chicken from baked chicken quarters. I also used a can of great northern beans and a can of pinto beans with jalapenos. The flavor was fantastic!

—MEAGANTEAL TASTEOFHOME.COM

EASY WHITE CHICKEN CHILI

CREAMY CHICKEN RICE SOUP

CREAMY CHICKEN RICE SOUP FAST FIX

I came up with this flavorful soup while making some adjustments to a favorite stovetop chicken casserole. We like this dish for lunch with rolls and fresh fruit.

—**JANICE MITCHELL** AURORA, CO

START TO FINISH: 30 MIN.
MAKES: 4 SERVINGS

- **1 tablespoon canola oil**
- **1 medium carrot, chopped**
- **1 celery rib, chopped**
- **½ cup chopped onion**
- **½ teaspoon minced garlic**
- **⅓ cup uncooked long grain rice**
- **¾ teaspoon dried basil**
- **¼ teaspoon pepper**
- **2 cans (14½ ounces each) reduced-sodium chicken broth**
- **3 tablespoons all-purpose flour**
- **1 can (5 ounces) evaporated milk**
- **2 cups cubed cooked chicken**

1. In a large saucepan, heat oil over medium-high heat; saute carrot, celery and onion until tender. Add garlic; cook and stir 1 minute. Stir in rice, seasonings and broth; bring to a boil. Reduce heat; simmer, covered, until rice is tender, about 15 minutes.

2. Mix flour and milk until smooth; stir into soup. Bring to a boil; cook and stir until thickened, about 2 minutes. Stir in chicken; heat through.

PER SERVING *1¼ cups: 322 cal., 11g fat (3g sat. fat), 73mg chol., 630mg sodium, 26g carb. (6g sugars, 1g fiber), 28g pro.* ***Diabetic Exchanges:*** *3 lean meat, 2 starch, 1 fat.*

MUSHROOM & BROCCOLI SOUP F C M

One of my girls won't eat meat and the other struggles to get enough fiber. This recipe is a great way to give them what they need in a form they love. I save broccoli stems in the freezer until I have about 2 small bags' worth, and then I make soup.

—**MARIA DAVIS** FLOWER MOUND, TX

PREP: 20 MIN. • **COOK:** 45 MIN.
MAKES: 8 SERVINGS

- **1 bunch broccoli (about 1½ pounds)**
- **1 tablespoon canola oil**
- **½ pound sliced fresh mushrooms**
- **1 tablespoon reduced-sodium soy sauce**
- **2 medium carrots, finely chopped**
- **2 celery ribs, finely chopped**
- **¼ cup finely chopped onion**
- **1 garlic clove, minced**
- **1 carton (32 ounces) vegetable broth**
- **2 cups water**
- **2 tablespoons lemon juice**

1. Cut broccoli florets into bite-size pieces. Peel and chop stalks.

2. In a large saucepan, heat oil over medium-high heat; saute mushrooms until tender, 4-6 minutes. Stir in soy sauce; remove from pan.

3. In same pan, combine broccoli stalks, carrots, celery, onion, garlic, broth and water; bring to a boil. Reduce heat; simmer, uncovered, until vegetables are softened, 25-30 minutes.

4. Puree soup using an immersion blender. Or, cool slightly and puree soup in a blender; return to pan. Stir in florets and mushrooms; bring to a boil. Reduce heat to medium; cook until broccoli is tender, 8-10 minutes, stirring soup occasionally. Stir in the lemon juice.

PER SERVING *¾ cup: 69 cal., 2g fat (0 sat. fat), 0 chol., 574mg sodium, 11g carb. (4g sugars, 3g fiber), 4g pro.* ***Diabetic Exchanges:*** *2 vegetable, ½ fat.*

MUSHROOM & BROCCOLI SOUP

POTATO CLAM CHOWDER

I ran across this recipe in one of my antique cookbooks. It's a timeless classic I like to prepare for friends and family throughout the year, but especially during the holidays.

—BETTY ANN MORGAN
UPPER MARLBORO, MD

PREP: 10 MIN. • **COOK:** 35 MIN.
MAKES: 6 SERVINGS

- **2 cans (6½ ounces each) minced clams**
- **2 bacon strips, chopped**
- **1 medium onion, chopped**
- **2 tablespoons all-purpose flour**
- **1 cup water**
- **1¾ pounds potatoes (about 4 medium), peeled and cut into ¾-in. cubes**
- **½ teaspoon salt**
- **¼ to ½ teaspoon dried thyme**
- **¼ teaspoon dried savory**
- **⅛ teaspoon pepper**
- **2 cups 2% milk**
- **2 tablespoons minced fresh parsley**

1. Drain clams, reserving clam juice. In a large saucepan, cook bacon over medium heat until crisp, stirring occasionally. Remove bacon with a slotted spoon; drain on paper towels.

2. Add onion to drippings; cook and stir 4-6 minutes or until tender. Stir in flour until blended. Gradually stir in water and reserved clam juice; cook and stir until bubbly.

3. Add potatoes and seasonings; bring to a boil, stirring frequently. Reduce heat; simmer, covered, 20-25 minutes or until potatoes are tender, stirring occasionally.

4. Stir in milk, parsley and clams; heat through. Top with bacon.

PER SERVING *1 cup: 201 cal., 6g fat (2g sat. fat), 34mg chol., 615mg sodium, 27g carb. (6g sugars, 2g fiber), 11g pro.* ***Diabetic Exchanges:*** *2 starch, 2 lean meat.*

SAUSAGE & LENTIL SOUP

SAUSAGE & LENTIL SOUP F

This recipe was given to me by my son, Chris, and we have it several times during the winter months.

—KATHY MAZUR SARASOTA, FL

PREP: 25 MIN. • **COOK:** 45 MIN.
MAKES: 12 SERVINGS (3¾ QUARTS)

- **1 package (19½ ounces) Italian turkey sausage links, casings removed**
- **1 large onion, chopped**
- **2 celery ribs, chopped**
- **1 medium carrot, chopped**
- **2 garlic cloves, minced**
- **1 bay leaf**
- **½ teaspoon fennel seed**
- **½ teaspoon dried oregano**
- **½ teaspoon dried thyme**
- **½ teaspoon pepper**
- **⅛ teaspoon crushed red pepper flakes, optional**
- **2 cups dried lentils, rinsed**
- **2 cans (14½ ounces each) no-salt-added diced tomatoes, undrained**
- **2 cartons (32 ounces each) reduced-sodium chicken broth**
- **Fat-free plain Greek yogurt and minced fresh parsley, optional**

1. In a 6-qt. stockpot, cook and crumble sausage over medium-high heat until no longer pink, 5-7 minutes; remove with a slotted spoon.

2. In same pot, saute onion, celery and carrot until tender, 4-6 minutes. Add garlic and seasonings; cook and stir 1 minute. Stir in sausage, lentils, tomatoes and broth; bring to a boil. Reduce heat; simmer, covered, until lentils are tender, 30-40 minutes, stirring occasionally. Remove bay leaf.

3. Transfer 5 cups soup to a blender; cool slightly. Cover; process until smooth. Return to pot; heat through. If desired, top servings with yogurt and parsley.

FREEZE OPTION *Freeze cooled soup in freezer containers. To use, partially thaw in refrigerator overnight. Heat soup through in a saucepan, stirring occasionally and adding a little broth or water if necessary.*

PER SERVING *1¼ cups: 187 cal., 3g fat (1g sat. fat), 17mg chol., 639mg sodium, 25g carb. (4g sugars, 5g fiber), 15g pro.* ***Diabetic Exchanges:*** *1½ starch, 1 lean meat.*

SOUPS

TURKEY & VEGETABLE BARLEY SOUP FAST FIX

I stirred up this turkey veggie soup using ingredients I already had in my fridge when I first made this. If you have them, corn, beans and celery are great in here, too.

—LISA WIGER ST. MICHAEL, MN

START TO FINISH: 30 MIN.
MAKES: 6 SERVINGS

- **1 tablespoon canola oil**
- **5 medium carrots, chopped**
- **1 medium onion, chopped**
- **⅔ cup quick-cooking barley**
- **6 cups reduced-sodium chicken broth**
- **2 cups cubed cooked turkey breast**
- **2 cups fresh baby spinach**
- **½ teaspoon pepper**

1. In a large saucepan, heat oil over medium-high heat. Add carrots and onion; cook and stir 4-5 minutes or until carrots are crisp-tender.
2. Stir in barley and broth; bring to a boil. Reduce heat; simmer, covered, 10-15 minutes or until carrots and barley are tender. Stir in turkey, spinach and pepper; heat through.

PER SERVING *1⅓ cups: 208 cal., 4g fat (1g sat. fat), 37mg chol., 662mg sodium, 23g carb. (4g sugars, 6g fiber), 21g pro.* ***Diabetic Exchanges:*** *2 lean meat, 1 starch, 1 vegetable, ½ fat.*

TURKEY & VEGETABLE BARLEY SOUP

GREEK TOMATO SOUP WITH ORZO

GREEK TOMATO SOUP WITH ORZO

My recipe for *manestra*, which means orzo in Greek, is a straightforward and very easy recipe. A few steps is all it takes to transform simple ingredients into a creamy, tomatoey one-pot wonder in about 30 minutes.

—KIKI VAGIANOS MELROSE, MA

PREP: 10 MIN. • **COOK:** 25 MIN.
MAKES: 4 SERVINGS

- **2 tablespoons olive oil**
- **1 medium onion, chopped**
- **1¼ cups uncooked whole wheat orzo pasta**
- **2 cans (14½ ounces each) whole tomatoes, undrained, coarsely chopped**
- **3 cups reduced-sodium chicken broth**
- **2 teaspoons dried oregano**
- **¼ teaspoon salt**
- **¼ teaspoon pepper**
- **Crumbled feta cheese and minced fresh basil, optional**

1. In large saucepan, heat oil over medium heat; saute onion until tender, 3-5 minutes. Add orzo; cook and stir until lightly toasted.
2. Stir in tomatoes, broth and seasonings; bring to a boil. Reduce heat; simmer, covered, until orzo is tender, 15-20 minutes, stirring occasionally. If desired, top with feta and basil.

FREEZE OPTION *Freeze cooled soup in freezer containers. To use, partially thaw in refrigerator overnight. Heat soup through in a saucepan, stirring occasionally and adding a little broth or water if necessary.*

PER SERVING *1 cup: 299 cal., 8g fat (1g sat. fat), 0 chol., 882mg sodium, 47g carb. (7g sugars, 12g fiber), 11g pro.*

HEALTH TIP *Using reduced-sodium chicken broth instead of regular saves more than 300 milligrams of sodium per serving. To save even more, look for unsalted chicken broth. Using unsalted broth can bring the sodium down to just 488 milligrams per serving. Check the labels, as salt content can vary among brands.*

CREAMY BUTTERNUT SOUP F

Thick and velvety, this soup topped with chives and a drizzle of sour cream looks as special as it tastes.

—**AMANDA SMITH** CINCINNATI, OH

PREP: 15 MIN. • **COOK:** 20 MIN.
MAKES: 10 SERVINGS (2½ QUARTS)

- **1 medium butternut squash, peeled, seeded and cubed (about 6 cups)**
- **3 medium potatoes (about 1 pound), peeled and cubed**
- **1 large onion, diced**
- **2 chicken bouillon cubes**
- **2 garlic cloves, minced**
- **5 cups water**
- **Sour cream and minced fresh chives, optional**

1. In a 6-qt. stockpot, combine first six ingredients; bring to a boil. Reduce heat; simmer, covered, until vegetables are tender, 15-20 minutes.
2. Puree soup using an immersion blender. Or, cool slightly and puree soup in batches in a blender; return to pan and heat through. If desired, serve with sour cream and chives.

PER SERVING *1 cup: 112 cal., 0 fat (0 sat. fat), 0 chol., 231mg sodium, 27g carb. (5g sugars, 4g fiber), 3g pro.* ***Diabetic Exchanges:*** *2 starch.*

ROASTED CAULIFLOWER & RED PEPPER SOUP

When cooler weather comes, soup is one of our favorite meals. I developed this recipe for my husband and me. I wanted it to be a healthier version of all the cream-based soups out there. After a bit of trial and error, this is the keeper.

—**ELIZABETH BRAMKAMP** GIG HARBOR, WA

PREP: 50 MIN. + STANDING
COOK: 25 MIN.
MAKES: 6 SERVINGS

- **2 medium sweet red peppers, halved and seeded**
- **1 large head cauliflower, broken into florets (about 7 cups)**
- **4 tablespoons olive oil, divided**
- **1 cup chopped sweet onion**
- **2 garlic cloves, minced**
- **2½ teaspoons minced fresh rosemary or ¾ teaspoon dried rosemary, crushed**
- **½ teaspoon paprika**
- **¼ cup all-purpose flour**
- **4 cups chicken stock**
- **1 cup 2% milk**
- **½ teaspoon salt**
- **¼ teaspoon pepper**
- **⅛ to ¼ teaspoon cayenne pepper**
- **Shredded Parmesan cheese, optional**

1. Preheat broiler. Place peppers on a foil-lined baking sheet, skin side up. Broil 4 in. from heat until skins are blistered, about 5 minutes. Transfer to a bowl; let stand, covered, 20 minutes. Change oven setting to bake; preheat oven to 400°.
2. Toss cauliflower with 2 tablespoons oil; spread in a 15x10x1-in. pan. Roast until tender, 25-30 minutes, stirring occasionally. Remove skin and seeds from peppers; chop peppers.
3. In a 6-qt. stockpot, heat remaining oil over medium heat. Add the onion; cook until golden and softened, 6-8 minutes, stirring occasionally. Add garlic, rosemary and paprika; cook and stir 1 minute. Stir in flour until blended; cook and stir 1 minute. Gradually stir in chicken stock. Bring to a boil, stirring constantly; cook and stir until thickened.
4. Stir in cauliflower and peppers. Puree soup using an immersion blender. Or, cool slightly and puree soup in batches in a blender; return to pot. Stir in milk and remaining seasonings; heat through. If desired, serve with cheese.

FREEZE OPTION *Freeze cooled soup in freezer containers. To use, partially thaw in refrigerator overnight. Heat soup through in a saucepan, stirring occasionally and adding a little stock or milk if necessary.*

PER SERVING *1 cup: 193 cal., 10g fat (2g sat. fat), 3mg chol., 601mg sodium, 19g carb. (8g sugars, 4g fiber), 8g pro.* ***Diabetic Exchanges:*** *2 vegetable, 2 fat, ½ starch.*

ROASTED CAULIFLOWER & RED PEPPER SOUP

TOMATO-ORANGE SOUP

Who knew orange and tomato were such a good pair? Whenever I serve this, I keep the recipe handy for requests.

—**BARBARA WOOD** ST. JOHN'S, NL

PREP: 30 MIN. • **COOK:** 1 HOUR • **MAKES:** 6 SERVINGS

- **3 pounds tomatoes (about 12 medium), halved**
- **2 tablespoons canola oil, divided**
- **2 medium onions, chopped**
- **2 garlic cloves, minced**
- **3 cups reduced-sodium chicken broth**
- **1 cup orange juice**
- **2 tablespoons tomato paste**
- **4 teaspoons grated orange peel**
- **1 tablespoon butter**
- **1 tablespoon minced fresh cilantro**
- **1 tablespoon honey**
- **¼ teaspoon salt**

1. Preheat oven to 450°. Place tomatoes in a 15x10x1-in. baking pan, cut side down; brush tops with 1 tablespoon oil. Roast for 20-25 minutes or until skins are blistered and charred. Remove and discard skins.

2. In a 6-qt. stockpot, heat remaining oil over medium-high heat. Add onions; cook and stir until tender. Add garlic; cook 1 minute longer. Stir in broth, orange juice, tomato paste and roasted tomatoes; bring to a boil. Reduce heat; simmer, uncovered, 45 minutes.

3. Stir in orange peel, butter, cilantro, honey and salt. Remove from heat; cool slightly. Process soup in batches in a blender until smooth. Return to pot; heat through.

PER SERVING *1 cup: 160 cal., 7g fat (2g sat. fat), 5mg chol., 419mg sodium, 22g carb. (15g sugars, 4g fiber), 5g pro.* ***Diabetic Exchanges:*** *2 vegetable, 1½ fat, ½ starch.*

TOMATO-ORANGE SOUP

VEGGIE THAI CURRY SOUP

VEGGIE THAI CURRY SOUP FAST FIX

My go-to Thai restaurant inspired this curry soup. Shiitake mushrooms are my favorite, but any fresh mushroom will work. Fresh basil and lime add a burst of bright flavors.

—**TRE BALCHOWSKY** SAUSALITO, CA

START TO FINISH: 30 MIN. • **MAKES:** 6 SERVINGS

- **1 package (8.8 ounces) thin rice noodles or uncooked angel hair pasta**
- **1 tablespoon sesame oil**
- **2 tablespoons red curry paste**
- **1 cup light coconut milk**
- **1 carton (32 ounces) reduced-sodium chicken or vegetable broth**
- **1 tablespoon reduced-sodium soy sauce or fish sauce**
- **1 package (14 ounces) firm tofu, drained and cubed**
- **1 can (8¾ ounces) whole baby corn, drained and cut in half**
- **1 can (5 ounces) bamboo shoots, drained**
- **1½ cups sliced fresh shiitake mushrooms**
- **½ medium sweet red pepper, cut into thin strips**
- **Torn fresh basil leaves and lime wedges**

1. Prepare noodles according to package directions.

2. Meanwhile, in a 6-qt. stockpot, heat oil over medium heat. Add curry paste; cook 30 seconds or until aromatic. Gradually whisk in coconut milk until blended. Stir in broth and soy sauce; bring to a boil.

3. Add tofu and vegetables to stockpot; cook 3-5 minutes or until vegetables are crisp-tender. Drain noodles; add to soup. Top each serving with basil; serve with lime wedges.

PER SERVING *1⅔ cups: 289 cal., 9g fat (3g sat. fat), 0 chol., 772mg sodium, 41g carb. (3g sugars, 2g fiber), 11g pro.* ***Diabetic Exchanges:*** *2½ starch, 1 medium-fat meat, ½ fat.*

SPINACH & WHITE BEAN SOUP F M FAST FIX

START TO FINISH: 30 MIN. • **MAKES:** 6 SERVINGS

- **2 teaspoons olive oil**
- **3 garlic cloves, minced**
- **3 cans (15 ounces each) cannellini beans, rinsed and drained, divided**
- **¼ teaspoon pepper**
- **1 carton (32 ounces) vegetable broth**
- **4 cups chopped fresh spinach (about 3 ounces)**
- **¼ cup thinly sliced fresh basil**
- **Shredded Parmesan cheese, optional**

1. In a large saucepan, heat oil over medium heat. Add garlic; cook and stir 30-45 seconds or until tender. Stir in two cans of beans, pepper and broth.

2. Puree mixture using an immersion blender. Or, cool slightly then puree in a blender and return to pan. Stir in remaining can of beans; bring to a boil. Reduce heat; simmer, covered, 15 minutes, stirring occasionally.

3. Stir in spinach and basil; cook, uncovered, 2-4 minutes or until spinach is wilted. If desired, serve with cheese.

PER SERVING *1¼ cups: 192 cal., 2g fat (0 sat. fat), 0 chol., 886mg sodium, 33g carb. (1g sugars, 9g fiber), 9g pro.*

HEALTH TIP *Reduced-sodium vegetable broth isn't widely available, but the organic versions of big-brand vegetable broths are typically lower in sodium than conventional versions.*

For me, soup is love, comfort, happiness and memories. With all its veggies and beans, this one appeals to my "kitchen sink" style of cooking.

—**ANNETTE PALERMO** BEACH HAVEN, NJ

MAKEOVER CURRIED CHICKEN RICE SOUP

CAROLINA SHRIMP SOUP

CAROLINA SHRIMP SOUP FAST FIX

Fresh shrimp from the Carolina coast is one of our favorite foods. We add kale, garlic, red peppers and black-eyed peas to complete this wholesome, filling soup.

—**MARY MARLOWE LEVERETTE** COLUMBIA, SC

START TO FINISH: 25 MIN. • **MAKES:** 6 SERVINGS

- **4 teaspoons olive oil, divided**
- **1 pound uncooked shrimp (31-40 per pound), peeled and deveined**
- **5 garlic cloves, minced**
- **1 bunch kale, trimmed and coarsely chopped (about 16 cups)**
- **1 medium sweet red pepper, cut into ¾-inch pieces**
- **3 cups reduced-sodium chicken broth**
- **1 can (15½ ounces) black-eyed peas, rinsed and drained**
- **¼ teaspoon salt**
- **¼ teaspoon pepper**
- **Minced fresh chives, optional**

1. In a 6-qt. stockpot, heat 2 teaspoons oil over medium-high heat. Add shrimp; cook and stir 2 minutes. Add garlic; cook 1-2 minutes longer or just until shrimp turns pink. Remove from pot.

2. In same pot, heat remaining oil over medium-high heat. Stir in kale and red pepper; cook, covered, 8-10 minutes or until kale is tender, stirring occasionally. Add broth; bring to a boil. Stir in peas, salt, pepper and shrimp; heat through. If desired, sprinkle servings with chives.

PER SERVING *1 cup: 188 cal., 5g fat (1g sat. fat), 92mg chol., 585mg sodium, 18g carb. (2g sugars, 3g fiber), 19g pro.* ***Diabetic Exchanges:*** *2 lean meat, 2 vegetable, ½ starch, ½ fat.*

HEALTH TIP *This soup's colorful mix of veggies means you're getting a variety of nutrients. Aim for lots of color when planning meals through the day.*

SOUPS

FRESH CORN & POTATO CHOWDER

This soup was one of my favorites as a child in upstate New York, and I still love it today. For extra depth, place the spent cob in the soup, simmer, then remove.

—TRACY BIVINS KNOB NOSTER, MO

PREP: 15 MIN. • **COOK:** 25 MIN.
MAKES: 6 SERVINGS

- **1 tablespoon butter**
- **1 medium onion, chopped**
- **1 pound red potatoes (about 3 medium), cubed**
- **1½ cups fresh or frozen corn (about 7 ounces)**
- **3 cups reduced-sodium chicken broth**
- **1¼ cups half-and-half cream, divided**
- **2 green onions, thinly sliced**
- **½ teaspoon salt**
- **¼ teaspoon freshly ground pepper**
- **3 tablespoons all-purpose flour**
- **1 tablespoon minced fresh parsley**

1. In a large saucepan, heat butter over medium-high heat. Add onion; cook and stir 2-4 minutes or until tender. Add potatoes, corn, broth, 1 cup cream, green onions, salt and pepper; bring to a boil. Reduce heat; simmer, covered, 12-15 minutes or until potatoes are tender.

2. In a small bowl, mix flour with the remaining cream until smooth; stir into soup. Return to a boil, stirring constantly; cook and stir 1-2 minutes or until soup is slightly thickened. Stir in parsley.

PER SERVING *1 cup: 200 cal., 8g fat (5g sat. fat), 30mg chol., 534mg sodium, 26g carb. (6g sugars, 3g fiber), 7g pro.* ***Diabetic Exchanges:*** *2 starch, 1½ fat.*

FRESH CORN & POTATO CHOWDER

WILD RICE MUSHROOM SOUP

WILD RICE MUSHROOM SOUP

Often mushrooms get used only as a seasoning or added flavor, but I think they are delicious enough to be the main part of a meal. This recipe uses a large quantity of mushrooms, and the result is delicious. Even though this contains some dairy, it freezes quite well!

—WENDY CAMPBELL NEW WILMINGTON, PA

PREP: 10 MIN. • **COOK:** 1 HOUR
MAKES: 8 SERVINGS (2 QUARTS)

- **½ cup uncooked wild rice**
- **1½ cups water**
- **8 ounces smoked turkey sausage, sliced**
- **⅓ cup all-purpose flour**
- **1 carton (32 ounces) reduced-sodium chicken broth, divided**
- **2 tablespoons butter**
- **1 large onion, chopped**
- **½ pound sliced fresh mushrooms**
- **1 cup whole milk**
- **¼ teaspoon pepper**

1. In a small saucepan, combine wild rice and water; bring to a boil. Reduce heat; simmer, covered, until rice is tender, 40-45 minutes.

2. In a large saucepan, cook and stir sausage over medium heat until lightly browned, 3-4 minutes. Remove from pan.

3. Mix flour and ½ cup broth until smooth. In same pan, heat butter over medium heat; saute the onion and mushrooms until tender, 4-5 minutes. Add remaining broth; gradually stir in flour mixture. Bring mixture to a boil; cook and stir until slightly thickened, 2-3 minutes. Add the milk, pepper, rice and sausage; heat through, stirring occasionally.

PER SERVING *1 cup: 157 cal., 6g fat (3g sat. fat), 28mg chol., 644mg sodium, 17g carb. (4g sugars, 1g fiber), 10g pro.* ***Diabetic Exchanges:*** *1 starch, 1 lean meat, 1 fat.*

DID YOU KNOW?

Wild rice is not a rice at all, but an ancient grass native to the northern U.S. and southern Canada near the Great Lakes, as well as parts of Asia. Today it is also farmed in California. An important food source for native Chippewa and Sioux tribes, the annual harvest continues to be meaningful both culturally and financially to Native Americans.

AUTUMN BISQUE M

(PICTURED ON P. 20)

I like cozy comfort soups that taste creamy but without the cream. This one's full of good stuff like rutabagas, leeks, fresh herbs and almond milk.

—**MERRY GRAHAM** NEWHALL, CA

PREP: 25 MIN. • **COOK:** 50 MIN.
MAKES: 12 SERVINGS (3½ QUARTS)

- ¼ cup buttery spread
- 2 teaspoons minced fresh chives
- 2 teaspoons minced fresh parsley
- ½ teaspoon grated lemon peel

BISQUE

- 2 tablespoons olive oil
- 2 large rutabagas, peeled and cubed (about 9 cups)
- 1 large celery root, peeled and cubed (about 3 cups)
- 3 medium leeks (white portion only), chopped (about 2 cups)
- 1 large carrot, cubed (about ⅔ cup)
- 3 garlic cloves, minced
- 7 cups vegetable stock
- 2 teaspoons minced fresh thyme
- 1½ teaspoons minced fresh rosemary
- 1 teaspoon salt
- ½ teaspoon coarsely ground pepper
- 2 cups almond milk
- 2 tablespoons minced fresh chives

1. Mix first four ingredients. Using a melon baller or 1-teaspoon measuring spoon, shape mixture into 12 balls. Freeze on a waxed paper-lined baking sheet until firm. Transfer to a freezer container; freeze up to 2 months.

2. In a 6-qt. stock pot, heat oil over medium heat; saute rutabagas, celery root, leeks and carrot 8 minutes. Add garlic; cook and stir 2 minutes. Stir in stock, herbs, salt and pepper; bring to a boil. Reduce heat and simmer, covered, until vegetables are tender, 30-35 minutes.

3. Puree soup using an immersion blender. Or, cool slightly and puree soup in batches in a blender; return to pan. Stir in almond milk; heat through. Top servings with chives and herbed buttery spread balls.

PER SERVING *1 cup: 146 cal., 7g fat (2g sat. fat), 0 chol., 672mg sodium, 20g carb. (9g sugars, 5g fiber), 3g pro.* ***Diabetic Exchanges:*** *1 starch, 1 fat.*

SPICY SWEET POTATO & CHICKPEA SOUP

I love hearty, healthy entree soups, and a bowl of this Southwestern sweet potato-chickpea soup really satisfies. I add a can of chickpeas for protein, making a big bowlful that's ideal for an easy dinner. This soup reheats and even freezes beautifully, so I often make a double batch.

—**JENNIFER FISHER** AUSTIN, TX

PREP: 20 MIN. • **COOK:** 25 MIN.
MAKES: 4 SERVINGS

- 2 teaspoons olive oil
- 1 medium onion, chopped
- 2 teaspoons ground ancho chili pepper
- ½ teaspoon ground cumin
- 1 pound sweet potatoes (about 2 medium), peeled and cut into 1-inch pieces
- 1 can (15 ounces) chickpeas, rinsed and drained
- 4 cups chicken stock
- ¼ cup water
- 6 bacon strips, cooked and crumbled
- 2 green onions, sliced
- Shaved Parmesan cheese, optional

1. In a 6-qt. stockpot, heat oil over medium-high heat; saute onion until tender, 4-6 minutes. Stir in spices. Add potatoes, chickpeas, stock and water; bring to a boil. Reduce heat; simmer, covered, until potatoes are tender, 15-20 minutes.

2. Puree soup using an immersion blender. Or, cool slightly and puree soup in batches in a blender; return to pan and heat through. Top with bacon, green onions and, if desired, cheese.

FREEZE OPTION *Freeze cooled soup in freezer containers. To use, partially thaw in refrigerator overnight. Heat soup through in a saucepan, stirring occasionally and adding a little stock or water if necessary.*

PER SERVING *1½ cups: 334 cal., 9g fat (2g sat. fat), 12mg chol., 880mg sodium, 48g carb. (16g sugars, 8g fiber), 15g pro.*

SPICY SWEET POTATO & CHICKPEA SOUP

49

46

39

Side Salads

"For an Italian twist on salad, I mix greens with red onion, mushrooms, olives, pepperoncini, lemon juice and seasoning. Add tomatoes and carrots, if you like."

—**DEBORAH LOOP** CLINTON TOWNSHIP, MI
about her recipe, Italian Salad with Lemon Vinaigrette , on page 51

DILL-MARINATED BROCCOLI S C M

A co-worker tipped me off to this splashy marinade for broccoli. The longer you wait, the better it gets. Add some fresh cauliflower if you have it.

—TIFFONY BUSH HUNTINGDON, PA

PREP: 15 MIN.+ MARINATING
MAKES: 8 SERVINGS

- **6 cups fresh broccoli florets**
- **1 cup canola oil**
- **1 cup cider vinegar**
- **2 tablespoons snipped fresh dill**
- **2 teaspoons sugar**
- **1 teaspoon garlic salt**
- **1 teaspoon salt**

1. Place broccoli in a large resealable plastic bag. Whisk together remaining ingredients; add to broccoli. Seal bag and turn to coat; refrigerate 4 hours or overnight.

2. To serve, drain broccoli, discarding marinade.

PER SERVING *1 serving: 79 cal., 7g fat (1g sat. fat), 0 chol., 119mg sodium, 3g carb. (0 sugars, 2g fiber), 2g pro.* ***Diabetic Exchanges:*** *1½ fat, 1 vegetable.*

DILL-MARINATED BROCCOLI

My sister gave me fresh tomatoes and basil, so I made a bread salad known as panzanella. The longer it sits, the more the bread soaks up the seasonings.

—JANNINE FISK MALDEN, MA

GARDEN BOUNTY PANZANELLA SALAD

GARDEN BOUNTY PANZANELLA SALAD M

PREP: 15 MIN. • **COOK:** 20 MIN.
MAKES: 16 SERVINGS (1 CUP EACH)

- **¼ cup olive oil**
- **12 ounces French or ciabatta bread, cut into 1-inch cubes (about 12 cups)**
- **4 large tomatoes, coarsely chopped**
- **1 English cucumber, coarsely chopped**
- **1 medium green pepper, cut into 1-inch pieces**
- **1 medium sweet yellow pepper, cut into 1-inch pieces**
- **1 small red onion, halved and thinly sliced**
- **½ cup coarsely chopped fresh basil**
- **¼ cup grated Parmesan cheese**
- **¾ teaspoon kosher salt**
- **¼ teaspoon coarsely ground pepper**
- **½ cup Italian salad dressing**

1. In a large skillet, heat 2 tablespoons oil over medium heat. Add half of the bread cubes; cook and stir until toasted, about 8 minutes. Remove from pan. Repeat with remaining oil and bread cubes.

2. Combine bread cubes, tomatoes, cucumber, peppers, onion, basil, cheese, salt and pepper. Toss with dressing.

PER SERVING *1 cup: 131 cal., 6g fat (1g sat. fat), 1mg chol., 310mg sodium, 18g carb. (3g sugars, 2g fiber), 3g pro.* ***Diabetic Exchanges:*** *1 starch, 1 vegetable, 1 fat.*

PESTO QUINOA SALAD C M (PICTURED ON P. 37)

(PICTURED ON P. 37)

My daughter-in-law got me hooked on quinoa, and I'm so glad she did! I've been substituting quinoa in some of my favorite pasta recipes, and this dish is the happy result of one of those experiments. I love using my garden tomatoes and peppers in this salad; however, sun-dried tomatoes and jarred roasted peppers are equally delicious!

—SUE GRONHOLZ BEAVER DAM, WI

PREP: 10 MIN. + CHILLING • **COOK:** 15 MIN.
MAKES: 4 SERVINGS

- **⅔ cup water**
- **⅓ cup quinoa, rinsed**
- **2 tablespoons prepared pesto**
- **1 tablespoon finely chopped sweet onion**
- **1 tablespoon olive oil**
- **1 teaspoon balsamic vinegar**
- **¼ teaspoon salt**
- **1 medium sweet red pepper, chopped**
- **1 cup cherry tomatoes, quartered**
- **⅔ cup fresh mozzarella cheese pearls (about 4 ounces)**
- **2 tablespoons minced fresh basil, optional**

1. In a small saucepan, bring water to a boil; stir in quinoa. Reduce heat; simmer, covered, until the liquid is absorbed, 10-12 minutes. Cool slightly.
2. Mix pesto, onion, oil, vinegar and salt; stir in pepper, tomatoes, cheese and quinoa. Refrigerate, covered, to allow flavors to blend, 1-2 hours. If desired, stir in basil.

PER SERVING *¾ cup: 183 cal., 11g fat (4g sat. fat), 15mg chol., 268mg sodium, 14g carb. (3g sugars, 2g fiber), 6g pro.* ***Diabetic Exchanges:*** *1 starch, 1 medium-fat meat, ½ fat.*

TOP TIP

Depending on your region, sweet onions may not be available in the fall and winter months. Luckily, red onion is a good substitute in this recipe.

GRILLED VEGETABLE SALAD WITH POPPY SEED DRESSING C FAST FIX

My Italian-style grilled veggies have a wonderful sweet and sour dressing. Best of all, I pick the fresh veggies and herbs from my garden.

—LAURA MAST DEFIANCE, OH

START TO FINISH: 25 MIN.
MAKES: 2 SERVINGS

- **2 tablespoons canola oil**
- **1 tablespoon cider vinegar**
- **2 teaspoons sugar**
- **½ teaspoon grated onion**
- **½ teaspoon poppy seeds**
- **¼ teaspoon ground mustard**
- **Dash salt**

SALAD

- **1 small zucchini, cut into ¾-inch pieces**
- **1 small sweet yellow pepper, cut into 1-inch pieces**
- **⅔ cup cherry tomatoes**
- **2 teaspoons olive oil**
- **¼ teaspoon salt**
- **⅛ teaspoon freshly ground pepper**
- **2 teaspoons minced fresh basil**
- **2 teaspoons minced fresh parsley**
- **1 teaspoon minced fresh thyme**

1. In a small bowl, whisk the first seven ingredients until blended. Refrigerate until serving.
2. In a large bowl, combine zucchini, yellow pepper and tomatoes. Add oil, salt and pepper; toss to coat. Transfer to a grill wok or an open grill basket; place on grill rack. Grill, covered, over medium-high heat 10-12 minutes or until vegetables are crisp-tender, stirring occasionally.
3. Transfer vegetables to a serving bowl; sprinkle with herbs. Serve with dressing.

NOTE *If you do not have a grill wok or basket, use a disposable foil pan. Poke holes in the bottom of the pan with a meat fork to allow liquid to drain.*

PER SERVING *1 cup: 219 cal., 19g fat (2g sat. fat), 0 chol., 378mg sodium, 11g carb. (8g sugars, 2g fiber), 2g pro.*

SIDE SALADS

CHUNKY VEGGIE SLAW

CHUNKY VEGGIE SLAW C M FAST FIX

So much for same ol' slaw—this snappy coleslaw gets a fresh approach when you add broccoli, cucumbers, snap peas and crunchy walnuts.

—**NICHOLAS KING** DULUTH, MN

START TO FINISH: 25 MIN.
MAKES: 14 SERVINGS (1 CUP EACH)

- **1 small head cabbage, chopped**
- **6 cups fresh broccoli florets**
- **1 medium cucumber, chopped**
- **2 celery ribs, sliced**
- **12 fresh sugar snap peas, halved**
- **1 small green pepper, chopped**
- **¾ cup buttermilk**
- **½ cup reduced-fat mayonnaise**
- **3 tablespoons cider vinegar**
- **2 tablespoons sugar**
- **½ teaspoon salt**
- **1 cup chopped walnuts, toasted**
- **2 green onions, thinly sliced**

In a large bowl, combine the first six ingredients. In a small bowl, whisk buttermilk, mayonnaise, vinegar, sugar and salt. Pour over salad; toss to coat. Top with walnuts and green onions. Refrigerate leftovers.

NOTE *To toast nuts, bake in a shallow pan in a 350° oven for 5-10 minutes or cook in a skillet over low heat until lightly browned, stirring occasionally.*

PER SERVING *1 cup: 125 cal., 9g fat (1g sat. fat), 4mg chol., 189mg sodium, 10g carb. (6g sugars, 3g fiber), 4g pro.* ***Diabetic Exchanges:*** *2 vegetable, 1½ fat.*

GREEK COUSCOUS SALAD

I love the fresh taste of crisp veggies in a satisfying salad, hearty enough for a full meal.

—**TERI RASEY** CADILLAC, MI

PREP: 15 MIN. • **COOK:** 5 MIN. + COOLING
MAKES: 12 SERVINGS

- **1 can (14½ ounces) reduced-sodium chicken broth**
- **1¾ cups uncooked whole wheat couscous (about 11 ounces)**

DRESSING

- **½ cup olive oil**
- **1½ teaspoons grated lemon peel**
- **¼ cup lemon juice**
- **1 teaspoon adobo seasoning**
- **¼ teaspoon salt**

SALAD

- **1 English cucumber, halved lengthwise and sliced**
- **2 cups grape tomatoes, halved**
- **1 cup coarsely chopped fresh parsley**
- **1 can (6½ ounces) sliced ripe olives, drained**
- **4 green onions, chopped**
- **½ cup crumbled feta cheese**

1. In a large saucepan, bring broth to a boil. Stir in couscous. Remove from heat; let stand, covered, until broth is absorbed, about 5 minutes. Transfer to a large bowl; cool completely.

2. Whisk together the dressing ingredients. Add cucumber, tomatoes, parsley, olives and green onions to couscous; stir in dressing. Gently stir in cheese. Serve immediately or refrigerate and serve cold.

PER SERVING *¾ cup: 335 cal., 18g fat (3g sat. fat), 4mg chol., 637mg sodium, 39g carb. (3g sugars, 7g fiber), 9g pro.*

GREEK COUSCOUS SALAD

CREAM-OF-THE-CROP VEGGIES

CREAM-OF-THE-CROP VEGGIES S C M

Veggies can be a hard sell for kids. So let them choose from the garden patch and they'll end up eating everything without a scrap left.

—**LORRAINE CALAND** SHUNIAH, ON

PREP: 20 MIN. • **COOK:** 15 MIN. + CHILLING
MAKES: 16 SERVINGS (¾ CUP EACH)

- **3 quarts water**
- **4 medium carrots, sliced**
- **1½ cups fresh or frozen peas**
- **2 small yellow summer squash, halved and cut into ½-inch slices**
- **1 pound fresh wax beans, trimmed and cut into 2-inch pieces**
- **1 pound fresh green beans, trimmed and cut into 2-inch pieces**
- **⅓ cup minced fresh chives**
- **⅓ cup mayonnaise**
- **⅓ cup creme fraiche or sour cream**
- **3 tablespoons thinly sliced fresh basil**
- **4 teaspoons snipped fresh dill**
- **½ teaspoon salt**
- **¼ teaspoon pepper**

1. In a Dutch oven over high heat, bring water to a boil. Add carrots and peas; cook, uncovered, 3 minutes. Add the squash and cook 1 minute longer or until crisp-tender. Remove vegetables and immediately drop into ice water. Drain and pat dry. Repeat with wax and green beans, cooking them separately until crisp-tender, about 3 minutes.

2. Place all vegetables in a large bowl. Sprinkle with chives; toss to combine.

3. In a small bowl, mix the remaining ingredients. Add to vegetables; toss gently to coat. Refrigerate, covered, 3-4 hours or until cold.

PER SERVING *¾ cup: 90 cal., 6g fat (2g sat. fat), 6mg chol., 117mg sodium, 8g carb. (3g sugars, 3g fiber), 2g pro.* ***Diabetic Exchanges:*** *1 vegetable, 1 fat.*

AVOCADO FRUIT SALAD WITH TANGERINE VINAIGRETTE M FAST FIX

On those long summer days when we just want to relax, I make a cool salad that includes avocado, berries and mint. The tangerine dressing is refreshingly different.

—**CAROLE RESNICK** CLEVELAND, OH

START TO FINISH: 25 MIN.
MAKES: 8 SERVINGS

- **3 medium ripe avocados, peeled and thinly sliced**
- **3 medium mangoes, peeled and thinly sliced**
- **1 cup fresh raspberries**
- **1 cup fresh blackberries**
- **¼ cup minced fresh mint**
- **¼ cup sliced almonds, toasted**

DRESSING

- **½ cup olive oil**
- **1 teaspoon grated tangerine or orange peel**
- **¼ cup tangerine or orange juice**
- **2 tablespoons balsamic vinegar**
- **½ teaspoon salt**
- **¼ teaspoon freshly ground pepper**

Arrange avocados and fruit on a serving plate; sprinkle with mint and almonds. In a small bowl, whisk dressing ingredients until blended; drizzle over salad.

NOTE *To toast nuts, bake in a shallow pan in a 350° oven for 5-10 minutes or cook in a skillet over low heat until lightly browned, stirring occasionally.*

PER SERVING *1 cup salad with 4 teaspoons dressing: 321 cal., 23g fat (3g sat. fat), 0 chol., 154mg sodium, 29g carb. (20g sugars, 8g fiber), 3g pro.*

AVOCADO FRUIT SALAD WITH TANGERINE VINAIGRETTE

SUMMER MACARONI SALAD M

When our family grills out, my mother asks me to make the macaroni salad. To make it extra creamy, I like to keep a small amount of dressing separate and stir it in just before serving.
—**CARLY CURTIN** ELLICOTT CITY, MD

PREP: 20 MIN. + CHILLING • **COOK:** 15 MIN.
MAKES: 16 SERVINGS (¾ CUP EACH)

- **1 package (16 ounces) elbow macaroni**
- **1 cup reduced-fat mayonnaise**
- **3 to 4 tablespoons water or 2% milk**
- **2 tablespoons red wine vinegar**
- **1 tablespoon sugar**
- **1½ teaspoons salt**
- **¼ teaspoon garlic powder**
- **¼ teaspoon pepper**
- **1 small sweet yellow, orange or red pepper, finely chopped**
- **1 small green pepper, finely chopped**
- **1 small onion, finely chopped**
- **1 celery rib, finely chopped**
- **2 tablespoons minced fresh parsley**

1. Cook macaroni according to package directions. Drain; rinse with cold water and drain again.
2. In a small bowl, mix mayonnaise, water, vinegar, sugar and seasonings until blended. In a large bowl, combine macaroni, peppers, onion and celery. Add 1 cup dressing; toss gently to coat. Refrigerate, covered, 2 hours or until cold. Cover and refrigerate remaining dressing to add just before serving.
3. To serve, stir in reserved dressing. Sprinkle with parsley.

PER SERVING *3/4 cup: 160 cal., 6g fat (1g sat. fat), 5mg chol., 320mg sodium, 24g carb. (3g sugars, 1g fiber), 4g pro.* ***Diabetic Exchanges:*** *1½ starch, 1 fat.*

SUMMER MACARONI SALAD

STRAWBERRY PASTA SALAD

STRAWBERRY PASTA SALAD S M

Bow tie pasta with strawberries makes a refreshing salad, especially with a little chopped mint. I multiply it for brunches, potlucks and even tailgates.
—**BARBARA LENTO** HOUSTON, PA

PREP: 20 MIN. • **COOK:** 15 MIN.
MAKES: 12 SERVINGS (⅔ CUP EACH)

- **½ pound uncooked mini farfalle or other bow tie pasta**
- **½ cup (4 ounces) lemon yogurt**
- **¼ cup canola oil**
- **2 tablespoons lemon juice**
- **½ teaspoon sea salt**
- **⅛ teaspoon cayenne pepper**
- **1 green onion, thinly sliced**
- **2 tablespoons crystallized ginger, finely chopped**
- **1 tablespoon pickled jalapeno slices, finely chopped**
- **1 pound fresh strawberries, quartered**
- **¼ cup slivered almonds, toasted**
- **Toasted flaked coconut and small fresh mint leaves, optional**

1. Cook pasta according to package directions. Drain pasta; rinse with cold water and drain well.
2. In a large bowl, whisk yogurt, oil, lemon juice, salt and cayenne until blended; stir in green onion, ginger and jalapeno. Add pasta and toss to coat.
3. Refrigerate, covered, until serving. Stir in strawberries and sprinkle with almonds just before serving. If desired, sprinkle with coconut and mint.

NOTE *To toast nuts and coconut, bake in separate shallow pans in a 350° oven for 5-10 minutes or until golden brown, stirring occasionally.*

PER SERVING *2/3 cup: 153 cal., 6g fat (1g sat. fat), 1mg chol., 96mg sodium, 21g carb. (5g sugars, 2g fiber), 4g pro.* ***Diabetic Exchanges:*** *1 starch, 1 fat, ½ fruit.*

SNAP PEA SALAD F C M FAST FIX

START TO FINISH: 20 MIN. • **MAKES:** 12 SERVINGS (¾ CUP EACH)

- **¼ cup white wine vinegar**
- **¼ cup Dijon mustard**
- **2 tablespoons minced fresh parsley**
- **2 tablespoons olive oil**
- **2 tablespoons honey**
- **1 tablespoon lemon juice**
- **1 teaspoon salt**
- **½ teaspoon pepper**
- **3 pounds fresh sugar snap peas**
- **Grated lemon peel, optional**

1. For vinaigrette, in a small bowl, whisk the first eight ingredients until blended. In a 6-qt. stockpot, bring 16 cups water to a boil. Add snap peas; cook, uncovered, 2-3 minutes or just until peas turn bright green. Remove the peas and immediately drop into ice water. Drain and pat dry; place in a large bowl.

2. Drizzle with vinaigrette and toss to coat. Serve salad immediately or refrigerate, covered, up to 4 hours before serving. If desired, sprinkle with lemon peel.

PER SERVING *¾ cup: 84 cal., 3g fat (0 sat. fat), 0 chol., 322mg sodium, 12g carb. (7g sugars, 3g fiber), 4g pro.* ***Diabetic Exchanges:*** *1 vegetable, ½ starch, ½ fat.*

HEALTH TIP *Sugar snap peas are a source of lutein and zeaxanthin, two carotenoids that can reduce the risk of chronic eye diseases.*

When snap peas are in season, we can't resist making this crunchy salad. I usually serve it cold, but it's also good warm, with the peas straight from the pot.
—**JEAN ECOS** HARTLAND, WI

SNAP PEA SALAD

ORANGE POMEGRANATE SALAD WITH HONEY

ORANGE POMEGRANATE SALAD WITH HONEY F S C M FAST FIX

I discovered this fragrant salad in a cooking class. If you can, try to find orange flower water (also called orange blossom water), which perks up the orange segments. But orange juice adds a nice zip, too!
—**CAROL RICHARDSON MARTY** LYNWOOD, WA

START TO FINISH: 15 MIN. • **MAKES:** 6 SERVINGS

- **5 medium oranges or 10 clementines**
- **½ cup pomegranate seeds**
- **2 tablespoons honey**
- **1 to 2 teaspoons orange flower water or orange juice**

1. Cut a thin slice from the top and bottom of each orange; stand orange upright on a cutting board. With a knife, cut off peel and outer membrane from oranges. Cut crosswise into ½-in. slices.

2. Arrange orange slices on a serving platter; sprinkle with pomegranate seeds. In a small bowl, mix honey and orange flower water; drizzle over fruit.

PER SERVING *⅔ cup: 62 cal., 0 fat (0 sat. fat), 0 chol., 2mg sodium, 15g carb. (14g sugars, 0 fiber), 1g pro.* ***Diabetic Exchanges:*** *1 fruit.*

SUMMER BUZZ FRUIT SALAD

RADISH, CUCUMBER AND GRAPEFRUIT SALAD F S C M

Looking for a light and refreshing way to round out your meal? Tart grapefruit complements crunchy radishes and cucumbers in this spring salad. It's a quick and healthy addition to any menu.
—**CONNIE BOLL** CHILTON, WI

PREP: 35 MIN.
MAKES: 10 SERVINGS

- **2 large red grapefruit**
- **1 pound radishes, thinly sliced (about 3 cups)**
- **1 English cucumber, thinly sliced**
- **4 green onions, thinly sliced**
- **2 tablespoons snipped fresh dill**

DRESSING

- **⅓ cup red grapefruit juice**
- **2 tablespoons honey**
- **1 tablespoon canola oil**
- **¼ teaspoon salt**
- **⅛ teaspoon pepper**
- **Sunflower kernels, optional**

1. Cut a thin slice from top and bottom of each grapefruit; stand upright on a cutting board. With a sharp knife, cut off peel and outer membrane from grapefruit. Remove fruit by cutting along the membrane of each segment. Halve large pieces if desired.
2. Combine the radishes, cucumber, green onions, dill and grapefruit in a large bowl. Whisk together grapefruit juice, honey, oil, salt and pepper; toss gently with radish mixture. If desired, sprinkle with sunflower kernels.

PER SERVING *3/4 cup: 63 cal., 2g fat (0 sat. fat), 0 chol., 79mg sodium, 12g carb. (10g sugars, 2g fiber), 1g pro.* ***Diabetic Exchanges:*** *1 vegetable, 1/2 fruit.*

SUMMER BUZZ FRUIT SALAD F S M FAST FIX

For picnics, cookouts and showers, we make a sweet salad of watermelon, cherries, blueberries and microgreens. No matter where I take it, it always delivers the wow factor.
—**KALISKA RUSSELL** TALKEETNA, AK

START TO FINISH: 15 MIN.
MAKES: 6 SERVINGS

- **2 cups watermelon balls**
- **2 cups fresh sweet cherries, pitted and halved**
- **1 cup fresh blueberries**
- **½ cup cubed English cucumber**
- **½ cup microgreens or torn mixed salad greens**
- **½ cup crumbled feta cheese**
- **3 fresh mint leaves, thinly sliced**
- **¼ cup honey**
- **1 tablespoon lemon juice**
- **1 teaspoon grated lemon peel**

Combine the first seven ingredients. In a small bowl, whisk together the remaining ingredients. Drizzle over salad; toss.

PER SERVING *3/4 cup: 131 cal., 2g fat (1g sat. fat), 5mg chol., 94mg sodium, 28g carb. (24g sugars, 2g fiber), 3g pro.* ***Diabetic Exchanges:*** *1 starch, 1 fruit.*

RADISH, CUCUMBER AND GRAPEFRUIT SALAD

BEET SALAD WITH LEMON DRESSING

BEET SALAD WITH LEMON DRESSING C M

I was looking for a recipe for pickled beets and saw one with lemon instead of vinegar. I immediately thought of making a tabbouleh-inspired salad with beets instead of tomatoes.

—**ANN SHEEHY** LAWRENCE, MA

PREP: 10 MIN. • **BAKE:** 1¼ HOURS
MAKES: 6 SERVINGS

- **3 medium fresh beets (about 1 pound)**
- **1 cup finely chopped English cucumber**
- **6 green onions, thinly sliced**
- **½ cup shredded carrot**
- **½ cup chopped sweet yellow or red pepper**
- **¼ cup finely chopped red onion**
- **¼ cup finely chopped radish**
- **¾ cup minced fresh parsley**

DRESSING

- **3 tablespoons olive oil**
- **2 teaspoons grated lemon peel**
- **3 tablespoons lemon juice**
- **1 garlic clove, minced**
- **¼ teaspoon salt**
- **¼ teaspoon pepper**

1. Preheat oven to 400°. Scrub beets and trim tops. Wrap beets in foil; place on a baking sheet. Bake until tender, 1¼ to 1½ hours. Cool slightly. Peel beets and cut into cubes.

2. Place the remaining vegetables and parsley in a large bowl. Whisk together the dressing ingredients; toss with the cucumber mixture. Gently stir in beets.

PER SERVING *⅔ cup: 116 cal., 7g fat (1g sat. fat), 0 chol., 173mg sodium, 13g carb. (8g sugars, 3g fiber), 2g pro.* ***Diabetic Exchanges:*** *1½ fat, 1 vegetable.*

EDAMAME CORN CARROT SALAD S C M

I created my salad recipe while trying to think of a protein-filled, nutritious and light dish for a summer potluck. It was super easy and visually quite colorful. Best of all, it was a success! Everyone, especially the vegetarians and vegans, loved it!

—**MAIAH MILLER** MONTEREY, CA

PREP: 25 MIN + CHILLING
MAKES: 8 SERVINGS

- **2½ cups frozen shelled edamame**
- **3 cups julienned carrots**
- **1½ cups frozen corn, thawed**
- **4 green onions, chopped**
- **2 tablespoons minced fresh cilantro**

VINAIGRETTE

- **3 tablespoons rice vinegar**
- **3 tablespoons lemon juice**
- **4 teaspoons canola oil**
- **2 garlic cloves, minced**
- **½ teaspoon salt**
- **½ teaspoon pepper**

1. Place the edamame in a small saucepan; add water to cover. Bring to a boil; cook 4-5 minutes or until tender. Drain and place in a large bowl; cool slightly.

2. Add carrots, corn, green onions and cilantro. Whisk together the vinaigrette ingredients; toss with salad. Refrigerate, covered, at least 2 hours before serving.

PER SERVING *⅔ cup: 111 cal., 5g fat (0 sat. fat), 0 chol., 135mg sodium, 14g carb. (4g sugars, 3g fiber), 5g pro.* ***Diabetic Exchanges:*** *1 starch, ½ fat.*

EDAMAME CORN CARROT SALAD

BASIL & HEIRLOOM TOMATO TOSS C M FAST FIX

START TO FINISH: 15 MIN.
MAKES: 4 SERVINGS

- **¼ cup olive oil**
- **3 tablespoons red wine vinegar**
- **2 teaspoons sugar**
- **1 garlic clove, minced**
- **¾ teaspoon salt**
- **¼ teaspoon ground mustard**
- **¼ teaspoon pepper**
- **2 large heirloom tomatoes, cut into ½-inch pieces**
- **1 medium sweet yellow pepper, cut into ½-inch pieces**
- **½ small red onion, thinly sliced**
- **1 tablespoon chopped fresh basil**

In a large bowl, whisk the first seven ingredients until blended. Add the remaining ingredients and toss gently to combine.

PER SERVING *1 cup: 162 cal., 14g fat (2g sat. fat), 0 chol., 449mg sodium, 10g carb. (5g sugars, 2g fiber), 1g pro.* ***Diabetic Exchanges:*** *3 fat, 1 vegetable.*

I came up with this garden-fresh salad to showcase the heirloom tomatoes and peppers we raised for our stall at the farmers market. Try out other types of basil like lemon, lime, licorice and cinnamon.
—SUE GRONHOLZ BEAVER DAM, WI

BASIL & HEIRLOOM TOMATO TOSS

CARAWAY COLESLAW WITH CITRUS MAYONNAISE C M

(PICTURED ON P. 37)

I always get requests to bring a big batch of this unique coleslaw to potlucks— proof positive that it's a keeper! I like to make it a day ahead so the flavors can blend.
—LILY JULOW LAWRENCEVILLE, GA

PREP: 20 MIN. + CHILLING
MAKES: 12 SERVINGS (⅔ CUP EACH)

- **1 medium head cabbage, finely shredded**
- **1 tablespoon sugar**
- **2 teaspoons salt**

DRESSING

- **⅔ cup reduced-fat mayonnaise**
- **⅓ cup orange juice**
- **3 tablespoons cider vinegar**
- **2 tablespoons caraway seeds**
- **2 teaspoons grated orange peel**
- **¼ teaspoon salt**
- **¼ teaspoon pepper**

1. Place cabbage in a colander over a plate. Sprinkle with sugar and salt; toss to coat. Let stand 1 hour.
2. In a small bowl, whisk the dressing ingredients until blended. Rinse the cabbage and drain well; place it in a large bowl. Add dressing; toss to coat. Refrigerate, covered, overnight.

PER SERVING *⅔ cup: 75 cal., 5g fat (1g sat. fat), 5mg chol., 366mg sodium, 8g carb. (5g sugars, 2g fiber), 1g pro.* ***Diabetic Exchanges:*** *1 vegetable, 1 fat.*

GARDEN CUCUMBER SALAD C M

If you like cucumber salad like I do, this one's a cool pick you're going to love. The mix of fresh veggies, feta and Greek seasoning is so refreshing when the sun's beating down.
—KATIE STANCZAK HOOVER, AL

PREP: 10 MIN. + CHILLING
MAKES: 12 SERVINGS (¾ CUP EACH)

- **4 medium cucumbers, cut into ½-inch pieces (about 7 cups)**
- **2 medium sweet red peppers, chopped**
- **1 cup cherry tomatoes, halved**
- **1 cup crumbled feta cheese**
- **½ cup finely chopped red onion**
- **½ cup olive oil**
- **¼ cup lemon juice**
- **1 tablespoon Greek seasoning**
- **½ teaspoon salt**

Place all ingredients in a large bowl; toss gently to combine. Refrigerate the salad, covered, at least 30 minutes before serving.

PER SERVING *¾ cup: 125 cal., 11g fat (2g sat. fat), 5mg chol., 431mg sodium, 5g carb. (3g sugars, 2g fiber), 3g pro.* ***Diabetic Exchanges:*** *2 fat, 1 vegetable.*

GARDEN CUCUMBER SALAD

RIBBON SALAD WITH ORANGE VINAIGRETTE

RIBBON SALAD WITH ORANGE VINAIGRETTE

C M FAST FIX

Zucchini, cucumbers and carrots are peeled into ribbons for this citrusy salad. We like to serve it for parties and special occasions.

—**NANCY HEISHMAN** LAS VEGAS, NV

START TO FINISH: 30 MIN.
MAKES: 8 SERVINGS

- **1 medium zucchini**
- **1 medium cucumber**
- **1 medium carrot**
- **3 medium oranges**
- **3 cups fresh baby spinach**
- **4 green onions, finely chopped**
- **½ cup chopped walnuts**
- **½ teaspoon salt**
- **½ teaspoon pepper**
- **½ cup golden raisins, optional**

VINAIGRETTE

- **¼ cup olive oil**
- **4 teaspoons white wine vinegar**
- **1 tablespoon finely chopped green onion**
- **2 teaspoons honey**
- **¼ teaspoon salt**
- **¼ teaspoon pepper**

1. Using a vegetable peeler, shave zucchini, cucumber and carrot lengthwise into very thin strips.
2. Finely grate enough peel from oranges to measure 2 tablespoons. Cut one orange crosswise in half; squeeze juice from orange to measure 1/2 cup. Reserve peel and juice for vinaigrette. Cut a thin slice from the top and bottom of remaining oranges; stand oranges upright on a cutting board. With a knife, cut off peel and outer membrane from orange. Cut along the membrane of each segment to remove fruit.
3. In a large bowl, combine spinach, orange sections, green onions, walnuts, salt, pepper and, if desired, raisins. Add vegetable ribbons; gently toss to combine. In a small bowl, combine vinaigrette ingredients. Add reserved orange peel and juice; whisk until blended. Drizzle half of the vinaigrette over salad; toss to coat. Serve with remaining vinaigrette.

PER SERVING *1½ cups: 162 cal., 12g fat (1g sat. fat), 0 chol., 240mg sodium, 14g carb. (9g sugars, 2g fiber), 3g pro.* ***Diabetic Exchanges:*** *2 fat, 1 vegetable, ½ starch.*

WATERMELON & SPINACH SALAD

C M FAST FIX

Summer is the perfect time to toss up my melon salad. You'd never expect it, but spinach is awesome in this recipe. You will eat it and feel cool on even the hottest days.

—**MARJORIE AU** HONOLULU, HI

START TO FINISH: 30 MIN.
MAKES: 8 SERVINGS

- **¼ cup rice vinegar or white wine vinegar**
- **1 tablespoon grated lime peel**
- **2 tablespoons lime juice**
- **2 tablespoons canola oil**
- **4 teaspoons minced fresh gingerroot**
- **2 garlic cloves, minced**
- **½ teaspoon salt**
- **¼ teaspoon sugar**
- **¼ teaspoon pepper**

SALAD

- **4 cups fresh baby spinach or arugula**
- **3 cups cubed seedless watermelon**
- **2 cups cubed cantaloupe**
- **2 cups cubed English cucumber**
- **½ cup chopped fresh cilantro**
- **2 green onions, chopped**

In a small bowl, whisk the first nine ingredients. In a large bowl, combine the salad ingredients. Drizzle the mixture with dressing and toss it to coat; serve immediately.

PER SERVING *1 cup: 84 cal., 4g fat (0 sat. fat), 0 chol., 288mg sodium, 13g carb. (10g sugars, 1g fiber), 1g pro.* ***Diabetic Exchanges:*** *1 vegetable, 1 fat, ½ fruit.*

WATERMELON & SPINACH SALAD

QUINOA TABBOULEH SALAD M (PICTURED ON P. 37)

This tabbouleh salad made with quinoa instead of bulgur is super simple and filling. Try red quinoa for a slightly earthier flavor.

—**LOGAN LEVANT** LOS ANGELES, CA

PREP: 15 MIN. • **COOK:** 15 MIN. + COOLING
MAKES: 6 SERVINGS

- **2 cups water**
- **1 cup quinoa, rinsed**
- **¾ cup packed fresh parsley sprigs, stems removed**
- **⅓ cup fresh mint leaves**
- **¼ cup coarsely chopped red onion**
- **1 garlic clove, minced**
- **1 cup grape tomatoes**
- **½ English cucumber, cut into 1-inch pieces**
- **2 tablespoons lemon juice**
- **2 tablespoons olive oil**
- **1 teaspoon salt**
- **½ teaspoon pepper**
- **¼ teaspoon ground allspice**

1. In a large saucepan, bring water to a boil. Add quinoa. Reduce heat; simmer, covered, 12-15 minutes or until liquid is absorbed. Remove from heat; fluff with a fork. Transfer to a large bowl; cool completely.

2. Place parsley, mint, onion and garlic in a food processor; pulse until finely chopped. Add tomatoes and cucumber; pulse until coarsely chopped. Add tomato mixture to the quinoa.

3. In a small bowl, whisk lemon juice, oil and seasonings until blended; drizzle over quinoa mixture and toss to coat. Serve at room temperature or refrigerate until serving.

NOTE *Look for quinoa in the cereal, rice or organic food aisle.*

PER SERVING *2/3 cup: 163 cal., 6g fat (1g sat. fat), 0 chol., 403mg sodium, 22g carb. (2g sugars, 3g fiber), 5g pro.* ***Diabetic Exchanges:*** *1½ starch, 1 fat.*

Tossing the cooked potatoes with stock and wine right after you drain them infuses them with flavor. The liquid absorbs like magic.

—**GEORGE LEVINTHAL** GOLETA, CA

RED, WHITE & BLUE POTATO SALAD

RED, WHITE & BLUE POTATO SALAD

PREP: 40 MIN. • **COOK:** 10 MIN.
MAKES: 12 SERVINGS (1 CUP EACH)

- **1¼ pounds small purple potatoes (about 11), quartered**
- **1 pound small Yukon Gold potatoes (about 9), quartered**
- **1 pound small red potatoes (about 9), quartered**
- **½ cup chicken stock**
- **¼ cup white wine or additional chicken stock**
- **2 tablespoons sherry vinegar**
- **2 tablespoons white wine vinegar**
- **1½ teaspoons Dijon mustard**
- **1½ teaspoons stone-ground mustard**
- **¾ teaspoon salt**
- **½ teaspoon coarsely ground pepper**
- **6 tablespoons olive oil**
- **3 celery ribs, chopped**
- **1 small sweet red pepper, chopped**
- **8 green onions, chopped**
- **¾ pound bacon strips, cooked and crumbled**
- **3 tablespoons each minced fresh basil, dill and parsley**
- **2 tablespoons toasted sesame seeds**

1. Place all potatoes in a Dutch oven; add water to cover. Bring to a boil. Reduce the heat; cook, uncovered, 10-15 minutes or until tender. Drain; transfer to a large bowl. Drizzle the potatoes with stock and wine; toss gently, allowing liquids to absorb.

2. In a small bowl, whisk vinegars, mustards, salt and pepper. Gradually whisk in oil until blended. Add vinaigrette, vegetables, bacon and herbs to potato mixture; toss. Sprinkle with sesame seeds. Serve warm.

PER SERVING *1 cup: 221 cal., 12g fat (2g sat. fat), 10mg chol., 405mg sodium, 22g carb. (2g sugars, 3g fiber), 7g pro.* ***Diabetic Exchanges:*** *2 fat, 1½ starch.*

BABY KALE SALAD WITH AVOCADO-LIME DRESSING

GREEN BEAN & POTATO SALAD M

For family reunions, my mom would make everybody's favorite green bean and potato salad. Now I'm the one who makes it and brings it.
—**CONNIE DICAVOLI** SHAWNEE, KS

PREP: 15 MIN. • **COOK:** 20 MIN. + CHILLING
MAKES: 10 SERVINGS

- **2 pounds red potatoes (about 6 medium), cubed**
- **1 pound fresh green beans, trimmed and halved**
- **1 small red onion, halved and thinly sliced**
- **¼ cup chopped fresh mint, optional**

DRESSING

- **½ cup canola oil**
- **¼ cup white vinegar**
- **2 tablespoons lemon juice**
- **1 teaspoon salt**
- **½ teaspoon garlic powder**
- **¼ teaspoon pepper**

1. Place potatoes in a 6-qt. stockpot; add water to cover. Bring to a boil. Reduce the heat; cook, uncovered, 10-15 minutes or until tender, adding green beans during the last 4 minutes of cooking. Drain.
2. Transfer potatoes and green beans to a large bowl; add onion and, if desired, mint. In a small bowl, whisk dressing ingredients until blended. Pour over potato mixture; toss gently to coat. Refrigerate, covered, at least 2 hours before serving.

PER SERVING *¾ cup: 183 cal., 11g fat (1g sat. fat), 0 chol., 245mg sodium, 19g carb. (2g sugars, 3g fiber), 3g pro.* ***Diabetic Exchanges:*** *2½ fat, 1 starch.*

BABY KALE SALAD WITH AVOCADO-LIME DRESSING F C M FAST FIX

We pull a bunch of ingredients from our garden when we make this salad of greens, zucchini and sweet onion. The yogurt dressing layers on big lime flavor.
—**SUZANNA ESTHER** STATE COLLEGE, PA

START TO FINISH: 20 MIN.
MAKES: 4 SERVINGS (¾ CUP DRESSING)

- **6 cups baby kale salad blend**
- **1 cup julienned zucchini**
- **½ cup thinly sliced sweet onion**
- **½ cup fat-free plain yogurt**
- **2 tablespoons lime juice**
- **1 garlic clove, minced**
- **¼ teaspoon salt**
- **⅛ teaspoon pepper**
- **½ medium ripe avocado, peeled**
- **3 green onions, chopped**
- **2 tablespoons minced fresh parsley**

In a large bowl, combine salad blend, zucchini and sweet onion. Place the remaining ingredients in a blender; cover and process until smooth. Divide the salad mixture among four plates; drizzle with dressing.

PER SERVING *1½ cups salad with 3 tablespoons dressing: 74 cal., 3g fat (1g sat. fat), 1mg chol., 197mg sodium, 10g carb. (4g sugars, 4g fiber), 4g pro.* ***Diabetic Exchanges:*** *2 vegetable, ½ fat.*

GREEN BEAN & POTATO SALAD

ITALIAN SALAD WITH LEMON VINAIGRETTE

C M FAST FIX (PICTURED ON P. 36)

For an Italian twist on salad, I mix greens with red onion, mushrooms, olives, pepperoncini, lemon juice and seasoning. Add tomatoes and carrots if you like.

—**DEBORAH LOOP** CLINTON TOWNSHIP, MI

START TO FINISH: 20 MIN.
MAKES: 8 SERVINGS (½ CUP VINAIGRETTE)

- **1 package (5 ounces) spring mix salad greens**
- **1 small red onion, thinly sliced**
- **1 cup sliced fresh mushrooms**
- **1 cup assorted olives, pitted and coarsely chopped**
- **8 pepperoncini**
- **Optional toppings: chopped tomatoes, shredded carrots and grated Parmesan cheese**

VINAIGRETTE

- **⅓ cup extra virgin olive oil**
- **3 tablespoons lemon juice**
- **1 teaspoon Italian seasoning**
- **¼ teaspoon salt**
- **¼ teaspoon pepper**

1. In a large bowl, combine the first five ingredients; toss lightly. If desired, add toppings.
2. Whisk vinaigrette ingredients until blended. Serve with salad.

PER SERVING *1¼ cups: 109 cal., 11g fat (1g sat. fat), 0 chol., 343mg sodium, 4g carb. (1g sugars, 1g fiber), 1g pro.* ***Diabetic Exchanges:*** *2 fat, 1 vegetable.*

READER RAVE

LOVE IT! I wish I could give it 10 stars! I omitted the olives because I don't like them, but I added cherry tomatoes and goat cheese, used a small Thai pepper instead of pepperoncini, and threw some croutons on top. The dressing is awesome. Thanks for the recipe!

—**HOMECHEFCOLLEEN**
TASTEOFHOME.COM

MICHIGAN CHERRY SALAD

MICHIGAN CHERRY SALAD

S M FAST FIX

This recipe reminds me of what I love about my home state: apple picking with my children, buying greens at the farmers market, and tasting cherries while on vacation.

—**JENNIFER GILBERT** BRIGHTON, MI

START TO FINISH: 15 MIN.
MAKES: 8 SERVINGS

- **7 ounces fresh baby spinach (about 9 cups)**
- **3 ounces spring mix salad greens (about 5 cups)**
- **1 large apple, chopped**
- **½ cup coarsely chopped pecans, toasted**
- **½ cup dried cherries**
- **¼ cup crumbled Gorgonzola cheese**

DRESSING

- **¼ cup fresh raspberries**
- **¼ cup red wine vinegar**
- **3 tablespoons cider vinegar**
- **3 tablespoons cherry preserves**
- **1 tablespoon sugar**
- **2 tablespoons olive oil**

1. In a large bowl, combine the first six ingredients.
2. Place the raspberries, vinegars, preserves and sugar in a blender. While processing, gradually add oil in a steady stream. Drizzle over salad; toss to coat.

NOTE *To toast nuts, bake in a shallow pan in a 350° oven for 5-10 minutes or cook in a skillet over low heat until lightly browned, stirring occasionally.*

PER SERVING *1½ cups: 172 cal., 10g fat (2g sat. fat), 3mg chol., 78mg sodium, 21g carb. (16g sugars, 3g fiber), 3g pro.* ***Diabetic Exchanges:*** *2 vegetable, 2 fat, 1 starch.*

59

64

61

Side Dishes

"This recipe was created as an attempt to use up a great turnip season from our garden as well as lighten up one of our favorite dishes. By using turnips in place of potatoes, I made a low-carb side. Now we rarely serve plain mashed potatoes!"

—COURTNEY STULTZ WEIR, KS
about her recipe, Mashed Peppery Turnips, on page 64

WARM TASTY GREENS WITH GARLIC C M FAST FIX

My farm box had too many greens, so I had to use them up somehow. This tasty idea uses kale, tomatoes and garlic in a dish that quickly disappears.
—**MARTHA NETH** AURORA, CO

START TO FINISH: 30 MIN.
MAKES: 4 SERVINGS

- **1 pound kale, trimmed and torn (about 20 cups)**
- **2 tablespoons olive oil**
- **¼ cup chopped oil-packed sun-dried tomatoes**
- **5 garlic cloves, minced**
- **2 tablespoons minced fresh parsley**
- **¼ teaspoon salt**

1. In a 6-qt. stockpot, bring 1 in. of water to a boil. Add the kale; cook, covered, 10-15 minutes or until tender. Remove with a slotted spoon; discard cooking liquid.
2. In same pot, heat oil over medium heat. Add tomatoes and garlic; cook and stir 1 minute. Add kale, parsley and salt; heat it through, stirring occasionally.
PER SERVING *2/3 cup: 137 cal., 9g fat (1g sat. fat), 0 chol., 216mg sodium, 14g carb. (0 sugars, 3g fiber), 4g pro.* ***Diabetic Exchanges:*** *2 vegetable, 2 fat.*

WARM TASTY GREENS WITH GARLIC

While traveling to Taiwan, we visited a restaurant where fresh vegetables including pumpkin were served. That inspired me to roast pumpkin with Brussels sprouts.
—**PAM CORRELL** BROCKPORT, PA

ROASTED PUMPKIN AND BRUSSELS SPROUTS

ROASTED PUMPKIN AND BRUSSELS SPROUTS M

PREP: 15 MIN. • **BAKE:** 35 MIN.
MAKES: 8 SERVINGS

- **1 medium pie pumpkin (about 3 pounds), peeled and cut into ¾-inch cubes**
- **1 pound fresh Brussels sprouts, trimmed and halved lengthwise**
- **4 garlic cloves, thinly sliced**
- **⅓ cup olive oil**
- **2 tablespoons balsamic vinegar**
- **1 teaspoon sea salt**
- **½ teaspoon coarsely ground pepper**
- **2 tablespoons minced fresh parsley**

1. Preheat the oven to 400°. In a large bowl, combine the pumpkin, Brussels sprouts and garlic. In a small bowl, whisk the oil, vinegar, salt and pepper; drizzle over the vegetables and toss to coat.
2. Transfer to a greased 15x10x1-in. baking pan. Roast 35-40 minutes or until tender, stirring once. Sprinkle with parsley.
PER SERVING *3/4 cup: 152 cal., 9g fat (1g sat. fat), 0 chol., 255mg sodium, 17g carb. (4g sugars, 3g fiber), 4g pro.* ***Diabetic Exchanges:*** *2 fat, 1 starch.*

SQUASH AND MUSHROOM MEDLEY

F C M FAST FIX

Bring the taste of summer to your dinner table with an easy zucchini and summer squash dish that is sure to go great with various main dishes.

—HEATHER ESPOSITO ROME, NY

START TO FINISH: 20 MIN.
MAKES: 5 SERVINGS

- **1 large yellow summer squash, chopped**
- **1 large zucchini, chopped**
- **1 medium onion, chopped**
- **2 teaspoons butter**
- **1 can (7 ounces) mushroom stems and pieces, drained**
- **2 garlic cloves, minced**
- **¼ teaspoon salt**
- **⅛ teaspoon pepper**

In a large skillet, saute the squash, zucchini and onion in butter until tender. Add the mushrooms, garlic, salt and pepper; saute 2-3 minutes longer or until heated through.

PER SERVING *1 cup: 58 cal., 2g fat (1g sat. fat), 4mg chol., 283mg sodium, 9g carb. (5g sugars, 3g fiber), 3g pro.* ***Diabetic Exchanges:*** *1 vegetable, ½ fat.*

ROASTED FRESH OKRA

C M FAST FIX

If you have picky eaters who worry about texture, roasted okra is marvelous. It's fine to crowd the pan because okra shrinks as it cooks.

—ANNA HUMPHREY GREENVILLE, NC

START TO FINISH: 25 MIN.
MAKES: 4 SERVINGS

- **1 pound fresh okra, trimmed and cut lengthwise in half**
- **3 tablespoons olive oil**
- **½ teaspoon salt**
- **¼ teaspoon pepper**

Preheat oven to 400°. Toss okra with oil, salt and pepper. Arrange in a 15x10x1-in. baking pan, cut side up. Roast 12-15 minutes or until tender and bottoms are lightly browned.

PER SERVING *⅔ cup: 115 cal., 10g fat (1g sat. fat), 0 chol., 302mg sodium, 5g carb. (3g sugars, 3g fiber), 2g pro.* ***Diabetic Exchanges:*** *2 fat, 1 vegetable.*

HEALTH TIP *New to okra? It's a rich source of vitamins K and C, low in calories, and naturally fat-free.*

RICE PILAF WITH APPLES & RAISINS

M FAST FIX

I love to make pilaf with apricots. I'm so glad I tried this variation of dried apples and golden raisins. Delicious!

—ELIZABETH DUMONT MADISON, MS

START TO FINISH: 25 MIN.
MAKES: 4 SERVINGS

- **2 tablespoons olive oil**
- **1 small onion, finely chopped**
- **1 cup uncooked jasmine rice**
- **1½ cups water**
- **¼ cup chopped dried apples**
- **¼ cup golden raisins**
- **1 teaspoon salt**
- **¼ teaspoon ground allspice**
- **¼ teaspoon ground cinnamon**
- **¼ teaspoon dried thyme**
- **⅛ teaspoon cayenne pepper**

1. In a large saucepan, heat the oil over medium heat; saute the onion until tender, 4-6 minutes. Add rice; cook and stir until lightly browned, 4-6 minutes.

2. Stir in the remaining ingredients; bring to a boil. Reduce heat; simmer, covered, until liquid is absorbed and rice is tender, 15-20 minutes. Fluff with a fork.

PER SERVING *¾ cup: 277 cal., 7g fat (1g sat. fat), 0 chol., 599mg sodium, 50g carb. (9g sugars, 2g fiber), 4g pro.*

RICE PILAF WITH APPLES & RAISINS

OVEN-ROASTED SPICED CARROTS C M

I started roasting veggies and serving them often with dinner. Now my children say, "Is it OK to finish the veggies?"

—JOAN DUCKWORTH LEE'S SUMMIT, MO

PREP: 15 MIN. • **BAKE:** 25 MIN. • **MAKES:** 8 SERVINGS

- **2 pounds carrots, cut into 2-inch pieces**
- **3 tablespoons olive oil**
- **½ teaspoon salt**
- **½ teaspoon ground coriander**
- **½ teaspoon ground cumin**
- **½ teaspoon pepper**
- **¼ teaspoon chili powder**
- **¼ teaspoon paprika**
- **⅛ teaspoon ground ginger**
- **⅛ teaspoon ground cinnamon**
- **Dash ground cloves**
- **Dash cayenne pepper**

1. Preheat the oven to 400°. In a large bowl, toss the carrots with oil. Mix the seasonings; sprinkle over the carrots and toss to coat.
2. Arrange the carrots in a single layer in a 15x10x1-in. baking pan that is coated with cooking spray. Roast for 25-30 minutes or until they are lightly browned and crisp-tender, stirring occasionally.

PER SERVING *¾ cup: 93 cal., 5g fat (1g sat. fat), 0 chol., 228mg sodium, 11g carb. (5g sugars, 3g fiber), 1g pro.* ***Diabetic Exchanges:*** *1 vegetable, 1 fat.*

ORZO WITH PEPPERS & SPINACH M FAST FIX

The bright colors from the bell peppers in this dish are eye-catching! As a bonus, sweet bell peppers are a good source of vitamin C, which helps the body fight infection and absorb folate and iron.

—TAMMI KETTENBACH JERSEYVILLE, IL

START TO FINISH: 30 MIN. • **MAKES:** 6 SERVINGS

- **1 cup uncooked orzo pasta (about 8 ounces)**
- **1 tablespoon olive oil**
- **1 each medium sweet orange, red and yellow peppers, chopped**
- **1 cup sliced fresh mushrooms**
- **3 garlic cloves, minced**
- **½ teaspoon Italian seasoning**
- **¼ teaspoon salt**
- **¼ teaspoon pepper**
- **2 cups fresh baby spinach**
- **½ cup grated Parmesan cheese**

1. Cook orzo according to package directions; drain.
2. Meanwhile, in large skillet, heat oil over medium-high heat; saute peppers and mushrooms until tender. Add garlic and seasonings; cook and stir 1 minute.
3. Stir in spinach until wilted. Stir in orzo and cheese; heat through.

PER SERVING *¾ cup: 196 cal., 5g fat (1g sat. fat), 6mg chol., 232mg sodium, 30g carb. (4g sugars, 2g fiber), 7g pro.* ***Diabetic Exchanges:*** *1½ starch, 1 vegetable, 1 fat.*

GRILLED VEGGIES WITH MUSTARD VINAIGRETTE C M

I make this healthy and inviting side dish whenever friends come over for a cookout. The honeyed vinaigrette lets the veggies shine.

—**SHELLY GRAVER** LANSDALE, PA

PREP: 20 MIN. • **GRILL:** 15 MIN.
MAKES: 10 SERVINGS (¾ CUP EACH)

- **¼ cup red wine vinegar**
- **1 tablespoon Dijon mustard**
- **1 tablespoon honey**
- **½ teaspoon salt**
- **⅛ teaspoon pepper**
- **¼ cup canola oil**
- **¼ cup olive oil**

VEGETABLES

- **2 large sweet onions**
- **2 medium zucchini**
- **2 yellow summer squash**
- **2 large sweet red peppers, halved and seeded**
- **1 bunch green onions, trimmed**
- **Cooking spray**

1. In a small bowl, whisk the first five ingredients. Then gradually whisk in the oils until blended.
2. Peel and quarter each sweet onion, leaving root ends intact. Cut zucchini and yellow squash lengthwise into ½-in.-thick slices. Lightly spritz onions, zucchini, yellow squash and remaining vegetables with cooking spray, turning to coat all sides.
3. Grill the sweet onions, covered, over medium heat 15-20 minutes until tender, turning occasionally. Grill zucchini, squash and peppers, covered, over medium heat 10-15 minutes or until crisp-tender and lightly charred, turning once. Grill green onions, covered, 2-4 minutes or until lightly charred, turning once.
4. Cut the vegetables into bite-size pieces; place in a large bowl. Add ½ cup vinaigrette and toss to coat. Serve with remaining vinaigrette.

PER SERVING *¾ cup: 155 cal., 12g fat (1g sat. fat), 0 chol., 166mg sodium, 13g carb. (8g sugars, 2g fiber), 2g pro.* ***Diabetic Exchanges:*** *2½ fat, 1 vegetable, ½ starch.*

LEMON-ROASTED ASPARAGUS

C M FAST FIX

When it comes to fixing asparagus, it's hard to go wrong. The springy flavors in this easy recipe burst with every bite.

—**JENN TIDWELL** FAIR OAKS, CA

START TO FINISH: 20 MIN. • **MAKES:** 8 SERVINGS

- **2 pounds fresh asparagus, trimmed**
- **¼ cup olive oil**
- **4 teaspoons grated lemon peel**
- **2 garlic cloves, minced**
- **½ teaspoon salt**
- **½ teaspoon pepper**

Preheat oven to 425°. Place asparagus in a greased 15x10x1-in. baking pan. Mix remaining ingredients; drizzle over the asparagus. Toss to coat. Roast for 8-12 minutes or until crisp-tender.

PER SERVING *75 cal., 7g fat (1g sat. fat), 0 chol., 154mg sodium, 3g carb. (1g sugars, 1g fiber), 2g pro.* ***Diabetic Exchanges:*** *1½ fat, 1 vegetable.*

BASIL GRILLED CORN ON THE COB

BASIL GRILLED CORN ON THE COB M

Corn on the cob is a comforting and cherished Midwest dish. It's amazing when grilled, and my recipe adds a few unexpected ingredients to make it taste even more like summertime.

—**CAITLIN DAWSON** MONROE, OH

PREP: 15 MIN. + SOAKING • **GRILL:** 20 MIN.
MAKES: 4 SERVINGS

- **4 medium ears sweet corn**
- **4 teaspoons butter, melted**
- **¾ teaspoon salt**
- **¼ teaspoon pepper**
- **16 fresh basil leaves**
- **½ medium lemon**
- **2 teaspoons minced fresh cilantro**
- **Additional butter, optional**

1. Place corn in a 6-qt. stockpot; cover with cold water. Soak 20 minutes; drain. Carefully peel back corn husks to within 1 in. of bottoms; remove silk. Brush butter over corn; sprinkle with salt and pepper. Press four basil leaves onto each cob. Rewrap corn in husks; secure with kitchen string.

2. Grill corn, covered, over medium heat 20-25 minutes or until tender, turning often. Cut string and peel back husks; discard basil leaves. Squeeze lemon juice over corn; sprinkle with cilantro. If desired, spread corn with additional butter.

PER SERVING *1 ear of corn: 125 cal., 5g fat (3g sat. fat), 10mg chol., 489mg sodium, 20g carb. (7g sugars, 2g fiber), 4g pro.* ***Diabetic Exchanges:*** *1 starch, 1 fat.*

PESTO PASTA & POTATOES M FAST FIX

Although this healthy pasta recipe is pretty simple to begin with, the cooking method makes it even simpler: You can throw the green beans and pasta into one big pot.

—**LAURA FLOWERS** MOSCOW, ID

START TO FINISH: 30 MIN.
MAKES: 12 SERVINGS

- **1½ pounds small red potatoes, halved**
- **12 ounces uncooked whole grain spiral pasta**
- **3 cups cut fresh or frozen green beans**
- **1 jar (6½ ounces) prepared pesto**
- **1 cup grated Parmigiano-Reggiano cheese**

1. Place potatoes in a large saucepan; add water to cover. Bring to a boil. Reduce heat; cook, uncovered, until tender, 8-10 minutes. Drain; transfer to a large bowl.

2. Meanwhile, cook pasta according to package directions, adding green beans during the last 5 minutes of cooking. Drain, reserving ¾ cup pasta water, and add to potatoes. Toss with pesto, cheese and enough pasta water to moisten.

PER SERVING *¾ cup: 261 cal., 10g fat (3g sat. fat), 11mg chol., 233mg sodium, 34g carb. (2g sugars, 5g fiber), 11g pro.* ***Diabetic Exchanges:*** *2 starch, 2 fat.*

PESTO PASTA & POTATOES

BEET AND SWEET POTATO FRIES M

(PICTURED ON P. 53)

Instead of offering traditional French fries, try these oven-baked root vegetables as a flavorful side dish.
—MARIE RIZZIO INTERLOCHEN, MI

PREP: 15 MIN. • **BAKE:** 20 MIN.
MAKES: 5 SERVINGS (½ CUP SAUCE)

- **½ cup reduced-fat mayonnaise**
- **1 teaspoon pink peppercorns, crushed**
- **½ teaspoon green peppercorns, crushed**
- **½ teaspoon coarsely ground pepper, divided**
- **1 large sweet potato (about 1 pound)**
- **2 tablespoons olive oil, divided**
- **½ teaspoon sea salt, divided**
- **2 large fresh beets (about 1 pound)**

1. In a small bowl, combine the mayonnaise, peppercorns and 1/4 teaspoon ground pepper. Cover and refrigerate until serving.
2. Peel and cut sweet potato in half widthwise; cut each half into 1/2-in. strips. Place in a small bowl. Add 1 tablespoon oil, 1/4 teaspoon salt and 1/8 teaspoon pepper; toss to coat. Spread onto a parchment paper-lined baking sheet.
3. Peel and cut beets in half; cut into 1/2-in. strips. Transfer to the same bowl; add the remaining oil, salt and pepper. Toss to coat. Spread onto another parchment paper-lined baking sheet.
4. Bake, uncovered, at 425° for 20-30 minutes or until tender, turning once. Serve with peppercorn mayonnaise.
PER SERVING *226 cal., 14g fat (2g sat. fat), 8mg chol., 455mg sodium, 25g carb. (14g sugars, 4g fiber), 3g pro.* ***Diabetic Exchanges:*** *2 starch, 2 fat.*

DID YOU KNOW?

Pink peppercorns are not peppercorns at all, but are related to mangoes and cashews. They may trigger an allergic response in those who have these allergies.

SMOKY CAULIFLOWER

SMOKY CAULIFLOWER

C M FAST FIX

Smoked Spanish paprika gives a simple side of roasted cauliflower even more depth of flavor. We're fans of roasted veggies of any kind, but this one is a definite favorite.
—JULIETTE MULHOLLAND CORVALLIS, OR

START TO FINISH: 30 MIN.
MAKES: 8 SERVINGS

- **1 large head cauliflower, broken into 1-inch florets (about 9 cups)**
- **2 tablespoons olive oil**
- **1 teaspoon smoked paprika**
- **¾ teaspoon salt**
- **2 garlic cloves, minced**
- **2 tablespoons minced fresh parsley**

1. Place cauliflower in a large bowl. Combine the oil, paprika and salt. Drizzle over cauliflower; toss to coat. Transfer to a 15x10x1-in. baking pan. Bake, uncovered, at 450° for 10 minutes.
2. Stir in garlic. Bake 10-15 minutes longer or until cauliflower is tender and lightly browned, stirring the dish occasionally. Sprinkle with parsley.
PER SERVING *3/4 cup: 58 cal., 4g fat (0 sat. fat), 0 chol., 254mg sodium, 6g carb. (3g sugars, 3g fiber), 2g pro.* ***Diabetic Exchanges:*** *1 vegetable, 1/2 fat.*
HEALTH TIP *Just 1/2 cup of cooked cauliflower provides nearly half the daily value for vitamin C, not to mention some sulfur-containing compounds that may help protect against certain cancers.*

BALSAMIC ZUCCHINI SAUTE

BALSAMIC ZUCCHINI SAUTE C M FAST FIX

This super-fast vegetarian dish is very flavorful and only uses a few ingredients, making it easy to whip up while your entree is cooking.

—**ELIZABETH BRAMKAMP** GIG HARBOR, WA

START TO FINISH: 20 MIN
MAKES: 4 SERVINGS

- **1 tablespoon olive oil**
- **3 medium zucchini, cut into thin slices**
- **½ cup chopped sweet onion**
- **½ teaspoon salt**
- **½ teaspoon dried rosemary, crushed**
- **¼ teaspoon pepper**
- **2 tablespoons balsamic vinegar**
- **⅓ cup crumbled feta cheese**

In a large skillet, heat oil over medium-high heat; saute zucchini and onion until crisp-tender, 6-8 minutes. Stir in seasonings. Add vinegar; cook and stir 2 minutes. Top with cheese.

PER SERVING *½ cup: 94 cal., 5g fat (2g sat. fat), 5mg chol., 398mg sodium, 9g carb. (6g sugars, 2g fiber), 4g pro.* ***Diabetic Exchanges:*** *1 vegetable, 1 fat.*

CURRIED SWEET POTATO WEDGES M FAST FIX

Sweet potatoes roasted with curry and smoked paprika delight everybody at our table. The mango chutney makes a tangy dip.

—**MAITREYI JOIS** STREAMWOOD, IL

START TO FINISH: 25 MIN.
MAKES: 4 SERVINGS

- **2 medium sweet potatoes (about 1 pound), cut into ½-inch wedges**
- **2 tablespoons olive oil**
- **1 teaspoon curry powder**
- **½ teaspoon salt**
- **½ teaspoon smoked paprika**
- **⅛ teaspoon coarsely ground pepper**
- **Minced fresh cilantro**
- **Mango chutney, optional**

1. Preheat oven to 425°. Place sweet potatoes in a large bowl. Mix the oil and seasonings; drizzle it over sweet potatoes and toss to coat. Transfer to an ungreased 15x10x1-in. baking pan.

2. Roast for 15-20 minutes or until the wedges are tender, turning them occasionally. Sprinkle with cilantro. If desired, serve with chutney.

PER SERVING *159 cal., 7g fat (1g sat. fat), 0 chol., 305mg sodium, 23g carb. (9g sugars, 3g fiber), 2g pro.* ***Diabetic Exchanges:*** *1½ starch, 1½ fat.*

GRILLED VEGETABLE PLATTER S C M

These pretty veggies are pefect for entertaining. Grilling brings out their natural sweetness, and the easy marinade really perks up the flavor.

—**HEIDI HALL** NORTH SAINT PAUL, MN

PREP: 20 MIN. + MARINATING
GRILL: 10 MIN. • **MAKES:** 6 SERVINGS

- **¼ cup olive oil**
- **2 tablespoons honey**
- **4 teaspoons balsamic vinegar**
- **1 teaspoon dried oregano**
- **½ teaspoon garlic powder**
- **⅛ teaspoon pepper**
- **Dash salt**
- **1 pound fresh asparagus, trimmed**
- **3 small carrots, cut in half lengthwise**
- **1 large sweet red pepper, cut into 1-inch strips**
- **1 medium yellow summer squash, cut into ½-inch slices**
- **1 medium red onion, cut into wedges**

1. In a small bowl, whisk the first seven ingredients. Place 3 tablespoons marinade in a large resealable plastic bag. Add the vegetables; seal bag and turn to coat. Marinate for 1½ hours at room temperature.

2. Transfer vegetables to a grilling grid; place grid on grill rack. Grill vegetables, covered, over medium heat for 8-12 minutes or until crisp-tender, turning occasionally.

3. Place the vegetables on a large serving plate and drizzle with the remaining marinade.

NOTE *If you do not have a grilling grid, use a disposable foil pan. Poke holes in the bottom of the pan with a meat fork to allow liquid to drain.*

PER SERVING *144 cal., 9g fat (1g sat. fat), 0 chol., 50mg sodium, 15g carb. (11g sugars, 3g fiber), 2g pro.* ***Diabetic Exchanges:*** *2 vegetable, 2 fat.*

GRILLED VEGETABLE PLATTER

GARLIC-HERB PATTYPAN SQUASH

GOLDEN ZUCCHINI PANCAKES M

If your garden is overflowing with zucchini, use it up by making these incredible pancakes. We squeeze the zucchini well before using to remove excess moisture.

—**TERRY ANN DOMINGUEZ** SILVER CITY, NM

PREP: 15 MIN. • **COOK:** 10 MIN./BATCH
MAKES: 8 ZUCCHINI PANCAKES

- **3 cups shredded zucchini**
- **2 large eggs**
- **2 garlic cloves, minced**
- **¾ teaspoon salt**
- **½ teaspoon pepper**
- **¼ teaspoon dried oregano**
- **½ cup all-purpose flour**
- **½ cup finely chopped sweet onion**
- **1 tablespoon butter**
- **Marinara sauce, warmed, optional**

1. Place the zucchini in a colander to drain; squeeze well to remove excess liquid. Pat dry.

2. In a large bowl, whisk eggs, garlic, salt, pepper and oregano until blended. Stir in flour just until moistened. Fold in zucchini and onion.

3. Lightly grease a griddle with butter; heat over medium heat. Drop zucchini mixture by ¼ cupfuls onto griddle; flatten to ½-in. thickness (3-in. diameter). Cook 4-5 minutes on each side or until golden brown. If desired, serve with marinara sauce.

PER SERVING *2 pancakes: 145 cal., 6g fat (3g sat. fat), 101mg chol., 510mg sodium, 18g carb. (3g sugars, 2g fiber), 6g pro.* ***Diabetic Exchanges:*** *1 starch, 1 fat.*

GOLDEN ZUCCHINI PANCAKES

GARLIC-HERB PATTYPAN SQUASH F C M FAST FIX

The first time I grew a garden, I harvested some summer squash and cooked it with garlic and herbs. Using pattypan squash is a creative twist.

—**KAYCEE MASON** SILOAM SPRINGS, AR

START TO FINISH: 25 MIN.
MAKES: 4 SERVINGS

- **5 cups halved small pattypan squash (about 1¼ pounds)**
- **1 tablespoon olive oil**
- **2 garlic cloves, minced**
- **½ teaspoon salt**
- **¼ teaspoon dried oregano**
- **¼ teaspoon dried thyme**
- **¼ teaspoon pepper**
- **1 tablespoon minced fresh parsley**

Preheat oven to 425°. Place squash in a greased 15x10x1-in. baking pan. Mix oil, garlic, salt, oregano, thyme and pepper; drizzle over squash. Toss to coat. Roast 15-20 minutes or until tender, stirring occasionally. Sprinkle with parsley.

PER SERVING *⅔ cup: 58 cal., 3g fat (0 sat. fat), 0 chol., 296mg sodium, 6g carb. (3g sugars, 2g fiber), 2g pro.* ***Diabetic Exchanges:*** *1 vegetable, ½ fat.*

TWICE-BAKED POTATOES SUPREME F S M

On Christmas Day, we invite all of our nearby relatives over for a special dinner. One way I make the meal memorable is with my twice-baked potatoes with a touch of cayenne and topped with Parmesan cheese.

—**RUTH ANDREWSON** LEAVENWORTH, WA

PREP: 15 MIN. • **BAKE:** 1 HOUR 20 MIN.
MAKES: 12 SERVINGS

- **8 large baking potatoes**
- **¼ cup butter, softened**
- **½ teaspoon salt**
- **½ teaspoon garlic powder**
- **½ teaspoon dried oregano**
- **¼ teaspoon cayenne pepper**
- **⅛ teaspoon celery salt**
- **⅓ to ½ cup whole milk**
- **Grated Parmesan cheese**
- **Paprika, optional**

1. Pierce the potatoes with a fork. Bake at 400° for 60-70 minutes or until tender. Cut the potatoes in half lengthwise; scoop out pulp, leaving a thin shell. Set 12 shell halves aside (discard remaining shells or save for another use).

2. In a large bowl, mash the pulp; add the butter, salt, garlic powder, oregano, cayenne, celery salt and enough milk to reach the desired consistency. Pipe or spoon into shells; place in two greased 13x9-in. baking pans. Sprinkle with Parmesan cheese and paprika if desired. Bake the dish, uncovered, at 350° for 20-25 minutes or until heated through.

PER SERVING *1 stuffed potato half: 199 cal., 0 fat (0 sat. fat), 1mg chol., 131mg sodium, 45g carb. (4g sugars, 4g fiber), 5g pro.*

TOP TIP

No whole milk in the house? Go ahead and use skim or low-fat milk in the recipe. If you have it, sub in a few teaspoons of half and half or cream for some of the requested milk.

ROASTED BROCCOLI & CAULIFLOWER

ROASTED BROCCOLI & CAULIFLOWER C M FAST FIX

When we make a time-consuming entree, we also do a quick broccoli and cauliflower side. The veggies are a good fit when you're watching calories.

—**DEBRA TOLBERT** DEVILLE, LA

START TO FINISH: 25 MIN.
MAKES: 8 SERVINGS

- **4 cups fresh cauliflowerets**
- **4 cups fresh broccoli florets**
- **10 garlic cloves, peeled and halved**
- **2 tablespoons olive oil**
- **½ teaspoon salt**
- **½ teaspoon pepper**

Preheat oven to 425°. In a large bowl, combine all ingredients; toss to coat. Transfer to two greased 15x10x1-in. baking pans. Roast 15-20 minutes or until tender.

PER SERVING *¾ cup: 58 cal., 4g fat (1g sat. fat), 0 chol., 173mg sodium, 6g carb. (2g sugars, 2g fiber), 2g pro.*
Diabetic Exchanges: *1 vegetable, ½ fat.*

SIDE DISHES

MASHED PEPPERY TURNIPS M FAST FIX

(PICTURED ON P. 52)

This recipe was created as an attempt to use up a great turnip season from our garden as well as lighten up one of our favorite dishes. By using turnips in place of potatoes, I made a low-carb side. Now we rarely serve plain mashed potatoes!
—COURTNEY STULTZ WEIR, KS

START TO FINISH: 30 MIN.
MAKES: 4 SERVINGS

- **4 medium turnips (about 1 pound), peeled and cut into 1¼-in. pieces**
- **1 large potato (about ¾ pound), peeled and cut into 1¼-in. pieces**
- **2 tablespoons reduced-fat cream cheese**
- **1 tablespoon butter**
- **1 tablespoon minced fresh parsley**
- **1 teaspoon sea salt**
- **½ teaspoon garlic powder**
- **¼ teaspoon pepper**
- **⅛ teaspoon chili powder**
- **⅛ teaspoon ground chipotle pepper**

1. Place turnips, potato and enough water to cover in a large saucepan; bring to a boil. Reduce heat; cook, uncovered, until tender, 15-20 minutes. Drain and return to pan.
2. Mash the vegetables to the desired consistency. Stir in the remaining ingredients.
PER SERVING *3/4 cup: 140 cal., 5g fat (3g sat. fat), 13mg chol., 608mg sodium, 23g carb. (5g sugars, 3g fiber), 3g pro.* ***Diabetic Exchanges:*** *1 1/2 starch, 1 fat.*

HOW-TO

MINCE PARSLEY WITHOUT THE MESS

Place parsley or cilantro sprigs in a small glass container and snip them with kitchen shears until chopped to the desired fineness. This is a helpful way to avoid dirtying a cutting board.

When we have company, these sprouts are my go-to side dish because they look and taste fantastic. Fancy them up a notch with pancetta instead of bacon.
—MANDY RIVERS LEXINGTON, SC

BRUSSELS SPROUTS WITH BACON & GARLIC

BRUSSELS SPROUTS WITH BACON & GARLIC C FAST FIX

START TO FINISH: 30 MIN.
MAKES: 12 SERVINGS (¾ CUP EACH)

- **2 pounds fresh Brussels sprouts (about 10 cups)**
- **8 bacon strips, coarsely chopped**
- **3 garlic cloves, minced**
- **¾ cup chicken broth**
- **½ teaspoon salt**
- **¼ teaspoon pepper**

1. Trim Brussels sprouts. Cut sprouts lengthwise in half; cut crosswise into thin slices. In a 6-qt. stockpot, cook bacon over medium heat until crisp, stirring occasionally. Add garlic; cook 30 seconds longer. Remove with a slotted spoon; drain on paper towels.
2. Add Brussels sprouts to bacon drippings; cook and stir 4-6 minutes or until sprouts begin to brown lightly. Stir in broth, salt and pepper; cook, covered, 4-6 minutes longer or until Brussels sprouts are tender. Stir in bacon mixture.
PER SERVING *3/4 cup: 109 cal., 8g fat (3g sat. fat), 13mg chol., 300mg sodium, 7g carb. (2g sugars, 3g fiber), 5g pro.* ***Diabetic Exchanges:*** *1 1/2 fat, 1 vegetable.*

RICH & CREAMY PARMESAN MASHED POTATOES

For special occasions, like my husband's birthday dinners, I mash my potatoes with cream cheese, sour cream and Parmesan. It's divine comfort food.

—**JO ANN BURRINGTON** OSCEOLA, IN

PREP: 15 MIN. • **COOK:** 25 MIN.
MAKES: 6 SERVINGS

- **2 pounds red potatoes, cut into ½-inch cubes (about 6 cups)**
- **1 cup chicken broth**
- **4 ounces reduced-fat cream cheese**
- **½ cup reduced-fat sour cream**
- **¼ cup grated Parmesan cheese**
- **¾ teaspoon salt**
- **Butter and additional grated Parmesan cheese, optional**

1. Place potatoes in a large saucepan; add broth. Bring to a boil. Reduce heat; simmer, covered, 15-20 minutes or until potatoes are tender. Uncover; cook 4-6 minutes longer or until broth is almost evaporated, stirring occasionally.

2. Reduce heat to low; stir in cream cheese until melted. Mash potatoes slightly, gradually adding sour cream, Parmesan cheese and salt; heat through. If desired, serve with butter and additional Parmesan cheese.

PER SERVING *2/3 cup: 199 cal., 7g fat (4g sat. fat), 24mg chol., 612mg sodium, 26g carb. (4g sugars, 3g fiber), 8g pro.* ***Diabetic Exchanges:*** *2 starch, 1 1/2 fat.*

ZESTY GARLIC BROCCOLI

F S C M FAST FIX

I've been a vegetarian for over 20 years and often experiment with flavors compatible with the many vegetables I prepare. My nephew thought this was one of my best creations.

—**LOUISA KEMYAN** PALM SPRINGS, CA

START TO FINISH: 15 MIN.
MAKES: 4 SERVINGS

- **4 cups fresh broccoli florets**
- **¼ cup water**
- **2 teaspoons olive oil**
- **1 to 2 garlic cloves, minced**
- **½ teaspoon salt**
- **Dash crushed red pepper flakes**

Place first five ingredients in a large saucepan; bring to a boil. Reduce heat; simmer, covered, until the broccoli is crisp-tender, 5 minutes. Drain. Toss with pepper flakes.

PER SERVING *1/2 cup: 42 cal., 3g fat (0 sat. fat), 0 chol., 49mg sodium, 4g carb. (1g sugars, 2g fiber), 2g pro.* ***Diabetic Exchanges:*** *1 vegetable, 1/2 fat.*

ROASTED VEGETABLES WITH SAGE

ROASTED VEGETABLES WITH SAGE M

When I can't decide what veggie to serve, I just roast a bunch. That's how we boost the veggie love at our house.

—**BETTY FULKS** ONIA, AR

PREP: 20 MIN. • **BAKE:** 35 MIN.
MAKES: 8 SERVINGS

- **5 cups cubed peeled butternut squash**
- **½ pound fingerling potatoes (about 2 cups)**
- **1 cup fresh Brussels sprouts, halved**
- **1 cup fresh baby carrots**
- **3 tablespoons butter**
- **1 tablespoon minced fresh sage or 1 teaspoon dried sage leaves**
- **1 garlic clove, minced**
- **½ teaspoon salt**

1. Preheat the oven to 425°. Place the vegetables in a large bowl. In a microwave, melt the butter; stir in remaining ingredients. Add to vegetables and toss to coat.

2. Transfer to a greased 15x10x1-in. baking pan. Roast 35-45 minutes or until tender, stirring occasionally.

PER SERVING *3/4 cup: 122 cal., 5g fat (3g sat. fat), 11mg chol., 206mg sodium, 20g carb. (4g sugars, 3g fiber), 2g pro.* ***Diabetic Exchanges:*** *1 starch, 1 fat.*

RICH & CREAMY PARMESAN MASHED POTATOES

Good Mornings

"With the abundance of zucchini my family has in the fall, this is the perfect dish to use what we have. Cheesy and rich, this is a warm, classic breakfast recipe sure to please!"

—**COLLEEN DOUCETTE** TRURO, NS
about her recipe, Roasted Vegetable Strata, on page 69

CALICO SCRAMBLED EGGS C M FAST FIX

When you're short on time and rushing to get a morning meal on the table, this recipe is eggs-actly what you need. There's a short ingredient list, and cooking is kept to a minimum.
—*TASTE OF HOME* TEST KITCHEN

START TO FINISH: 15 MIN.
MAKES: 4 SERVINGS

- **8 large eggs**
- **¼ cup 2% milk**
- **⅛ to ¼ teaspoon dill weed**
- **⅛ to ¼ teaspoon salt**
- **⅛ to ¼ teaspoon pepper**
- **1 tablespoon butter**
- **½ cup chopped green pepper**
- **¼ cup chopped onion**
- **½ cup chopped fresh tomato**

1. In a bowl, whisk the first five ingredients until blended. In a 12-in. nonstick skillet, heat the butter over medium-high heat. Add green pepper and onion; cook and stir until tender. Remove from pan.
2. In same pan, pour in egg mixture; cook and stir over medium heat until eggs begin to thicken. Add tomato and pepper mixture; cook until heated through and no liquid egg remains, stirring gently.
PER SERVING *1 cup: 188 cal., 13g fat (5g sat. fat), 381mg chol., 248mg sodium, 4g carb. (3g sugars, 1g fiber), 14g pro.* ***Diabetic Exchanges:*** *2 medium-fat meat, ½ fat.*

CALICO SCRAMBLED EGGS

LEMON-RASPBERRY RICOTTA PANCAKES

LEMON-RASPBERRY RICOTTA PANCAKES M FAST FIX

I was raised in a home where stacks of freshly cooked pancakes were the norm every Sunday morning. I keep the tradition alive, making pancakes for my own family with almond milk, ricotta and raspberries.
—ANITA ARCHIBALD AURORA, ON

START TO FINISH: 30 MIN.
MAKES: 24 PANCAKES

- **1½ cups cake or all-purpose flour**
- **¼ cup sugar**
- **2 teaspoons baking powder**
- **¼ teaspoon salt**
- **¼ teaspoon ground cinnamon**
- **1 cup unsweetened almond milk**
- **1 cup part-skim ricotta cheese**
- **3 large eggs, separated**
- **2 teaspoons grated lemon peel**
- **3 tablespoons lemon juice**
- **1 teaspoon almond extract**
- **1 cup fresh or frozen raspberries**
- **Whipped cream, maple syrup and additional raspberries**

1. In a large bowl, whisk flour, sugar, baking powder, salt and cinnamon. In another bowl, whisk almond milk, ricotta, egg yolks, lemon peel, lemon juice and extract until blended. Add to dry ingredients, stirring just until moistened. In a clean small bowl, beat egg whites until stiff but not dry. Fold into batter. Gently stir in raspberries.
2. Lightly grease a griddle; heat over medium heat. Pour the batter by ¼ cupfuls onto griddle. Cook until bubbles on top begin to pop and bottoms are golden brown. Turn; cook until second side is golden brown. Serve with whipped cream, syrup and additional raspberries.
PER SERVING *3 pancakes: 203 cal., 5g fat (2g sat. fat), 79mg chol., 254mg sodium, 31g carb. (7g sugars, 2g fiber), 8g pro.* ***Diabetic Exchanges:*** *2 starch, 1 medium-fat meat.*

ROASTED VEGETABLE STRATA F M (PICTURED ON P. 66)

With the abundance of zucchini my family has in the fall, this is the perfect dish to use what we have. Cheesy and rich, this is a warm, classic breakfast recipe sure to please!

—COLLEEN DOUCETTE TRURO, NS

PREP: 55 MIN. + CHILLING • **BAKE:** 40 MIN.
MAKES: 8 SERVINGS

- **3 large zucchini, halved lengthwise and cut into ¾-inch slices**
- **1 each medium red, yellow and orange peppers, cut into 1-inch pieces**
- **2 tablespoons olive oil**
- **1 teaspoon dried oregano**
- **½ teaspoon salt**
- **½ teaspoon pepper**
- **½ teaspoon dried basil**
- **1 medium tomato, chopped**
- **1 loaf (1 pound) unsliced crusty Italian bread**
- **½ cup shredded sharp cheddar cheese**
- **½ cup shredded Asiago cheese**
- **6 large eggs**
- **2 cups fat-free milk**

1. Preheat oven to 400°. Toss zucchini and peppers with oil and seasonings; transfer to a 15x10x1-in. pan. Roast until tender, 25-30 minutes, stirring once. Stir in tomato; cool slightly.

2. Trim ends from bread; cut bread into 1-in. slices. In a greased 13x9-in. baking dish, layer half of each of the following: bread, roasted vegetables and cheeses. Repeat layers. Whisk together eggs and milk; pour evenly over top. Refrigerate, covered, 6 hours or overnight.

3. Preheat oven to 375°. Remove casserole from refrigerator while oven heats. Bake, uncovered, until golden brown, 40-50 minutes. Let stand for 5-10 minutes before cutting.

FREEZE OPTION *Cover and freeze unbaked casserole. To use, partially thaw in refrigerator overnight. Remove from refrigerator 30 minutes before baking. Preheat oven to 375°. Bake casserole as directed, increasing time as necessary for a thermometer to read 165°.*

PER SERVING *1 piece: 349 cal., 14g fat (5g sat. fat), 154mg chol., 642mg sodium, 40g carb. (9g sugars, 4g fiber), 17g pro.* ***Diabetic Exchanges:*** *2 starch, 1 medium-fat meat, 1 vegetable, 1 fat.*

ARUGULA & MUSHROOM BREAKFAST PIZZA M

It's a challenge to be creative with breakfast every morning, and I like to come up with fun foods the kids will love. This is a great recipe for the kids to help make. It's also convenient to prep ahead and freeze for a weekday.

—MELISSA PELKEY HASS WALESKA, GA

PREP: 20 MIN. • **BAKE:** 15 MIN.
MAKES: 6 SERVINGS

- **1 prebaked 12-inch thin whole wheat pizza crust**
- **¾ cup reduced-fat ricotta cheese**
- **1 teaspoon garlic powder**
- **1 teaspoon paprika, divided**
- **1 cup sliced baby portobello mushrooms**
- **½ cup julienned soft sun-dried tomatoes (not packed in oil)**
- **3 cups fresh arugula or baby spinach**
- **2 tablespoons balsamic vinegar**
- **2 tablespoons olive oil**
- **¼ teaspoon salt, divided**
- **¼ teaspoon pepper, divided**
- **6 large eggs**

1. Preheat oven to 450°. Place crust on a pizza pan. Spread with ricotta cheese; sprinkle with garlic powder and ½ teaspoon paprika. Top with mushrooms and tomatoes.

2. With clean hands, massage arugula with vinegar, oil and ⅛ teaspoon each salt and pepper until softened; arrange over pizza.

3. Using a spoon, make six indentations in arugula; carefully break an egg into each. Sprinkle with the remaining paprika, salt and pepper. Bake until egg whites are completely set and yolks begin to thicken but are not hard, 12-15 minutes.

NOTE *This recipe was tested with sun-dried tomatoes that can be used without soaking. When using other sun-dried tomatoes that are not oil-packed, cover with boiling water and let stand until soft. Drain before using.*

PER SERVING *1 slice: 299 cal., 13g fat (4g sat. fat), 194mg chol., 464mg sodium, 31g carb. (8g sugars, 5g fiber), 15g pro.* ***Diabetic Exchanges:*** *2 medium-fat meat, 1½ starch, 1 vegetable, 1 fat.*

ARUGULA & MUSHROOM BREAKFAST PIZZA

HASH BROWN QUICHE CUPS

HASH BROWN QUICHE CUPS C FAST FIX

Quiche cups are my showstopper potluck dish. Hash browns and Asiago cheese make up the crusts. Eggs, spinach and bacon do the rest.

—**NICOLE STONE** GILBERTVILLE, IA

START TO FINISH: 30 MIN. • **MAKES:** 4 SERVINGS

- **1 large egg**
- **¼ teaspoon salt**
- **⅛ teaspoon pepper**
- **2 cups frozen shredded hash brown potatoes, thawed**
- **¼ cup shredded Asiago cheese**

FILLING

- **3 large eggs**
- **1 tablespoon minced fresh chives**
- **⅓ cup shredded Colby-Monterey Jack cheese**
- **⅓ cup fresh baby spinach, thinly sliced**
- **2 bacon strips, cooked and crumbled**

1. Preheat oven to 400°. Grease eight muffin cups.
2. In a bowl, whisk egg, salt and pepper until blended; stir in potatoes and Asiago cheese. To form crusts, press about 1/4 cup potato mixture onto bottom and up sides of each prepared muffin cup. Bake 14-17 minutes or until light golden brown.
3. For filling, in a small bowl, whisk eggs and chives until blended; stir in cheese and spinach. Spoon into crusts; top with bacon. Bake 6-8 minutes longer or until a knife inserted near the center comes out clean.

PER SERVING *2 mini quiches: 180 cal., 11g fat (5g sat. fat), 205mg chol., 375mg sodium, 8g carb. (1g sugars, 0 fiber), 12g pro.* ***Diabetic Exchanges:*** *2 medium-fat meat, 1/2 starch.*

HAWAIIAN BREAKFAST HASH

PREP: 10 MIN. • **COOK:** 30 MIN. • **MAKES:** 6 SERVINGS

- **4 bacon strips, chopped**
- **1 tablespoon canola or coconut oil**
- **2 large sweet potatoes (about 1½ pounds), peeled and cut into ½-inch pieces**
- **½ teaspoon salt**
- **¼ teaspoon chili powder**
- **¼ teaspoon paprika**
- **¼ teaspoon pepper**
- **⅛ teaspoon ground cinnamon**
- **2 cups cubed fresh pineapple (½-inch cubes)**

1. In a large skillet, cook bacon over medium heat until crisp, stirring occasionally. Remove with a slotted spoon; drain on paper towels. Discard drippings.
2. In same pan, heat oil over medium heat. Add potatoes and seasonings; cook and stir 15 minutes. Add pineapple; cook and stir until potatoes are tender and browned, 8-10 minutes. Sprinkle with bacon.

PER SERVING *⅔ cup: 194 cal., 5g fat (1g sat. fat), 6mg chol., 309mg sodium, 35g carb. (17g sugars, 4g fiber), 4g pro.* ***Diabetic Exchanges:*** *2 starch, 1 fat.*

Breakfast is our favorite meal, and we love a good variety of dishes. This hash brown recipe is full of flavor and possibilities. Top with some eggs or spinach for an extra twist! —**COURTNEY STULTZ** WEIR, KS

HAWAIIAN BREAKFAST HASH

EGG & HASH BROWN BREAKFAST CUPS C FAST FIX

When I want to deliver homey breakfast comfort, I turn sausage, eggs and hash browns into easy muffin-style cups. They're winners for dinner, too.

—**SUSAN STETZEL** GAINESVILLE, NY

START TO FINISH: 30 MIN. • **MAKES:** 2 SERVINGS

- **3 uncooked turkey breakfast sausage links (1 ounce each), casings removed**
- **3 tablespoons chopped green pepper**
- **2 tablespoons chopped onion**
- **½ cup frozen cubed hash brown potatoes**
- **⅓ cup fat-free milk**
- **¼ cup egg substitute**
- **3 tablespoons reduced-fat biscuit/baking mix**
- **⅛ teaspoon pepper**
- **2 tablespoons shredded reduced-fat cheddar cheese**

1. Preheat oven to 400°. In a nonstick skillet coated with cooking spray, cook and stir sausage with green pepper and onion over medium heat until no longer pink, breaking sausage into small pieces. Stir in potatoes. Divide among four muffin cups coated with cooking spray.

2. Whisk together milk, egg substitute, baking mix and pepper; pour into cups. Sprinkle with cheese. Bake until a knife inserted in center comes out clean, 13-15 minutes.

PER SERVING *2 egg cups: 158 cal., 5g fat (2g sat. fat), 28mg chol., 435mg sodium, 15g carb. (4g sugars, 1g fiber), 13g pro.* ***Diabetic Exchanges:*** *1 starch, 1 medium-fat meat.*

HONEY-YOGURT BERRY SALAD

F M FAST FIX (PICTURED ON P. 67)

I wanted my family to eat more fruit but not more sugary ingredients. This lovely salad lets the simple goodness of berries shine.

—**BETSY KING** DULUTH, MN

START TO FINISH: 10 MIN. • **MAKES:** 8 SERVINGS

- **1½ cups sliced fresh strawberries**
- **1½ cups fresh raspberries**
- **1½ cups fresh blueberries**
- **1½ cups fresh blackberries**
- **1 cup (8 ounces) reduced-fat plain yogurt**
- **1 tablespoon honey**
- **¼ teaspoon grated orange peel**
- **1 tablespoon orange juice**

Place berries in a glass bowl; toss to combine. In a small bowl, mix remaining ingredients. Spoon over berries.

PER SERVING *¾ cup fruit with 2 tablespoons yogurt mixture: 76 cal., 1g fat (0 sat. fat), 2mg chol., 23mg sodium, 16g carb. (11g sugars, 4g fiber), 3g pro.* ***Diabetic Exchanges:*** *1 fruit.*

FULL GARDEN FRITTATA

FULL GARDEN FRITTATA C M

I was cooking for a health-conscious friend and wanted to serve a frittata. To brighten it up, I added classic bruschetta toppings. This has become a staple in my recipe book.

—**MELISSA ROSENTHAL** VISTA, CA

PREP: 25 MIN. • **BAKE:** 10 MIN. • **MAKES:** 2 SERVINGS

- **4 large eggs**
- **⅓ cup 2% milk**
- **¼ teaspoon salt, divided**
- **⅛ teaspoon coarsely ground pepper**
- **2 teaspoons olive oil**
- **½ medium zucchini, chopped**
- **½ cup chopped baby portobello mushrooms**
- **¼ cup chopped onion**
- **1 garlic clove, minced**
- **2 tablespoons minced fresh basil**
- **1 teaspoon minced fresh oregano**
- **1 teaspoon minced fresh parsley**
- **Optional toppings: halved grape tomatoes, small fresh mozzarella cheese balls and thinly sliced fresh basil**

1. Preheat the oven to 375°. In a bowl, whisk eggs, milk, ⅛ teaspoon salt and pepper. In an 8-in. ovenproof skillet, heat oil over medium-high heat. Add zucchini, mushrooms and onion; cook and stir until tender. Add garlic, herbs and remaining salt; cook 1 minute longer. Pour in egg mixture.

2. Bake, uncovered, 10-15 minutes or until eggs are set. Cut into four wedges. If desired, serve with toppings.

PER SERVING *2 wedges: 227 cal., 15g fat (4g sat. fat), 375mg chol., 463mg sodium, 7g carb. (5g sugars, 1g fiber), 15g pro.* ***Diabetic Exchanges:*** *2 medium-fat meat, 1 vegetable, 1 fat.*

STRAWBERRY-CARROT SMOOTHIES F S M FAST FIX

My children dislike veggies, but they love smoothies. This smoothie packs in lots of good-for-you fruits and veggies. To my kids, it's just a super delicious breakfast.

—**ELISABETH LARSEN** PLEASANT GROVE, UT

START TO FINISH: 5 MIN.
MAKES: 5 SERVINGS

- **2 cups (16 ounces) reduced-fat plain Greek yogurt**
- **1 cup carrot juice**
- **1 cup orange juice**
- **1 cup frozen pineapple chunks**
- **1 cup frozen unsweetened sliced strawberries**

Place all ingredients in a blender; cover and process until smooth.

PER SERVING *1 cup: 141 cal., 2g fat (1g sat. fat), 5mg chol., 79mg sodium, 20g carb. (15g sugars, 1g fiber), 10g pro.* ***Diabetic Exchanges:*** *1 fruit, 1/2 reduced-fat milk.*

HEALTH TIP *Yogurt's combination of carbohydrate and protein helps give you long-lasting energy. It's also a rich source of phosphorous, which is vital to energy production and storage.*

ASPARAGUS-MUSHROOM FRITTATA

STRAWBERRY-CARROT SMOOTHIES

ASPARAGUS-MUSHROOM FRITTATA C M

My Aunt Paulina, who is Sicilian, inspired this fluffy frittata. I remember visiting her garden, picking fresh veggies and watching her cook. Her wild asparagus frittata was my favorite.

—**CINDY ESPOSITO** BLOOMFIELD, NJ

PREP: 25 MIN. • **BAKE:** 20 MIN.
MAKES: 8 SERVINGS

- **8 large eggs**
- **½ cup whole-milk ricotta cheese**
- **2 tablespoons lemon juice**
- **½ teaspoon salt**
- **¼ teaspoon pepper**
- **1 tablespoon olive oil**
- **1 package (8 ounces) frozen asparagus spears, thawed**
- **1 large onion, halved and thinly sliced**
- **½ cup finely chopped sweet red or green pepper**
- **¼ cup sliced baby portobello mushrooms**

1. Preheat oven to 350°. In a large bowl, whisk eggs, ricotta cheese, lemon juice, salt and pepper. In a 10-in. ovenproof skillet, heat oil over medium heat. Add asparagus, onion, red pepper and mushrooms; cook and stir 6-8 minutes or until onion and pepper are tender.

2. Remove from heat; remove the asparagus from skillet. Reserve eight spears; cut remaining asparagus into 2-in. pieces. Return cut asparagus to skillet; stir in egg mixture. Arrange reserved asparagus spears over eggs to resemble spokes of a wheel.

3. Bake, uncovered, 20-25 minutes or until eggs are completely set. Let stand 5 minutes. Cut into wedges.

PER SERVING *1 wedge: 135 cal., 8g fat (3g sat. fat), 192mg chol., 239mg sodium, 7g carb. (2g sugars, 1g fiber), 9g pro.* ***Diabetic Exchanges:*** *1 medium-fat meat, 1 vegetable, 1/2 fat.*

APPLE-SAGE SAUSAGE PATTIES C

(PICTURED ON P. 67)

Apple and sausage naturally go together. Add sage, and you've got a standout patty. They're freezer friendly, so I make them ahead and grab when needed.

—SCARLETT ELROD NEWNAN, GA

PREP: 35 MIN. + CHILLING
COOK: 10 MIN./BATCH
MAKES: 16 PATTIES

- **1 large apple**
- **1 large egg, lightly beaten**
- **½ cup chopped fresh parsley**
- **3 to 4 tablespoons minced fresh sage**
- **2 garlic cloves, minced**
- **1¼ teaspoons salt**
- **½ teaspoon pepper**
- **½ teaspoon crushed red pepper flakes**
- **1¼ pounds lean ground turkey**
- **6 teaspoons olive oil, divided**

1. Peel and coarsely shred apple; place apple in a colander over a plate. Let stand 15 minutes. Squeeze and blot dry with paper towels.

2. In a large bowl, combine egg, parsley, sage, garlic, seasonings and apple. Add turkey; mix lightly but thoroughly. Shape into sixteen 2-in. patties. Place patties on waxed paper-lined baking sheets. Refrigerate, covered, 8 hours or overnight.

3. In a large nonstick skillet, heat 2 teaspoons oil over medium heat. In batches, cook patties 3-4 minutes on each side or until golden brown and a thermometer reads 165°, adding additional oil as needed.

FREEZE OPTION *Place uncooked patties on plastic wrap-lined baking sheets; wrap and freeze until firm. Remove from pans and transfer to resealable plastic bags; return to freezer. To use, cook frozen patties as directed, increasing time to 4-5 minutes on each side.*

PER SERVING *1 patty: 79 cal., 5g fat (1g sat. fat), 36mg chol., 211mg sodium, 2g carb. (1g sugars, 0 fiber), 8g pro.* ***Diabetic Exchanges:*** *1 lean meat, ½ fat.*

LANCE'S OWN FRENCH TOAST M FAST FIX

When my son, Lance, helps me make this French toast, he knows what order to add the ingredients and even how much to measure out. It's great for the whole family!

—JANNA STEELE MAGEE, MS

START TO FINISH: 25 MIN.
MAKES: 6 SERVINGS

- **4 large eggs**
- **1 cup 2% milk**
- **1 tablespoon honey**
- **½ teaspoon ground cinnamon**
- **⅛ teaspoon pepper**
- **12 slices whole wheat bread**
- **Cinnamon sugar, optional**
- **Vanilla frosting, optional**

1. In a shallow bowl, whisk eggs, milk, honey, cinnamon and pepper. Dip both sides of bread in egg mixture. Cook on a greased hot griddle 3-4 minutes on each side or until golden brown.

2. If desired, sprinkle with cinnamon sugar or frost with vanilla icing.

FREEZE OPTION *Cool French toast on wire racks. Freeze between layers of waxed paper in a resealable plastic freezer bag. To use, reheat French toast in a toaster oven on medium setting. Or, microwave each French toast on high for 30-60 seconds or until heated through.*

PER SERVING *2 slices: 218 cal., 6g fat (2g sat. fat), 144mg chol., 331mg sodium, 28g carb. (8g sugars, 4g fiber), 13g pro.* ***Diabetic Exchanges:*** *2 starch, 1 medium-fat meat.*

LANCE'S OWN FRENCH TOAST

SPICED APRICOT BAKED OATMEAL

SPICED APRICOT BAKED OATMEAL M

Eat these spiced oatmeal squares while they're still warm for a cozy morning treat. I freeze mine in single servings so I can grab, microwave and go when I get to work. I'm not afraid to say I have the best breakfast in the office.

—ELLIE MARTIN CLIFFE MILWAUKEE, WI

PREP: 15 MIN. • **BAKE:** 25 MIN.
MAKES: 12 SERVINGS

- **¾ cup packed brown sugar**
- **3 teaspoons pumpkin pie spice**
- **2 teaspoons baking powder**
- **½ teaspoon salt**
- **¼ teaspoon ground cardamom**
- **3 cups old-fashioned oats**
- **½ cup chopped dried apricots**
- **½ cup chopped pecans, toasted**
- **3 large eggs**
- **1½ cups fat-free milk**
- **½ cup unsweetened applesauce**
- **1½ teaspoons vanilla extract**
- **¼ cup butter, melted**

TOPPINGS

- **3 cups vanilla yogurt**
- **½ cup apricot preserves, warmed**

1. Preheat oven to 350°. In a large bowl, mix the first five ingredients; stir in oats, apricots and pecans. In another bowl, whisk together the eggs, milk, applesauce and vanilla; gradually whisk in melted butter. Stir into oat mixture.

2. Transfer to a greased 11x7-in. baking dish. Bake, uncovered, for 25-30 minutes or until set and edges are lightly browned. Cut into twelve portions; serve with toppings.

FREEZE OPTION *Freeze cooled portions of oatmeal in resealable plastic freezer bags. To use, microwave each portion on high for 20-30 seconds or until heated through. Serve with toppings.*

NOTE *To toast nuts, bake in a shallow pan in a 350° oven for 5-10 minutes or cook in a skillet over low heat until lightly browned, stirring occasionally.*

PER SERVING *1 piece with ¼ cup yogurt and 2 teaspoons preserves: 327 cal., 11g fat (4g sat. fat), 60mg chol., 280mg sodium, 52g carb. (33g sugars, 3g fiber), 9g pro.*

SOUTHWEST BREAKFAST POCKETS M FAST FIX

I came up with this after my second son was born. The two are just 17 months apart, so we needed meals that were fast, tasty and kept us going all morning.

—KOLEEN O'MALLEY-ELLINGSON
SIOUX FALLS, SD

START TO FINISH: 20 MIN.
MAKES: 2 SERVINGS

- **2 large eggs**
- **2 large egg whites**
- **1 teaspoon olive oil**
- **1 small onion, chopped**
- **1 garlic clove, minced**
- **½ cup canned pinto beans, rinsed and drained**
- **4 whole wheat pita pocket halves, warmed**
- **¼ cup salsa**
- **Sliced avocado, optional**

1. Whisk together eggs and egg whites. In a large nonstick skillet, heat the oil over medium heat; saute onion until tender, 3-4 minutes. Add garlic; cook and stir 1 minute. Add eggs and beans; cook and stir until eggs are thickened and no liquid egg remains.

2. Spoon into pitas. Serve with salsa and, if desired, avocado.

PER SERVING *339 cal., 9g fat (2g sat. fat), 186mg chol., 580mg sodium, 47g carb. (4g sugars, 7g fiber), 19g pro.* ***Diabetic Exchanges:*** *3 starch, 2 medium-fat meat.*

HOW-TO

CHOP AN ONION

Peel onion and cut in half from root to top. Leaving root attached, place flat side down on work surface. Cut vertically through the onion, leaving the root end uncut. Cut across the onion, discarding root end. The closer the cuts, the more finely chopped the onion will be. This method can also be used for shallots.

SOUTHWEST BREAKFAST POCKETS

BERRY-TOPPED COFFEE CAKE M

This tasty, wholesome coffee cake is loaded with fresh berries. It's perfect for those with a sweet tooth.

—**HEATHER O'NEILL** TROY, OH

PREP: 25 MIN. • **BAKE:** 45 MIN. + COOLING
MAKES: 10 SERVINGS

- **⅓ cup butter, softened**
- **⅔ cup sugar**
- **1 large egg**
- **2 teaspoons grated lemon peel**
- **¾ cup all-purpose flour**
- **¾ cup whole wheat flour**
- **½ teaspoon baking powder**
- **¼ teaspoon salt**
- **¼ teaspoon baking soda**
- **½ cup reduced-fat sour cream**

TOPPING

- **⅓ cup sugar**
- **2 teaspoons all-purpose flour**
- **½ teaspoon ground cinnamon**
- **1 cup fresh or frozen blueberries, thawed**
- **½ cup fresh or frozen unsweetened raspberries, thawed**

GLAZE

- **⅓ cup confectioners' sugar**
- **2 teaspoons fat-free milk**
- **⅛ teaspoon vanilla extract**

1. Preheat oven to 350°. Grease a 9-in. springform pan.

2. Cream butter and sugar until light and fluffy. Beat in egg and lemon peel. In another bowl, whisk together flours, baking powder, salt and baking soda; add to creamed mixture alternately with sour cream, beating well (batter will be thick). Spread batter into the prepared pan.

3. For topping, mix sugar, flour and cinnamon; toss gently with berries. Distribute over batter to within 1 in. of sides. Bake until a toothpick inserted in center comes out clean, 45-50 minutes. Cool on a wire rack 10 minutes. Remove rim from pan.

4. Mix glaze ingredients. Drizzle over warm coffee cake.

PER SERVING *1 slice: 246 cal., 8g fat (5g sat. fat), 36mg chol., 180mg sodium, 42g carb. (27g sugars, 2g fiber), 4g pro.*

BERRY-TOPPED COFFEE CAKE

GREAT GRANOLA S M

Nuts, dried fruit and more make a crunchy homemade topping for yogurt or for eating by the handful. It makes a delicious gift.

—**JOHNNA JOHNSON** SCOTTSDALE, AZ

PREP: 25 MIN. • **BAKE:** 25 MIN. + COOLING
MAKES: 7 CUPS

- **2 cups old-fashioned oats**
- **½ cup chopped almonds**
- **½ cup salted pumpkin seeds or pepitas**
- **½ cup chopped walnuts**
- **¼ cup chopped pecans**
- **¼ cup sesame seeds**
- **¼ cup sunflower kernels**
- **⅓ cup honey**
- **¼ cup packed brown sugar**
- **¼ cup maple syrup**
- **2 tablespoons toasted wheat germ**
- **2 tablespoons canola oil**
- **1 teaspoon ground cinnamon**
- **1 teaspoon vanilla extract**
- **1 package (7 ounces) dried fruit bits**

1. In a large bowl, combine the first seven ingredients; set aside.

2. In a small saucepan, combine the honey, brown sugar, syrup, wheat germ, oil and cinnamon. Cook and stir over medium heat for 4-5 minutes or until smooth. Remove from the heat; stir in vanilla. Pour over oat mixture and toss to coat.

3. Transfer to a greased 15x10x1-in. baking pan. Bake mixture at 350° for 22-27 minutes or until golden brown, stirring occasionally. Cool completely on a wire rack. Stir in fruit bits. Store in an airtight container.

PER SERVING *½ cup: 264 cal., 12g fat (1g sat. fat), 0 chol., 14mg sodium, 37g carb. (21g sugars, 4g fiber), 6g pro.*

TOP TIP

Pecans have a higher fat content than other nuts, so be careful that they don't go rancid. They'll stay fresh for twice as long in the freezer as they would at room temperature.

GREEK VEGGIE OMELET

GREEK VEGGIE OMELET

C M FAST FIX

This is a family favorite in my house. It's very quick and satisfying and not to mention, yummy!

—**SHARON MANNIX** WINDSOR, NY

START TO FINISH: 20 MIN.
MAKES: 2 SERVINGS

- **4 large eggs**
- **2 tablespoons fat-free milk**
- **⅛ teaspoon salt**
- **3 teaspoons olive oil, divided**
- **2 cups sliced baby portobello mushrooms**
- **¼ cup finely chopped onion**
- **1 cup fresh baby spinach**
- **3 tablespoons crumbled feta cheese**
- **2 tablespoons sliced ripe olives**
- **Freshly ground pepper**

1. Whisk together the eggs, milk and salt. In a large nonstick skillet, heat 2 teaspoons oil over medium-high heat; cook mushrooms and onion until golden brown, 5-6 minutes. Stir in spinach until wilted; remove from pan.

2. In same pan, heat remaining oil over medium-low heat. Pour in egg mixture. As eggs set, push cooked portions toward the center, letting t he uncooked eggs flow underneath. When eggs are thickened and no liquid egg remains, spoon vegetables on one side; sprinkle with cheese and olives. Fold to close; cut in half to serve. Sprinkle with pepper.

PER SERVING *1/2 omelet: 271 cal., 19g fat (5g sat. fat), 378mg chol., 475mg sodium, 7g carb. (3g sugars, 2g fiber), 18g pro.* ***Diabetic Exchanges:*** *2 medium-fat meat, 2 fat, 1 vegetable.*

WHOLE GRAIN BANANA PANCAKES

M FAST FIX

START TO FINISH: 30 MIN.
MAKES: 8 SERVINGS

- **1 cup whole wheat flour**
- **1 cup all-purpose flour**
- **4 teaspoons baking powder**
- **1 teaspoon ground cinnamon**
- **½ teaspoon salt**
- **2 large eggs**
- **2 cups fat-free milk**
- **⅔ cup mashed ripe banana (about 1 medium)**
- **1 tablespoon olive oil**
- **1 tablespoon maple syrup**
- **½ teaspoon vanilla extract**
- **Sliced bananas and additional syrup, optional**

1. Whisk together first five ingredients. In another bowl, whisk together eggs, milk, mashed banana, oil, 1 tablespoon syrup and vanilla. Add to flour mixture; stir just until moistened.

2. Preheat a griddle coated with cooking spray over medium heat. Pour batter by 1/4 cupfuls onto griddle; cook until bubbles on top begin to pop and bottoms are golden brown. Turn; cook until the second side is golden brown. If desired, serve with sliced bananas and additional syrup.

FREEZE OPTION *Freeze cooled pancakes between layers of waxed paper in a resealable plastic freezer bag. To use, place pancakes on an ungreased baking sheet, cover with foil and reheat in preheated 375° oven until heated through, 10-15 minutes. Or, place a stack of two pancakes on a microwave-safe plate, microwave on high until heated, 45-60 seconds.*

PER SERVING *2 pancakes: 186 cal., 4g fat (1g sat. fat), 48mg chol., 392mg sodium, 32g carb. (7g sugars, 3g fiber), 7g pro.* ***Diabetic Exchanges:*** *2 starch, 1/2 fat.*

My kids love homemade banana bread, so why not make it in pancake form? These freeze well for a special breakfast any day.

—**ALLY BILLHORN** WILTON, IA

WHOLE GRAIN BANANA PANCAKES

WHOLE WHEAT PECAN WAFFLES M FAST FIX

(PICTURED ON P. 67)

We bought a waffle iron, and a recipe came with it. After a few changes, we came up with these delicious waffles.

—SARAH MORRIS JOPLIN, MO

START TO FINISH: 30 MIN.
MAKES: 8 SERVINGS

- **2 cups whole wheat pastry flour**
- **2 tablespoons sugar**
- **3 teaspoons baking powder**
- **½ teaspoon salt**
- **2 large eggs, separated**
- **1¾ cups fat-free milk**
- **¼ cup canola oil**
- **½ cup chopped pecans**

1. Preheat waffle maker. Whisk together first four ingredients. In another bowl, whisk together egg yolks, milk and oil; add to flour mixture, stirring until moistened.

2. In a clean bowl, beat egg whites on medium speed until stiff but not dry. Fold into batter. Bake waffles according to manufacturer's directions until golden brown, sprinkling with pecans after pouring.

FREEZE OPTION *Cool waffles on wire racks. Freeze between layers of waxed paper in a resealable plastic freezer bag. Reheat waffles in a toaster or toaster oven on medium setting.*

PER SERVING *2 (4-in.) waffles: 241 cal., 14g fat (1g sat. fat), 48mg chol., 338mg sodium, 24g carb. (6g sugars, 3g fiber), 7g pro.* ***Diabetic Exchanges:*** *2½ fat, 1½ starch.*

TOP TIP

Whole wheat pastry flour is made from soft wheat, which contains less gluten than hard wheat, the ingredient in regular whole wheat flour. Pastry flour produces lighter, more tender and flaky biscuits, pie crusts and baked goods. If you need a substitute, try a 50-50 mix of cake or all-purpose and whole wheat flours.

SAUSAGE TORTILLA BREAKFAST BAKE

SAUSAGE TORTILLA BREAKFAST BAKE C

This is perfect for the holidays. It combines the spices of the Southwest with the comfort of a hearty morning breakfast. The recipe can be spiced up by adding cayenne and hot peppers, or mellowed by replacing the tomatoes and green chilies with mild salsa. The versatility and ease of preparation have made it a longtime favorite of my family.

—DARLENE BUERGER PEORIA, AZ

PREP: 25 MIN. • **BAKE:** 25 MIN. + STANDING
MAKES: 6 SERVINGS

- **8 ounces bulk lean turkey breakfast sausage**
- **½ cup canned diced tomatoes and green chilies**
- **6 corn tortillas (6 inches)**
- **½ cup shredded Monterey Jack cheese**
- **¼ cup shredded pepper jack cheese**
- **2 green onions, chopped**
- **6 large eggs**
- **¾ cup fat-free milk**
- **¾ teaspoon paprika**
- **¼ teaspoon ground cumin**
- **Salsa, optional**
- **Reduced-fat sour cream, optional**
- **Additional chopped green onions, optional**

1. Preheat oven to 350°. In a large skillet, cook and crumble sausage over medium heat until no longer pink, 4-6 minutes. Stir in tomatoes.

2. Coat a 9-in. pie plate with cooking spray; place in a 15x10x1-in. baking pan. Lie pie plate with tortillas. Sprinkle with half of each of the following: sausage mixture, cheeses and green onions. Repeat layers.

3. In a bowl, whisk together eggs, milk, paprika and cumin; pour slowly over layers. Bake, uncovered, until set, 25-30 minutes. Let stand 10 minutes. Cut into wedges. If desired, serve with remaining ingredients.

PER SERVING *1 piece: 268 cal., 14g fat (5g sat. fat), 240mg chol., 646mg sodium, 14g carb. (2g sugars, 2g fiber), 22g pro.* ***Diabetic Exchanges:*** *3 medium-fat meat, 1 starch.*

WINTER HERB TEA MIX

F S C M FAST FIX

This caffeine-free option is a blend of mint, sage, rosemary, thyme and honey that melts away any day's troubles.
—**SUE GRONHOLZ** BEAVER DAM, WI

START TO FINISH: 10 MIN.
MAKES: 18 SERVINGS (9 TABLESPOONS TEA MIX)

- **6 tablespoons dried mint**
- **1 tablespoon dried sage leaves**
- **1 tablespoon dried rosemary, crushed**
- **1 tablespoon dried thyme**

ADDITIONAL INGREDIENTS (FOR EACH SERVING)

- **1 cup boiling water**
- **1 teaspoon honey**
- **1 lemon wedge**

In a small airtight container, combine the herbs. Store in a cool dry place for up to 6 months.

TO PREPARE TEA *Put 1½ teaspoons tea mix in a glass measuring cup. With the end of a wooden spoon handle, crush mixture until aromas are released. Add boiling water. Cover and steep for 10 minutes. Strain tea into a mug, discarding herbs. Stir in honey; serve with lemon.*

PER SERVING *1 cup hot tea: 27 cal., 0 fat (0 sat. fat), 0 chol., 2mg sodium, 7g carb. (6g sugars, 1g fiber), 0 pro.*

WINTER HERB TEA MIX

YUMMY ZUCCHINI COFFEE CAKE

YUMMY ZUCCHINI COFFEE CAKE

M

The first time I made this, I gave some to my daughter, who hates zucchini, and she said it was the best thing I ever made! It has been an excellent and wholesome way to use up all of the zucchini from my garden. If using thawed shredded zucchini, make sure to drain very well.
—**TAMMY KIRSCH** ARCADE, NY

PREP: 25 MIN. • **BAKE:** 35 MIN. + COOLING
MAKES: 16 SERVINGS

- **⅓ cup packed brown sugar**
- **¼ cup all-purpose flour**
- **¼ cup quick-cooking oats**
- **2 tablespoons butter, softened**
- **½ teaspoon ground cinnamon**

BATTER

- **1½ cups quick-cooking oats**
- **1 cup all-purpose flour**
- **¾ cup whole wheat flour**
- **1¼ teaspoons ground cinnamon**
- **1 teaspoon baking powder**
- **1 teaspoon baking soda**
- **½ teaspoon salt**
- **¼ teaspoon ground nutmeg**
- **⅓ cup butter, softened**
- **1 cup packed light brown sugar**
- **1½ teaspoons vanilla extract**
- **2 large eggs**
- **⅓ cup reduced-fat sour cream**
- **2½ cups shredded zucchini (about 2 medium)**
- **Confectioners' sugar**

1. Preheat oven to 350°. Coat a 10-in. fluted tube pan with cooking spray; dust lightly with flour, tapping out the excess.

2. Mix first five ingredients with a fork until crumbly. Sprinkle onto bottom of prepared pan.

3. For batter, mix oats, flours, cinnamon, baking powder, baking soda, salt and nutmeg. In another bowl, beat butter and brown sugar until crumbly; beat in vanilla and eggs, one at a time. Add oat mixture alternately with sour cream, beating well (batter will be thick). Fold in zucchini. Pour over crumb mixture.

4. Bake until a toothpick put in center comes out clean, 35-40 minutes. Cool 10 minutes before removing to a wire rack. Serve warm or at room temperature; dust with confectioners' sugar before serving.

PER SERVING *1 slice: 223 cal., 7g fat (4g sat. fat), 38mg chol., 244mg sodium, 37g carb. (19g sugars, 2g fiber), 4g pro.*

COLORFUL BROCCOLI CHEDDAR CASSEROLE F M

When we have houseguests, we make our broccoli and cheese strata the night before so we can relax and visit while it bubbles in the oven.

—**GALE LALMOND** DEERING, NH

PREP: 25 MIN. + CHILLING • **BAKE:** 50 MIN.
MAKES: 8 SERVINGS

- **1 tablespoon olive oil**
- **6 green onions, sliced**
- **2 cups fresh broccoli florets, chopped**
- **1 medium sweet red pepper, finely chopped**
- **2 garlic cloves, minced**
- **⅛ teaspoon pepper**
- **5 whole wheat English muffins, split, toasted and quartered**
- **1½ cups shredded reduced-fat cheddar cheese, divided**
- **8 large eggs**
- **2½ cups fat-free milk**
- **2 tablespoons Dijon mustard**
- **½ teaspoon hot pepper sauce, optional**

1. In a large skillet, heat oil over medium-high heat. Add green onions; cook and stir until tender. Add the broccoli, red pepper and garlic; cook and stir 4-5 minutes or until tender. Transfer to a large bowl and season with pepper.

2. Place English muffins in a greased 13x9-in. baking dish, cut sides up. Top muffins with vegetable mixture and sprinkle with 1 cup cheese.

3. In a large bowl, whisk eggs, milk, mustard and, if desired, hot sauce. Pour over top. Refrigerate, covered, overnight.

4. Remove from the refrigerator 30 minutes before baking. Preheat oven to 350°. Bake casserole, covered, 30 minutes. Sprinkle with remaining cheese. Bake, uncovered, for 20-30 minutes longer or until egg mixture is set. Let stand 5 minutes before cutting.

PER SERVING *1 piece: 273 cal., 12g fat (5g sat. fat), 228mg chol., 529mg sodium, 25g carb. (9g sugars, 4g fiber), 19g pro.* ***Diabetic Exchanges:*** *2 medium-fat meat, 1½ starch, ½ fat.*

BLUEBERRY-ORANGE BLINTZES

BLUEBERRY-ORANGE BLINTZES S M

Blintzes are aces for brunch time because I can easily make the crepes ahead. They taste so indulgent that guests don't know they're lower in fat and calories.

—**MARY JOHNSON** COLOMA, WI

PREP: 15 MIN. + CHILLING • **BAKE:** 25 MIN.
MAKES: 6 SERVINGS

- **1 large egg**
- **1 cup fat-free milk**
- **¾ cup all-purpose flour**
- **1 carton (15 ounces) part-skim ricotta cheese**
- **6 tablespoons orange marmalade, divided**
- **1 tablespoon sugar**
- **⅛ teaspoon ground cinnamon**
- **2 cups fresh blueberries or raspberries, divided**
- **⅔ cup reduced-fat sour cream**

1. In a large bowl, whisk egg, milk and flour until blended. Refrigerate, covered, 1 hour.

2. Preheat oven to 350°. Place a 6-in. nonstick skillet coated with cooking spray over medium heat. Stir batter; fill a ¼-cup measure halfway with batter and pour into center of pan. Quickly lift and tilt pan to coat bottom evenly. Cook until top appears dry; turn crepe over and cook 15-20 seconds longer or until bottom is cooked. Remove to a wire rack. Repeat with remaining batter.

3. In a small bowl, mix ricotta cheese, 2 tablespoons marmalade, sugar and cinnamon. Spoon about 2 tablespoons mixture onto each crepe; top with about 1 tablespoon blueberries. Fold opposite sides of crepes over filling, forming a rectangular bundle.

4. Place blintzes on a 15x10x1-in. baking pan coated with cooking spray, seam side down. Bake, uncovered, 10-15 minutes or until heated through. Serve blintzes with sour cream and the remaining marmalade and blueberries.

FREEZE OPTION *Freeze cooled crepes between layers of waxed paper in a resealable plastic freezer bag. To use, thaw overnight in refrigerator overnight. Proceed as directed.*

PER SERVING *2 blintzes with toppings: 301 cal., 9g fat (5g sat. fat), 63mg chol., 129mg sodium, 42g carb. (23g sugars, 2g fiber), 14g pro.* ***Diabetic Exchanges:*** *2 starch, 2 lean meat, ½ fruit.*

HEALTH TIP *Use reduced-fat ricotta cheese instead of part-skim and save 30 calories and 3 grams fat.*

CUCUMBER MELON SMOOTHIES F S M FAST FIX

My cool honeydew and cucumber smoothie has only five ingredients. I sometimes add a small avocado to make it extra creamy.

—**CRYSTAL SCHLUETER** NORTHGLENN, CO

START TO FINISH: 15 MIN.
MAKES: 6 SERVINGS

- **2 cups reduced-fat plain Greek yogurt**
- **⅓ cup honey**
- **3 cups chopped honeydew**
- **2 medium cucumbers, peeled, seeded and chopped**
- **1 to 2 tablespoons fresh mint leaves, optional**
- **2 cups crushed ice cubes**

Place half of each of the following in a blender: yogurt, honey, honeydew, cucumber and, if desired, mint. Cover; process until blended. Add 1 cup ice; cover and process until smooth. Pour into three glasses; repeat with remaining ingredients.

PER SERVING *1 cup: 155 cal., 2g fat (1g sat. fat), 4mg chol., 48mg sodium, 28g carb. (26g sugars, 2g fiber), 9g pro.*

CHORIZO & GRITS BREAKFAST BOWLS

FAST FIX

START TO FINISH: 30 MIN.
MAKES: 6 SERVINGS

- **2 teaspoons olive oil**
- **1 package (12 ounces) fully cooked chorizo chicken sausages or flavor of choice, sliced**
- **1 large zucchini, chopped**
- **3 cups water**
- **¾ cup quick-cooking grits**
- **1 can (15 ounces) black beans, rinsed and drained**
- **½ cup shredded cheddar cheese**
- **6 large eggs**
- **Pico de gallo and chopped fresh cilantro, optional**

1. In a large nonstick skillet, heat oil over medium heat. Add sausage; cook and stir 2-3 minutes or until lightly browned. Add zucchini; cook and stir 4-5 minutes longer or until tender. Remove from pan; keep warm.

2. Meanwhile, in a large saucepan, bring water to a boil. Slowly stir in grits. Reduce heat to medium-low; cook, covered, about 5 minutes or until thickened, stirring occasionally. Stir in beans and cheese until blended. Remove from heat.

3. Wipe skillet clean; coat with cooking spray and place over medium heat. In batches, break eggs, one at a time, into pan. Immediately reduce heat to low; cook until whites are completely set and yolks begin to thicken but are not hard, about 5 minutes.

4. To serve, divide grits mixture among six bowls. Top with chorizo mixture, eggs and, if desired, pico de gallo and cilantro.

PER SERVING *344 cal., 14g fat (5g sat. fat), 239mg chol., 636mg sodium, 30g carb. (4g sugars, 4g fiber), 24g pro.* ***Diabetic Exchanges:*** *3 medium-fat meat, 2 starch.*

HEALTH TIP *Pulses like black beans are part of the legume family and a rich source of iron, which helps transport oxygen to muscles.*

Growing up, I bonded with my dad over chorizo and eggs. My fresh approach combines them with grits and black beans. Add a spoonful of pico de gallo.

—**JENN TIDWELL** FAIR OAKS, CA

CHORIZO & GRITS BREAKFAST BOWLS

94

92

85

Slow Cooker

"This cool and always refreshing dessert is fancy enough to take to a gathering. You can make it ahead of time and freeze it. Make sure you wrap it well in airtight wrap and only add the peaches and whipped cream after it thaws."

—JOAN ENGELHARDT LATROBE, PA
about her recipe, Peachy Summer Cheesecake, on page 87

SLOW COOKER DRESSING

Here's an easy dressing that's perfect for Thanksgiving get-togethers. Once it's in the slow cooker, you're free to turn your attention to the other dishes.

—RITA NODLAND BISMARCK, ND

PREP: 15 MIN. • **COOK:** 3 HOURS
MAKES: 8 SERVINGS

- **2 tablespoons olive oil**
- **1 medium celery rib, chopped**
- **1 small onion, chopped**
- **8 cups unseasoned stuffing cubes**
- **1 teaspoon poultry seasoning**
- **¼ teaspoon salt**
- **¼ teaspoon pepper**
- **2 cups reduced-sodium chicken broth**

1. In a large skillet, heat oil over medium-high heat; saute celery and onion until tender. Place stuffing cubes, celery mixture and seasonings in a large bowl; toss to combine. Gradually stir in broth.

2. Transfer to a greased 5-qt. slow cooker. Cook, covered, on low until heated through, 3-4 hours.

PER SERVING *½ cup: 226 cal., 5g fat (0 sat. fat), 0 chol., 635mg sodium, 40g carb. (3g sugars, 3g fiber), 8g pro.*

SLOW COOKER DRESSING

SLOW COOKER BEEF TOSTADAS

SLOW COOKER BEEF TOSTADAS

I dedicate these tostadas to my husband, the only Italian man I know who can't get enough of Mexican flavors. Pile on your best toppings.

—TERESA DEVONO RED LION, PA

PREP: 20 MIN. • **COOK:** 6 HOURS
MAKES: 6 SERVINGS

- **1 large onion, chopped**
- **¼ cup lime juice**
- **1 jalapeno pepper, seeded and minced**
- **1 serrano pepper, seeded and minced**
- **1 tablespoon chili powder**
- **3 garlic cloves, minced**
- **½ teaspoon ground cumin**
- **1 beef top round steak (about 1½ pounds)**
- **1 teaspoon salt**
- **½ teaspoon pepper**
- **¼ cup chopped fresh cilantro**
- **12 corn tortillas (6 inches)**
- **Cooking spray**

TOPPINGS

- **1½ cups shredded lettuce**
- **1 medium tomato, finely chopped**
- **¾ cup shredded sharp cheddar cheese**
- **¾ cup reduced-fat sour cream, optional**

1. Place the first seven ingredients in a 3- or 4-qt. slow cooker. Cut steak in half and sprinkle with salt and pepper; add to slow cooker. Cook, covered, on low 6-8 hours or until meat is tender.

2. Remove meat; cool slightly. Shred meat with two forks. Return beef to slow cooker and stir in cilantro; heat through. Spritz both sides of the tortillas with cooking spray. Place in a single layer on baking sheets; broil 1-2 minutes on each side or until crisp. Spoon beef mixture over tortillas; top with lettuce, tomato, cheese and, if desired, sour cream.

NOTE *Wear disposable gloves when cutting hot peppers; the oils can burn skin. Avoid touching your face.*

PER SERVING *2 tostadas: 372 cal., 13g fat (6g sat. fat), 88mg chol., 602mg sodium, 30g carb. (5g sugars, 5g fiber), 35g pro.* ***Diabetic Exchanges:*** *4 lean meat, 2 starch, ½ fat.*

TOP TIP

Sharp cheddar cheese's flavor is more pronounced than regular cheddar. It's useful in light cooking because you can get more flavor while using less cheese.

AUTUMN APPLE CHICKEN (PICTURED ON P. 83)

I'd just been apple picking and wanted to bake something new with the bounty. Slow-cooking chicken with apples and barbecue sauce filled my whole house with the most delicious smell. We couldn't wait to eat.

—**CAITLYN HAUSER** BROOKLINE, NH

PREP: 20 MIN. • **COOK:** 3½ HOURS
MAKES: 4 SERVINGS

- **1 tablespoon canola oil**
- **4 bone-in chicken thighs (about 1½ pounds), skin removed**
- **¼ teaspoon salt**
- **¼ teaspoon pepper**
- **2 medium Fuji or Gala apples, coarsely chopped**
- **1 medium onion, chopped**
- **1 garlic clove, minced**
- **⅓ cup barbecue sauce**
- **¼ cup apple cider or juice**
- **1 tablespoon honey**

1. In a large skillet, heat oil over medium heat. Brown chicken thighs on both sides; sprinkle with salt and pepper. Transfer to a 3-qt. slow cooker; top with apples.
2. Add onion to same skillet; cook and stir over medium heat 2-3 minutes or until tender. Add garlic; cook 1 minute longer. Stir in barbecue sauce, apple cider and honey; increase heat to medium-high. Cook 1 minute, stirring to loosen browned bits from pan. Pour over chicken and apples. Cook, covered, on low 3½-4½ hours or until chicken is tender.

FREEZE OPTION *Freeze cooled chicken mixture in freezer containers. To use, partially thaw in refrigerator overnight. Heat through in a covered saucepan, stirring occasionally.*

PER SERVING *1 chicken thigh with ½ cup apple mixture: 333 cal., 13g fat (3g sat. fat), 87mg chol., 456mg sodium, 29g carb. (22g sugars, 3g fiber), 25g pro.* ***Diabetic Exchanges:*** *4 lean meat, 1½ starch, ½ fruit.*

TURKEY CHILI

I've taken my mother's milder recipe for chili and made it thicker and more robust. It's a favorite, especially in fall and winter.

—**CELESTA ZANGER** BLOOMFIELD HILLS, MI

PREP: 20 MIN. • **COOK:** 6½ HOURS
MAKES: 12 SERVINGS

- **1 pound lean ground turkey**
- **¾ cup chopped celery**
- **¾ cup chopped onion**
- **¾ cup chopped green pepper**
- **2 tablespoons chili powder**
- **1 teaspoon ground cumin**
- **¼ teaspoon pepper**
- **⅛ to ¼ teaspoon cayenne pepper**
- **2 cans (14½ ounces each) no-salt-added diced tomatoes, undrained**
- **1 jar (24 ounces) meatless pasta sauce**
- **1 can (16 ounces) hot chili beans, undrained**
- **1½ cups water**
- **½ cup frozen corn**
- **1 can (16 ounces) kidney beans, rinsed and drained**
- **1 can (15 ounces) pinto beans, rinsed and drained**
- **Sour cream, optional**

1. In a large skillet, cook and crumble turkey with celery, onion and pepper over medium-high heat until no longer pink, 6-8 minutes. Transfer to a 5-qt. slow cooker. Stir in the seasonings, tomatoes, spaghetti sauce, chili beans, water and corn.
2. Cook, covered, on high 1 hour. Reduce setting to low; cook, covered, until flavors are blended, 5-6 hours.
3. Stir in kidney and pinto beans; cook, covered, on low 30 minutes longer. If desired, serve chili with sour cream.

PER SERVING *1 cup: 200 cal., 4g fat (1g sat. fat), 26mg chol., 535mg sodium, 29g carb. (8g sugars, 8g fiber), 15g pro.* ***Diabetic Exchanges:*** *2 lean meat, 2 vegetable, 1 starch.*

TURKEY CHILI

As a busy mom, I love my slow cooker meals! Beef tips remind me of a childhood favorite. I cook them with mushrooms and red wine for an amazing dish.

—AMY LENTS GRAND FORKS, ND

SLOW COOKER BEEF TIPS

SLOW COOKER BEEF TIPS C

PREP: 25 MIN. • **COOK:** 6¼ HOURS • **MAKES:** 4 SERVINGS

- **½ pound sliced baby portobello mushrooms**
- **1 small onion, halved and sliced**
- **1 beef top sirloin steak (1 pound), cubed**
- **½ teaspoon salt**
- **¼ teaspoon pepper**
- **2 teaspoons olive oil**
- **⅓ cup dry red wine or beef broth**
- **2 cups beef broth**
- **1 tablespoon Worcestershire sauce**
- **2 tablespoons cornstarch**
- **¼ cup cold water**
- **Hot cooked mashed potatoes**

1. Place mushrooms and onion in a 3-qt. slow cooker. Sprinkle beef with salt and pepper. In a large skillet, heat 1 teaspoon oil over medium-high heat; brown meat in batches, adding more oil as needed. Transfer meat to slow cooker.

2. Add wine to skillet, stirring to loosen browned bits from pan. Stir in broth and Worcestershire sauce; pour over meat. Cook, covered, on low 6-8 hours or until meat is tender.

3. In a small bowl, mix cornstarch and cold water until smooth; gradually stir into slow cooker. Cook, covered, on high 15-30 minutes or until gravy is thickened. Serve with mashed potatoes.

PER SERVING *1 cup: 212 cal., 7g fat (2g sat. fat), 46mg chol., 836mg sodium, 8g carb. (2g sugars, 1g fiber), 27g pro.* ***Diabetic Exchanges:*** *3 lean meat, ½ starch, ½ fat.*

BEEF & VEGGIE SLOPPY JOES

I'm always looking for ways to serve my family healthy and delicious food, so I started experimenting with my favorite veggies and ground beef. I came up with this winning dish that my kids actually request!

—MEGAN NIEBUHR YAKIMA, WA

PREP: 35 MIN. • **COOK:** 5 HOURS • **MAKES:** 10 SERVINGS

- **4 medium carrots, shredded**
- **1 medium yellow summer squash, shredded**
- **1 medium zucchini, shredded**
- **1 medium sweet red pepper, finely chopped**
- **2 medium tomatoes, seeded and chopped**
- **1 small red onion, finely chopped**
- **½ cup ketchup**
- **3 tablespoons minced fresh basil or 3 teaspoons dried basil**
- **3 tablespoons molasses**
- **2 tablespoons cider vinegar**
- **2 garlic cloves, minced**
- **½ teaspoon salt**
- **½ teaspoon pepper**
- **2 pounds lean ground beef (90% lean)**
- **10 whole wheat hamburger buns, split**

1. In a 5- or 6-qt. slow cooker, combine the first 13 ingredients. In a large skillet, cook beef over medium heat 8-10 minutes or until no longer pink, breaking into crumbles. Drain; transfer beef to slow cooker. Stir to combine.

2. Cook, covered, on low 5-6 hours or until heated through and vegetables are tender. Using a slotted spoon, serve beef mixture on buns.

PER SERVING *1 sandwich: 316 cal., 10g fat (3g sat. fat), 57mg chol., 565mg sodium, 36g carb. (15g sugars, 5g fiber), 22g pro.* ***Diabetic Exchanges:*** *2 starch, 2 lean meat, 1 vegetable.*

BEEF & VEGGIE SLOPPY JOES

SLOW-COOKED BREAKFAST APPLE COBBLER

SLOW-COOKED BREAKFAST APPLE COBBLER S M

This is a great recipe to serve on Christmas morning or any other cold morning. The apples can be peeled if preferred.

—MARIETTA SLATER JUSTIN, TX

PREP: 15 MIN. • **COOK:** 6 HOURS • **MAKES:** 6 SERVINGS

- **6 medium apples, cut into ½-inch wedges**
- **1 tablespoon butter**
- **3 tablespoons honey**
- **½ teaspoon ground cinnamon**
- **¼ cup dried cranberries**
- **2 cups granola without raisins**
- **Milk and maple syrup, optional**

1. Place apples in a greased 3-qt. slow cooker. In a microwave, melt butter; stir in honey and cinnamon. Drizzle over apples. Sprinkle cranberries and granola over top.

2. Cook, covered, on low until apples are tender, 6-8 hours. If desired, serve with milk and syrup.

PER SERVING *¾ cup: 289 cal., 8g fat (1g sat. fat), 5mg chol., 31mg sodium, 58g carb. (31g sugars, 11g fiber), 7g pro.*

PEACHY SUMMER CHEESECAKE M (PICTURED ON P. 82)

This cool and always refreshing dessert is fancy enough to take to a gathering. You can make it ahead of time and freeze it. Make sure you wrap it well in airtight wrap and only add the peaches and whipped cream after it thaws.

—JOAN ENGELHARDT LATROBE, PA

PREP: 25 MIN. • **COOK:** 2½ HOURS + CHILLING
MAKES: 6 SERVINGS

- **1 package (8 ounces) reduced-fat cream cheese**
- **4 ounces fat-free cream cheese**
- **½ cup sugar**
- **½ cup reduced-fat sour cream**
- **2 tablespoons unsweetened apple juice**
- **1 tablespoon all-purpose flour**
- **½ teaspoon vanilla**
- **3 large eggs, lightly beaten**
- **2 medium ripe peaches, peeled and thinly sliced**

1. Pour 1 in. water into a 6-qt. slow cooker. Layer two 24-in. pieces of foil; roll up lengthwise to make a 1-in.-thick roll. Shape into a ring; place in slow cooker to make a rack.

2. Grease a 6-in. springform pan; place on a double thickness of heavy-duty foil (about 12 in. square). Wrap securely around pan.

3. In a large bowl, beat the cream cheeses and sugar until smooth. Beat in the sour cream, apple juice, flour and vanilla extract.

4. Add eggs; beat on low speed just until blended. Pour into prepared pan. Center pan on foil rack, not allowing sides to touch slow cooker. Cover slow cooker with a double layer of white paper towels; place lid securely over towels. Cook, covered, on low 2½ hours.

5. Turn off slow cooker, but do not remove lid. Let stand 1 hour. Remove springform pan from slow cooker; remove foil from pan. Cool cheesecake on a wire rack 1 hour.

6. Loosen sides from springform pan with a knife. Refrigerate cheesecake overnight, covering when cooled. To serve, remove rim from the springform pan. Serve cheesecake with peaches.

NOTE *The 6-in. springform pan is available from Wilton Industries. Call 800-794-5866 or visit its website at wilton.com.*

PER SERVING *1 slice with 3 tablespoons peaches: 268 cal., 12g fat (7g sat. fat), 129mg chol., 342mg sodium, 27g carb. (25g sugars, 1g fiber), 12g pro.*

TOP TIP

For a hazelnut-kissed variation, toss the peach slices with 4 teaspoons hazelnut liqueur and some chopped toasted hazelnuts. You could also replace 1½ teaspoons of the apple juice with hazelnut liqueur.

SLOW COOKER CURRY PORK

SLOW COOKER CURRY PORK

I'm a busy stay-at-home mom, and the slow cooker helps me create delicious dishes like this pork without a lot of prep time. I add a splash of coconut milk.

—**BEVERLY PEYCHAL** WAUKESHA, WI

PREP: 15 MIN.
COOK: 3½ HOURS + STANDING
MAKES: 10 SERVINGS

- **1½ teaspoons salt**
- **1½ teaspoons hot or regular curry powder**
- **1 teaspoon ground cumin**
- **1 teaspoon dried oregano**
- **¾ teaspoon onion powder**
- **¾ teaspoon garlic powder**
- **½ teaspoon pepper**
- **¼ teaspoon cayenne pepper**
- **¼ teaspoon paprika**
- **¼ teaspoon ground chipotle pepper**
- **1½ pounds potatoes, cut into ½-inch pieces**
- **4 medium carrots, thinly sliced**
- **3 cups cubed peeled butternut squash (about 1 pound)**
- **1 can (14½ ounces) reduced-sodium chicken broth**
- **1 boneless pork loin roast (3 to 4 pounds)**

1. In a small bowl, mix seasonings. In a 6-qt. slow cooker, combine the vegetables, broth and 2 teaspoons seasoning mixture. Rub remaining seasoning mixture over roast; place over vegetables. Cook, covered, on low 3½-4½ hours or until meat and vegetables are tender (a thermometer inserted into roast should read at least 145°).

2. Remove roast from slow cooker; tent with foil. Let stand 15 minutes before slicing. Serve with vegetables.

PER SERVING *4 ounces cooked pork with ½ cup vegetables: 261 cal., 7g fat (2g sat. fat), 68mg chol., 523mg sodium, 21g carb. (3g sugars, 4g fiber), 29g pro.* ***Diabetic Exchanges:*** *4 lean meat, 1½ starch.*

SLOW COOKER FRITTATA PROVENCAL C M

PREP: 30 MIN. • **COOK:** 3 HOURS
MAKES: 6 SERVINGS

- **½ cup water**
- **1 tablespoon olive oil**
- **1 medium Yukon Gold potato, peeled and sliced**
- **1 small onion, thinly sliced**
- **½ teaspoon smoked paprika**
- **12 large eggs**
- **1 teaspoon minced fresh thyme or ¼ teaspoon dried thyme**
- **1 teaspoon hot pepper sauce**
- **½ teaspoon salt**
- **¼ teaspoon pepper**
- **1 log (4 ounces) fresh goat cheese, coarsely crumbled, divided**
- **½ cup chopped soft sun-dried tomatoes (not packed in oil)**

1. Layer two 24-in. pieces of aluminum foil; starting with a long side, fold up foil to create a 1-in.-wide strip. Shape strip into a coil to make a rack for bottom of a 6-qt. oval slow cooker. Add water to slow cooker; set foil rack in water.

2. In a large skillet, heat oil over medium-high heat. Add potato and onion; cook and stir 5-7 minutes or until potato is lightly browned. Stir in paprika. Transfer to a greased 1½-qt. baking dish (dish must fit in slow cooker).

3. In a large bowl, whisk eggs, thyme, pepper sauce, salt and pepper; stir in 2 ounces cheese. Pour over potato mixture. Top with the tomatoes and remaining goat cheese. Place dish on foil rack.

4. Cook, covered, on low 3 hours or until eggs are set and a knife inserted near the center comes out clean.

NOTE *This recipe was tested with sun-dried tomatoes that are ready to use without soaking. When using other sun-dried tomatoes that are not oil-packed, cover with boiling water and let stand until soft. Drain before using.*

PER SERVING *1 wedge: 245 cal., 14g fat (5g sat. fat), 385mg chol., 338mg sodium, 12g carb. (4g sugars, 2g fiber), 15g pro.* ***Diabetic Exchanges:*** *2 medium-fat meat, 1 starch, ½ fat.*

SLOW COOKER
FRITTATA PROVENCAL

LENTIL PUMPKIN SOUP F M

Plenty of seasonings brighten up my pumpkin soup. It's just the thing we need on nippy days and nights.

—**LAURA MAGEE** HOULTON, WI

PREP: 15 MIN. • **COOK:** 7 HOURS • **MAKES:** 6 SERVINGS

- **1 pound red potatoes (about 4 medium), cut into 1-inch pieces**
- **1 can (15 ounces) solid-pack pumpkin**
- **1 cup dried lentils, rinsed**
- **1 medium onion, chopped**
- **3 garlic cloves, minced**
- **½ teaspoon ground ginger**
- **½ teaspoon pepper**
- **⅛ teaspoon salt**
- **2 cans (14½ ounces each) vegetable broth**
- **1½ cups water**
- **Minced fresh cilantro, optional**

In a 3- or 4-qt. slow cooker, combine first 10 ingredients. Cook, covered, on low 7-9 hours or until potatoes and lentils are tender. If desired, sprinkle servings with cilantro.

PER SERVING *1⅓ cups: 210 cal., 1g fat (0 sat. fat), 0 chol., 463mg sodium, 42g carb. (5g sugars, 7g fiber), 11g pro.*
Diabetic Exchanges: *3 starch, 1 lean meat.*

HULI HULI CHICKEN THIGHS

I'm allergic to store-bought barbecue sauces, so when I found a marinade recipe I could use, I tweaked it a little and began using it with chicken thighs. My fiance loves this tender chicken over Parmesan couscous.

—**ERIN ROCKWELL** LOWELL, MA

PREP: 10 MIN. • **COOK:** 4 HOURS • **MAKES:** 8 SERVINGS

- **1 cup crushed pineapple, drained**
- **¾ cup ketchup**
- **⅓ cup reduced-sodium soy sauce**
- **3 tablespoons brown sugar**
- **3 tablespoons lime juice**
- **1 garlic clove, minced**
- **8 boneless skinless chicken thighs (about 2 pounds)**
- **Hot cooked rice**
- **Thinly sliced green onions, optional**

1. Mix first six ingredients. Place chicken in a 3-qt. slow cooker; top with pineapple mixture.
2. Cook, covered, on low until chicken is tender, 4-5 hours. Serve with rice. If desired, top with green onions.

PER SERVING *239 cal., 8g fat (2g sat. fat), 76mg chol., 733mg sodium, 19g carb. (16g sugars, 0 fiber), 22g pro.*
Diabetic Exchanges: *3 lean meat, 1 starch.*

SPICED CARROTS & BUTTERNUT SQUASH

SPICED CARROTS & BUTTERNUT SQUASH F M

When I've got a lot going on, my slow cooker is my go-to tool for cooking veggies. I toss in cumin and chili powder to bring out their natural sweetness.

—COURTNEY STULTZ WEIR, KS

PREP: 15 MIN. • **COOK:** 4 HOURS • **MAKES:** 6 SERVINGS

- **5 large carrots, cut into ½-inch pieces (about 3 cups)**
- **2 cups cubed peeled butternut squash (1-inch pieces)**
- **1 tablespoon balsamic vinegar**
- **1 tablespoon olive oil**
- **1 tablespoon honey**
- **1 teaspoon ground cinnamon**
- **½ teaspoon salt**
- **½ teaspoon ground cumin**
- **¼ teaspoon chili powder**

Place carrots and squash in a 3-qt. slow cooker. In a small bowl, mix remaining ingredients; drizzle over vegetables and toss to coat. Cook, covered, on low 4-5 hours or until vegetables are tender. Gently stir before serving.

PER SERVING *2/3 cup: 85 cal., 3g fat (0 sat. fat), 0 chol., 245mg sodium, 16g carb. (8g sugars, 3g fiber), 1g pro.* ***Diabetic Exchanges:*** *1 vegetable, 1/2 starch, 1/2 fat.*

TURKEY STUFFED PEPPERS

I created this as a healthier alternative to traditional stuffed peppers. I work 12-hour shifts as a nurse, so I often rely on the slow cooker for feeding my family.

—MANDY PEMBERTON DENHAM SPRINGS, LA

PREP: 35 MIN. • **COOK:** 4 HOURS • **MAKES:** 6 SERVINGS

- **2 medium sweet yellow or orange peppers**
- **2 medium sweet red peppers**
- **2 medium green peppers**
- **1 pound lean ground turkey**
- **1 small red onion, finely chopped**
- **1 small zucchini, shredded**
- **2 cups cooked brown rice**
- **1 jar (16 ounces) spaghetti sauce, divided**
- **1 tablespoon Creole seasoning**
- **¼ teaspoon pepper**
- **2 tablespoons shredded Parmesan cheese**

1. Cut tops from peppers and remove seeds. Finely chop enough tops to measure 1 cup for filling.
2. In a large skillet, cook turkey, onion and reserved chopped peppers over medium heat 6-8 minutes or until turkey is no longer pink and vegetables are tender, breaking up turkey into crumbles; drain.
3. Add zucchini; cook and stir 2 minutes longer. Stir in rice, 2/3 cup spaghetti sauce, Creole seasoning and pepper.
4. Spread 1/2 cup spaghetti sauce onto the bottom of a greased 6-qt. slow cooker. Fill peppers with turkey mixture; place over sauce. Pour remaining spaghetti sauce over peppers; sprinkle with cheese.
5. Cook, covered, on low 4-5 hours or until peppers are tender and filling is heated through.

NOTE *The following spices may be substituted for 1 teaspoon Creole seasoning: 1/4 teaspoon each salt, garlic powder and paprika; and a pinch each of dried thyme, ground cumin and cayenne pepper.*

PER SERVING *1 stuffed pepper: 290 cal., 10g fat (3g sat. fat), 63mg chol., 818mg sodium, 31g carb. (9g sugars, 5g fiber), 19g pro.* ***Diabetic Exchanges:*** *3 lean meat, 1 1/2 starch, 1 vegetable.*

HEALTH TIP *Cooked long grain and instant brown rice are very similar nutritionally, so go ahead and take a shortcut.*

TURKEY STUFFED PEPPERS

SIMPLE VEGETARIAN SLOW-COOKED BEANS

SIMPLE VEGETARIAN SLOW-COOKED BEANS F M

When I have a hungry family to feed, these tasty beans with spinach, tomatoes and carrots are a go-to dish. This veggie delight is frequently on the menu.

—**JENNIFER REID** FARMINGTON, ME

PREP: 15 MIN. • **COOK:** 4 HOURS
MAKES: 8 SERVINGS

- **4 cans (15½ ounces each) great northern beans, rinsed and drained**
- **4 medium carrots, finely chopped (about 2 cups)**
- **1 cup vegetable stock**
- **6 garlic cloves, minced**
- **2 teaspoons ground cumin**
- **¾ teaspoon salt**
- **⅛ teaspoon chili powder**
- **4 cups fresh baby spinach, coarsely chopped**
- **1 cup oil-packed sun-dried tomatoes, patted dry and chopped**
- **⅓ cup minced fresh cilantro**
- **⅓ cup minced fresh parsley**

In a 3-qt. slow cooker, combine the first seven ingredients. Cook, covered, on low 4-5 hours or until carrots are tender, adding spinach and tomatoes during the last 10 minutes of cooking. Stir in cilantro and parsley.

PER SERVING *¾ cup: 229 cal., 3g fat (0 sat. fat), 0 chol., 672mg sodium, 40g carb. (2g sugars, 13g fiber), 12g pro.*

SESAME PULLED PORK SANDWICHES

PREP: 15 MIN. • **COOK:** 4½ HOURS
MAKES: 12 SERVINGS

- **3 pork tenderloins (1 pound each)**
- **1¾ cups reduced-fat sesame ginger salad dressing, divided**
- **¼ cup packed brown sugar**

SLAW

- **1 package (14 ounces) coleslaw mix**
- **4 green onions, chopped**
- **¼ cup minced fresh cilantro**
- **2 tablespoons reduced-fat sesame ginger salad dressing**
- **2 teaspoons sesame oil**
- **1 teaspoon sugar**
- **1 teaspoon reduced-sodium soy sauce**

TO SERVE

- **12 multigrain hamburger buns, split**
- **Wasabi mayonnaise, optional**

1. Place tenderloins in a 5-qt. slow cooker coated with cooking spray; pour ¾ cup salad dressing over pork, turning to coat. Cook, covered, on low 4-5 hours or until meat is tender.

2. Remove pork; cool slightly. Shred meat into bite-size pieces; return to slow cooker. Stir in brown sugar and remaining salad dressing. Cook, covered, for 30-45 minutes or until heated through.

3. Combine slaw ingredients. Serve pork on buns with slaw and, if desired, mayonnaise.

NOTE *This recipe was tested with Newman's Own Sesame Ginger Dressing.*

PER SERVING *1 sandwich: 324 cal., 9g fat (2g sat. fat), 64mg chol., 756mg sodium, 33g carb. (14g sugars, 3g fiber), 27g pro.* ***Diabetic Exchanges:*** *3 lean meat, 2 starch.*

HEALTH TIP *Cuts of pork with loin in the name, like pork tenderloin and pork loin, are some of the leanest options. However, pork tenderloin will shred much more easily than pork loin, making it a great lean meat choice for pulled pork sandwiches.*

I wanted to build a better pork sandwich, and this Asian-style filling was a huge hit with my husband and co-workers. Bring on the wasabi mayo.
—**REBECCA COOK** HELOTES, TX

SESAME PULLED PORK SANDWICHES

CHICKEN MOLE [C]

If you're not familiar with mole, don't be afraid to try this versatile Mexican sauce. I love sharing the recipe because it's a good, simple introduction to mole.

—**DARLENE MORRIS** FRANKLINTON, LA

PREP: 25 MIN. • **COOK:** 6 HOURS
MAKES: 12 SERVINGS

- **12 bone-in chicken thighs (about 4½ pounds), skin removed**
- **1 teaspoon salt**

MOLE SAUCE

- **1 can (28 ounces) whole tomatoes, drained**
- **1 medium onion, chopped**
- **2 dried ancho chilies, stems and seeds removed**
- **½ cup sliced almonds, toasted**
- **¼ cup raisins**
- **3 ounces bittersweet chocolate, chopped**
- **3 tablespoons olive oil**
- **1 chipotle pepper in adobo sauce**
- **3 garlic cloves, peeled and halved**
- **¾ teaspoon ground cumin**
- **½ teaspoon ground cinnamon**
- **Fresh cilantro leaves, optional**

1. Sprinkle chicken with salt; place in a 5- or 6-qt. slow cooker. Place the tomatoes, onion, chilies, almonds, raisins, chocolate, oil, chipotle pepper, garlic, cumin and cinnamon in a food processor; cover and process until blended. Pour over chicken.

2. Cover and cook on low for 6-8 hours or until chicken is tender; skim fat. Serve chicken with sauce, and sprinkle with cilantro if desired.

FREEZE OPTION *Cool chicken in mole sauce. Freeze in freezer containers. To use, partially thaw in refrigerator overnight. Heat through slowly in a covered skillet or Dutch oven until a thermometer inserted into chicken reads 165°, stirring occasionally and adding a little broth or water if necessary.*

PER SERVING *1 chicken thigh with 1/3 cup sauce: 311 cal., 18g fat (5g sat. fat), 86mg chol., 378mg sodium, 12g carb. (7g sugars, 3g fiber), 26g pro.*

MEDITERRANEAN POT ROAST DINNER

MEDITERRANEAN POT ROAST DINNER

I first made this recipe one cold winter day. My family and I were having a blast sledding and playing in the snow all day, and when we came inside supper was ready! This pot roast is perfect served with mashed potatoes, rice or crusty dinner rolls.

—**HOLLY BATTISTE** BARRINGTON, NJ

PREP: 30 MIN. • **COOK:** 8 HOURS
MAKES: 8 SERVINGS

- **2 pounds potatoes (about 6 medium), peeled and cut into 2-inch pieces**
- **5 medium carrots (about ¾ pound), cut into 1-inch pieces**
- **2 tablespoons all-purpose flour**
- **1 boneless beef chuck roast (3 to 4 pounds)**
- **1 tablespoon olive oil**
- **8 large fresh mushrooms, quartered**
- **2 celery ribs, chopped**
- **1 medium onion, thinly sliced**
- **¼ cup sliced Greek olives**
- **½ cup minced fresh parsley, divided**
- **1 can (14½ ounces) fire-roasted diced tomatoes, undrained**
- **1 tablespoon minced fresh oregano or 1 teaspoon dried oregano**
- **1 tablespoon lemon juice**
- **2 teaspoons minced fresh rosemary or ½ teaspoon dried rosemary, crushed**
- **2 garlic cloves, minced**
- **¾ teaspoon salt**
- **¼ teaspoon pepper**
- **¼ teaspoon crushed red pepper flakes, optional**

1. Place the potatoes and carrots in a 6-qt. slow cooker. Sprinkle flour over all surfaces of roast. In a large skillet, heat oil over medium-high heat. Brown roast on all sides. Place over vegetables.

2. Add mushrooms, celery, onion, olives and 1/4 cup parsley to slow cooker. In a small bowl, mix the remaining ingredients; pour over top.

3. Cook, covered, on low 8-10 hours or until meat and vegetables are tender. Remove beef. Stir remaining parsley into vegetables. Serve beef with vegetables.

PER SERVING *5 ounces cooked beef with 1 cup vegetables: 422 cal., 18g fat (6g sat. fat), 111mg chol., 538mg sodium, 28g carb. (6g sugars, 4g fiber), 37g pro.* ***Diabetic Exchanges:*** *5 lean meat, 1½ starch, 1 vegetable, ½ fat.*

SOUTHWESTERN BREAKFAST SLOW COOKER CASSEROLE

(PICTURED ON P. 83)

I created this recipe for a breakfast-for-dinner meal one day, and now it's become a favorite on chilly mornings. Such a wonderful aroma! Using extra-sharp cheddar cheese instead of the milder types allows you to use less, while giving you an extra boost of flavor.

—**LISA RENSHAW** KANSAS CITY, MO

PREP: 20 MIN.
COOK: 2½ HOURS + STANDING
MAKES: 8 SERVINGS

- **4 large eggs**
- **8 large egg whites**
- **1⅔ cups fat-free milk**
- **3 teaspoons chili powder**
- **½ teaspoon ground cumin**
- **½ teaspoon pepper**
- **½ teaspoon cayenne pepper**
- **1 can (15 ounces) black beans, rinsed and drained**
- **1 can (7 ounces) Mexicorn, drained**
- **1 cup cubed fully cooked ham**
- **1 cup (4 ounces) shredded extra-sharp cheddar cheese**
- **1 can (4 ounces) chopped green chilies, drained**
- **6 slices whole wheat bread, lightly toasted and cubed**
- **Pico de gallo, optional**

1. In a large bowl, whisk together first seven ingredients. Stir in beans, corn, ham, cheese and chilies. Stir in bread to moisten. Transfer to a 5-qt. slow cooker coated with cooking spray.

2. Cook, covered, on low until a knife inserted near the center comes out clean, 2½-3½ hours. Let stand, uncovered, 10 minutes before serving. If desired, serve with pico de gallo.

PER SERVING *1¼ cups: 270 cal., 9g fat (4g sat. fat), 119mg chol., 771mg sodium, 25g carb. (5g sugars, 4g fiber), 21g pro.* ***Diabetic Exchanges:*** *3 lean meat, 1½ starch.*

CILANTRO & LIME CHICKEN WITH SCOOPS C

I came up with this recipe when I was preparing for a large party, and I wanted a healthy Tex-Mex chicken to serve in tortilla cups. This party dish can be made ahead of time, freeing you up for time-sensitive dishes. You can serve it in tortilla chip cups or any other savory crispy cup you can find. Leftovers are great over salad greens or wrapped up in a tortilla as a burrito.

—**LORI TERRY** CHICAGO, IL

PREP: 15 MIN. • **COOK:** 3½ HOURS
MAKES: 16 SERVINGS (¼ CUP EACH)

- **1 pound boneless skinless chicken breasts**
- **2 teaspoons chili powder**
- **2 tablespoons lime juice**
- **1½ cups frozen petite corn (about 5 ounces), thawed**
- **1½ cups chunky salsa**
- **1½ cups (6 ounces) finely shredded cheddar cheese**
- **1 medium sweet red pepper, finely chopped**
- **4 green onions, thinly sliced**
- **Baked tortilla chip scoops**
- **Minced fresh cilantro**

1. Place chicken in a 1½-qt. slow cooker; sprinkle with chili powder and lime juice. Cook, covered, on low until tender, 3-4 hours.

2. Remove chicken; discard cooking juices. Shred chicken with two forks; return to slow cooker. Add corn and salsa; cook, covered, on low until heated through, about 30 minutes, stirring occasionally.

3. Transfer to a large bowl; stir in cheese, pepper and green onions. Serve with tortilla scoops; sprinkle with cilantro.

PER SERVING *¼ cup chicken mixture: 97 cal., 4g fat (2g sat. fat), 26mg chol., 183mg sodium, 5g carb. (2g sugars, 1g fiber), 9g pro.* ***Diabetic Exchanges:*** *1 medium-fat meat.*

CILANTRO & LIME CHICKEN WITH SCOOPS

ITALIAN CABBAGE SOUP

ITALIAN CABBAGE SOUP F

After doing yardwork on a windy day, we love to come in for a light but hearty soup like this one. It's brimming with cabbage, veggies and white beans. It goes well with a crusty bread.

—JENNIFER STOWELL MONTEZUMA, IA

PREP: 15 MIN. • **COOK:** 6 HOURS
MAKES: 8 SERVINGS (2 QUARTS)

- **4 cups chicken stock**
- **1 can (6 ounces) tomato paste**
- **1 small head cabbage (about 1½ pounds), shredded**
- **4 celery ribs, chopped**
- **2 large carrots, chopped**
- **1 small onion, chopped**
- **1 can (15½ ounces) great northern beans, rinsed and drained**
- **2 garlic cloves, minced**
- **2 fresh thyme sprigs**
- **1 bay leaf**
- **½ teaspoon salt**
- **Shredded Parmesan cheese, optional**

1. In a 5- or 6-qt. slow cooker, whisk together stock and tomato paste. Stir in the vegetables, beans, garlic and seasonings. Cook, covered, on low until vegetables are tender, 6-8 hours.

2. Remove thyme sprigs and bay leaf. If desired, serve with cheese.

PER SERVING *1 cup: 111 cal., 0 fat (0 sat. fat), 0 chol., 537mg sodium, 21g carb. (7g sugars, 6g fiber), 8g pro.*
***Diabetic Exchanges:** 1½ starch.*

HARVEST TIME CHICKEN WITH COUSCOUS F

Even on busy days, I can start this chicken in a slow cooker and still get to work on time. When I come home, I add spinach salad and crescent rolls.

—HEIDI RUDOLPH OREGON, IL

PREP: 30 MIN. • **COOK:** 3 HOURS
MAKES: 6 SERVINGS

- **2 medium sweet potatoes (about 1¼ pounds), peeled and cut into ½-inch pieces**
- **1 medium sweet red pepper, coarsely chopped**
- **1½ pounds boneless skinless chicken breasts**
- **1 can (14½ ounces) stewed tomatoes, undrained**
- **½ cup peach or mango salsa**
- **¼ cup golden raisins**
- **½ teaspoon salt**
- **¼ teaspoon ground cumin**
- **¼ teaspoon ground cinnamon**
- **¼ teaspoon pepper**

COUSCOUS

- **1 cup water**
- **½ teaspoon salt**
- **1 cup uncooked whole wheat couscous**

1. In a 4-qt. slow cooker, layer sweet potatoes, red pepper and chicken breasts. In a small bowl, mix tomatoes, salsa, raisins and seasonings; pour over chicken. Cook, covered, on low 3-4 hours or until sweet potatoes and chicken are tender.

2. About 10 minutes before serving, prepare couscous. In a small saucepan, bring water and salt to a boil. Stir in couscous. Remove from heat; let stand, covered, 5 minutes or until water is absorbed. Fluff with a fork.

3. Remove chicken from slow cooker; coarsely shred with two forks. Return chicken to slow cooker, stirring gently to combine. Serve with couscous.

FREEZE OPTION *Place cooled chicken mixture in freezer containers. To use, partially thaw in refrigerator overnight. Microwave, covered, on high in a microwave-safe dish until heated through, stirring gently and adding a little broth or water if necessary.*

PER SERVING *1⅓ cups chicken mixture with ½ cup couscous: 351 cal., 3g fat (1g sat. fat), 63mg chol., 699mg sodium, 52g carb. (15g sugars, 7g fiber), 30g pro.*

HARVEST TIME CHICKEN WITH COUSCOUS

100

106

102

Beef Entrees

"It really is possible to find a dish that's low in fat, easy to prepare and delicious, all at once. This Italian pot roast will have you going for seconds."

—MARGRET RUBBO LIVONIA, MI
about her recipe, Italian-Style Pot Roast, on page 109

ONE-POT SAUCY BEEF ROTINI FAST FIX

My husband loves pasta. On Spaghetti Day, as he calls it, I make a one-pot saucy rotini that keeps everyone happy.

—LORRAINE CALAND SHUNIAH, ON

START TO FINISH: 30 MIN.
MAKES: 4 SERVINGS

- **¾ pound lean ground beef (90% lean)**
- **2 cups sliced fresh mushrooms**
- **1 medium onion, chopped**
- **3 garlic cloves, minced**
- **¾ teaspoon Italian seasoning**
- **2 cups tomato basil pasta sauce**
- **¼ teaspoon salt**
- **2½ cups water**
- **3 cups uncooked whole wheat rotini (about 8 ounces)**
- **¼ cup grated Parmesan cheese**

1. In a 6-qt. stockpot, cook the first five ingredients over medium-high heat 6-8 minutes or until beef is no longer pink, breaking up beef into crumbles; drain.

2. Add pasta sauce, salt and water; bring to a boil. Stir in rotini; return to a boil. Reduce heat; simmer, covered, 8-10 minutes or until pasta is al dente, stirring occasionally. Serve with cheese.

PER SERVING *1½ cups: 414 cal., 11g fat (4g sat. fat), 57mg chol., 806mg sodium, 49g carb. (12g sugars, 8g fiber), 28g pro.*

ONE-POT SAUCY BEEF ROTINI

CHIPOTLE CHILI SLOPPY JOES

My husband didn't like sloppy joes until he tried my rendition with its smoky heat. If you need to dial down the fiery zip, reduce the peppers.

—BRITTANY ALLYN MESA, AZ

CHIPOTLE CHILI SLOPPY JOES

PREP: 15 MIN. • **COOK:** 20 MIN.
MAKES: 6 SERVINGS

- **1 pound lean ground beef (90% lean)**
- **1 cup finely chopped sweet onion**
- **½ cup finely chopped green pepper**
- **1 jalapeno pepper, seeded and finely chopped, optional**
- **½ cup chili sauce**
- **½ cup water**
- **1 to 2 chipotle peppers in adobo sauce, finely chopped**
- **1 tablespoon packed brown sugar**
- **1 teaspoon yellow mustard**
- **6 kaiser rolls or hamburger buns, split**
- **2 tablespoons butter, softened**
- **Pickle slices, optional**

1. Preheat broiler. In a large skillet, cook beef, onion, green pepper and, if desired, jalapeno over medium heat 5-7 minutes or until beef is no longer pink, breaking up the meat into crumbles; drain.

2. Stir in chili sauce, water, chipotle peppers, brown sugar and mustard; bring to a boil. Simmer, uncovered, 8-10 minutes or until slightly thickened, stirring occasionally.

3. Lightly spread cut sides of rolls with butter; arrange on a baking sheet, buttered side up. Broil 3-4 in. from heat until lightly toasted, about 30 seconds. Fill with beef mixture and, if desired, pickles.

FREEZE OPTION *Freeze cooled meat mixture in freezer containers. To use, partially thaw in refrigerator overnight. Heat through in a saucepan, stirring occasionally and adding a little water if necessary.*

PER SERVING *1 sandwich: 313 cal., 12g fat (5g sat. fat), 57mg chol., 615mg sodium, 32g carb. (11g sugars, 2g fiber), 19g pro.* ***Diabetic Exchanges:*** *2 starch, 2 lean meat, 1 fat.*

BALSAMIC BEEF KABOB SANDWICHES

This dish is popular wherever it goes. The flavorful sandwiches will surely be the highlight of your summer barbecue.

—PEGGY LABOR LOUISVILLE, KY

PREP: 15 MIN. + MARINATING
GRILL: 10 MIN.
MAKES: 8 SERVINGS

- **¼ cup balsamic vinegar**
- **¼ cup olive oil**
- **2 garlic cloves, minced**
- **1 teaspoon dried rosemary, crushed**
- **½ teaspoon pepper, divided**
- **¼ teaspoon salt, divided**
- **1½ pounds beef top sirloin steak, cut into ¼-inch-thick strips**
- **2 medium onions**
- **8 naan flatbreads**
- **2 cups chopped heirloom tomatoes**

1. Mix first four ingredients; stir in 1/4 teaspoon pepper and 1/8 teaspoon salt. Toss with beef strips; let stand 20 minutes.

2. Cut each onion into eight wedges; thread onto metal or soaked wooden skewers. Thread beef strips, weaving back and forth, onto separate skewers.

3. Grill onions, covered, over medium heat until tender, 5-7 minutes per side. Grill beef, covered, over medium heat until desired doneness, 3-4 minutes per side. Grill flatbreads until lightly browned, 1-2 minutes per side.

4. Toss tomatoes with the remaining pepper and salt. Remove onion and beef from skewers; serve on flatbreads. Top with tomatoes.

PER SERVING *1 sandwich: 353 cal., 14g fat (3g sat. fat), 39mg chol., 595mg sodium, 34g carb. (7g sugars, 2g fiber), 23g pro.* ***Diabetic Exchanges:*** *3 lean meat, 2 starch, 1½ fat.*

TOP TIP

Three ounces (a serving the size of a deck of cards) of cooked sirloin steak, pork loin, tuna, chicken or turkey breast provides about 25 grams of protein.

BBQ BEEF & VEGETABLE STIR-FRY

FAST FIX

This was a spur-of-the-moment experiment when we wanted to eat something nice and hearty, but also easy. I created this from steak, peppers and onion on hand. For a twist, try the filling in tortillas for fajitas.

—ROCHELLE M. DICKSON POTWIN, KS

START TO FINISH: 25 MIN.
MAKES: 4 SERVINGS

- **1 beef top sirloin steak (1 pound), cut into thin strips**
- **3 tablespoons reduced-sodium soy sauce**
- **1 garlic clove, minced**
- **¼ teaspoon pepper**
- **1 large sweet onion, halved and sliced**
- **1 medium green pepper, cut into thin strips**
- **1 medium sweet red pepper, cut into thin strips**
- **¼ cup barbecue sauce**
- **3 cups hot cooked brown rice**

1. Toss beef with soy sauce, garlic and pepper. Place a large nonstick skillet coated with cooking spray over medium-high heat. Add beef mixture; stir-fry 2-3 minutes or until beef is browned. Remove from pan.

2. Add vegetables; stir-fry 3-4 minutes or until crisp-tender. Stir in barbecue sauce and beef; heat through. Serve with rice.

PER SERVING *1 cup beef mixture with 3/4 cup rice: 387 cal., 6g fat (2g sat. fat), 46mg chol., 673mg sodium, 51g carb. (12g sugars, 5g fiber), 30g pro.* ***Diabetic Exchanges:*** *3 starch, 3 lean meat, 1 vegetable.*

BBQ BEEF & VEGETABLE STIR-FRY

GREAT-GRANDMA'S ITALIAN MEATBALLS C

A classic Italian dish isn't complete without homemade meatballs. This versatile recipe can be used in other dishes starring meatballs, too.

—AUDREY COLANTINO WINCHESTER, MA

PREP: 30 MIN. • **BAKE:** 20 MIN. • **MAKES:** 8 SERVINGS

- **2 teaspoons olive oil**
- **1 medium onion, chopped**
- **3 garlic cloves, minced**
- **¾ cup seasoned bread crumbs**
- **½ cup grated Parmesan cheese**
- **2 large eggs, lightly beaten**
- **1 teaspoon each dried basil, oregano and parsley flakes**
- **¾ teaspoon salt**
- **1 pound lean ground turkey**
- **1 pound lean ground beef (90% lean)**
- **Hot cooked pasta and pasta sauce, optional**

1. Preheat oven to 375°. In a small skillet, heat oil over medium-high heat. Add onion; cook and stir 3-4 minutes or until tender. Add garlic; cook 1 minute longer. Cool slightly.
2. In a large bowl, combine bread crumbs, cheese, eggs, seasonings and onion mixture. Add turkey and beef; mix lightly but thoroughly. Shape into 1½-in. balls.
3. Place meatballs on a rack coated with cooking spray in a 15x10x1-in. baking pan. Bake 18-22 minutes or until lightly browned and cooked through. If desired, serve with pasta and pasta sauce.

PER SERVING *271 cal., 13g fat (5g sat. fat), 125mg chol., 569mg sodium, 10g carb. (1g sugars, 1g fiber), 27g pro.* ***Diabetic Exchanges:*** *4 lean meat, 1 fat, ½ starch.*

GREAT-GRANDMA'S ITALIAN MEATBALLS

FETA MUSHROOM BURGERS

FETA MUSHROOM BURGERS FAST FIX

My son-in-law gave me this recipe and I tweaked it to make it healthier. The burgers are so quick to whip up on the grill.

—DOLORES BLOCK FRANKENMUTH, MI

START TO FINISH: 25 MIN. • **MAKES:** 6 SERVINGS

- **1 pound lean ground beef (90% lean)**
- **3 Italian turkey sausage links (4 ounces each), casings removed**
- **2 teaspoons Worcestershire sauce**
- **½ teaspoon garlic powder**
- **2 tablespoons balsamic vinegar**
- **1 tablespoon olive oil**
- **6 large portobello mushrooms, stems removed**
- **1 large onion, cut into ½-inch slices**
- **6 tablespoons crumbled feta or blue cheese**
- **6 whole wheat hamburger buns or sourdough rolls, split**
- **10 fresh basil leaves, thinly sliced**

1. Combine the first four ingredients; mix lightly but thoroughly. Shape into six ½-in.-thick patties. Mix vinegar and oil; brush over mushrooms.
2. Place burgers, mushrooms and onion on an oiled grill rack over medium heat. Grill, covered, over medium heat 4-6 minutes per side or until a thermometer inserted into burger reads 165° and mushrooms and onion are tender.
3. Fill mushroom caps with cheese; grill, covered, until cheese is melted, 1-2 minutes. Grill buns, cut side down, until toasted, 30-60 seconds. Serve burgers on buns; top with mushrooms, basil and onion.

PER SERVING *1 burger: 371 cal., 15g fat (5g sat. fat), 72mg chol., 590mg sodium, 31g carb. (8g sugars, 5g fiber), 28g pro.* ***Diabetic Exchanges:*** *4 lean meat, 2 starch, 1 vegetable, ½ fat.*

SMOKY ESPRESSO STEAK C FAST FIX

This juicy steak rubbed with espresso, cocoa and pumpkin pie spice is one of my husband's favorites. We usually grill it, but broiling works for the chilly months.

—DEBORAH BIGGS OMAHA, NE

START TO FINISH: 30 MIN. • **MAKES:** 4 SERVINGS

- **3 teaspoons instant espresso powder**
- **2 teaspoons brown sugar**
- **1½ teaspoons smoked or regular paprika**
- **1 teaspoon salt**
- **1 teaspoon baking cocoa**
- **¼ teaspoon pumpkin pie spice**
- **¼ teaspoon pepper**
- **1 pound beef flat iron or top sirloin steak (¾ inch thick)**

1. Preheat broiler. Mix first seven ingredients; rub over both sides of steak. Place steak on a broiler pan; let stand 10 minutes.

2. Broil steak 3-4 in. from heat 4-6 minutes on each side or until meat reaches desired doneness (for medium-rare, a thermometer should read 145°; medium, 160°). Let stand 5 minutes before slicing.

PER SERVING *3 ounces cooked beef: 216 cal., 12g fat (5g sat. fat), 73mg chol., 661mg sodium, 4g carb. (2g sugars, 0 fiber), 22g pro.* ***Diabetic Exchanges:*** *3 lean meat.*

SMOKY ESPRESSO STEAK

HEARTY GARDEN SPAGHETTI

HEARTY GARDEN SPAGHETTI

My husband and I wanted a pleasing dish that didn't leave a ton of leftovers. My spaghetti with beef and fresh veggies is perfectly filling for four.

—WANDA QUIST LOVELAND, CO

PREP: 15 MIN. • **COOK:** 30 MIN. • **MAKES:** 4 SERVINGS

- **1 pound lean ground beef (90% lean)**
- **1 small onion, finely chopped**
- **1 medium sweet red pepper, finely chopped**
- **1 medium zucchini, finely chopped**
- **½ pound sliced fresh mushrooms**
- **1 can (8 ounces) tomato sauce**
- **2 teaspoons Italian seasoning**
- **½ teaspoon salt**
- **¼ teaspoon pepper**
- **8 ounces uncooked multigrain spaghetti**
- **Grated Parmesan cheese, optional**

1. In a Dutch oven coated with cooking spray, cook beef, onion and red pepper over medium-high heat 5-7 minutes or until beef is no longer pink, breaking up the meat into crumbles; drain.

2. Add zucchini and mushrooms; cook 3-5 minutes longer or until tender. Stir in tomato sauce and seasonings; bring to a boil. Reduce heat; simmer, covered, 15 minutes to allow flavors to blend. Meanwhile, cook spaghetti according to package directions.

3. Serve spaghetti with sauce and, if desired, cheese.

PER SERVING *1¼ cups sauce with 1 cup spaghetti: 432 cal., 11g fat (4g sat. fat), 71mg chol., 649mg sodium, 48g carb. (6g sugars, 7g fiber), 36g pro.* ***Diabetic Exchanges:*** *3 lean meat, 2½ starch, 2 vegetable.*

GARLIC SPAGHETTI SQUASH WITH MEAT SAUCE F

PREP: 15 MIN. • **BAKE:** 45 MIN.
MAKES: 4 SERVINGS

- **1 medium spaghetti squash (about 4 pounds)**
- **1 pound lean ground beef (90% lean)**
- **2 cups sliced fresh mushrooms**
- **4 garlic cloves, minced, divided**
- **4 plum tomatoes, chopped**
- **2 cups pasta sauce**
- **½ teaspoon pepper, divided**
- **1 tablespoon olive oil**
- **¼ teaspoon salt**
- **Grated Parmesan cheese, optional**

1. Preheat oven to 375°. Cut squash lengthwise in half; remove and discard seeds. Place squash in a 13x9-in. baking pan, cut side down; add ½ in. of hot water. Bake, uncovered, for 40 minutes. Drain water from pan; turn squash cut side up. Bake for 5-10 minutes longer or until squash is tender.

2. Meanwhile, in a large skillet, cook beef and mushrooms over medium heat 6-8 minutes or until beef is no longer pink, breaking up beef into crumbles; drain. Add half of the garlic; cook and stir 1 minute. Stir in tomatoes, pasta sauce and ¼ teaspoon pepper; bring to a boil. Reduce heat; simmer, uncovered, 15-20 minutes.

3. When squash is cool enough to handle, use a fork to separate strands. In a large skillet, heat oil over medium heat. Add remaining garlic; cook and stir 1 minute. Stir in squash, salt and remaining pepper; heat through. Serve with meat sauce and, if desired, cheese.

PER SERVING *1¼ cups squash with 1 cup sauce: 443 cal., 17g fat (5g sat. fat), 71mg chol., 770mg sodium, 49g carb. (12g sugars, 11g fiber), 29g pro.* ***Diabetic Exchanges:*** *3 starch, 3 lean meat, 1 vegetable, ½ fat.*

I was looking for satisfying, comforting meals without pasta or potatoes. When tinkering with this recipe, I discovered that spaghetti squash makes a great pasta replacement. —**BECKY RUFF** MCGREGOR, IA

GARLIC SPAGHETTI SQUASH WITH MEAT SAUCE

SUMMER SALAD WITH CITRUS VINAIGRETTE

S FAST FIX

I live in Orange County, which is so named for its beautiful orange groves. This salad is one of my favorite ways to use the fresh oranges. It makes a nice light supper on a hot day.
—**CAROLYN WILLIAMS** COSTA MESA, CA

START TO FINISH: 20 MIN.
MAKES: 4 SERVINGS

- **3 tablespoons red wine vinegar**
- **3 tablespoons orange juice**
- **2 teaspoons honey**
- **1½ teaspoons Dijon mustard**
- **1 teaspoon olive oil**

SALAD

- **1 tablespoon canola oil**
- **1 pound beef top sirloin steak, cut into thin strips**
- **½ teaspoon salt, optional**
- **4 cups torn romaine**
- **2 large oranges, peeled and sectioned**
- **½ cup sliced fresh strawberries**
- **¼ cup chopped walnuts, toasted, optional**

1. Whisk together first five ingredients.

2. For salad, in a large skillet, heat oil over medium-high heat; stir-fry beef until browned, 1-3 minutes. Remove from heat. If desired, sprinkle with salt.

3. Place romaine, fruit and beef in a serving dish. Toss with vinaigrette. If desired, top with walnuts. Serve immediately.

PER SERVING *1½ cups: 265 cal., 10g fat (2g sat. fat), 46mg chol., 101mg sodium, 19g carb. (14g sugars, 4g fiber), 26g pro.* ***Diabetic Exchanges:*** *3 lean meat, 1 vegetable, 1 fat, ½ starch, ½ fruit.*

ITALIAN PIZZA MEAT LOAF C

If you have kids who protest when they hear that meat loaf is on the menu, just try keeping them away from this saucy creation packed with pizza flavors. One bite and there's no turning back!

—**HANNAH KLEINHANS** MILWAUKEE, WI

PREP: 20 MIN. • **BAKE:** 50 MIN. + STANDING
MAKES: 2 LOAVES (8 SERVINGS EACH)

- **3 large eggs, lightly beaten**
- **1 large onion, finely chopped**
- **2 cans (2¼ ounces each) sliced ripe olives, drained**
- **¾ cup dry bread crumbs**
- **⅔ cup 2% milk**
- **⅔ cup jarred pizza sauce**
- **2 tablespoons Worcestershire sauce**
- **2½ teaspoons dried basil**
- **2½ teaspoons dried oregano**
- **1½ teaspoons pepper**
- **1¼ teaspoons salt**
- **3 pounds lean ground beef (90% lean)**
- **Additional pizza sauce (warmed) and shredded part-skim mozzarella cheese, optional**

1. Preheat oven to 350°. In a large bowl, combine first 11 ingredients. Add beef; mix lightly but thoroughly. Divide mixture between two greased 9x5-in. loaf pans.

2. Bake until a thermometer reads 160°, 50-60 minutes. If desired, top with additional sauce and cheese.

FREEZE OPTION *Shape meat loaves in plastic wrap-lined 9x5-in. loaf pans; cover and freeze until firm. Remove from pans and wrap securely in foil; return to freezer. To use, unwrap meat loaves and bake in pans as directed, increasing time to 1¼-1½ hours or until a thermometer inserted in center reads 160°. Top as desired.*

PER SERVING *1 slice: 193 cal., 9g fat (3g sat. fat), 89mg chol., 408mg sodium, 7g carb. (2g sugars, 1g fiber), 19g pro.* ***Diabetic Exchanges:*** *2 lean meat, ½ starch.*

SPINACH STEAK PINWHEELS C FAST FIX

Bacon and spinach bring plenty of flavor to these sirloin steak spirals. It's an easy dish to make and great to grill at a cookout.

—**HELEN VAIL** GLENSIDE, PA

START TO FINISH: 25 MIN.
MAKES: 6 SERVINGS

- **1½ pounds beef top sirloin steak**
- **8 bacon strips, cooked**
- **1 package (10 ounces) frozen chopped spinach, thawed and squeezed dry**
- **¼ cup grated Parmesan cheese**
- **½ teaspoon salt**
- **⅛ teaspoon cayenne pepper**

1. Lightly score steak by making shallow diagonal cuts at 1-in. intervals into top of steak; repeat cuts in the opposite direction. Cover steak with plastic wrap; pound with a meat mallet to ½-in. thickness. Remove plastic.

2. Place bacon widthwise at center of steak. In a bowl, mix remaining ingredients; spoon over bacon. Starting at a short side, roll up steak jelly-roll style; secure with toothpicks. Cut into six slices.

3. Moisten a paper towel with cooking oil; using long-handled tongs, rub on grill rack to coat lightly. Grill pinwheels, covered, over medium heat 5-6 minutes on each side or until beef reaches desired doneness (for medium-rare, a thermometer should read 145°; medium, 160°). Discard toothpicks before serving.

PER SERVING *1 pinwheel: 227 cal., 10g fat (4g sat. fat), 60mg chol., 536mg sodium, 3g carb. (0 sugars, 1g fiber), 31g pro.* ***Diabetic Exchanges:*** *4 lean meat, 1 fat.*

HEALTH TIP *Spinach is loaded with vitamin K, which plays an important role in bone health.*

PEPPER-CRUSTED SIRLOIN ROAST

BARLEY BEEF BURGERS FAST FIX

I stirred cooked barley and barbecue sauce into hamburger patties to make them moist and flavorful. It's an ingenious way to work grains into a meal.

—**ROSELLA PETERS** GULL LAKE, SK

START TO FINISH: 30 MIN.
MAKES: 2 SERVINGS

- **½ cup water**
- **¼ cup quick-cooking barley**
- **½ small onion, halved**
- **1 tablespoon barbecue sauce**
- **1½ teaspoons all-purpose flour**
- **¼ teaspoon salt**
- **⅛ teaspoon pepper**
- **½ pound lean ground beef**
- **2 hamburger buns, split**
- **Optional toppings: lettuce leaves, tomato slices and onion slices**

1. In a small saucepan, bring water to a boil. Stir in barley. Reduce heat; simmer, covered, 8-10 minutes or until barley is tender. Remove from heat; let stand 5 minutes. Cool slightly.
2. Place onion and barley in a food processor; process until finely chopped. Remove to a bowl; stir in barbecue sauce, flour, salt and pepper. Add beef; mix lightly but thoroughly. Shape into two ½-in. thick patties.
3. Grill, covered, over medium heat 4-5 minutes on each side or until a thermometer reads 160°. Serve on buns with toppings as desired.

PER SERVING *1 burger: 395 cal., 12g fat (4g sat. fat), 69mg chol., 625mg sodium, 42g carb. (5g sugars, 5g fiber), 29g pro.* ***Diabetic Exchanges:*** *3 lean meat, 2½ starch, 2 fat.*

HEALTH TIP *Including barley adds 3 grams fiber and saves 5 grams fat compared with an all-beef burger the same size.*

BARLEY BEEF BURGERS

PEPPER-CRUSTED SIRLOIN ROAST S C

Dinner guests will be surprised to hear this festive entree only calls for five ingredients. It's the perfect choice for serving a large group.

—**MARY ANN GRIFFIN** BOWLING GREEN, KY

PREP: 15 MIN.
BAKE: 2 HOURS + STANDING
MAKES: 16 SERVINGS

- **2 tablespoons Dijon mustard**
- **1 tablespoon coarsely ground pepper**
- **1 tablespoon minced fresh mint or 1 teaspoon dried mint**
- **1 tablespoon minced fresh rosemary or 1 teaspoon dried rosemary, crushed**
- **1 beef sirloin tip roast (4 pounds)**

1. Preheat oven to 350°. Mix first four ingredients.
2. Place roast on a rack in a roasting pan; spread with mustard mixture. Roast until desired doneness (for medium-rare, a thermometer should read 145°; medium, 160°), 2¼ to 3 hours.
3. Remove from oven; tent with foil. Let stand 15 minutes before slicing.

PER SERVING *3 ounces cooked beef: 146 cal., 5g fat (2g sat. fat), 72mg chol., 78mg sodium, 1g carb. (0 sugars, 0 fiber), 23g pro.* ***Diabetic Exchanges:*** *3 lean meat.*

ASPARAGUS BEEF STIR-FRY ON POTATOES

This is my light and quick version of a steak dinner that I created when I had leftover grilled steak and asparagus. The hands-on time is minimal, and the dish is full of flavor and very satisfying.

—**FRANCES PIETSCH** FLOWER MOUND, TX

PREP: 25 MIN. • **COOK:** 15 MIN.
MAKES: 4 SERVINGS

- **2 large baking potatoes (about 12 ounces each)**
- **2 tablespoons butter**
- **¼ cup reduced-sodium soy sauce**
- **2 teaspoons balsamic vinegar**
- **2 teaspoons canola oil, divided**
- **1 pound beef top sirloin steak, cut into thin strips**
- **1½ cups cut fresh asparagus (1 inch)**
- **1½ cups sliced fresh mushrooms**
- **¼ teaspoon salt**
- **⅛ teaspoon pepper**

1. Scrub potatoes; pierce several times with a fork. Place potatoes on a microwave-safe plate. Microwave, uncovered, on high until tender, 12-16 minutes, turning once. Cool slightly.
2. In a small saucepan, melt butter over medium heat. Heat until golden brown, 3-4 minutes, stirring constantly. Remove from heat; stir in soy sauce and vinegar. Keep warm.
3. In a large skillet, heat 1 teaspoon oil over medium-high heat; stir-fry beef until browned, 2-3 minutes. Remove from pan.
4. In same pan, stir-fry asparagus and mushrooms in remaining oil until asparagus is crisp-tender, 2-3 minutes. Stir in beef, salt and pepper; heat through.
5. Cut potatoes lengthwise in half; fluff pulp with a fork. Top with beef mixture; drizzle with sauce.

NOTE *This recipe was tested in a 1,100-watt microwave.*

PER SERVING *½ baked potato with 1 cup beef mixture and 1 tablespoon sauce: 387 cal., 13g fat (6g sat. fat), 61mg chol., 832mg sodium, 37g carb. (4g sugars, 5g fiber), 31g pro.* ***Diabetic Exchanges:*** *4 lean meat, 2 starch, 1½ fat.*

CABBAGE ROLL SKILLET

CABBAGE ROLL SKILLET

Have a nice big helping of of this quicker take on something our grandmothers would have made. We like it over brown rice. It also freezes well.

—**SUSAN CHICKNESS** PICTOU COUNTY, NS

PREP: 15 MIN. • **COOK:** 20 MIN.
MAKES: 6 SERVINGS

- **1 can (28 ounces) whole plum tomatoes, undrained**
- **1 pound extra-lean ground beef (95% lean)**
- **1 large onion, chopped**
- **1 can (8 ounces) tomato sauce**
- **2 tablespoons cider vinegar**
- **1 tablespoon brown sugar**
- **1 teaspoon dried oregano**
- **1 teaspoon dried thyme**
- **½ teaspoon pepper**
- **1 small head cabbage, thinly sliced (about 6 cups)**
- **1 medium green pepper, cut into thin strips**
- **4 cups hot cooked brown rice**

1. Drain tomatoes, reserving liquid; coarsely chop tomatoes. In a large nonstick skillet, cook beef and onion over medium-high heat 6-8 minutes or until the beef is no longer pink, breaking up beef into crumbles. Stir in tomato sauce, vinegar, brown sugar, seasonings, chopped tomatoes and the reserved liquid.
2. Add the cabbage and pepper; cook, covered, for 6 minutes, stirring occasionally. Cook, uncovered, for 6-8 minutes or until cabbage is tender. Serve with rice.

PER SERVING *1⅓ cups with ⅔ cup rice: 332 cal., 5g fat (2g sat. fat), 43mg chol., 439mg sodium, 50g carb. (12g sugars, 9g fiber), 22g pro.* ***Diabetic Exchanges:*** *3 starch, 3 lean meat.*

DID YOU KNOW?

Oregano comes in two types. The sweet Mediterranean one is often simply labeled oregano. It belongs to the mint family. Mexican oregano, a member of the verbena family, has a more intense flavor and citrusy notes.

GREEK-STYLE RAVIOLI

ANCHO GARLIC STEAKS WITH SUMMER SALSA

C FAST FIX

START TO FINISH: 30 MIN.
MAKES: 4 SERVINGS

- **2 boneless beef top loin steaks (1¼ inches thick and 8 ounces each)**
- **2 teaspoons ground ancho chili pepper**
- **1 teaspoon garlic salt**

SALSA

- **1 cup seeded diced watermelon**
- **1 cup fresh blueberries**
- **1 medium tomato, chopped**
- **¼ cup finely chopped red onion**
- **1 tablespoon minced fresh mint**
- **1½ teaspoons grated fresh gingerroot**
- **¼ teaspoon salt**

1. Rub steaks with chili pepper and garlic salt. Grill, covered, over medium heat or broil 4 in. from the heat for 7-9 minutes on each side or until meat reaches desired doneness (for medium-rare, a thermometer should read 145°; medium, 160°).
2. In a bowl, combine the salsa ingredients. Cut steak into slices; serve with salsa.

NOTE *Top loin steak may be labeled as strip steak, Kansas City steak, New York strip steak, ambassador steak or boneless club steak in your region.*

PER SERVING *3 ounces cooked beef with ½ cup salsa: 195 cal., 5g fat (2g sat. fat), 50mg chol., 442mg sodium, 10g carb. (7g sugars, 2g fiber), 25g pro.* ***Diabetic Exchanges:*** *3 lean meat, ½ fruit.*

GREEK-STYLE RAVIOLI

FAST FIX

Here's a flavorful Greek twist on an Italian classic. It's an easy weekday meal that's become one of our favorites. My husband and I enjoy it with warm garlic cheese toast.

—**HETTI WILLIAMS** RAPID CITY, SD

START TO FINISH: 25 MIN.
MAKES: 2 SERVINGS

- **12 frozen cheese ravioli**
- **⅓ pound lean ground beef (90% lean)**
- **1 cup canned diced tomatoes with basil, oregano and garlic**
- **1 cup fresh baby spinach**
- **¼ cup sliced ripe olives**
- **¼ cup crumbled feta cheese**

1. Cook ravioli according to package directions; drain. Meanwhile, in a skillet, cook beef over medium heat 4-6 minutes or until no longer pink; drain. Stir in tomatoes; bring to a boil. Reduce heat; simmer, uncovered, for 10 minutes, stirring occasionally.
2. Add ravioli, spinach and olives; heat through, stirring gently to combine. Sprinkle with cheese.

PER SERVING *1¼ cups: 333 cal., 12g fat (5g sat. fat), 61mg chol., 851mg sodium, 28g carb. (5g sugars, 4g fiber), 23g pro.* ***Diabetic Exchanges:*** *3 lean meat, 2 starch, ½ fat.*

MOM'S SPANISH RICE

FAST FIX (PICTURED ON P. 97)

My mom is famous for her Spanish rice. When I want a taste of home, I pull out this recipe and prepare it for my own family.

—**JOAN HALLFORD** NORTH RICHLAND HILLS, TX

START TO FINISH: 20 MIN.
MAKES: 4 SERVINGS

- **1 pound lean ground beef (90% lean)**
- **1 large onion, chopped**
- **1 medium green pepper, chopped**
- **1 can (15 ounces) tomato sauce**
- **1 can (14½ ounces) no-salt-added diced tomatoes, drained**
- **1 teaspoon ground cumin**
- **1 teaspoon chili powder**
- **½ teaspoon garlic powder**
- **¼ teaspoon salt**
- **2⅔ cups cooked brown rice**

1. In a large skillet, cook beef, onion and pepper over medium heat for 6-8 minutes or until beef is no longer pink and onion is tender, breaking up beef into crumbles; drain.
2. Stir in tomato sauce, tomatoes and seasonings; bring to a boil. Add rice; heat through, stirring occasionally.

PER SERVING *1½ cups: 395 cal., 11g fat (4g sat. fat), 71mg chol., 757mg sodium, 46g carb. (8g sugars, 6g fiber), 29g pro.* ***Diabetic Exchanges:*** *3 lean meat, 2 starch, 2 vegetable.*

TOP TIP

A thrifty alternative to purchasing garlic salt is to mix up your own: Just combine 1 teaspoon garlic powder with 3 teaspoons of table salt or other fine-grained salt. The ratio works the same for onion salt, too.

The first time I tasted this, I was amazed how well the blueberries and watermelon go with the peppery steak. Use whatever fruits are in season so you can serve this anytime. —**VERONICA CALLAGHAN** GLASTONBURY, CT

ANCHO GARLIC STEAKS WITH SUMMER SALSA

ONE-POT BEEF & PEPPER STEW

I love most things made with green peppers, tomatoes or green chilies. I was wanting to prepare a quick and satisfying dish one evening and came up with this recipe with things I had on hand.

—SANDRA CLARK SIERRA VISTA, AZ

PREP: 10 MIN. • **COOK:** 30 MIN.
MAKES: 8 SERVINGS

- **1 pound lean ground beef (90% lean)**
- **3 cans (14½ ounces each) diced tomatoes, undrained**
- **4 large green peppers, coarsely chopped**
- **1 large onion, chopped**
- **2 cans (4 ounces each) chopped green chilies**
- **3 teaspoons garlic powder**
- **1 teaspoon pepper**
- **¼ teaspoon salt**
- **2 cups uncooked instant rice**
- **Hot pepper sauce, optional**

1. In a 6-qt. stockpot, cook beef over medium heat 6-8 minutes or until no longer pink, breaking into crumbles; drain. Add tomatoes, green peppers, onion, chilies and seasonings; bring to a boil. Reduce heat; simmer, covered, 20-25 minutes or until vegetables are tender.

2. Prepare rice according to package directions. Serve with stew and, if desired, pepper sauce.

PER SERVING *1½ cups: 244 cal., 5g fat (2g sat. fat), 35mg chol., 467mg sodium, 35g carb. (8g sugars, 5g fiber), 15g pro.* ***Diabetic Exchanges:*** *2 lean meat, 2 vegetable, 1½ starch.*

ONE-POT BEEF & PEPPER STEW

SPECIAL OCCASION BEEF BOURGUIGNON

SPECIAL OCCASION BEEF BOURGUIGNON

I've found many rich and satisfying variations for beef bourguignon, including an intriguing peasant version that used beef cheeks for the meat and a rustic table wine. To make this stew gluten-free, use white rice flour instead of all-purpose.

—LEO COTNOIR JOHNSON CITY, NY

PREP: 50 MIN. • **BAKE:** 2 HOURS
MAKES: 8 SERVINGS

- **4 bacon strips, chopped**
- **1 beef sirloin tip roast (2 pounds), cut into 1½-inch cubes and patted dry**
- **¼ cup all-purpose flour**
- **½ teaspoon salt**
- **½ teaspoon pepper**
- **1 tablespoon canola oil**
- **2 medium onions, chopped**
- **2 medium carrots, coarsely chopped**
- **½ pound medium fresh mushrooms, quartered**
- **4 garlic cloves, minced**
- **1 tablespoon tomato paste**
- **2 cups dry red wine**
- **1 cup beef stock**
- **2 bay leaves**
- **½ teaspoon dried thyme**
- **8 ounces uncooked egg noodles**
- **Minced fresh parsley**

1. Preheat oven to 325°. In a Dutch oven, cook bacon over medium-low heat until crisp, stirring occasionally. Remove with a slotted spoon, reserving drippings; drain on paper towels.

2. In batches, brown beef in drippings over medium-high heat; remove from pan. Toss with flour, salt and pepper.

3. In same pan, heat 1 tablespoon oil over medium heat; saute onions, carrots and mushrooms until onions are tender, 4-5 minutes. Add garlic and tomato paste; cook and stir 1 minute. Add wine and stock, stirring to loosen browned bits from pan. Add herbs, bacon and beef; bring to a boil.

4. Transfer to oven; bake, covered, until meat is tender, 2-2¼ hours. Remove bay leaves.

5. To serve, cook noodles according to package directions; drain. Serve stew with noodles; sprinkle with parsley.

FREEZE OPTION *Freeze cooled stew in freezer containers. To use, partially thaw in refrigerator overnight. Heat through in a saucepan, stirring occasionally and adding a little stock or broth if necessary.*

PER SERVING *⅔ cup stew with ⅔ cup noodles: 422 cal., 14g fat (4g sat. fat), 105mg chol., 357mg sodium, 31g carb. (4g sugars, 2g fiber), 31g pro.* ***Diabetic Exchanges:*** *4 lean meat, 2 fat, 1½ starch, 1 vegetable.*

ITALIAN-STYLE POT ROAST (PICTURED ON P. 96)

It really is possible to find a dish that's low in fat, easy to prepare and delicious, all at once. This Italian pot roast will have you going for seconds.

—**MARGRET RUBBO** LIVONIA, MI

PREP: 40 MIN. • **BAKE:** 2¼ HOURS
MAKES: 8 SERVINGS

- **1 beef rump roast or bottom round roast (2 pounds)**
- **½ teaspoon salt**
- **¼ teaspoon pepper**
- **2 tablespoons canola oil, divided**
- **2 medium onions, halved and sliced**
- **1 medium green pepper, halved and sliced**
- **4 garlic cloves, minced**
- **½ cup dry red wine or reduced-sodium beef broth**
- **1 can (28 ounces) whole tomatoes, undrained**
- **1 can (15 ounces) tomato sauce**
- **2 teaspoons Italian seasoning**
- **2 teaspoons reduced-sodium soy sauce**
- **1 teaspoon Worcestershire sauce**
- **1 pound small red potatoes, quartered**
- **6 medium carrots, cut into 2-inch pieces**
- **4 celery ribs, cut into 2-inch pieces**

1. Preheat oven to 325°. Pat roast dry with a paper towel; sprinkle with salt and pepper. In a Dutch oven, heat 1 tablespoon oil over medium-high heat. Brown roast on all sides. Remove from pan.

2. In same pan, heat remaining oil over medium heat; cook and stir the onions and pepper until tender, 4-6 minutes. Add garlic; cook and stir 1 minute.

3. Add wine, stirring to loosen browned bits from pan; stir in tomatoes, tomato sauce, Italian seasoning, soy sauce and Worcestershire sauce. Add roast and remaining vegetables; bring to a boil.

4. Transfer to oven; bake, covered, until meat is fork-tender, 2¼-2½ hours.

FREEZE OPTION *Place sliced pot roast and vegetables in freezer containers; top with sauce. Cool and freeze. To use, partially thaw in refrigerator overnight. Heat through in a covered saucepan, stirring gently and adding a little broth if necessary.*

PER SERVING *288 cal., 10g fat (2g sat. fat), 68mg chol., 685mg sodium, 25g carb. (8g sugars, 6g fiber), 26g pro.* ***Diabetic Exchanges:*** *3 lean meat, 1½ starch, 1 fat.*

STRAWBERRY-BLUE CHEESE STEAK SALAD

C FAST FIX

At lunch with a friend, she told me about a steak salad she'd had at a party. It sounded so fantastic, I had to try it. My family would eat it nonstop if they could.

—**ALMA WINBERRY** GREAT FALLS, MT

START TO FINISH: 30 MIN.
MAKES: 4 SERVINGS

- **1 beef top sirloin steak (¾ inch thick and 1 pound)**
- **½ teaspoon salt**
- **¼ teaspoon pepper**
- **2 teaspoons olive oil**
- **2 tablespoons lime juice**

SALAD

- **1 bunch romaine, torn (about 10 cups)**
- **2 cups fresh strawberries, halved**
- **¼ cup thinly sliced red onion**
- **¼ cup crumbled blue cheese**
- **¼ cup chopped walnuts, toasted**
- **Reduced-fat balsamic vinaigrette**

1. Season steak with salt and pepper. In a large skillet, heat oil over medium heat. Add steak; cook 5-7 minutes on each side until meat reaches desired doneness (for medium-rare, a thermometer should read 145°; medium, 160°). Remove from pan; let stand 5 minutes. Cut steak into bite-size strips; toss with lime juice.

2. On a platter, combine romaine, strawberries and onion; top with steak. Sprinkle with cheese and walnuts. Serve with vinaigrette.

NOTE *To toast nuts, cook in a skillet over low heat until lightly browned, stirring occasionally.*

PER SERVING *289 cal., 15g fat (4g sat. fat), 52mg chol., 452mg sodium, 12g carb. (5g sugars, 4g fiber), 29g pro.* ***Diabetic Exchanges:*** *4 lean meat, 2 vegetable, 2 fat, ½ fruit.*

HEALTH TIP *If you're looking to trim calories, leave off the walnuts and blue cheese; they're adding almost 40 calories per serving.*

STRAWBERRY-BLUE CHEESE STEAK SALAD

129 120 131

Chicken Favorites

“We love Mexican night at our house, and I re-create dishes from our favorite restaurants. This burrito-inspired dish is ready for the table in almost no time!”

—**KRISTA MARSHALL** FORT WAYNE, IN
about her recipe, Chicken Burrito Skillet, on page 113

APPLE-GLAZED CHICKEN THIGHS C FAST FIX

My pickatarian child is choosy, but willing to eat this chicken glazed with apple juice and thyme. I dish it up with mashed potatoes and green beans.
—**KERRY PICARD** SPOKANE, WA

START TO FINISH: 25 MIN.
MAKES: 6 SERVINGS

- **6 boneless skinless chicken thighs (1½ pounds)**
- **¾ teaspoon seasoned salt**
- **¼ teaspoon pepper**
- **1 tablespoon canola oil**
- **1 cup unsweetened apple juice**
- **1 teaspoon minced fresh thyme or ¼ teaspoon dried thyme**

1. Sprinkle chicken with seasoned salt and pepper. In a large skillet, heat oil over medium-high heat. Brown the chicken on both sides. Remove from pan.
2. Add juice and thyme to skillet. Bring to a boil, stirring to loosen browned bits from pan; cook until liquid is reduced by half. Return chicken to pan; cook, covered, over medium heat 3-4 minutes longer or until a thermometer inserted into chicken reads 170°.
PER SERVING *1 chicken thigh with about 1 tablespoon glaze: 204 cal., 11g fat (2g sat. fat), 76mg chol., 255mg sodium, 5g carb. (4g sugars, 0 fiber), 21g pro.* ***Diabetic Exchanges:*** *3 lean meat, ½ fat.*

BACON & SWISS CHICKEN SANDWICHES

APPLE-GLAZED CHICKEN THIGHS

BACON & SWISS CHICKEN SANDWICHES FAST FIX

I tried to create this sandwich from one my daughter had at a local restaurant, and now she has me make it instead. She likes to dip her sandwich into extra honey mustard sauce.
—**MARILYN MOBERG** PAPILLION, NE

START TO FINISH: 25 MIN.
MAKES: 4 SERVINGS

- **¼ cup reduced-fat mayonnaise**
- **1 tablespoon Dijon mustard**
- **1 tablespoon honey**
- **4 boneless skinless chicken breast halves (4 ounces each)**
- **½ teaspoon Montreal steak seasoning**
- **4 slices Swiss cheese**
- **4 whole wheat hamburger buns, split**
- **2 bacon strips, cooked and crumbled**
- **Lettuce leaves and tomato slices, optional**

1. In a small bowl, mix mayonnaise, mustard and honey. Pound chicken with a meat mallet to ½-in. thickness. Sprinkle chicken with steak seasoning. Grill the chicken, covered, over medium heat or broil 4 in. from heat for 4-6 minutes on each side or until a thermometer reads 165°. Top with the cheese during the last minute of cooking.
2. Grill buns over medium heat, cut side down, for 30-60 seconds or until toasted. Serve chicken on buns with bacon, mayonnaise mixture and, if desired, lettuce and tomato.
PER SERVING *1 sandwich: 410 cal., 17g fat (6g sat. fat), 91mg chol., 667mg sodium, 29g carb. (9g sugars, 3g fiber), 34g pro.* ***Diabetic Exchanges:*** *4 lean meat, 2 starch, 2 fat.*

TOP TIP

I always fry 2 pounds or more of bacon at a time, drain the slices well, then freeze them. The slices don't stick together, so it's easy to remove a few from the bag for a sandwich or to crumble for a recipe.
—**SHIRLEY M.** GOLDSBORO, NC

CHICKEN BURRITO SKILLET (PICTURED ON P. 110)

We love Mexican night at our house, and I re-create dishes from our favorite restaurants. This burrito-inspired dish is ready for the table in almost no time!

—**KRISTA MARSHALL** FORT WAYNE, IN

PREP: 15 MIN. • **COOK:** 30 MIN.
MAKES: 6 SERVINGS

- **1 pound boneless skinless chicken breasts, cut into 1½-inch pieces**
- **⅛ teaspoon salt**
- **⅛ teaspoon pepper**
- **2 tablespoons olive oil, divided**
- **1 cup uncooked long grain rice**
- **1 can (15 ounces) black beans, rinsed and drained**
- **1 can (14½ ounces) diced tomatoes, drained**
- **1 teaspoon ground cumin**
- **½ teaspoon onion powder**
- **½ teaspoon garlic powder**
- **½ teaspoon chili powder**
- **2½ cups reduced-sodium chicken broth**
- **1 cup shredded Mexican cheese blend**
- **1 medium tomato, chopped**
- **3 green onions, chopped**

1. Toss chicken with salt and pepper. In a large skillet, heat 1 tablespoon oil over medium-high heat; saute chicken until browned, about 2 minutes. Remove from pan.

2. In same pan, heat remaining oil over medium-high heat; saute rice until lightly browned, 1-2 minutes. Stir in beans, canned tomatoes, seasonings and broth; bring to a boil. Place the chicken on top (do not stir into rice). Simmer, covered, until rice is tender and the chicken is no longer pink, 20-25 minutes.

3. Remove from heat; sprinkle with cheese. Let stand, covered, until cheese is melted. Top with tomato and green onions.

PER SERVING *1⅓ cups: 403 cal., 13g fat (4g sat. fat), 58mg chol., 690mg sodium, 43g carb. (4g sugars, 5g fiber), 27g pro.* ***Diabetic Exchanges:*** *3 starch, 3 lean meat, 1½ fat.*

LEMON CHICKEN WITH ORZO

Here's a dish that's light and summery but still satisfies. My kids love all the veggies—for real! If you like a lot of lemon, stir in an extra splash of lemon juice just before serving.

—**SHANNON HUMPHREY** HAMPTON, VA

PREP: 20 MIN. • **COOK:** 20 MIN.
MAKES: 4 SERVINGS

- **⅓ cup all-purpose flour**
- **1 teaspoon garlic powder**
- **1 pound boneless skinless chicken breasts**
- **¾ teaspoon salt, divided**
- **½ teaspoon pepper**
- **2 tablespoons olive oil**
- **1 can (14½ ounces) reduced-sodium chicken broth**
- **1¼ cups uncooked whole wheat orzo pasta**
- **2 cups chopped fresh spinach**
- **1 cup grape tomatoes, halved**
- **3 tablespoons lemon juice**
- **2 tablespoons minced fresh basil**
- **Lemon wedges, optional**

1. In a shallow bowl, mix flour and garlic powder. Cut chicken into 1½-in. pieces; pound each with a meat mallet to ¼-in. thickness. Sprinkle with ½ teaspoon salt and pepper. Dip both sides of chicken in flour mixture to coat lightly; shake off excess.

2. In a large skillet, heat oil over medium heat. Add chicken; cook 3-4 minutes on each side until golden brown and chicken is no longer pink. Remove from pan; keep warm. Wipe skillet clean.

3. In same pan, bring broth to a boil; stir in orzo. Return to a boil. Reduce heat; simmer, covered, 8-10 minutes or until tender. Stir in the spinach, tomatoes, lemon juice, basil and remaining salt; remove from heat. Return chicken to pan. If desired, serve with lemon wedges.

PER SERVING *1¼ cups: 399 cal., 11g fat (2g sat. fat), 63mg chol., 807mg sodium, 43g carb. (2g sugars, 9g fiber), 32g pro.* ***Diabetic Exchanges:*** *3 lean meat, 2 starch, 1½ fat, 1 vegetable.*

LEMON CHICKEN WITH ORZO

HONEY MUSTARD APPLE CHICKEN SAUSAGE FAST FIX

I threw this recipe together one day and it made a fantastic lunch. It's a great way to use up leftover sausage and rice from dinner the night before.

—**JULIE PUDERBAUGH** BERWICK, PA

START TO FINISH: 20 MIN. • **MAKES:** 4 SERVINGS

- **¼ cup honey mustard**
- **2 tablespoons apple jelly**
- **1 tablespoon water**
- **1 tablespoon olive oil**
- **2 medium apples, sliced**
- **1 package (12 ounces) fully cooked apple chicken sausage links or flavor of your choice, sliced**
- **Hot cooked rice**

1. In a small bowl, whisk honey mustard, jelly and water until blended. In a large skillet, heat oil over medium heat. Add apples; cook and stir 2-3 minutes or until tender. Remove from pan.

2. Add sausage to skillet; cook and stir 2-4 minutes or until browned. Return apples to skillet. Add mustard mixture; cook and stir 1-2 minutes or until thickened. Serve with rice.

PER SERVING *3/4 cup sausage mixture: 288 cal., 12g fat (3g sat. fat), 61mg chol., 609mg sodium, 34g carb. (28g sugars, 2g fiber), 15g pro.*

HONEY MUSTARD APPLE CHICKEN SAUSAGE

COOL & CRUNCHY CHICKEN SALAD

COOL & CRUNCHY CHICKEN SALAD

C FAST FIX

When the weather sizzles, get your chill on with a cool chicken salad. Mine uses grapes, pecans and celery for that signature crunch.

—**SARAH SMILEY** BANGOR, ME

START TO FINISH: 25 MIN. • **MAKES:** 6 SERVINGS

- **½ cup reduced-fat mayonnaise**
- **2 tablespoons minced fresh parsley**
- **1 tablespoon lemon juice**
- **1 tablespoon cider vinegar**
- **1 teaspoon spicy brown mustard**
- **½ teaspoon sugar**
- **¼ teaspoon salt**
- **¼ teaspoon pepper**
- **3 cups cubed cooked chicken**
- **1 cup seedless red grapes, halved**
- **1 cup thinly sliced celery**
- **1 cup pecan halves, toasted**
- **Lettuce leaves**

In a large bowl, mix the first eight ingredients until blended. Add chicken, grapes, celery and pecans; toss to coat. Serve on lettuce.

NOTE *To toast nuts, bake in a shallow pan in a 350° oven for 5-10 minutes or cook in a skillet over low heat until lightly browned, stirring occasionally.*

PER SERVING *1 cup: 340 cal., 24g fat (3g sat. fat), 69mg chol., 311mg sodium, 10g carb. (7g sugars, 2g fiber), 22g pro.* ***Diabetic Exchanges:*** *3 lean meat, 3 fat, 1/2 starch.*

TANDOORI CHICKEN THIGHS C FAST FIX

I spent some time in India and I love reminders of this vibrant culture, so serving this tandoori chicken makes me happy. Paired with warmed naan bread and a cool tomato and cucumber salad, it makes a whole meal.

—CLAIRE ELSTON SPOKANE, WA

START TO FINISH: 30 MIN. • **MAKES:** 4 SERVINGS

- **1 cup (8 ounces) reduced-fat plain yogurt**
- **1 tablespoon minced fresh gingerroot**
- **1 teaspoon ground cumin**
- **1 garlic clove, minced**
- **¾ teaspoon kosher salt**
- **½ teaspoon curry powder**
- **½ teaspoon pepper**
- **¼ teaspoon cayenne pepper**
- **4 boneless skinless chicken thighs (about 1 pound)**

1. In a small bowl, mix the first eight ingredients until blended. Add chicken to marinade; turn to coat. Let stand 10 minutes.

2. Place chicken on greased grill rack. Grill, covered, over medium heat 6-8 minutes on each side or until a thermometer reads 170°.

PER SERVING *1 chicken thigh: 193 cal., 9g fat (3g sat. fat), 78mg chol., 333mg sodium, 4g carb. (3g sugars, 0 fiber), 23g pro.* ***Diabetic Exchanges:*** *3 lean meat, 1/2 fat.*

TANDOORI CHICKEN THIGHS

Our go-to meal has always been baked chicken thighs. This easy grilled version takes the cooking outside with a zesty rub of turmeric, paprika and chili powder. **—BILL STALEY** MONROEVILLE, PA

SPICE-RUBBED CHICKEN THIGHS

SPICE-RUBBED CHICKEN THIGHS

C FAST FIX

START TO FINISH: 20 MIN. • **MAKES:** 6 SERVINGS

- **1 teaspoon salt**
- **1 teaspoon garlic powder**
- **1 teaspoon onion powder**
- **1 teaspoon dried oregano**
- **½ teaspoon ground turmeric**
- **½ teaspoon paprika**
- **¼ teaspoon chili powder**
- **¼ teaspoon pepper**
- **6 boneless skinless chicken thighs (about 1½ pounds)**

1. In a small bowl, mix the first eight ingredients. Sprinkle over both sides of chicken.

2. Moisten a paper towel with cooking oil; using long-handled tongs, rub on grill rack to coat lightly. Grill chicken, covered, over medium heat or broil 4 in. from heat for 6-8 minutes on each side or until a thermometer reads 170°.

PER SERVING *1 chicken thigh: 169 cal., 8g fat (2g sat. fat), 76mg chol., 460mg sodium, 1g carb. (0 sugars, 0 fiber), 21g pro.* ***Diabetic Exchanges:*** *3 lean meat.*

DESERT OASIS CHICKEN

FAST FIX

Boneless skinless chicken breasts pair nicely with sweet and spicy ingredients, like the ones in this recipe.

—**ROXANNE CHAN** ALBANY, CA

START TO FINISH: 20 MIN.
MAKES: 4 SERVINGS

- **¼ teaspoon salt**
- **¼ teaspoon ground cinnamon**
- **¼ teaspoon ground cumin**
- **¼ teaspoon crushed red pepper flakes**
- **4 boneless skinless chicken breast halves (5 ounces each)**
- **1 tablespoon olive oil**
- **1 cup canned apricot halves, sliced**
- **⅓ cup dried tropical fruit**
- **¼ cup water**
- **1 tablespoon honey**

1. Mix first four ingredients. Pound chicken breasts with a meat mallet to flatten slightly. Rub with oil; sprinkle with seasonings.

2. In a large skillet, brown chicken on both sides. Add apricots, tropical fruit, water and honey; bring to a boil. Reduce heat; simmer, covered, for 5-6 minutes or until a thermometer inserted into chicken reads 165°.

PER SERVING *1 chicken breast with 1/4 cup apricot mixture: 288 cal., 7g fat (2g sat. fat), 78mg chol., 230mg sodium, 27g carb. (24g sugars, 2g fiber), 29g pro.*

MEDITERRANEAN CHICKEN PASTA

On special days, I make this cheesy pasta bake loaded with chicken and all sorts of veggies. Want a vegetarian version? Use vegetable stock and garbanzo beans.

—**LIZ BELLVILLE** HAVELOCK, NC

PREP: 25 MIN. • **COOK:** 20 MIN.
MAKES: 8 SERVINGS

- **1 package (12 ounces) uncooked tricolor spiral pasta**
- **2 tablespoons olive oil, divided**
- **1 pound boneless skinless chicken breasts, cut into ½-inch pieces**
- **1 large sweet red pepper, chopped**
- **1 medium onion, chopped**
- **3 garlic cloves, peeled and thinly sliced**
- **1 cup white wine or reduced-sodium chicken broth**
- **¼ cup julienned soft sun-dried tomatoes (not packed in oil)**
- **1 teaspoon dried basil**
- **1 teaspoon Italian seasoning**
- **½ teaspoon salt**
- **¼ teaspoon crushed red pepper flakes**
- **¼ teaspoon pepper**
- **1 can (14½ ounces) reduced-sodium chicken broth**
- **1 can (14 ounces) water-packed quartered artichoke hearts, drained**
- **1 package (6 ounces) fresh baby spinach**
- **1 cup (4 ounces) crumbled feta cheese**
- **Thinly sliced fresh basil leaves and shaved Parmesan cheese, optional**

1. Cook pasta according to the package directions. In a 6-qt. stockpot, heat 1 tablespoon oil over medium-high heat. Add chicken; cook and stir 4-6 minutes or until no longer pink. Remove from pot.

2. In same pot, heat remaining oil over medium heat. Add red pepper and onion; cook and stir 4-5 minutes or until onion is tender. Add the garlic; cook 1 minute longer. Add wine, sun-dried tomatoes and seasonings; bring to a boil. Reduce heat; simmer 5 minutes, stirring to loosen browned bits from pot.

3. Add the broth and artichoke hearts; return mixture to a boil. Stir in the spinach and chicken; cook just until spinach is wilted.

4. Drain pasta; stir into the chicken mixture. Stir in feta cheese. If desired, top each serving with basil and Parmesan cheese.

NOTE *This recipe was tested with sun-dried tomatoes that can be used without soaking. When using other sun-dried tomatoes that are not oil-packed, cover with boiling water and let stand until soft. Drain before using.*

PER SERVING *1½ cups: 357 cal., 8g fat (2g sat. fat), 39mg chol., 609mg sodium, 42g carb. (4g sugars, 4g fiber), 23g pro.* ***Diabetic Exchanges:*** *2 starch, 2 lean meat, 1½ fat, 1 vegetable.*

MEDITERRANEAN CHICKEN PASTA

MARINATED CHICKEN & ZUCCHINI KABOBS

MARINATED CHICKEN & ZUCCHINI KABOBS

These tasty and healthy kabobs are a family favorite. You can change them up with turkey tenderloins and other veggies, like summer squash or sweet bell peppers.

—TAMMY SLADE STANSBURY PARK, UT

PREP: 25 MIN. + MARINATING
GRILL: 10 MIN. • **MAKES:** 8 SERVINGS

- **¾ cup lemon-lime soda**
- **½ cup reduced-sodium soy sauce**
- **½ cup canola oil, divided**
- **2 pounds boneless skinless chicken breasts or turkey breast tenderloins, cut into 1-inch cubes**
- **3 medium zucchini, cut into 1-inch pieces**
- **2 medium red onions, cut into 1-inch pieces**
- **½ teaspoon salt**
- **¼ teaspoon pepper**

1. In a large resealable plastic bag, combine soda, soy sauce and 1/4 cup oil. Add chicken; seal bag and turn to coat. Refrigerate 8 hours or overnight.

2. Drain chicken, discarding the marinade. On eight metal or soaked wooden skewers, alternately thread chicken and vegetables. Brush the vegetables with remaining oil; sprinkle with salt and pepper. On a greased grill, cook kabobs, covered, over medium heat 8-10 minutes or until chicken is no longer pink and vegetables are tender, turning occasionally.

PER SERVING *1 kabob: 224 cal., 11g fat (1g sat. fat), 63mg chol., 344mg sodium, 6g carb. (3g sugars, 1g fiber), 24g pro.* ***Diabetic Exchanges:*** *3 lean meat, 2 fat, 1 vegetable.*

BRUSCHETTA CHICKEN WRAPS FAST FIX

As an Italian-American, I love the garlic, tomatoes and basil that traditionally go into bruschetta. This recipe was created in celebration of the first tomatoes to come out of the garden.

—GINA RINE CANFIELD, OH

START TO FINISH: 30 MIN.
MAKES: 4 SERVINGS

- **2 plum tomatoes, finely chopped (about 1 cup)**
- **1 cup fresh baby spinach, coarsely chopped**
- **¼ cup finely chopped red onion**
- **1 tablespoon shredded Parmesan or Romano cheese**
- **1 tablespoon minced fresh basil**
- **1 teaspoon olive oil**
- **1 teaspoon balsamic vinegar**
- **⅛ teaspoon plus ¼ teaspoon pepper, divided**
- **Dash garlic powder**
- **4 boneless skinless chicken breast halves (4 ounces each)**
- **½ teaspoon salt**
- **2 ounces fresh mozzarella cheese, cut into 4 slices**
- **4 whole wheat tortillas (8 inches)**

1. In a small bowl, mix tomatoes, spinach, onion, Parmesan cheese, basil, oil, vinegar, 1/8 teaspoon pepper and garlic powder.

2. Moisten a paper towel with cooking oil; using long-handled tongs, rub on grill rack to coat lightly. Sprinkle the chicken with salt and the remaining pepper; place on grill rack. Grill, covered, over medium heat for 4-6 minutes on each side or until a thermometer reads 165°.

3. Top each chicken breast with a cheese slice; cover and grill for 1-2 minutes longer or until the cheese is melted. Grill the tortillas over medium heat for 20-30 seconds or until heated through.

4. Place chicken on center of each tortilla; top with about 1/4 cup tomato mixture. Fold bottom of tortilla over filling; fold both sides to close.

PER SERVING *1 wrap: 330 cal., 10g fat (3g sat. fat), 75mg chol., 569mg sodium, 25g carb. (3g sugars, 3g fiber), 31g pro.* ***Diabetic Exchanges:*** *3 lean meat, 2 starch, 1 fat.*

BRUSCHETTA CHICKEN WRAPS

SPICY LEMON CHICKEN KABOBS

SPICY LEMON CHICKEN KABOBS S C

When I see Meyer lemons in the store, I know that spring has arrived. I like using them for these smoky kabobs, but regular grilled lemons work, too.
—**TERRI CRANDALL** GARDNERVILLE, NV

PREP: 15 MIN. + MARINATING
GRILL: 10 MIN.
MAKES: 6 SERVINGS

- **¼ cup lemon juice**
- **4 tablespoons olive oil, divided**
- **3 tablespoons white wine**
- **1½ teaspoons crushed red pepper flakes**
- **1 teaspoon minced fresh rosemary or ¼ teaspoon dried rosemary, crushed**
- **1½ pounds boneless skinless chicken breasts, cut into 1-inch cubes**
- **2 medium lemons, halved**
- **Minced chives**

1. In a large resealable plastic bag, combine lemon juice, 3 tablespoons oil, wine, pepper flakes and rosemary. Add chicken; seal bag and turn to coat. Refrigerate up to 3 hours.
2. Drain chicken and discard the marinade. Thread chicken onto six metal or soaked wooden skewers. Grill, covered, over medium heat 10-12 minutes or until no longer pink, turning once. Place lemons on grill, cut side down. Grill 8-10 minutes or until lightly browned. Squeeze lemons over chicken. Drizzle with remaining oil; sprinkle with chives.
PER SERVING *1 kabob: 182 cal., 8g fat (2g sat. fat), 63mg chol., 55mg sodium, 2g carb. (1g sugars, 1g fiber), 23g pro.* ***Diabetic Exchanges:*** *3 lean meat, 1 fat.*

TOP TIP

Be careful not to marinate chicken and seafood for too long in acidic ingredients such as lemon juice or wine. The acid breaks down fibers and can cause a mushy texture if left on too long.

CHICKEN WITH FIRE-ROASTED TOMATOES

My skillet chicken with the colors and flavors of Italy is so easy. The fire-roasted tomatoes sound complicated, but all you have to do is open a can and add to the chicken! —**MARGARET WILSON** SAN BERNARDINO, CA

CHICKEN WITH FIRE-ROASTED TOMATOES C FAST FIX

START TO FINISH: 30 MIN.
MAKES: 4 SERVINGS

- **2 tablespoons salt-free garlic herb seasoning blend**
- **½ teaspoon salt**
- **¼ teaspoon Italian seasoning**
- **¼ teaspoon pepper**
- **⅛ teaspoon crushed red pepper flakes, optional**
- **4 boneless skinless chicken breast halves (6 ounces each)**
- **1 tablespoon olive oil**
- **1 can (14½ ounces) fire-roasted diced tomatoes, undrained**
- **¾ pound fresh green beans, trimmed**
- **2 tablespoons water**
- **1 tablespoon butter**
- **Hot cooked pasta, optional**

1. Mix the first five ingredients; sprinkle over both sides of chicken breasts. In a large skillet, heat oil over medium heat. Brown chicken on both sides. Add tomatoes; bring to a boil. Reduce heat; simmer, covered, for 10-12 minutes or until a thermometer inserted into chicken reads 165°.
2. Meanwhile, in a 2-qt. microwave-safe dish, combine green beans and water; microwave, covered, on high for 3-4 minutes or just until tender. Drain.
3. Remove chicken from skillet; keep warm. Stir butter and beans into the tomato mixture. Serve with chicken and, if desired, pasta.
PER SERVING *1 chicken breast half with 1 cup bean mixture: 294 cal., 10g fat (3g sat. fat), 102mg chol., 681mg sodium, 12g carb. (5g sugars, 4g fiber), 37g pro.* ***Diabetic Exchanges:*** *5 lean meat, 1 vegetable, 1 fat.*

ITALIAN SPAGHETTI WITH CHICKEN & ROASTED VEGETABLES

ITALIAN SPAGHETTI WITH CHICKEN & ROASTED VEGETABLES

When I get a craving for homemade tomato sauce, I make a zesty batch to toss with chicken and veggies. The flavors do wonders for penne, too.

—**CARLY CURTIN** ELLICOTT CITY, MD

PREP: 25 MIN. • **COOK:** 25 MIN.
MAKES: 6 SERVINGS

- **3 plum tomatoes, seeded and chopped**
- **2 medium zucchini, cubed**
- **1 medium yellow summer squash, cubed**
- **2 tablespoons olive oil, divided**
- **2 teaspoons Italian seasoning, divided**
- **8 ounces uncooked whole wheat spaghetti**
- **1 pound boneless skinless chicken breasts, cubed**
- **½ teaspoon garlic powder**
- **½ cup reduced-sodium chicken broth**
- **⅓ cup dry red wine or additional reduced-sodium chicken broth**
- **4 cans (8 ounces each) no-salt-added tomato sauce**
- **1 can (6 ounces) tomato paste**
- **¼ cup minced fresh basil**
- **2 tablespoons minced fresh oregano**
- **¼ teaspoon salt**
- **6 tablespoons shredded Parmesan cheese**

1. Preheat oven to 425°. In a large bowl, combine tomatoes, zucchini and squash. Add 1 tablespoon of oil and 1 teaspoon Italian seasoning. Transfer to a 15x10x1-in. baking pan coated with cooking spray. Bake 15-20 minutes or until tender.
2. Meanwhile, cook the spaghetti according to package directions. Sprinkle chicken with garlic powder and remaining Italian seasoning. In a large nonstick skillet, heat remaining oil over medium heat. Add chicken; cook until no longer pink. Remove from skillet.
3. Add broth and wine to skillet, stirring to loosen browned bits from pan. Stir in tomato sauce, tomato paste, basil, oregano and salt. Bring to a boil. Return chicken to skillet. Reduce heat; simmer, covered, for 4-6 minutes or until the sauce is slightly thickened.
4. Drain spaghetti. Add spaghetti and vegetables to tomato mixture; heat through. Sprinkle with cheese.

PER SERVING *1⅔ cups spaghetti with 1 tablespoon cheese: 379 cal., 9g fat (2g sat. fat), 45mg chol., 345mg sodium, 49g carb. (14g sugars, 8g fiber), 26g pro.* ***Diabetic Exchanges:*** *2½ starch, 2 lean meat, 2 vegetable, 1 fat.*

CHICKEN NICOISE SALAD

C FAST FIX (PICTURED ON P. 111)

This salad makes it easy to eat what's good for you. It's versatile, so you can use asparagus in place of green beans and salmon instead of tuna, or add garden tomatoes.

—**NICHOLAS MONFRE** OAK RIDGE, NJ

START TO FINISH: 30 MIN.
MAKES: 4 SERVINGS

- **½ pound fresh green beans, trimmed and halved (about 1 cup)**

DRESSING

- **¼ cup olive oil**
- **2 teaspoons grated lemon peel**
- **2 tablespoons lemon juice**
- **2 garlic cloves, minced**
- **1 teaspoon Dijon mustard**
- **⅛ teaspoon salt**
- **Dash pepper**

SALAD

- **1 can (5 ounces) light tuna in water, drained and flaked**
- **2 tablespoons sliced ripe olives, drained**
- **1 teaspoon capers, rinsed and drained**
- **2 cups torn mixed salad greens**
- **1 package (6 ounces) ready-to-use Southwest-style grilled chicken breast strips**
- **1 small red onion, halved and thinly sliced**
- **1 medium sweet red pepper, julienned**
- **2 hard-cooked large eggs, cut into wedges**

1. In a saucepan, cook green beans in boiling water just until crisp-tender. Remove and immediately drop into ice water to cool. Drain; pat dry.
2. Meanwhile, whisk together dressing ingredients. In a small bowl, lightly toss tuna with olives and capers.
3. Line platter with salad greens; top with tuna mixture, green beans and the remaining ingredients. Serve with dressing.

PER SERVING *289 cal., 18g fat (3g sat. fat), 142mg chol., 562mg sodium, 9g carb. (3g sugars, 3g fiber), 24g pro.*

JAMAICAN CHICKEN WITH COUSCOUS

JAMAICAN CHICKEN WITH COUSCOUS FAST FIX

"Fantabulous" is a word I reserve for dishes like this jerk-seasoned chicken. Fresh pineapple and cilantro are delicious, delightful counterpoints to the warm spices.

—**JONI HILTON** ROCKLIN, CA

START TO FINISH: 30 MIN.
MAKES: 6 SERVINGS

- **1 can (20 ounces) unsweetened pineapple tidbits, undrained**
- **1 teaspoon salt, divided**
- **1 cup uncooked whole wheat couscous**
- **⅓ cup all-purpose flour**
- **2 tablespoons minced fresh cilantro**
- **1½ pounds boneless skinless chicken breasts, cut into ½-inch-thick strips**
- **2 teaspoons Caribbean jerk seasoning**
- **3 tablespoons olive oil, divided**
- **Additional minced fresh cilantro, optional**

1. In a large saucepan, combine pineapple and ½ teaspoon salt; bring to a boil. Stir in couscous. Remove from heat; let stand, covered, for 5 minutes or until liquid is absorbed. Fluff with a fork.

2. Meanwhile, in a shallow bowl, mix flour and 2 tablespoons cilantro. Toss chicken with jerk seasoning and the remaining salt. Add to flour mixture, a few pieces at a time, and toss to coat lightly; shake off any excess.

3. In a large skillet, heat 1 tablespoon oil. Add a third of the chicken; cook 1-2 minutes on each side or until no longer pink. Repeat twice with oil and chicken. Serve with couscous. If desired, sprinkle with cilantro.

PER SERVING *3 ounces cooked chicken with ⅔ cup couscous mixture: 374 cal., 10g fat (2g sat. fat), 63mg chol., 542mg sodium, 42g carb. (12g sugars, 5g fiber), 29g pro.* ***Diabetic Exchanges:*** *3 starch, 3 lean meat, 1 fat.*

WILD RICE SALAD

I modified a recipe I received years ago and came up with this versatile salad. It makes a refreshing chilled salad on a hot day, but we also enjoy it at room temperature or warmed in the microwave during the cooler months.

—**ROBIN THOMPSON** ROSEVILLE, CA

PREP: 1¼ HOURS + CHILLING
MAKES: 4 SERVINGS

- **3 cups water**
- **1 cup uncooked wild rice**
- **2 chicken bouillon cubes**
- **4½ teaspoons butter**
- **1 cup cut fresh green beans**
- **1 cup cubed cooked chicken breast**
- **1 medium tomato, chopped**
- **1 bunch green onions, sliced**
- **¼ cup rice vinegar**
- **1 tablespoon sesame oil**
- **1 garlic clove, minced**
- **½ teaspoon dried tarragon**
- **¼ teaspoon pepper**

1. In a large saucepan, bring the water, rice, bouillon and butter to a boil. Reduce heat; cover and simmer for 45-60 minutes or until rice is tender. Drain if necessary; transfer to a large bowl and cool completely.

2. Place green beans in a steamer basket; place in a small saucepan over 1 in. of water. Bring to a boil; cover and steam for 8-10 minutes or until crisp-tender.

3. Add the chicken, tomato, onions and green beans to the rice; stir until blended. Combine the remaining ingredients; drizzle over mixture and toss to coat. Refrigerate until chilled.

PER SERVING *1½ cups: 330 cal., 10g fat (4g sat. fat), 39mg chol., 618mg sodium, 43g carb. (3g sugars, 4g fiber), 18g pro.* ***Diabetic Exchanges:*** *2 starch, 2 fat, 1 lean meat, 1 vegetable.*

WILD RICE SALAD

ROASTED CHICKEN WITH POTATO WEDGES

ROASTED CHICKEN WITH POTATO WEDGES

I grow herbs and dry them for use all year. Knowing that the rosemary and thyme are from our garden makes this cozy roast chicken dinner even better.
—**TANYA BORKHOLDER** MILFORD, IN

PREP: 10 MIN. • **BAKE:** 30 MIN.
MAKES: 4 SERVINGS

- 2 large potatoes (about 1½ pounds)
- 2 teaspoons olive oil
- 2 teaspoons Montreal steak seasoning

CHICKEN

- 4 bone-in chicken thighs
- 4 chicken drumsticks
- 1 tablespoon hot water
- 2 teaspoons butter
- 1 teaspoon dried rosemary, crushed
- 1 teaspoon dried thyme
- ¼ teaspoon kosher salt
- ¼ teaspoon pepper

1. Preheat oven to 450°. Cut each potato lengthwise into 12 wedges; toss with oil and steak seasoning. Arrange in a single layer in a greased 15x10x1-in. baking pan. Roast on a lower oven rack 30-35 minutes or until tender and lightly browned, turning occasionally.
2. Place chicken in a large bowl. In a small bowl, combine the remaining ingredients; add to chicken and toss to coat. Transfer to a rack in a broiler pan, skin side up. Place on an oven rack above potatoes; roast 30-35 minutes or until a thermometer inserted in chicken reads 170°-175°. Serve with potato wedges.

PER SERVING *1 thigh and 1 drumstick (skin removed) with 6 potato wedges: 447 cal., 17g fat (5g sat. fat), 133mg chol., 596mg sodium, 33g carb. (1g sugars, 4g fiber), 41g pro.* ***Diabetic Exchanges:*** *5 lean meat, 2 starch, 2 fat.*

GRECIAN PASTA & CHICKEN SKILLET

PREP: 30 MIN. • **COOK:** 10 MIN
MAKES: 4 SERVINGS

- 1 can (14½ ounces) reduced-sodium chicken broth
- 1 can (14½ ounces) no-salt-added diced tomatoes, undrained
- ¾ pound boneless skinless chicken breasts, cut into 1-inch pieces
- ½ cup white wine or water
- 1 garlic clove, minced
- ½ teaspoon dried oregano
- 4 ounces multigrain thin spaghetti
- 1 jar (7½ ounces) marinated quartered artichoke hearts, drained and coarsely chopped
- 2 cups fresh baby spinach
- ¼ cup roasted sweet red pepper strips
- ¼ cup sliced ripe olives
- 1 green onion, finely chopped
- 2 tablespoons minced fresh parsley
- ½ teaspoon grated lemon peel
- 2 tablespoons lemon juice
- 1 tablespoon olive oil
- ½ teaspoon pepper
- Crumbled reduced-fat feta cheese, optional

1. In a large skillet, combine the first six ingredients; add spaghetti. Bring to a boil. Cook 5-7 minutes or until chicken is no longer pink and spaghetti is tender.
2. Stir in artichoke hearts, spinach, red pepper, olives, green onion, parsley, lemon peel, lemon juice, oil and pepper. Cook and stir 2-3 minutes or until spinach is wilted. If desired, sprinkle with cheese.

PER SERVING *1½ cups: 373 cal., 15g fat (3g sat. fat), 47mg chol., 658mg sodium, 30g carb. (8g sugars, 4g fiber), 25g pro.* ***Diabetic Exchanges:*** *2 starch, 2 lean meat, 2 fat, 1 vegetable.*

We love a homemade meal at the end of the day. But the prep involved? Not so much. My Greek-inspired pasta is lemony, herby and thankfully, easy.
—**ROXANNE CHAN** ALBANY, CA

GRECIAN PASTA & CHICKEN SKILLET

STRAWBERRY MINT CHICKEN C FAST FIX

I hand-picked wild strawberries for this saucy chicken dish. We love it with fresh spring greens and a sweet white wine.

—**ALICIA DUERST** MENOMONIE, WI

START TO FINISH: 30 MIN.
MAKES: 4 SERVINGS

- **1 tablespoon cornstarch**
- **1 tablespoon sugar**
- **⅛ teaspoon ground nutmeg**
- **⅛ teaspoon pepper**
- **½ cup water**
- **1 cup fresh strawberries, coarsely chopped**
- **½ cup white wine or white grape juice**
- **2 teaspoons minced fresh mint**

CHICKEN

- **4 boneless skinless chicken breast halves (6 ounces each)**
- **½ teaspoon salt**
- **¼ teaspoon pepper**
- **Sliced green onion**

1. In a small saucepan, mix the first five ingredients until smooth; stir in strawberries and wine. Bring to a boil. Reduce heat; simmer, uncovered, 3-5 minutes or until thickened and strawberries are softened, stirring occasionally. Remove from heat; stir in mint.

2. Moisten a paper towel with cooking oil; using long-handled tongs, rub on grill rack to coat lightly. Sprinkle the chicken with salt and pepper.

3. Grill chicken, covered, over medium heat 5-7 minutes on each side or until a thermometer reads 165°; brush occasionally with 1/4 cup sauce during the last 4 minutes. Serve with remaining sauce. Sprinkle with green onion.

PER SERVING *1 chicken breast half with 1/4 cup sauce: 224 cal., 4g fat (1g sat. fat), 94mg chol., 378mg sodium, 8g carb. (5g sugars, 1g fiber), 35g pro.* ***Diabetic Exchanges:*** *5 lean meat, 1/2 starch.*

CHICKEN WITH MANGO-CUCUMBER SALSA

CHICKEN WITH MANGO-CUCUMBER SALSA FAST FIX

I put this dish together after looking for something quick and easy without too much indoor cooking. My husband prefers this grilled chicken a little spicy.

—**LINDA TRINGALI** MONROE TOWNSHIP, NJ

START TO FINISH: 30 MIN.
MAKES: 4 SERVINGS (4 CUPS SALSA)

- **2 tablespoons lemon juice**
- **1 tablespoon lime juice**
- **2 teaspoons minced fresh cilantro or parsley**
- **¼ teaspoon ground cumin**
- **¼ teaspoon salt**
- **⅛ teaspoon pepper**
- **1 medium cucumber, diced**
- **1 medium mango, peeled and diced**
- **1 medium tomato, chopped**
- **¼ cup finely chopped red onion**

CHICKEN

- **4 boneless skinless chicken breast halves (6 ounces each)**
- **1 tablespoon olive oil**
- **1 teaspoon chili powder**
- **½ teaspoon salt**
- **¼ teaspoon pepper**

1. For dressing, in a small bowl, mix the first six ingredients. Place the cucumber, mango, tomato and onion in a large bowl; toss with dressing.

2. Brush chicken with oil; sprinkle with seasonings. Grill chicken, covered, over medium heat or broil 4 in. from heat 4-5 minutes on each side or until a thermometer reads 165°. Serve with salsa.

NOTE *Add 3 cups cooked whole wheat couscous to the colorful salsa to turn it into a hearty side dish.*

PER SERVING *1 chicken breast half with 1 cup salsa: 285 cal., 8g fat (2g sat. fat), 94mg chol., 547mg sodium, 18g carb. (14g sugars, 3g fiber), 36g pro.* ***Diabetic Exchanges:*** *5 lean meat, 1 starch, 1/2 fat.*

BAKED CHICKEN CHALUPAS

I wanted an easy alternative to deep-fried chalupas, so I bake them with filling on top.

—**MAGDALENA FLORES** ABILENE, TX

PREP: 20 MIN. • **BAKE:** 15 MIN. • **MAKES:** 6 SERVINGS

- **6 corn tortillas (6 inches)**
- **2 teaspoons olive oil**
- **¾ cup shredded part-skim mozzarella cheese**
- **2 cups chopped cooked chicken breast**
- **1 can (14½ ounces) diced tomatoes with mild green chilies, undrained**
- **1 teaspoon garlic powder**
- **1 teaspoon onion powder**
- **1 teaspoon ground cumin**
- **¼ teaspoon salt**
- **¼ teaspoon pepper**
- **½ cup finely shredded cabbage**

1. Preheat oven to 350°. Place tortillas on an ungreased baking sheet. Brush each tortilla with olive oil and sprinkle with cheese.

2. Place chicken, tomatoes and seasonings in a large skillet; cook and stir over medium heat 6-8 minutes or until most of the liquid is evaporated. Spoon over tortillas. Bake for 15-18 minutes or until tortillas are crisp and cheese is melted. Top with cabbage.

PER SERVING *1 chalupa: 206 cal., 6g fat (2g sat. fat), 45mg chol., 400mg sodium, 17g carb. (3g sugars, 3g fiber), 19g pro.* ***Diabetic Exchanges:*** *2 lean meat, 1 starch, 1/2 fat.*

BAKED CHICKEN CHALUPAS

CHICKEN TZATZIKI CUCUMBER BOATS

CHICKEN TZATZIKI CUCUMBER BOATS FAST FIX

I've tended a garden for decades, and these colorful boats made from cucumbers hold my fresh tomatoes, peas and dill. It's absolute garden greatness.

—**RONNA FARLEY** ROCKVILLE, MD

START TO FINISH: 15 MIN. • **MAKES:** 2 SERVINGS

- **2 medium cucumbers**
- **½ cup fat-free plain Greek yogurt**
- **2 tablespoons mayonnaise**
- **½ teaspoon garlic salt**
- **3 teaspoons snipped fresh dill, divided**
- **1 cup chopped cooked chicken breast**
- **1 cup chopped seeded tomato (about 1 large), divided**
- **½ cup fresh or frozen peas, thawed**

1. Cut each cucumber lengthwise in half; scoop out pulp, leaving a 1/4-in. shell. In a bowl, mix yogurt, mayonnaise, garlic salt and 1 teaspoon dill; gently stir in chicken, 3/4 cup tomato and peas.

2. Spoon into cucumber shells. Top with the remaining tomato and dill.

PER SERVING *2 filled cucumber halves: 322 cal., 13g fat (2g sat. fat), 59mg chol., 398mg sodium, 18g carb. (10g sugars, 6g fiber), 34g pro.* ***Diabetic Exchanges:*** *4 lean meat, 2 vegetable, 2 fat, 1/2 starch.*

HEALTH TIP *Skip the peas for a fast and refreshing low-carb lunch or supper.*

MAPLE-ROASTED CHICKEN & ACORN SQUASH

When I became a new mother, my mom helped me find comforting recipes to have on hand. This terrific roast chicken is a happy discovery.

—SARA EILERS SURPRISE, AZ

PREP: 15 MIN. • **BAKE:** 35 MIN. • **MAKES:** 6 SERVINGS

- **1 medium acorn squash**
- **4 medium carrots, chopped (about 2 cups)**
- **1 medium onion, cut into 1-inch pieces**
- **6 bone-in chicken thighs (about 2¼ pounds)**
- **½ cup maple syrup**
- **1 teaspoon salt**
- **½ teaspoon coarsely ground pepper**

1. Preheat oven to 450°. Cut squash lengthwise in half; remove and discard seeds. Cut each half crosswise into ½-in. slices; discard ends. Place squash, carrots and onion in a greased 13x9-in. baking pan; top with chicken, skin side down. Roast 10 minutes.

2. Turn chicken over; drizzle with the maple syrup and sprinkle with salt and pepper. Roast 25-30 minutes longer or until a thermometer inserted in chicken reads 170°-175° and vegetables are tender.

PER SERVING *363 cal., 14g fat (4g sat. fat), 81mg chol., 497mg sodium, 36g carb. (23g sugars, 3g fiber), 24g pro.* ***Diabetic Exchanges:*** *3 lean meat, 2 starch, 1 vegetable.*

MAPLE-ROASTED CHICKEN & ACORN SQUASH

RASPBERRY PECAN CHICKEN SALAD

RASPBERRY PECAN CHICKEN SALAD FAST FIX

I gave this sweet-savory chicken salad a little zip with Chinese five-spice powder, which tastes a bit like pumpkin pie spice. Sprinkle some on roasted carrots for an awesome meal.

—LISA RENSHAW KANSAS CITY, MO

START TO FINISH: 15 MIN. • **MAKES:** 6 SERVINGS

- **1 carton (6 ounces) orange yogurt**
- **½ cup mayonnaise**
- **¼ teaspoon Chinese five-spice powder**
- **3 cups cubed cooked chicken**
- **2 green onions, chopped**
- **¼ cup sliced celery**
- **¼ cup chopped pecans, toasted**
- **1 cup fresh raspberries**
- **12 slices multigrain bread**

In a large bowl, mix yogurt, mayonnaise and five-spice powder. Stir in chicken, green onions, celery and pecans. Gently stir in raspberries. Serve on bread.

NOTE *To toast nuts, cook in a skillet over low heat until lightly browned, stirring occasionally.*

PER SERVING *477 cal., 26g fat (4g sat. fat), 70mg chol., 378mg sodium, 31g carb. (10g sugars, 6g fiber), 29g pro.*

FETA CHICKEN BURGERS

FAST FIX

START TO FINISH: 30 MIN.
MAKES: 6 SERVINGS

- **¼ cup finely chopped cucumber**
- **¼ cup reduced-fat mayonnaise**

BURGERS

- **½ cup chopped roasted sweet red pepper**
- **1 teaspoon garlic powder**
- **½ teaspoon Greek seasoning**
- **¼ teaspoon pepper**
- **1½ pounds lean ground chicken**
- **1 cup (4 ounces) crumbled feta cheese**
- **6 whole wheat hamburger buns, split and toasted**
- **Lettuce leaves and tomato slices, optional**

1. Preheat broiler. Mix cucumber and mayonnaise. For burgers, mix red pepper and seasonings. Add chicken and cheese; mix lightly but thoroughly (mixture will be sticky). Shape into six ½-in.-thick patties.
2. Broil burgers 4 in. from heat until a thermometer reads 165°, 3-4 minutes per side. Serve in buns with cucumber sauce. If desired, top burgers with lettuce and tomato.

FREEZE OPTION *Place uncooked patties on a plastic wrap-lined baking sheet; wrap and freeze until firm. Remove from pan and transfer to a large resealable plastic bag; return to freezer. To use, broil the frozen patties as directed, increasing cook time as necessary.*

PER SERVING *1 burger with 1 tablespoon sauce: 356 cal., 14g fat (5g sat. fat), 95mg chol., 703mg sodium, 25g carb. (5g sugars, 4g fiber), 31g pro.* ***Diabetic Exchanges:*** *5 lean meat, 2 starch, ½ fat.*

My friends always request these tasty chicken burgers on the grill. I sometimes add olives to punch up the flavor! Try them with the mayo topping.
—**ANGELA ROBINSON** FINDLAY, OH

FETA CHICKEN BURGERS

PESTO RICE-STUFFED CHICKEN C

Juicy stuffed chicken is light, fresh and feels extra special. The quick prep lets it fit right into any busy schedule. Substitute shredded cheese for the pesto if you have picky eaters.
—**RACHEL DION** PORT CHARLOTTE, FL

PREP: 20 MIN. • **BAKE:** 20 MIN.
MAKES: 8 SERVINGS

- **¾ cup uncooked instant rice**
- **½ cup chopped seeded tomato**
- **¼ cup prepared pesto**
- **⅛ teaspoon salt**
- **8 boneless skinless chicken breast halves (6 ounces each)**
- **2 tablespoons canola oil, divided**

1. Preheat oven to 375°. Cook rice according to package directions.
2. In a small bowl, combine tomato, pesto, salt and rice. Cut a pocket horizontally in the thickest part of each chicken breast. Fill each with 3 tablespoons rice mixture; secure with toothpicks.
3. In a large skillet, heat 1 tablespoon oil over medium-high heat. In batches, brown chicken breasts on each side, adding more oil as needed. Transfer to a greased 15x10x1-in. baking pan.
4. Bake 18-22 minutes or until chicken is no longer pink. Discard toothpicks before serving.

PER SERVING *1 stuffed chicken breast half: 278 cal., 10g fat (2g sat. fat), 94mg chol., 210mg sodium, 9g carb. (1g sugars, 0 fiber), 35g pro.* ***Diabetic Exchanges:*** *5 lean meat, 1 fat, ½ starch.*

PESTO RICE-STUFFED CHICKEN

SESAME CHICKEN NOODLE SALAD

When I don't have much time, I go straight to this recipe. It's quick, easy and you can use almost anything you have left over in the fridge.

—JESSIE APFE BERKELEY, CA

PREP: 25 MIN. • **COOK:** 15 MIN.
MAKES: 4 SERVINGS

- **8 ounces uncooked whole wheat angel hair pasta**
- **2 cups cubed cooked chicken breast**
- **1½ cups coleslaw mix**
- **1 can (11 ounces) mandarin oranges, drained**
- **1 medium sweet red pepper, julienned**
- **1 cup fresh sugar snap peas, trimmed and halved**
- **3 green onions, chopped**
- **¼ teaspoon salt**
- **⅔ cup reduced-fat Asian toasted sesame salad dressing**
- **¼ cup chopped salted peanuts**

1. Cook pasta according to package directions.

2. In a large bowl, combine chicken, coleslaw mix, oranges, red pepper, snap peas and green onions; sprinkle with salt and toss to combine.

3. Drain the pasta and rinse in cold water. Add pasta and dressing to the chicken mixture; toss to coat. Sprinkle with peanuts.

PER SERVING *2 cups: 519 cal., 11g fat (1g sat. fat), 54mg chol., 631mg sodium, 72g carb. (25g sugars, 10g fiber), 35g pro.*

HEALTH TIP *Whole grain brown rice noodles are available, but they can be hard to find. Whole wheat angel hair pasta is a healthy stand-in, and it adds 6 grams of fiber per serving.*

SESAME CHICKEN NOODLE SALAD

SAUSAGE & VEGETABLE SKILLET DINNER

SAUSAGE & VEGETABLE SKILLET DINNER FAST FIX

I threw this together one night trying to use up produce before going out of town. Who knew it was going to be such a hit! Now it's a go-to recipe that I use when I don't have much time to cook or wash dishes.

—ELIZABETH KELLEY CHICAGO, IL

START TO FINISH: 30 MIN.
MAKES: 4 SERVINGS

- **1 tablespoon olive oil**
- **1 package (12 ounces) fully cooked Italian chicken sausage links, cut into 1-inch pieces**
- **1 large onion, chopped**
- **3 garlic cloves, minced**
- **¼ teaspoon crushed red pepper flakes**
- **2 pounds red potatoes (about 7 medium), thinly sliced**
- **1 package (10 ounces) frozen corn**
- **1¼ cups vegetable broth**
- **¼ teaspoon pepper**
- **2 cups fresh baby spinach**

1. In a 12-in. skillet, heat oil over medium-high heat. Add the sausage and onion; cook and stir until the sausage is browned and onion is tender. Add the garlic and pepper flakes; cook 1 minute longer.

2. Add the potatoes, corn, broth and pepper; bring to a boil. Reduce heat; simmer, covered, 12-15 minutes or until potatoes are tender. Add spinach; cook just until wilted.

PER SERVING *2 cups: 413 cal., 11g fat (3g sat. fat), 65mg chol., 804mg sodium, 58g carb. (6g sugars, 7g fiber), 22g pro.*

READER RAVE

Another fast and easy dinner. I used turkey kielbasa (I prefer it to chicken sausage) and added zucchini as well. It turned out delicious!

—CHICKLUVS2COOK
TASTEOFHOME.COM

PARMESAN CHICKEN WITH ARTICHOKE HEARTS

I've liked the chicken and artichoke combo for a long time, so here's my own lemony twist. With all the praise it gets, this dinner is so much fun to serve.

—**CARLY GILES** HOPUIAM, WA

PREP: 20 MIN. • **BAKE:** 20 MIN.
MAKES: 4 SERVINGS

- **4 boneless skinless chicken breast halves (6 ounces each)**
- **3 teaspoons olive oil, divided**
- **1 teaspoon dried rosemary, crushed**
- **½ teaspoon dried thyme**
- **½ teaspoon pepper**
- **2 cans (14 ounces each) water-packed artichoke hearts, drained and quartered**
- **1 medium onion, coarsely chopped**
- **½ cup white wine or reduced-sodium chicken broth**
- **2 garlic cloves, chopped**
- **¼ cup shredded Parmesan cheese**
- **1 lemon, cut into 8 slices**
- **2 green onions, thinly sliced**

1. Preheat oven to 375°. Place the chicken in a 15x10x1-in. baking pan coated with cooking spray; drizzle with 1½ teaspoons oil. In a small bowl, mix rosemary, thyme and pepper; sprinkle half over chicken.
2. In a large bowl, combine artichoke hearts, onion, wine, garlic and the remaining oil and herb mixture; toss to coat. Arrange around chicken. Top chicken with cheese and lemon.
3. Roast 20-25 minutes or until a thermometer inserted into chicken reads 165°. Sprinkle with green onions.

PER SERVING *1 chicken breast half with ¾ cup artichoke mixture: 339 cal., 9g fat (3g sat. fat), 98mg chol., 667mg sodium, 18g carb. (2g sugars, 1g fiber), 42g pro.* ***Diabetic Exchanges:*** *5 lean meat, 1 vegetable, 1 fat, ½ starch.*

PARMESAN CHICKEN WITH ARTICHOKE HEARTS

ROASTED CHICKEN THIGHS WITH PEPPERS & POTATOES (PICTURED ON P. 111)

My family loves this dish! It looks and tastes really special, but it is quite simple to make. It uses olive oil and fresh herbs from my garden.

—**PATRICIA PRESCOTT** MANCHESTER, NH

PREP: 20 MIN. • **BAKE:** 35 MIN.
MAKES: 8 SERVINGS

- **2 pounds red potatoes (about 6 medium)**
- **2 large sweet red peppers**
- **2 large green peppers**
- **2 medium onions**
- **2 tablespoons olive oil, divided**
- **4 teaspoons minced fresh thyme or 1½ teaspoons dried thyme, divided**
- **3 teaspoons minced fresh rosemary or 1 teaspoon dried rosemary, crushed, divided**
- **8 boneless skinless chicken thighs (about 2 pounds)**
- **½ teaspoon salt**
- **¼ teaspoon pepper**

1. Preheat oven to 450°. Cut potatoes, peppers and onions into 1-in. pieces. Place vegetables in a roasting pan. Drizzle with 1 tablespoon oil; sprinkle with 2 teaspoons each fresh thyme and rosemary and toss to coat. Place chicken over vegetables. Brush the chicken with remaining oil; sprinkle with remaining thyme and rosemary. Sprinkle vegetables and chicken with salt and pepper.
2. Roast 35-40 minutes or until a thermometer inserted into chicken reads 170° and vegetables are tender.

PER SERVING *1 chicken thigh with 1 cup vegetables: 308 cal., 12g fat (3g sat. fat), 76mg chol., 221mg sodium, 25g carb. (5g sugars, 4g fiber), 24g pro.* ***Diabetic Exchanges:*** *3 lean meat, 1 starch, 1 vegetable, ½ fat.*

HEARTY CHICKEN GYROS

HEARTY CHICKEN GYROS

I love reinventing classic recipes to fit our taste and healthy lifestyle. This recipe is quick to prepare and can be served with oven fries or on its own. You can add Greek olives, omit the onion or even use cubed pork tenderloin for a new taste.

—**KAYLA DOUTHITT** ELIZABETHTOWN, KY

PREP: 30 MIN. + MARINATING
COOK: 5 MIN. • **MAKES:** 6 SERVINGS

- **1½ pounds boneless skinless chicken breasts, cut into ½-inch cubes**
- **½ cup salt-free lemon-pepper marinade**
- **3 tablespoons minced fresh mint**

SAUCE

- **½ cup fat-free plain Greek yogurt**
- **2 tablespoons lemon juice**
- **1 teaspoon dill weed**
- **½ teaspoon garlic powder**

ASSEMBLY

- **1 medium cucumber, seeded and chopped**
- **1 medium tomato, chopped**
- **¼ cup finely chopped onion**
- **6 whole wheat pita pocket halves, warmed**
- **⅓ cup crumbled feta cheese**

1. Place chicken, marinade and mint in a large resealable plastic bag; seal bag and turn to coat. Refrigerate up to 6 hours.
2. Drain chicken, discarding the marinade. Place a large nonstick skillet over medium-high heat. Add chicken; cook and stir 4-6 minutes or until no longer pink.
3. In a small bowl, mix the sauce ingredients. In another bowl, combine cucumber, tomato and onion. Serve chicken in pita pockets with vegetable mixture, sauce and cheese.

PER SERVING *1 gyro: 248 cal., 4g fat (2g sat. fat), 66mg chol., 251mg sodium, 22g carb. (4g sugars, 3g fiber), 30g pro.* ***Diabetic Exchanges:*** *3 lean meat, 1½ starch, ½ fat.*

CITRUS-SPICED ROAST CHICKEN C

I am the designated Thanksgiving host in my family because of my chipotle citrus roast turkey. Even finicky eaters love it. That's why I use the same recipe for chicken, so we can enjoy it year-round.

—**ROBIN HAAS** CRANSTON, RI

PREP: 20 MIN. • **BAKE:** 1 HOUR + STANDING
MAKES: 6 SERVINGS

- **3 tablespoons orange marmalade**
- **4½ teaspoons chopped chipotle peppers in adobo sauce**
- **3 garlic cloves, minced**
- **¾ teaspoon salt, divided**
- **½ teaspoon ground cumin**
- **1 broiler/fryer chicken (4 pounds)**

1. Preheat oven to 350°. Mix the marmalade, chipotle peppers, garlic, 1/2 teaspoon salt and cumin. With fingers, carefully loosen skin from chicken; rub mixture under the skin.
2. Place chicken on a rack in a shallow roasting pan, breast side up. Tuck wings under chicken; tie drumsticks together. Rub skin with remaining salt. Roast for 1-1¼ hours or until a thermometer inserted in thickest part of thigh reads 170°-175°; cover with foil halfway through cooking to prevent overbrowning.
3. Remove chicken from oven; let stand, loosely covered, 15 minutes before carving. Remove and discard skin before serving.

PER SERVING *4 ounces cooked chicken (skin removed): 239 cal., 8g fat (2g sat. fat), 98mg chol., 409mg sodium, 8g carb. (6g sugars, 0 fiber), 32g pro.* ***Diabetic Exchanges:*** *4 lean meat.*

CITRUS-SPICED ROAST CHICKEN

OVEN CHICKEN CORDON BLEU C FAST FIX

(PICTURED ON P. 111)

My son loves chicken Cordon Bleu, so I created this recipe with all the yummy flavors he craves, ready in a 30-minute meal. The leftovers freeze well, too.
—**RONDA EAGLE** GOOSE CREEK, SC

START TO FINISH: 30 MIN.
MAKES: 6 SERVINGS

- **6 boneless skinless chicken breast halves (4 ounces each)**
- **¼ teaspoon salt**
- **¼ teaspoon pepper**
- **6 slices deli ham**
- **3 slices aged Swiss cheese, halved**
- **1 cup panko (Japanese) bread crumbs**
- **Cooking spray**

SAUCE

- **2 tablespoons all-purpose flour**
- **1 cup 2% milk**
- **½ cup dry white wine**
- **⅓ cup finely shredded Swiss cheese**
- **¼ teaspoon salt**
- **⅛ teaspoon pepper**

1. Preheat oven to 375°. Sprinkle chicken breasts with salt and pepper; place in a greased 13x9-in. baking dish.
2. Top each with one slice of ham and a half slice of cheese, folding ham in half and covering chicken as much as possible. Sprinkle with bread crumbs. Carefully spritz bread crumbs with cooking spray, keeping crumbs in place. Bake 15-20 minutes or until golden brown and a thermometer inserted into chicken reads 165°.
3. For sauce, in a small saucepan, whisk flour and milk until smooth. Bring mixture to a boil, stirring constantly; cook and stir 1-2 minutes or until thickened.
4. Reduce heat to medium. Stir in wine and cheese; cook and stir 2-3 minutes or until cheese is melted and sauce is thickened and bubbly. Stir in salt and pepper. Keep warm over low heat until ready to serve. Serve with chicken.

PER SERVING *1 chicken breast half with 3 tablespoons sauce: 285 cal., 9g fat (4g sat. fat), 89mg chol., 490mg sodium, 12g carb. (3g sugars, 0 fiber), 33g pro.* ***Diabetic Exchanges:*** *4 lean meat, 1 starch.*

Everyone goes for this super moist, garlicky chicken, including my fussy kids. For your holiday buffet or family gathering, serve it with rice or noodles.
—**CAROLE LOTITO** HILLSDALE, NJ

ASIAN GLAZED CHICKEN THIGHS

ASIAN GLAZED CHICKEN THIGHS C FAST FIX

START TO FINISH: 25 MIN.
MAKES: 4 SERVINGS

- **¼ cup rice vinegar**
- **3 tablespoons reduced-sodium soy sauce**
- **2 tablespoons honey**
- **2 teaspoons canola oil**
- **4 boneless skinless chicken thighs (about 1 pound)**
- **3 garlic cloves, minced**
- **1 teaspoon minced fresh gingerroot or ½ teaspoon ground ginger**
- **Toasted sesame seeds, optional**

1. In a small bowl, whisk vinegar, soy sauce and honey until blended. In a large nonstick skillet, heat oil over medium-high heat. Brown chicken on both sides.
2. Add garlic and ginger to skillet; cook and stir 1 minute (do not allow garlic to brown). Stir in vinegar mixture; bring to a boil. Reduce heat; simmer, covered, 8-10 minutes or until a thermometer inserted into chicken reads 170°.
3. Uncover; simmer 1-2 minutes longer or until sauce is slightly thickened. If desired, cut into bite-size pieces and sprinkle with sesame seeds before serving.

PER SERVING *247 cal., 11g fat (2g sat. fat), 76mg chol., 735mg sodium, 15g carb. (14g sugars, 0 fiber), 22g pro.* ***Diabetic Exchanges:*** *3 lean meat, 1 starch, ½ fat.*

HOW-TO

PEEL GARLIC

Using the blade of a chef's knife, crush garlic. Peel away skin. If you don't have a large knife, use a can to crush the garlic.

136

143

147

Turkey Specialties

"I love turkey in any way, shape or form. I feel the same about Swiss chard or any leafy greens, so I decided to combine the two in this delicious, healthy meal. To complete the dinner, I make extra spice rub and toss it with oil and new potatoes, then roast them in the oven along with the turkey."

—**SUSAN BICKTA** KUTZTOWN, PA
about her recipe, Spiced Turkey with Swiss Chard, on page 137

TURKEY & FRUIT SALAD FAST FIX

We have our own turkeys, so I am always on the lookout for good recipes that are a little different. This is a good way to use up leftover turkey.

—**HARRIET STICHTER** MILFORD, IN

START TO FINISH: 25 MIN.
MAKES: 5 SERVINGS

- **¼ cup fat-free plain yogurt**
- **¼ cup reduced-fat mayonnaise**
- **1 tablespoon honey**
- **1 tablespoon spicy brown mustard**
- **½ teaspoon dried marjoram**
- **⅛ teaspoon ground ginger**
- **3 cups cubed cooked turkey breast**
- **1 large red apple, finely chopped**
- **2 celery ribs, thinly sliced**
- **½ cup dried cranberries**
- **¼ cup chopped walnuts, toasted**

Mix first six ingredients. In a large bowl, combine remaining ingredients. Stir in yogurt mixture. Refrigerate, covered, until serving.

PER SERVING *1 cup: 278 cal., 9g fat (1g sat. fat), 77mg chol., 208mg sodium, 23g carb. (17g sugars, 2g fiber), 28g pro.* ***Diabetic Exchanges:*** *3 lean meat, 1 starch, 1 fat.*

TURKEY & FRUIT SALAD

SAUSAGE-TOPPED WHITE PIZZA

SAUSAGE-TOPPED WHITE PIZZA FAST FIX

I love cooking, and I learned from Nana and Mom. Pizza is easily one of my favorite dishes to prepare. I switched up this recipe to make it my own.

—**TRACY BROWN** RIVER EDGE, NJ

START TO FINISH: 30 MIN.
MAKES: 6 SERVINGS

- **2 hot Italian turkey sausage links, casings removed**
- **1 cup reduced-fat ricotta cheese**
- **¼ teaspoon garlic powder**
- **1 prebaked 12-inch thin whole wheat pizza crust**
- **1 medium sweet red pepper, julienned**
- **1 small onion, halved and thinly sliced**
- **½ teaspoon Italian seasoning**
- **¼ teaspoon freshly ground pepper**
- **¼ teaspoon crushed red pepper flakes, optional**
- **½ cup shredded part-skim mozzarella cheese**
- **2 cups arugula or baby spinach**

1. Preheat oven to 450°. In a large skillet, cook and crumble sausage over medium-high heat until no longer pink, 4-6 minutes. Mix ricotta cheese and garlic powder.

2. Place crust on a baking sheet; spread with ricotta cheese mixture. Top with sausage, red pepper and onion; sprinkle with seasonings, then with mozzarella cheese.

3. Bake on a lower oven rack until edge is lightly browned and cheese is melted, 8-10 minutes. Top pizza with arugula.

PER SERVING *1 slice: 242 cal., 8g fat (4g sat. fat), 30mg chol., 504mg sodium, 28g carb. (5g sugars, 4g fiber), 16g pro.* ***Diabetic Exchanges:*** *2 starch, 2 medium-fat meat.*

TOP TIP

If you lack Italian seasoning, you can mix up your own with equal amounts of basil, rosemary, thyme and oregano.

TURKEY SLOPPY JOES FAST FIX

This is a wonderful sandwich for family meals or parties. Once the meat is browned, the mixture simmers for just 10 minutes, so it's perfect for spur-of-the-moment backyard picnics.
—**SUE ANN O'BUCK** SINKING SPRING, PA

START TO FINISH: 25 MIN.
MAKES: 6 SERVINGS

- **1 pound lean ground turkey**
- **¼ cup chopped onion**
- **½ cup no-salt-added ketchup**
- **3 tablespoons barbecue sauce**
- **1 tablespoon white vinegar**
- **1 tablespoon prepared mustard**
- **1½ teaspoons Worcestershire sauce**
- **½ teaspoon celery seed**
- **¼ teaspoon pepper**
- **6 whole wheat hamburger buns, split**

1. In a large skillet, cook and crumble turkey with onion over medium heat until no longer pink, 5-7 minutes.
2. Stir in all remaining ingredients except buns; bring to a boil. Reduce heat; simmer, uncovered, 10 minutes, stirring occasionally. Serve on buns.
PER SERVING *1 sandwich: 259 cal., 9g fat (2g sat. fat), 60mg chol., 395mg sodium, 29g carb. (10g sugars, 4g fiber), 18g pro.* ***Diabetic Exchanges:*** *2 starch, 2 lean meat.*

TURKEY BREAST WITH CRANBERRY BROWN RICE

PREP: 20 MIN. • **BAKE:** 45 MIN. + STANDING
MAKES: 6 SERVINGS

- **2 tablespoons jellied cranberry sauce**
- **2 tablespoons chopped celery**
- **2 tablespoons minced red onion**
- **1 tablespoon olive oil**
- **1½ teaspoons minced fresh parsley**
- **½ teaspoon grated orange peel**
- **⅛ teaspoon garlic powder**
- **½ teaspoon poultry seasoning, divided**
- **1 boneless skinless turkey breast half (2 pounds)**
- **½ teaspoon kosher salt**
- **¼ teaspoon pepper**
- **¼ cup orange juice**

RICE

- **1⅓ cups uncooked long grain brown rice**
- **2⅔ cups water**
- **¼ cup chopped celery**
- **3 tablespoons minced red onion**
- **¾ teaspoon salt**
- **¼ teaspoon pepper**
- **⅔ cup dried cranberries**
- **⅓ cup sliced almonds, toasted**
- **1 tablespoon minced fresh parsley**
- **½ teaspoon grated orange peel**

1. Preheat oven to 350°. Mix first seven ingredients and 1/4 teaspoon poultry seasoning.
2. Place turkey in a greased foil-lined 13x9-in. baking pan; rub with salt, pepper and the remaining poultry seasoning. Spread with cranberry mixture. Roast until a thermometer reads 165°, 45-55 minutes, drizzling with orange juice halfway.
3. Meanwhile, in a saucepan, combine first six rice ingredients; bring to a boil. Reduce heat; simmer, covered, until rice is tender and liquid is absorbed, 40-45 minutes. Stir in remaining ingredients.
4. Remove turkey from oven; tent with foil. Let stand 10 minutes before slicing. Serve with rice.
NOTE *To toast nuts, bake in a shallow pan in a 350° oven for 5-10 minutes or cook in a skillet over low heat until lightly browned, stirring occasionally.*
PER SERVING *5 ounces cooked turkey with 2/3 cup rice: 465 cal., 11g fat (1g sat. fat), 86mg chol., 642mg sodium, 50g carb. (13g sugars, 5g fiber), 42g pro.* ***Diabetic Exchanges:*** *5 lean meat, 3 starch, 1 1/2 fat.*

As a single retiree, I roast a turkey breast half instead of making a whole turkey dinner. This is a perfect meal for anyone cooking for themselves, and it also leaves enough leftovers for sandwiches and tacos.
—**NANCY HEISHMAN** LAS VEGAS, NV

TURKEY BREAST WITH CRANBERRY BROWN RICE

TURKEY MEDALLIONS WITH TOMATO SALAD

TURKEY MEDALLIONS WITH TOMATO SALAD C

This is a quick-to-cook meal using turkey medallions with a crisp coating. The turkey is enhanced by the bright flavor of a simple tomato salad.

—**GILDA LESTER** MILLSBORO, DE

PREP: 30 MIN. • **COOK:** 15 MIN. • **MAKES:** 6 SERVINGS

2 tablespoons olive oil
1 tablespoon red wine vinegar
½ teaspoon sugar
¼ teaspoon dried oregano
¼ teaspoon salt
1 medium green pepper, coarsely chopped
1 celery rib, coarsely chopped
¼ cup chopped red onion
1 tablespoon thinly sliced fresh basil
3 medium tomatoes

TURKEY

1 large egg
2 tablespoons lemon juice
1 cup panko (Japanese) bread crumbs
½ cup grated Parmesan cheese
½ cup finely chopped walnuts
1 teaspoon lemon-pepper seasoning
1 package (20 ounces) turkey breast tenderloins
¼ teaspoon salt
¼ teaspoon pepper
3 tablespoons olive oil, divided
Additional fresh basil

1. Whisk together first five ingredients. Stir in green pepper, celery, onion and basil. Cut tomatoes into wedges; cut wedges in half. Stir into pepper mixture.

2. In a shallow bowl, whisk together egg and lemon juice. In another shallow bowl, toss bread crumbs with cheese, walnuts and lemon pepper.

3. Cut tenderloins crosswise into 1-in. slices; flatten slices with a meat mallet to ½-in. thickness. Sprinkle with salt and pepper. Dip in egg mixture, then in crumb mixture, patting to adhere.

4. In a large skillet, heat 1 tablespoon oil over medium-high heat. Add a third of the turkey; cook until golden brown, 2-3 minutes per side. Repeat twice with remaining oil and turkey. Serve with tomato mixture; sprinkle with basil.

PER SERVING *1 serving: 351 cal., 21g fat (3g sat. fat), 68mg chol., 458mg sodium, 13g carb. (4g sugars, 2g fiber), 29g pro.*

HEALTH TIP *At just 13 grams of carbohydrates, this is a hearty option for anyone looking to cut carbs.*

ORANGE-WILD RICE SALAD WITH SMOKED TURKEY F (PICTURED ON P. 133)

For picnics and potlucks, we make a salad of smoked turkey, wild rice and dried cherries. The citrus dressing is refreshing and light.

—**SHARON TIPTON** CASSELBERRY, FL

PREP: 10 MIN. • **COOK:** 30 MIN. + COOLING • **MAKES:** 4 SERVINGS

2 packages (2¾ ounces each) quick-cooking wild rice
½ pound deli smoked turkey, cubed (about 1¾ cups)
1 cup orange sections
1 celery rib, chopped
⅓ cup dried cherries

DRESSING

6 tablespoons orange juice
2 tablespoons lemon juice
1 tablespoon Dijon mustard
1½ teaspoons olive oil
¼ teaspoon salt
¼ teaspoon freshly ground pepper

1. Cook wild rice according to package directions. Transfer to a large bowl; cool completely.

2. Add turkey, oranges, celery and cherries to cooled rice. In a small bowl, whisk dressing ingredients. Pour over the salad; toss to coat. Refrigerate, covered, until cold.

PER SERVING *1¼ cups: 303 cal., 3g fat (0 sat. fat), 20mg chol., 678mg sodium, 50g carb. (17g sugars, 4g fiber), 19g pro.*

TURKEY MEAT LOAF C

I first made this recipe when my husband and I had to start watching our diets. Since then, I've been asked to make this many times.

—RUBY RATH NEW HAVEN, IN

PREP: 15 MIN. • **BAKE:** 1 HOUR + STANDING
MAKES: 10 SERVINGS

- **1 cup quick-cooking oats**
- **1 medium onion, chopped**
- **½ cup shredded carrot**
- **½ cup fat-free milk**
- **¼ cup egg substitute**
- **2 tablespoons ketchup**
- **1 teaspoon garlic powder**
- **¼ teaspoon pepper**
- **2 pounds ground turkey breast**

TOPPING

- **¼ cup ketchup**
- **¼ cup quick-cooking oats**

1. Preheat oven to 350°. Combine first eight ingredients. Add turkey; mix lightly but thoroughly.

2. Transfer to a 9x5-in. loaf pan coated with cooking spray. Mix topping ingredients; spread over loaf. Bake until a thermometer reads 165°, 60-65 minutes. Let stand 10 minutes before slicing.

PER SERVING *1 slice: 195 cal., 8g fat (2g sat. fat), 63mg chol., 188mg sodium, 12g carb. (4g sugars, 1g fiber), 20g pro.* ***Diabetic Exchanges:*** *3 lean meat, 1 starch.*

TURKEY MEAT LOAF

SPICED TURKEY WITH SWISS CHARD C (PICTURED ON P. 132)

I love turkey in any way, shape or form. I feel the same about Swiss chard or any leafy greens, so I decided to combine the two in this delicious, healthy meal. To complete the dinner, I make extra spice rub and toss it with oil and new potatoes, then roast them in the oven along with the turkey.

—SUSAN BICKTA KUTZTOWN, PA

PREP: 25 MIN. + CHILLING • **BAKE:** 20 MIN. + STANDING
MAKES: 4 SERVINGS

- **¾ teaspoon smoked paprika**
- **½ teaspoon dried parsley flakes**
- **½ teaspoon kosher salt**
- **½ teaspoon freshly ground pepper**
- **¼ teaspoon onion powder**
- **Pinch cayenne pepper**
- **1 package (20 ounces) turkey breast tenderloins**
- **1 tablespoon olive oil**

SWISS CHARD

- **1 tablespoon butter**
- **1 large bunch Swiss chard, trimmed and chopped**
- **¾ cup reduced-sodium chicken broth**
- **⅛ teaspoon freshly ground pepper**
- **Minced fresh parsley, optional**

1. Preheat oven to 375°. Mix first six ingredients; rub over tenderloins. Refrigerate, covered, 30 minutes.

2. In a large ovenproof skillet, heat the oil over medium-high heat, brown tenderloins on all sides. Transfer skillet to oven; roast turkey until a thermometer reads 165°, 20-25 minutes. Remove from pan; tent with foil. Let stand 10 minutes before slicing.

3. In same skillet, heat butter over medium-high heat; saute chard 5 minutes. Stir in broth and pepper. Reduce heat to medium. Cook, covered, until tender, about 5 minutes, stirring occasionally. Serve with turkey. If desired, sprinkle turkey with parsley.

PER SERVING *3 ounces cooked turkey and ½ cup chard: 228 cal., 8g fat (2g sat. fat), 64mg chol., 633mg sodium, 4g carb. (1g sugars, 2g fiber), 37g pro.*

HEALTH TIP *The dark green color of Swiss chard is a clue that it's an excellent source of immune-boosting vitamin A.*

TOP TIP

Smoked paprika's rich, smoky and slightly sweet flavor adds complexity to dishes. The spice is especially good in lentil and bean soups and vegetable recipes, where it lends a robust, meaty flavor. You also could use it in recipes that call for ground chipotle pepper. Just add cayenne or chili powder to boost the heat—if desired.

GREEK SAUSAGE PITAS

GREEK SAUSAGE PITAS

FAST FIX

I nicknamed my sandwich Thor's Pita because it's robust and lightning-quick. The ingredient amounts don't really matter. Use more or less depending on what you have.

—TERESA ALEKSANDROV YPSILANTI, MI

START TO FINISH: 20 MIN.
MAKES: 4 SERVINGS

- **4 whole wheat pita breads (6 inches)**
- **1 cup plain yogurt**
- **2 green onions, chopped**
- **2 tablespoons minced fresh parsley**
- **1 teaspoon lemon juice**
- **1 garlic clove, minced**
- **¾ pound Italian turkey sausage links or other sausage links of your choice, casings removed**
- **1 medium cucumber, seeded and chopped**
- **1 medium tomato, chopped**
- **Additional minced fresh parsley**

1. Preheat oven to 325°. Wrap pita breads in foil; warm in oven while preparing toppings.

2. In a small bowl, mix yogurt, green onions, parsley, lemon juice and garlic. In a large skillet, cook sausage over medium heat 4-6 minutes or until no longer pink, breaking into crumbles.

3. To assemble, spoon sausage over pitas. Top with cucumber, tomato and yogurt mixture; sprinkle with additional parsley.

PER SERVING *1 open-faced sandwich: 309 cal., 9g fat (3g sat. fat), 39mg chol., 667mg sodium, 42g carb. (5g sugars, 6g fiber), 19g pro.* ***Diabetic Exchanges:*** *3 starch, 2 lean meat.*

MIGHTY HERO SANDWICH

FAST FIX

My friend Valerie is a gracious hostess who once served us this Dagwood sandwich. It's easy and colorful, and the marinated veggies give it all kinds of oomph.

—KELLEY BOYCE TULSA, OK

START TO FINISH: 30 MIN.
MAKES: 8 SERVINGS

- **¼ cup balsamic vinegar**
- **1 tablespoon minced fresh parsley**
- **1 tablespoon olive oil**
- **2 garlic cloves, minced**
- **¼ teaspoon dried oregano**
- **¼ teaspoon pepper**
- **1 large tomato, halved and sliced**
- **1 cup sliced fresh mushrooms**
- **2 thin slices red onion, separated into rings**
- **1 round loaf (1 pound) sourdough bread**
- **1 small zucchini, shredded**
- **½ pound sliced deli turkey**
- **6 slices part-skim mozzarella cheese**

1. In a large bowl, whisk the first six ingredients until blended. Add tomato, mushrooms and onion; toss gently to coat. Let stand 15 minutes.

2. Meanwhile, cut loaf horizontally in half. Hollow out both parts, leaving a 1/2-in.-thick shell (save removed bread for another use).

3. Drain marinated vegetables, reserving marinade. Brush marinade over inside of bread halves. Top the bottom half with the zucchini. Layer with half of the marinated vegetables, 1/4 pound turkey and three slices cheese; repeat layers. Replace top of loaf. Cut into wedges.

PER SERVING *1 piece: 233 cal., 7g fat (3g sat. fat), 24mg chol., 636mg sodium, 26g carb. (6g sugars, 1g fiber), 16g pro.* ***Diabetic Exchanges:*** *2 starch, 2 lean meat, 1/2 fat.*

MIGHTY HERO SANDWICH

TURKEY TENDERLOINS WITH SHALLOT BERRY SAUCE C

This dish is so easy to make and comes together in a snap! The original recipe called for chicken and apricot, but I switched out turkey and berry jam to use up some Thanksgiving leftovers. I was thrilled with how well it turned out.
—**KENDRA DOSS** COLORADO SPRINGS, CO

PREP: 15 MIN. • **COOK:** 25 MIN.
MAKES: 8 SERVINGS

- **4 turkey breast tenderloins (12 ounces each)**
- **½ teaspoon salt**
- **½ teaspoon pepper**
- **1 tablespoon olive oil**
- **¼ cup chicken broth**

SAUCE

- **1 tablespoon olive oil**
- **5 shallots, thinly sliced**
- **¼ teaspoon salt**
- **¼ teaspoon pepper**
- **½ cup chicken broth**
- **¼ cup balsamic vinegar**
- **3 tablespoons seedless raspberry jam**

1. Sprinkle the turkey with salt and pepper. In a large skillet, heat oil over medium heat; brown tenderloins in batches. Cook, covered, 8-10 minutes longer or until a thermometer reads 165°. Remove from pan; keep warm.
2. Add broth to skillet; increase heat to medium-high. Cook, stirring to loosen browned bits from the pan; remove from heat.
3. Meanwhile, in another skillet, heat oil over medium-high heat. Add shallots, salt and pepper; cook and stir until shallots are tender. Add broth, stirring to loosen browned bits from pan. Stir in vinegar and jam. Bring to a boil; cook until slightly thickened, 4-5 minutes, stirring occasionally.
4. Slice tenderloins; drizzle with pan juices. Serve with berry sauce.
PER SERVING *1 serving: 258 cal., 6g fat (0 sat. fat), 68mg chol., 414mg sodium, 12g carb. (8g sugars, 0 fiber), 43g pro.* ***Diabetic Exchanges:*** *5 lean meat, 1 starch, 1/2 fat.*

SAUSAGE & FETA STUFFED TOMATOES

SAUSAGE & FETA STUFFED TOMATOES

C FAST FIX

START TO FINISH: 25 MIN.
MAKES: 4 SERVINGS

- **3 Italian turkey sausage links (4 ounces each), casings removed**
- **1 cup crumbled feta cheese, divided**
- **8 plum tomatoes**
- **¼ teaspoon salt**
- **¼ teaspoon pepper**
- **3 tablespoons balsamic vinegar**
- **Minced fresh parsley**

1. Preheat oven to 350°. In a large skillet, cook sausage over medium heat 4-6 minutes or until no longer pink, breaking into crumbles. Transfer to a small bowl; stir in 1/2 cup cheese.
2. Cut tomatoes in half lengthwise. Scoop out pulp, leaving a 1/2-in. shell; discard pulp. Sprinkle the tomatoes with salt and pepper; transfer to an ungreased 13x9-in. baking dish. Spoon sausage mixture into tomato shells; drizzle with vinegar. Sprinkle with remaining cheese.
3. Bake, uncovered, 10-12 minutes or until heated through. Sprinkle with parsley.
PER SERVING *4 stuffed tomato halves: 200 cal., 10g fat (4g sat. fat), 46mg chol., 777mg sodium, 12g carb. (8g sugars, 3g fiber), 16g pro.* ***Diabetic Exchanges:*** *2 medium-fat meat, 1 vegetable, 1/2 starch.*

I love this recipe because it looks beautiful, tastes delicious, and is a very healthy alternative to turkey and dressing! Chicken broth may be substituted if turkey broth is not available. —JOYCE CONWAY WESTERVILLE, OH

MUSHROOM-STUFFED TURKEY TENDERLOINS

MUSHROOM-STUFFED TURKEY TENDERLOINS

F C

PREP: 30 MIN. • **BAKE:** 15 MIN.
MAKES: 4 SERVINGS

- **1 package (8 ounces) frozen artichoke hearts, thawed and chopped**
- **½ pound baby portobello mushrooms, chopped**
- **2½ cups reduced-sodium chicken broth, divided**
- **2 tablespoons lemon juice**
- **¼ cup panko (Japanese) bread crumbs**
- **1 package (20 ounces) turkey breast tenderloins**
- **½ teaspoon salt**
- **¼ teaspoon pepper**
- **2 tablespoons all-purpose flour**
- **1 teaspoon grated lemon peel**

1. Preheat oven to 400°. Place the artichoke hearts, mushrooms, 1/2 cup broth and the lemon juice in a large saucepan; bring to a boil. Reduce heat; simmer, uncovered, until mushrooms are tender and liquid is evaporated, 7-9 minutes. Stir in bread crumbs; cool slightly.

2. Cut each tenderloin horizontally through the center to within 1/4 in. of the opposite edge; open flat. Using a sharp knife, remove white tendons. Cover with plastic wrap; pound each with a meat mallet to even thickness. Remove plastic; spread tops with artichoke mixture. Starting at a long side, roll up jelly-roll style; tie at 3-in. intervals with kitchen string.

3. Place 1 in. apart in a 13x9-in. baking pan, seam side down; pour 1 cup broth over top. Sprinkle with salt and pepper. Bake, uncovered, until a thermometer reads 165°, about 15-20 minutes.

4. Remove turkey from pan; tent with foil and let stand 5 minutes. Meanwhile, in a small saucepan, whisk flour and remaining broth until smooth; stir in pan juices. Bring to a boil; cook and stir until gravy is thickened, 2-3 minutes.

5. Remove string; cut tenderloins into slices. Serve with gravy; sprinkle with lemon peel.

PER SERVING *1 serving: 228 cal., 3g fat (0 sat. fat), 56mg chol., 776mg sodium, 14g carb. (3g sugars, 4g fiber), 41g pro.* ***Diabetic Exchanges:*** *4 lean meat, 1 vegetable, 1/2 starch.*

GRILLED ITALIAN TURKEY BURGERS FAST FIX

These turkey burgers are awesome at a cookout, especially if you're trying to eat healthy. Try topping them with a little marinara or steak sauce.

—**DARLA ANDREWS** SCHERTZ, TX

START TO FINISH: 30 MIN.
MAKES: 4 SERVINGS

- **½ pound sliced baby portobello mushrooms**
- **2 cups chopped fresh spinach**

BURGERS

- **2 large egg whites, lightly beaten**
- **½ cup panko (Japanese) bread crumbs**
- **2 tablespoons minced fresh parsley**
- **2 tablespoons ketchup**
- **1 tablespoon brown sugar**
- **1 tablespoon Worcestershire sauce**
- **2 teaspoons paprika**
- **2 teaspoons prepared pesto**
- **½ teaspoon garlic powder**
- **1 pound lean ground turkey**
- **4 slices reduced-fat provolone cheese**
- **4 whole wheat hamburger buns, split**

1. Place a large nonstick skillet coated with cooking spray over medium-high heat. Add mushrooms; cook and stir until tender, 3-4 minutes. Add the spinach; cook and stir just until wilted.

2. Mix first nine burger ingredients. Add turkey; mix lightly but thoroughly. Shape into four 1/2-in.-thick patties.

3. Place the burgers on an oiled grill rack over medium heat. Grill burgers, covered, until a thermometer reads 165°, 4-6 minutes per side. Top with cheese; grill, covered, until cheese is melted, 1-2 minutes.

4. Serve on buns. Top with mushroom mixture.

PER SERVING *1 burger: 423 cal., 16g fat (5g sat. fat), 88mg chol., 663mg sodium, 37g carb. (11g sugars, 5g fiber), 36g pro.* ***Diabetic Exchanges:*** *4 lean meat, 2 starch, 1 vegetable, 1 fat.*

GRILLED ITALIAN TURKEY BURGERS

SMOKED TURKEY AND APPLE SALAD FAST FIX

This refreshing salad is a great main course for a summer lunch or light dinner. The dressing's Dijon flavor goes nicely with the turkey, and the apples add crunch.

—**CAROLYN JOHNS** LACEY, WA

START TO FINISH: 20 MIN.
MAKES: 4 SERVINGS

- **5 tablespoons olive oil**
- **2 tablespoons cider vinegar**
- **1 tablespoon Dijon mustard**
- **½ teaspoon lemon-pepper seasoning**

SALAD

- **6 to 8 cups watercress or torn romaine**
- **1 medium carrot, julienned**
- **10 cherry tomatoes, halved**
- **8 ounces sliced deli smoked turkey, cut into strips**
- **4 medium apples, sliced**
- **⅓ cup chopped walnuts, toasted**

1. For dressing, whisk together the first four ingredients.

2. Place watercress on a platter; top with carrot, tomatoes, turkey and apples. Drizzle with dressing; top with walnuts. Serve immediately.

PER SERVING *1 serving: 382 cal., 25g fat (3g sat. fat), 20mg chol., 576mg sodium, 27g carb. (18g sugars, 7g fiber), 15g pro.*

SMOKED TURKEY AND APPLE SALAD

SMOTHERED TURKEY CUTLETS

SMOTHERED TURKEY CUTLETS

Why have turkey just for Thanksgiving? This is an easy recipe that makes it feel like the holidays any day of the week.

—**LISA KEYS** KENNET SQUARE, PA

PREP: 30 MIN. • **BAKE:** 5 MIN
MAKES: 4 SERVINGS

- **1 cup mild chunky salsa**
- **¼ cup dried cranberries**
- **1 tablespoon chopped fresh cilantro**
- **1 cup orange sections, cut into 1-inch pieces**
- **2 tablespoons all-purpose flour**
- **1 teaspoon ground cumin**
- **1 large egg**
- **1 tablespoon water**
- **1 cup panko (Japanese) bread crumbs**
- **¼ cup grated Parmesan cheese**
- **4 turkey breast cutlets (2½ ounces each)**
- **½ teaspoon pepper**
- **⅛ teaspoon salt**
- **2 tablespoons olive oil, divided**
- **½ cup shredded sharp cheddar cheese**
- **½ medium ripe avocado, cubed**
- **Additional chopped cilantro**
- **Reduced-fat sour cream, optional**

1. Preheat oven to 350°. Mix salsa, cranberries and cilantro; gently stir in oranges. In a shallow bowl, mix flour and cumin. In another shallow bowl, whisk together egg and water. In a third bowl, toss bread crumbs with Parmesan cheese.

2. Sprinkle cutlets with pepper and salt; coat lightly with flour mixture, shaking off excess. Dip in egg mixture, then in crumb mixture, patting firmly.

3. In a large skillet, heat 1 tablespoon oil over medium heat; add 2 cutlets, cook until golden brown, 1-2 minutes per side. Transfer cutlets to a foil-lined baking sheet. Repeat with remaining oil and turkey.

4. Sprinkle cutlets with cheddar cheese; bake until cheese is melted and turkey is no longer pink, 4-6 minutes. Top with avocado, salsa mixture, additional cilantro and, if desired, sour cream.

PER SERVING *1 serving: 401 cal., 19g fat (5g sat. fat), 106mg chol., 638mg sodium, 31g carb. (12g sugars, 4g fiber), 26g pro.*

BARBECUED BASIL TURKEY BURGERS FAST FIX

(PICTURED ON P. 133)

My husband built me a patio planter for herbs, so I made a turkey burger featuring fresh basil. We add toppings like provolone, red onion and tomatoes.

—**DENISE MILLER** GREELEY, CO

START TO FINISH: 30 MIN.
MAKES: 4 SERVINGS

- **¼ cup chopped fresh basil**
- **3 tablespoons mesquite smoke-flavored barbecue sauce**
- **2 tablespoons quick-cooking oats or oat bran**
- **1 garlic clove, minced**
- **¼ teaspoon garlic salt**
- **⅛ teaspoon pepper**
- **1 pound lean ground turkey**
- **4 whole wheat or multigrain hamburger buns, split**
- **Optional toppings: sliced provolone cheese, red onion slices, sliced tomato, fresh basil leaves and additional barbecue sauce**

1. In a large bowl, combine first six ingredients. Add turkey; mix lightly but thoroughly. Shape into four ½-in.-thick patties.

2. On a lightly greased grill rack, grill burgers, covered, over medium heat 5-7 minutes on each side or until a thermometer reads 165°. Grill buns over medium heat, cut side down, for 30-60 seconds or until toasted. Serve burgers on buns with toppings of your choice.

PER SERVING *1 burger: 315 cal., 11g fat (3g sat. fat), 78mg chol., 482mg sodium, 29g carb. (8g sugars, 4g fiber), 27g pro.* ***Diabetic Exchanges:*** *3 lean meat, 2 starch.*

TOP TIP

Lean ground turkey (93% lean) contains 53% less fat and 38% less saturated fat than regular ground turkey (85% lean). Be sure to oil the grill rack to keep lean meats like turkey burgers and seafood from sticking.

ITALIAN SAUSAGE ORZO

This light dish is perfect for any night of the week, and it looks as good as it tastes! If you have leftover sauteed mushrooms or other vegetables, toss them in as well.

—**LISA SPEER** PALM BEACH, FL

PREP: 15 MIN. • **COOK:** 25 MIN.
MAKES: 6 SERVINGS

- **8 cups water**
- **3 teaspoons reduced-sodium chicken bouillon granules**
- **1½ cups uncooked whole wheat orzo pasta (about 8 ounces)**
- **1 package (19½ ounces) Italian turkey sausage links, casings removed**
- **½ cup chopped sweet onion**
- **2 garlic cloves, minced**
- **3 plum tomatoes, chopped**
- **½ cup chopped roasted sweet red pepper**
- **⅛ teaspoon salt**
- **⅛ teaspoon pepper**
- **⅛ teaspoon crushed red pepper flakes**
- **⅓ cup chopped fresh basil**
- **¼ cup grated Parmesan cheese**

1. In a large saucepan, bring water and bouillon to a boil. Stir in orzo; return to a boil. Cook until al dente, 8-10 minutes. Drain orzo, reserving ¾ cup cooking liquid.

2. In a large skillet coated with cooking spray, cook and crumble sausage with onion and garlic over medium heat until no longer pink, 6-8 minutes. Stir in tomatoes, roasted pepper, salt, pepper, pepper flakes and orzo. Heat through over medium-low heat; stir in reserved cooking liquid to moisten if desired. Remove from heat; stir in bail and cheese.

PER SERVING *1 cup: 265 cal., 7g fat (2g sat. fat), 37mg chol., 623mg sodium, 32g carb. (2g sugars, 7g fiber), 16g pro.* ***Diabetic Exchanges:*** *2 starch, 2 lean meat.*

ITALIAN SAUSAGE ORZO

TURKEY CURRY WITH RICE

TURKEY CURRY WITH RICE FAST FIX

When I have leftover turkey and a hankering for non-holiday food, I make turkey curry with carrots, cauliflower and mango chutney to spoon over rice.

—NANCY HEISHMAN LAS VEGAS, NV

START TO FINISH: 30 MIN. • **MAKES:** 6 SERVINGS

1⅓ cups chicken broth
2 tablespoons curry powder
2 tablespoons minced fresh cilantro
3 garlic cloves, minced
¾ teaspoon salt
½ teaspoon ground cardamom
½ teaspoon pepper
3 medium carrots, thinly sliced
1 medium onion, finely chopped
1 package (16 ounces) frozen cauliflower, thawed
3 cups chopped cooked turkey
½ cup mango chutney
2 teaspoons all-purpose flour
1 cup coconut milk
4½ cups hot cooked rice
Additional mango chutney, optional

1. In a large saucepan, mix the first seven ingredients. Add carrots and onion; bring to a boil. Reduce heat; simmer, covered, 3-5 minutes or until carrots are crisp-tender. Add cauliflower; cook, covered, 4-6 minutes longer or until vegetables are tender.

2. Stir in turkey and chutney; heat through. In a small bowl, mix flour and coconut milk until smooth; stir into turkey mixture. Bring to a boil, stirring constantly; cook and stir 1-2 minutes or until slightly thickened. Serve with rice and, if desired, additional chutney.

PER SERVING *1 cup turkey mixture with 3/4 cup rice: 363 cal., 9g fat (7g sat. fat), 1mg chol., 787mg sodium, 64g carb. (16g sugars, 5g fiber), 7g pro.*

RED BEANS AND SAUSAGE FAST FIX

Turkey sausage makes this traditional dish more health-conscious, while a zesty blend of seasonings adds some spark.

—CATHY WEBSTER MORRIS, IL

START TO FINISH: 25 MIN. • **MAKES:** 6 SERVINGS

1 tablespoon canola oil
1 medium green pepper, diced
1 medium onion, chopped
2 garlic cloves, minced
2 cans (16 ounces each) kidney beans, rinsed and drained
½ pound smoked turkey sausage, sliced
1 teaspoon Cajun seasoning
⅛ teaspoon hot pepper sauce
¾ cup water
Hot cooked rice, optional

1. In a large saucepan, heat oil over medium heat; saute pepper and onion until tender. Add garlic; cook and stir 1 minute.

2. Stir in the beans, sausage, Cajun seasoning, pepper sauce and water; bring to a boil. Reduce the heat; simmer, uncovered, until heated through, 5-7 minutes. If desired, serve with rice.

PER SERVING *2/3 cup bean mixture: 212 cal., 4g fat (1g sat. fat), 24mg chol., 706mg sodium, 27g carb. (4g sugars, 8g fiber), 16g pro.* ***Diabetic Exchanges:*** *2 lean meat, 1 1/2 starch, 1/2 fat.*

RED BEANS AND SAUSAGE

BULGUR JAMBALAYA

BULGUR JAMBALAYA FAST FIX

I like making this dish because it allows me to stay on track for my weight loss without giving up foods I love.

—**NICHOLAS MONFRE** OAK RIDGE, NJ

START TO FINISH: 30 MIN. • **MAKES:** 4 SERVINGS

- **8 ounces boneless skinless chicken breasts, cut into ¾-inch pieces**
- **1 teaspoon Cajun seasoning**
- **2 teaspoons olive oil**
- **6 ounces smoked turkey sausage, sliced**
- **1 medium sweet red pepper, diced**
- **2 celery ribs, diced**
- **1 small onion, chopped**
- **½ cup no-salt-added tomato sauce**
- **1 cup bulgur**
- **1 cup reduced-sodium chicken broth**
- **¾ cup water**
- **¼ teaspoon cayenne pepper, optional**

1. Toss chicken with Cajun seasoning. In a large saucepan, heat oil over medium heat; saute chicken until browned, 2-3 minutes. Remove from pan.

2. In the same pan, saute the sausage until browned, 1-2 minutes. Add red pepper, celery and onion; cook and stir 2 minutes. Stir in tomato sauce; cook 30 seconds. Stir in bulgur, broth, water, chicken and, if desired, cayenne; bring to a boil. Reduce heat; simmer, covered, until bulgur is tender and liquid is almost absorbed, about 10 minutes, stirring occasionally.

PER SERVING *1 cup: 287 cal., 6g fat (2g sat. fat), 58mg chol., 751mg sodium, 34g carb. (5g sugars, 6g fiber), 24g pro.* ***Diabetic Exchanges:*** *3 lean meat, 2 starch, ½ fat.*

ASPARAGUS TURKEY STIR-FRY C FAST FIX

When people try this dish, they ask for the recipe, just as I did when I first tasted it at my friend's house. Coated with a delicious lemon sauce, this simple skillet dinner is sure to satisfy on the busiest of nights. It a great way to use up leftover turkey.

—**MAY EVANS** CORINTH, KY

START TO FINISH: 20 MIN. • **MAKES:** 4 SERVINGS

- **2 teaspoons cornstarch**
- **¼ cup chicken broth**
- **1 tablespoon lemon juice**
- **1 teaspoon soy sauce**
- **1 pound turkey breast tenderloins, cut into ½-inch strips**
- **1 garlic clove, minced**
- **2 tablespoons canola oil, divided**
- **1 pound fresh asparagus, trimmed and cut into 1½-inch pieces**
- **1 jar (2 ounces) sliced pimientos, drained**

1. In a small bowl, combine the cornstarch, broth, lemon juice and soy sauce until smooth; set aside. In a large skillet or wok, stir-fry turkey and garlic in 1 tablespoon oil until meat is no longer pink; remove and keep warm.

2. Stir-fry asparagus in remaining oil until crisp-tender. Add pimientos. Stir broth mixture and add to the pan; cook and stir for 1 minute or until thickened. Return turkey to the pan; heat through.

PER SERVING *1¼ cups: 205 cal., 9g fat (1g sat. fat), 56mg chol., 204mg sodium, 5g carb. (1g sugars, 1g fiber), 28g pro.* ***Diabetic Exchanges:*** *3 lean meat, 1½ fat, 1 vegetable.*

ASPARAGUS TURKEY STIR-FRY

ZUCCHINI CRUSTED PIZZA C

Great flavor, nutritious, versatile, easy to prep ahead, fun to make with kids, quadruples nicely. What's not to like?

—**RUTH HARTUNIAN-ALUMBAUGH** WILLIMANTIC, CT

PREP: 25 MIN. • **BAKE:** 25 MIN.
MAKES: 6 SERVINGS

- **2 large eggs, lightly beaten**
- **2 cups shredded zucchini (about 2 medium), squeezed dry**
- **½ cup shredded part-skim mozzarella cheese**
- **½ cup grated Parmesan cheese**
- **¼ cup all-purpose flour**
- **1 tablespoon olive oil**
- **1 tablespoon minced fresh basil**
- **1 teaspoon minced fresh thyme**

TOPPINGS

- **1 jar (12 ounces) roasted sweet red peppers, julienned**
- **1 cup shredded part-skim mozzarella cheese**
- **½ cup sliced turkey pepperoni**

1. Preheat oven to 450°. Mix first eight ingredients; transfer to a 12-in. pizza pan coated generously with cooking spray. Spread mixture to an 11-in. circle.
2. Bake mixture until light golden brown, 13-16 minutes. Reduce oven setting to 400°. Add toppings. Bake until cheese is melted, 10-12 minutes.

PER SERVING *1 slice: 219 cal., 12g fat (5g sat. fat), 95mg chol., 680mg sodium, 10g carb. (4g sugars, 1g fiber), 14g pro.* ***Diabetic Exchanges:*** *2 medium-fat meat, ½ starch, ½ fat.*

ZUCCHINI CRUSTED PIZZA

A Waldorf salad inspired my pasta dish. I use smoked turkey, apples, strawberries and orecchiette. Rotisserie chicken and other fruits would also taste great.
—**SONYA LABBE** WEST HOLLYWOOD, CA

MODERN WALDORF SALAD

MODERN WALDORF SALAD FAST FIX

START TO FINISH: 30 MIN.
MAKES: 4 SERVINGS

- **2 cups uncooked orecchiette or small tube pasta (about 6 ounces)**
- **¼ cup reduced-fat plain yogurt**
- **2 tablespoons mayonnaise**
- **2 tablespoons 2% milk**
- **4 teaspoons Dijon mustard**
- **½ teaspoon dried thyme, optional**
- **1 medium apple, chopped**
- **1 tablespoon lemon juice**
- **½ pound thick-sliced deli smoked turkey, cut into bite-size pieces**
- **1 cup quartered fresh strawberries**
- **1 celery rib, sliced**
- **¼ cup toasted chopped walnuts, optional**

1. Cook pasta according to package directions. Drain; rinse with cold water and drain well.
2. Meanwhile, in a small bowl, mix yogurt, mayonnaise, milk, mustard and, if desired, thyme until blended. Toss apple with lemon juice.
3. In a large bowl, combine pasta, apple, turkey, strawberries and celery. Add dressing; toss gently to coat. If desired, sprinkle with walnuts. Refrigerate until serving.

PER SERVING *1½ cups: 313 cal., 8g fat (1g sat. fat), 24mg chol., 606mg sodium, 42g carb. (8g sugars, 3g fiber), 19g pro.* ***Diabetic Exchanges:*** *2 starch, 2 lean meat, 1 fat, ½ fruit.*

TURKEY TOSSED SALAD C

FAST FIX (PICTURED ON P. 133)

I played around with my best friend's recipe for chicken salad until I had one that was perfect for Thanksgiving leftovers. This salad is light and refreshing—the perfect antidote for heavy holiday eating.

—**KRISTY DILLS** FLINTSTONE, GA

START TO FINISH: 25 MIN.
MAKES: 12 SERVINGS

- **1 package (10 ounces) ready-to-serve salad greens**
- **4 cups shredded cooked turkey**
- **1 cup crumbled blue cheese**
- **½ cup sliced almonds**
- **½ cup dried cranberries**
- **¼ cup chopped celery**
- **¼ cup chopped red onion**
- **1 snack-size cup (4 ounces) mandarin oranges**
- **¼ cup orange juice**
- **2 tablespoons sugar**
- **2 tablespoons olive oil**
- **2 tablespoons cider vinegar**
- **Dash each salt and pepper**

1. In a large bowl, combine first seven ingredients. Drain oranges, reserving syrup, and place in bowl.

2. In a small bowl, whisk together remaining ingredients and reserved syrup; toss with salad. Serve immediately.

PER SERVING *1½ cups: 199 cal., 10g fat (3g sat. fat), 44mg chol., 211mg sodium, 11g carb. (8g sugars, 1g fiber), 17g pro.* ***Diabetic Exchanges:*** *2 lean meat, 2 fat, 1 vegetable.*

ASIAN LETTUCE WRAPS C FAST FIX

This recipe replicates the lettuce wraps found in national restaurants, but it's healthier! The filling can be made up to an hour ahead and chilled.

—**LINDA ROWLEY** RICHARDSON, TX

START TO FINISH: 25 MIN.
MAKES: 4 SERVINGS

- **1 tablespoon canola oil**
- **1 pound lean ground turkey**
- **1 jalapeno pepper, seeded and minced**
- **2 green onions, thinly sliced**
- **2 garlic cloves, minced**
- **2 tablespoons minced fresh basil**
- **2 tablespoons lime juice**
- **2 tablespoons reduced-sodium soy sauce**
- **1 to 2 tablespoons chili garlic sauce**
- **1 tablespoon sugar or sugar substitute blend equivalent to 1 tablespoon sugar**
- **12 Bibb or Boston lettuce leaves**
- **1 medium cucumber, julienned**
- **1 medium carrot, julienned**
- **2 cups bean sprouts**

1. In a large skillet, heat oil over medium heat. Add turkey; cook 6-8 minutes or until no longer pink, breaking into crumbles. Add the jalapeno, green onions and garlic; cook 2 minutes longer. Stir in basil, lime juice, soy sauce, chili garlic sauce and sugar; heat through.

2. To serve, place turkey mixture in lettuce leaves; top with cucumber, carrot and bean sprouts. Fold lettuce over filling.

PER SERVING *3 lettuce wraps: 259 cal., 12g fat (3g sat. fat), 78mg chol., 503mg sodium, 12g carb. (6g sugars, 3g fiber), 26g pro.* ***Diabetic Exchanges:*** *3 lean meat, 1 vegetable, ½ starch, ½ fat.*

ASIAN LETTUCE WRAPS

160

165

164

Pork, Ham & More

"These pork chops are perfect for a summer dinner party. They're beautiful and easy, and they have a lot of flavors. I recommend using bone-in pork chops."

—**CLARK CASTLE** NEW ORLEANS, LA
about his recipe, Jalapeno-Peach Pork Chops, on page 150

JALAPENO-PEACH PORK CHOPS FAST FIX

(PICTURED ON P. 148)

These pork chops are perfect for a summer dinner party. They're beautiful and easy, and they have a lot of flavors. I recommend using bone-in pork chops.

—**CLARK CASTLE** NEW ORLEANS, LA

START TO FINISH: 25 MIN.
MAKES: 4 SERVINGS

- **4 bone-in pork loin chops (¾ inch thick and 7 ounces each)**
- **½ teaspoon salt**
- **¼ teaspoon pepper**
- **1 tablespoon butter**
- **1 tablespoon olive oil**
- **2 medium ripe peaches, peeled and sliced**
- **¼ cup pepper jelly**
- **2 teaspoons minced seeded jalapeno pepper, optional**

1. Sprinkle chops with salt and pepper. In a skillet, heat butter and oil over medium heat; cook chops until a thermometer reads 145°, 3-5 minutes per side. Remove from pan; keep warm.

2. Add peaches, pepper jelly and, if desired, jalapeno to pan; cook and stir until the peaches are softened, 2-3 minutes. Serve with chops.

PER SERVING *1 pork chop with 1/4 cup peach mixture: 345 cal., 15g fat (5g sat. fat), 94mg chol., 387mg sodium, 22g carb. (17g sugars, 1g fiber), 31g pro.*

HOW-TO

PEEL PEACHES

1. Carefully place peaches in boiling water for 10-20 seconds or until skins split.

2. Remove with a slotted spoon. Immediately place in ice water. Use a paring knife to peel. If stubborn areas won't peel, boil fruit a few seconds longer.

GRILLED PORK TACOS

GRILLED PORK TACOS FAST FIX

My family raves about this moist pork with smoked paprika and pineapple. I dish it up next to brown rice and a salad of avocado and tomatoes.

—**E. GELESKY** BALA CYNWYD, PA

START TO FINISH: 30 MIN.
MAKES: 4 SERVINGS

- **1 pound boneless pork ribeye chops, cut into ¾-inch cubes**
- **2 tablespoons plus 2 teaspoons lime juice, divided**
- **1 teaspoon smoked or regular paprika**
- **½ teaspoon salt**
- **¼ teaspoon pepper**
- **¾ cup canned black beans, rinsed and drained**
- **½ cup canned unsweetened pineapple tidbits plus 1 tablespoon reserved juice**
- **2 tablespoons finely chopped red onion**
- **2 tablespoons chopped fresh cilantro**
- **4 flour tortillas (6 to 8 inches), warmed**
- **Reduced-fat sour cream or plain yogurt, optional**

1. In a large bowl, toss pork with 2 tablespoons lime juice and the seasonings; let stand 5 minutes. Meanwhile, in a small bowl, mix beans, pineapple with reserved juice, onion, cilantro and remaining lime juice.

2. Thread pork onto four metal or soaked wooden skewers. Moisten a paper towel with cooking oil; using long-handled tongs, rub on grill rack to coat lightly. Grill kabobs, covered, over medium heat 6-8 minutes or until tender, turning occasionally.

3. Remove pork from skewers; serve in tortillas. Top with bean mixture and, if desired, sour cream.

PER SERVING *1 taco with 1/4 cup salsa: 383 cal., 16g fat (6g sat. fat), 66mg chol., 636mg sodium, 31g carb. (6g sugars, 4g fiber), 27g pro.* ***Diabetic Exchanges:*** *3 starch, 3 medium-fat meat.*

MELON ARUGULA SALAD WITH HAM FAST FIX

My summer dining guests always appreciate the healthy antioxidants in this melon salad. I like to save my melon rinds, cut them into large wedges and use them as a serving dish. It makes a lovely presentation and is easy to clean up.
—**SHAWN JACKSON** FISHERS, IN

START TO FINISH: 20 MIN.
MAKES: 8 SERVINGS

- **¼ cup olive oil**
- **3 tablespoons white wine vinegar**
- **3 tablespoons honey**
- **3 cups cubed watermelon**
- **2 cups cubed honeydew**
- **2½ cups cubed fully cooked ham**
- **1 small cucumber, coarsely chopped**
- **8 cups fresh arugula**
- **¾ cup crumbled feta cheese**

1. In a large bowl, whisk together oil, vinegar and honey. Add both melons, ham and cucumber; toss to coat.
2. To serve, arrange arugula on a platter. Top with melon mixture; sprinkle with cheese.
PER SERVING *2 cups: 202 cal., 10g fat (3g sat. fat), 32mg chol., 646mg sodium, 17g carb. (15g sugars, 2g fiber), 12g pro.* ***Diabetic Exchanges:*** *2 lean meat, 1½ fat, 1 vegetable, ½ fruit.*
HEALTH TIP *Swap cantaloupe for honeydew and get a boost of vitamin A. One cup of cantaloupe has a whopping 120% of the daily value, whereas honeydew only provides 2%. Most other nutrient amounts are similar between the melons.*

MELON ARUGULA SALAD WITH HAM

I needed to use pork tenderloin from my fridge, but I didn't want to wait for it to roast. I tried this, and it was not only quick but my family loves it. You can play with different preserves to make your favorite flavors. —**MILDRED LYNN CARUSO** BRIGHTON, TN

APRICOT-ROSEMARY PORK MEDALLIONS

APRICOT-ROSEMARY PORK MEDALLIONS

PREP: 10 MIN. • **COOK:** 30 MIN.
MAKES: 8 SERVINGS

- **2 pork tenderloins (1 pound each)**
- **½ cup seasoned bread crumbs**
- **2 tablespoons olive oil**
- **6 cups fresh broccoli florets**
- **⅔ cup apricot preserves**
- **¼ cup white wine or chicken broth**
- **2 teaspoons minced fresh rosemary or ½ teaspoon dried rosemary, crushed**
- **½ teaspoon salt**
- **⅛ teaspoon pepper**
- **5⅓ cups hot cooked brown rice**

1. Cut each tenderloin crosswise into eight 1-in. slices. Place bread crumbs in a shallow bowl. Dip the pork slices in crumbs, patting to help coating adhere. In a large nonstick skillet, heat oil over medium heat. Add pork in batches; cook 3-4 minutes on each side or until a thermometer reads 145°.
2. Meanwhile, in a large saucepan, place steamer basket over 1 in. of water. Place broccoli in basket. Bring water to a boil. Reduce heat to maintain a simmer; steam, covered, 4-6 minutes or until tender.
3. In a small saucepan, mix preserves, wine, rosemary, salt and pepper. Cook and stir mixture over medium-low heat 3-5 minutes or until preserves are melted. Serve with pork, broccoli, rice.
PER SERVING *404 cal., 9g fat (2g sat. fat), 64mg chol., 321mg sodium, 53g carb. (12g sugars, 4g fiber), 28g pro.*

SKILLET PORK CHOPS WITH APPLES

SKILLET PORK CHOPS WITH APPLES C

Our family loves to use apples to brighten savory dishes. We tried many pork and apple recipes to find the perfect pairing, and this recipe is what it came to be.

—AMANDA JOBE OLATHE, KS

PREP: 15 MIN. • **COOK:** 20 MIN.
MAKES: 4 SERVINGS

- **4 boneless pork loin chops (4 ounces each and ¾ inch thick)**
- **1 teaspoon dried oregano, divided**
- **½ teaspoon salt**
- **¼ teaspoon coarsely ground pepper**
- **1½ teaspoons canola oil**
- **2 small apples, cut into ½-inch slices**
- **1 cup sliced sweet onion (¼ inch thick)**
- **⅓ cup unsweetened applesauce**
- **¼ cup cider vinegar**

1. Sprinkle the pork chops with 1/2 teaspoon oregano, salt and pepper. Place a large nonstick skillet coated with cooking spray over medium-high heat. Brown the pork chops, about 3 minutes per side; remove from pan.
2. In same pan, heat oil over medium-high heat. Add apples, onion and remaining oregano; cook and stir 6-8 minutes or until apples are tender.
3. Reduce heat to medium; stir in applesauce and vinegar. Return chops to pan; cook, covered, 4-6 minutes or until tender. Let stand 5 minutes before serving.

PER SERVING *1 pork chop with 1/2 cup apple mixture: 215 cal., 8g fat (2g sat. fat), 55mg chol., 329mg sodium, 12g carb. (8g sugars, 2g fiber), 22g pro.* ***Diabetic Exchanges:*** *3 lean meat, 1/2 fruit, 1/2 fat.*

FRIED GREEN TOMATO STACKS

This dish is for lovers of red and green tomatoes. When I ran across this recipe, I knew I had to try it. It has proved to be so tasty!

—BARBARA MOHR MILLINGTON, MI

PREP: 20 MIN. • **COOK:** 15 MIN.
MAKES: 4 SERVINGS

- **¼ cup fat-free mayonnaise**
- **¼ teaspoon grated lime peel**
- **2 tablespoons lime juice**
- **1 teaspoon minced fresh thyme or ¼ teaspoon dried thyme**
- **½ teaspoon pepper, divided**
- **¼ cup all-purpose flour**
- **2 large egg whites, lightly beaten**
- **¾ cup cornmeal**
- **¼ teaspoon salt**
- **2 medium green tomatoes**
- **2 medium red tomatoes**
- **2 tablespoons canola oil**
- **8 slices Canadian bacon**

1. Mix the first four ingredients and 1/4 teaspoon pepper; refrigerate until serving. Place flour in a shallow bowl; place egg whites in a separate shallow bowl. In a third bowl, mix cornmeal, salt and remaining pepper.
2. Cut each tomato crosswise into four slices. Lightly coat each slice in flour; shake off excess. Dip in egg whites, then in cornmeal mixture.
3. In a large nonstick skillet, heat oil over medium heat. In batches, cook tomatoes until golden brown, 4-5 minutes per side.
4. In the same pan, lightly brown Canadian bacon on both sides. For each serving, stack one slice each green tomato, bacon and red tomato. Serve with sauce.

PER SERVING *1 stack: 284 cal., 10g fat (1g sat. fat), 16mg chol., 679mg sodium, 37g carb. (6g sugars, 3g fiber), 12g pro.* ***Diabetic Exchanges:*** *2 starch, 1 1/2 fat, 1 lean meat, 1 vegetable.*

FRIED GREEN TOMATO STACKS

CHARD & BACON LINGUINE

MOM'S GARLIC PORK ROAST C

My mom cooked for my 10 siblings and me, so she usually prepared simple, hearty meals. She always treated us to this pork roast on special occasions.

—**RUBY WILLIAMS** BOGALUSA, LA

PREP: 10 MIN.
BAKE: 1 HOUR 15 MIN. + STANDING
MAKES: 8 SERVINGS

- **½ cup chopped celery**
- **½ medium green pepper, finely chopped**
- **½ cup thinly sliced green onions**
- **8 garlic cloves, minced**
- **1 bone-in pork loin roast (5 pounds)**
- **1 teaspoon salt**
- **¼ teaspoon cayenne pepper**

1. Preheat oven to 350°. In a small bowl, mix celery, green pepper, green onions and garlic.

2. Place the roast in a roasting pan, fat side up. With a sharp knife, make deep slits into top of roast, cutting between ribs. Fill slits with vegetable mixture. Sprinkle roast with salt and cayenne.

3. Roast until the meat reaches desired doneness (for medium-rare, a thermometer should read 145°; medium, 160°), 1¼ to 1½ hours. Remove roast from oven; tent with foil. Let stand 15 minutes before carving.

PER SERVING *298 cal., 13g fat (5g sat. fat), 114mg chol., 399mg sodium, 2g carb. (1g sugars, 1g fiber), 40g pro.* ***Diabetic Exchanges:*** *5 lean meat.*

MOM'S GARLIC PORK ROAST

CHARD & BACON LINGUINE FAST FIX

I use Swiss chard in every way I can, and that includes stirring it into this breezy linguine. When you're short on time, this dish keeps life simple.

—**DIANE NEMITZ** LUDINGTON, MI

START TO FINISH: 30 MIN.
MAKES: 4 SERVINGS

- **8 ounces uncooked whole wheat linguine**
- **4 bacon strips, chopped**
- **4 garlic cloves, minced**
- **½ cup reduced-sodium chicken broth**
- **½ cup dry white wine or additional chicken broth**
- **¼ teaspoon salt**
- **6 cups chopped Swiss chard (about 6 ounces)**
- **⅓ cup shredded Parmesan cheese**

1. Cook linguine according to package directions; drain. Meanwhile, in a large skillet, cook bacon over medium heat until crisp, stirring occasionally. Add garlic; cook 1 minute longer.

2. Add broth, wine, salt and Swiss chard to skillet; bring to a boil. Cook and stir 4-5 minutes or until chard is tender.

3. Add linguine; heat through, tossing to combine. Sprinkle with cheese.

PER SERVING *1 cup: 353 cal., 14g fat (5g sat. fat), 23mg chol., 633mg sodium, 47g carb. (2g sugars, 7g fiber), 14g pro.* ***Diabetic Exchanges:*** *3 starch, 1 medium-fat meat, 1 vegetable.*

HEALTH TIP *The dark green color of Swiss chard is a clue that it's an excellent source of immune-boosting vitamin A.*

A dear friend from the Philippines gave me this pork recipe that's so tempting. We never have leftovers. Try it with meats such as chicken, sausage or Spam.
—PRISCILLA GILBERT INDIAN HARBOUR BEACH, FL

PORK PANCIT

PORK PANCIT FAST FIX

START TO FINISH: 30 MIN. • **MAKES:** 6 SERVINGS

- **8 ounces uncooked vermicelli or angel hair pasta**
- **1 pound boneless pork loin chops (½ inch thick), cut into thin strips**
- **3 tablespoons canola oil, divided**
- **4 garlic cloves, minced**
- **1½ teaspoons salt, divided**
- **1 medium onion, halved and thinly sliced**
- **2½ cups shredded cabbage**
- **1 medium carrot, julienned**
- **1 cup fresh snow peas**
- **¼ teaspoon pepper**

1. Break vermicelli in half; cook according to package directions. Drain.
2. Meanwhile, in a bowl, toss pork with 2 tablespoons oil, garlic and ½ teaspoon salt. Place a large skillet over medium-high heat. Add half of the pork mixture; stir-fry 2-3 minutes or until browned. Remove from pan. Repeat with remaining pork mixture.
3. In same skillet, heat remaining oil over medium-high heat. Add onion; stir-fry 1-2 minutes or until tender. Add remaining vegetables; stir-fry 3-5 minutes or until crisp-tender. Stir in pepper and remaining salt. Return pork to pan. Add vermicelli; heat through, tossing to combine.
PER SERVING *1⅓ cups: 326 cal., 12g fat (2g sat. fat), 36mg chol., 627mg sodium, 34g carb. (3g sugars, 3g fiber), 21g pro.* ***Diabetic Exchanges:*** *2 starch, 2 lean meat, 1 vegetable, 1 fat.*

MARINATED GRILLED LAMB C

It's fun to fire up the grill on Easter, especially if you live in a cold climate! A mild marinade fabulously flavors the lamb.
—*TASTE OF HOME* TEST KITCHEN

PREP: 10 MIN. + MARINATING • **GRILL:** 1½ HOURS + STANDING
MAKES: 10 SERVINGS

- **¼ cup lemon juice**
- **¼ cup dry white wine or chicken broth**
- **3 tablespoons olive oil**
- **8 garlic cloves, minced**
- **3 tablespoons minced fresh rosemary**
- **1 tablespoon minced fresh thyme**
- **1 tablespoon minced fresh oregano**
- **1 teaspoon salt**
- **½ teaspoon coarsely ground pepper**
- **1 boneless leg of lamb (3 to 4 pounds), trimmed and untied**
- **1 sprig fresh rosemary**
- **Additional salt and pepper**

1. In a large resealable plastic bag, combine first nine ingredients; add lamb. Seal bag and turn to coat; refrigerate 4 hours.
2. Prepare grill for indirect medium heat. Drain lamb, discarding marinade. Place rosemary sprig on lamb; roll up and tie with kitchen string, leaving a portion of the sprig exposed. If desired, sprinkle with additional salt and pepper.
3. Grill the lamb, covered, over indirect medium heat 1½ to 2 hours or until the meat reaches desired doneness (for medium-rare, a thermometer should read 145°; medium, 160°; well-done, 170°). Remove from grill; tent with foil and let stand 15 minutes before slicing. Discard rosemary sprig before serving.
MARINATED ROAST LAMB *Prepare lamb as directed. Place on a rack in a shallow roasting pan; roast at 325° for 1½ to 2 hours or until meat reaches desired doneness (for medium-rare, a thermometer should read 145°; medium, 160°; well-done, 170°).*
PER SERVING *4 ounces cooked lamb: 225 cal., 12g fat (4g sat. fat), 82mg chol., 304mg sodium, 2g carb. (0 sugars, 0 fiber), 26g pro.* ***Diabetic Exchanges:*** *4 lean meat, 1 fat.*

QUICK HAWAIIAN PIZZA FAST FIX

Our family never quite liked the taste of canned pizza sauce, so one time I tried mixing some barbecue sauce into spaghetti sauce to add some sweetness. I've made my pizzas with this special and easy sauce ever since, and my family loves it!
—**TONYA SCHIELER** CARMEL, IN

START TO FINISH: 25 MIN. • **MAKES:** 6 SLICES

- **1 prebaked 12-inch thin whole wheat pizza crust**
- **½ cup marinara sauce**
- **¼ cup barbecue sauce**
- **1 medium sweet yellow or red pepper, chopped**
- **1 cup cubed fresh pineapple**
- **½ cup chopped fully cooked ham**
- **1 cup shredded part-skim mozzarella cheese**
- **½ cup shredded cheddar cheese**

1. Preheat oven to 425°. Place crust on a baking sheet. Mix marinara and barbecue sauces; spread over crust.
2. Top with remaining ingredients. Bake until crust is browned and cheese is melted, 10-15 minutes.

PER SERVING *1 slice: 290 cal., 10g fat (5g sat. fat), 29mg chol., 792mg sodium, 36g carb. (11g sugars, 5g fiber), 16g pro.* ***Diabetic Exchanges:*** *2 starch, 2 lean meat, 1/2 fat.*

QUICK HAWAIIAN PIZZA

CHARDONNAY PORK CHOPS

CHARDONNAY PORK CHOPS C FAST FIX

I began perfecting these juicy chops when I moved to another state and missed my stepdad's best pork recipe. His dish inspired my version, which includes a wine sauce.
—**JOLEEN THOMPSON** FARMINGTON, MN

START TO FINISH: 25 MIN. • **MAKES:** 4 SERVINGS

- **4 bone-in pork loin chops (6 ounces each)**
- **½ teaspoon salt**
- **¼ teaspoon pepper**
- **1 cup seasoned bread crumbs**
- **1 tablespoon olive oil**
- **3 green onions, chopped**
- **2 garlic cloves, minced**
- **1 cup chardonnay or chicken broth**
- **2 tablespoons lemon juice**
- **1 teaspoon dried rosemary, crushed**

1. Sprinkle pork chops with salt and pepper. Place bread crumbs in a shallow bowl. Dip pork chops in bread crumbs to coat both sides; shake off excess. In a large skillet, heat oil over medium heat; cook chops 4-5 minutes on each side or until golden brown and thermometer reads 145°. Remove from pan and keep warm.
2. In same pan, add green onions and garlic; cook and stir 1-2 minutes or until tender. Add chardonnay, stirring to loosen browned bits from the pan. Bring to a boil; cook 1-2 minutes or until liquid is reduced by half. Stir in lemon juice and rosemary. Serve pork chops with sauce.

PER SERVING *1 pork chop with 3 tablespoons sauce: 270 cal., 11g fat (3g sat. fat), 74mg chol., 509mg sodium, 9g carb. (1g sugars, 1g fiber), 28g pro.* ***Diabetic Exchanges:*** *4 lean meat, 1/2 starch, 1/2 fat.*

EGG ROLL NOODLE BOWL

EGG ROLL NOODLE BOWL

We truly love egg rolls, but they can be challenging to make. Simplify everything with this deconstructed version made on the stovetop.

—**COURTNEY STULTZ** WEIR, KS

START TO FINISH: 30 MIN.
MAKES: 4 SERVINGS

- **1 tablespoon sesame oil**
- **½ pound ground pork**
- **1 tablespoon soy sauce**
- **1 garlic clove, minced**
- **1 teaspoon ground ginger**
- **½ teaspoon salt**
- **¼ teaspoon ground turmeric**
- **¼ teaspoon pepper**
- **6 cups shredded cabbage (about 1 small head)**
- **2 large carrots, shredded (about 2 cups)**
- **4 ounces rice noodles**
- **3 green onions, thinly sliced**
- **Additional soy sauce, optional**

1. In a large skillet, heat the oil over medium-high heat; cook and crumble pork until browned, 4-6 minutes. Stir in soy sauce, garlic and seasonings. Add the cabbage and carrots; cook 4-6 minutes longer or until vegetables are tender, stirring occasionally.

2. Cook rice noodles according to package directions; drain and immediately add to pork mixture, tossing to combine. Sprinkle with green onions. If desired, serve with additional soy sauce.

PER SERVING *1½ cups: 302 cal., 12g fat (4g sat. fat), 38mg chol., 652mg sodium, 33g carb. (2g sugars, 4g fiber), 14g pro.* ***Diabetic Exchanges:*** *2 medium-fat meat, 2 vegetable, 1½ starch, ½ fat.*

PORK TENDERLOIN WITH SWEET POTATO RAGOUT

With the taste of sweet potatoes and pork, this combination is a perfect dish to serve on a fall evening.

—**GREG FONTENOT** THE WOODLANDS, TX

PREP: 1 HOUR • **GRILL:** 20 MIN.
MAKES: 6 SERVINGS (3 CUPS RAGOUT)

- **2 tablespoons olive oil**
- **1 large onion, chopped**
- **2 garlic cloves, minced**
- **1 large navel orange**
- **¼ cup packed brown sugar**
- **¼ cup balsamic vinegar**
- **⅛ teaspoon plus ½ teaspoon salt, divided**
- **1 can (15¾ ounces) cut sweet potatoes in syrup, undrained**
- **1 can (14½ ounces) diced tomatoes, undrained**
- **2 medium tart apples, peeled and chopped**
- **2 pork tenderloins (¾ pound each)**
- **½ teaspoon pepper**

1. In a large skillet, heat the oil over medium heat. Add onion; cook and stir 4-5 minutes or until softened. Reduce heat to medium-low; cook 20-25 minutes or until golden brown, stirring occasionally. Add garlic; cook 1 minute longer.

2. Finely grate peel from orange. Cut orange crosswise in half; squeeze juice from orange. Stir brown sugar, vinegar, ⅛ teaspoon salt, orange peel and the orange juice into onion mixture. Bring to a boil; cook 6-8 minutes or until liquid is almost evaporated.

3. Stir in sweet potatoes, tomatoes and the apples. Return to a boil. Reduce heat; simmer, uncovered, 20-25 minutes or until apples are tender and liquid is almost evaporated, stirring occasionally.

4. Sprinkle pork with pepper and remaining salt. Grill, covered, over medium heat 18-22 minutes or until a thermometer reads 145°, turning occasionally. Let stand 5 minutes before slicing. Serve with ragout.

PER SERVING *3 ounces cooked pork with ½ cup ragout: 344 cal., 9g fat (2g sat. fat), 64mg chol., 436mg sodium, 42g carb. (34g sugars, 5g fiber), 25g pro.*

PORK TENDERLOIN WITH SWEET POTATO RAGOUT

TARRAGON-DIJON PORK CHOPS

TARRAGON-DIJON PORK CHOPS C FAST FIX

For my smoky chops, I add tarragon for a hint of herbs. If you like a lot of sauce, double or triple the ingredients.

—**JULIE DANLER** BEL AIRE, KS

START TO FINISH: 30 MIN.
MAKES: 4 SERVINGS

- **4 boneless pork loin chops (¾ inch thick and 6 ounces each)**
- **½ teaspoon garlic powder**
- **¼ teaspoon pepper**
- **2 tablespoons olive oil, divided**
- **1 pound sliced fresh mushrooms**
- **4 green onions, chopped**
- **¼ cup Dijon mustard**
- **1 to 1½ teaspoons chipotle or other hot pepper sauce**
- **1 tablespoon red wine, optional**
- **1 tablespoon minced fresh tarragon**

1. Preheat oven to 400°. Sprinkle chops with garlic powder and pepper. In a large ovenproof skillet, heat 1 tablespoon oil over medium heat. Brown chops on both sides; remove from pan.

2. In same skillet, heat remaining oil over medium-high heat. Add the mushrooms and green onions; cook and stir 3 minutes. Place chops over mushroom mixture. Bake, uncovered, 8-10 minutes or until a thermometer inserted in pork reads 145°.

3. Meanwhile, in a small bowl, mix mustard, pepper sauce and, if desired, wine; spread over chops. Bake 2 minutes longer. Sprinkle with tarragon.

PER SERVING *1 pork chop with 1⁄3 cup mushroom mixture: 334 cal., 17g fat (5g sat. fat), 82mg chol., 417mg sodium, 8g carb. (3g sugars, 2g fiber), 37g pro.* ***Diabetic Exchanges:*** *5 lean meat, 1½ fat, 1 vegetable.*

QUICK TACOS AL PASTOR FAST FIX

My husband and I tried pork and pineapple tacos at a truck stand in Hawaii. Something about them was so tasty, so I decided to create my own version at home.

—**LORI MCLAIN** DENTON, TX

START TO FINISH: 25 MIN.
MAKES: 4 SERVINGS (2 TACOS EACH)

- **1 package (15 ounces) refrigerated pork roast au jus**
- **1 cup well-drained unsweetened pineapple chunks, divided**
- **1 tablespoon canola oil**
- **½ cup enchilada sauce**
- **8 corn tortillas (6 inches), warmed**
- **½ cup finely chopped onion**
- **¼ cup chopped fresh cilantro**
- **Optional ingredients: crumbled queso fresco, salsa verde and lime wedges**

1. Coarsely shred pork, reserving juices. In a small bowl, crush half of the pineapple with a fork.

2. In a large nonstick skillet, heat oil over medium-high heat. Add whole pineapple chunks; cook 2-3 minutes or until lightly browned, turning occasionally. Remove from pan.

3. Add enchilada sauce and crushed pineapple to same skillet; stir in the pork and reserved juices. Cook over medium-high heat 4-6 minutes or until liquid is evaporated, stirring occasionally.

4. Serve in tortillas with pineapple chunks, onion and cilantro. If desired, top with cheese and salsa and serve with lime wedges.

PER SERVING *2 tacos: 317 cal., 11g fat (3g sat. fat), 57mg chol., 573mg sodium, 36g carb. (12g sugars, 5g fiber), 24g pro.* ***Diabetic Exchanges:*** *3 lean meat, 2 starch, 1 fat.*

QUICK TACOS AL PASTOR

Get out there and fire up the grill for pork kabobs, a tasty alternative to chicken and beef. These sweet and gingery beauties make dinnertime happy.
—**TONYA BURKHARD** PALM COAST, FL

PLUM-GLAZED PORK KABOB

SPICE-RUBBED LAMB CHOPS C

One of my favorite meals is lamb! My girls, Hanna and Amani, love watching me make these chops, but they love eating them even more.
—**NAREMAN DIETZ** BEVERLY HILLS, MI

PREP: 15 MIN. + CHILLING • **BAKE:** 5 MIN.
MAKES: 2 SERVINGS

- **2 teaspoons lemon juice**
- **2 teaspoons Worcestershire sauce**
- **1½ teaspoons pepper**
- **1¼ teaspoons ground cumin**
- **1¼ teaspoons curry powder**
- **1 garlic clove, minced**
- **½ teaspoon sea salt**
- **½ teaspoon onion powder**
- **½ teaspoon crushed red pepper flakes**
- **4 lamb rib chops**
- **1 tablespoon olive oil**

1. Mix the first nine ingredients; spread over chops. Refrigerate, covered, overnight.
2. Preheat the oven to 450°. In an ovenproof skillet, heat the oil over medium-high heat; brown the chops, about 2 minutes per side. Transfer to oven; roast until desired doneness (for medium-rare, a thermometer should read 145°; medium, 160°), 3-4 minutes.
PER SERVING *2 lamb chops: 290 cal., 17g fat (4g sat. fat), 90mg chol., 620mg sodium, 5g carb. (1g sugars, 2g fiber), 29g pro.* ***Diabetic Exchanges:*** *4 lean meat, 1½ fat.*

PLUM-GLAZED PORK KABOBS C FAST FIX

START TO FINISH: 30 MIN.
MAKES: 6 SERVINGS

- **⅓ cup plum jam**
- **2 tablespoons reduced-sodium soy sauce**
- **1 garlic clove, minced**
- **½ teaspoon ground ginger**
- **1 medium sweet red pepper**
- **1 medium green pepper**
- **1 small red onion**
- **2 pork tenderloins (¾ pound each)**

1. For glaze, in a small bowl, mix the jam, soy sauce, garlic and ginger. Cut vegetables and pork into 1-in. pieces. On six metal or soaked wooden skewers, alternately thread pork and vegetables.
2. Moisten a paper towel with cooking oil; using tongs, rub on grill rack to coat lightly. Grill the kabobs, covered, over medium heat 12-15 minutes or until pork is tender, turning occasionally and brushing with ¼ cup glaze during the last 5 minutes. Brush with remaining glaze before serving.
PER SERVING *1 kabob: 196 cal., 4g fat (1g sat. fat), 64mg chol., 239mg sodium, 15g carb. (12g sugars, 1g fiber), 24g pro.* ***Diabetic Exchanges:*** *3 lean meat, 1 starch.*

DID YOU KNOW?

Worcestershire sauce was originally considered a mistake. In 1835, an English lord commissioned two chemists to duplicate a sauce he had tried in India. The pungent batch was disappointing and wound up in their cellar. When the pair stumbled upon the aged concoction 2 years later, they were pleasantly surprised.

SPICE-RUBBED LAMB CHOPS

SUNDAY PORK ROAST C

(PICTURED ON P. 149)

My mom would prepare this delectable main dish for the customers at the three restaurants she and my dad owned. The herb rub gives it a remarkable flavor.

—SANDI PICHON MEMPHIS, TN

PREP: 20 MIN.
BAKE: 1 HOUR 10 MIN. + STANDING
MAKES: 12 SERVINGS

- **2 medium onions, chopped**
- **2 medium carrots, chopped**
- **1 celery rib, chopped**
- **4 tablespoons all-purpose flour, divided**
- **1 bay leaf, finely crushed**
- **½ teaspoon dried thyme**
- **1¼ teaspoons salt, divided**
- **1¼ teaspoons pepper, divided**
- **1 boneless pork loin roast (3 to 4 pounds)**
- **⅓ cup packed brown sugar**

1. Preheat the oven to 350°. Place vegetables on bottom of a shallow roasting pan. Mix 2 tablespoons flour, bay leaf, thyme, and 1 teaspoon each salt and pepper; rub over roast. Place roast on top of vegetables, fat side up. Add 1 cup water to pan.
2. Roast 1 hour, basting once with pan juices if desired. Sprinkle brown sugar over roast. Roast 10-15 minutes longer or until a thermometer reads 140°. (Temperature of roast will continue to rise about 5-10° upon standing.)
3. Remove roast to a platter. Tent with foil; let stand 15 minutes before slicing.
4. Strain drippings from roasting pan into a measuring cup; skim fat. Add enough water to the drippings to measure 1½ cups.
5. In a small saucepan over medium heat, whisk remaining flour and ⅓ cup water until smooth. Gradually whisk in drippings mixture and remaining salt and pepper. Bring to a boil over medium-high heat, stir constantly; cook and stir 2 minutes or until thickened. Serve roast with gravy.

FREEZE OPTION *Freeze cooled sliced pork and gravy in freezer containers. To use, partially thaw in refrigerator overnight. Heat through in a covered saucepan, gently stirring and adding a little broth or water if necessary.*

PER SERVING *3 ounces cooked pork with about 2 tablespoons gravy: 174 cal., 5g fat (2g sat. fat), 57mg chol., 280mg sodium, 8g carb. (6g sugars, 0 fiber), 22g pro.* ***Diabetic Exchanges:*** *3 lean meat, ½ starch.*

BERNIE'S PORK CHOP SANDWICHES FAST FIX

My aunt worked in Butte, Montana, and whenever we visited we had pork chop sandwiches. This recipe is a take on that sandwich.

—JEANETTE KOTECKI HELENA, MT

START TO FINISH: 25 MIN.
MAKES: 4 SERVINGS

- **¾ cup cornmeal**
- **1 cup all-purpose flour**
- **½ teaspoon onion powder**
- **½ teaspoon garlic powder**
- **½ teaspoon dry mustard**
- **½ teaspoon paprika**
- **1 cup fat-free milk**
- **4 boneless pork loin chops (3 ounces each)**
- **½ teaspoon salt**
- **¼ teaspoon pepper**
- **2 tablespoons canola oil**
- **4 whole wheat hamburger buns, split and warmed**
- **Thinly sliced onion, optional**
- **Pickle slices, optional**
- **Prepared mustard, optional**

1. Place cornmeal in a shallow bowl. In another bowl, mix flour and spices; add the milk, stirring just until dry ingredients are moistened. Pound chops with a meat mallet to ¼-in. thickness; season with salt and pepper.
2. In two batches, heat oil in a large skillet over medium heat. Lightly coat chops with cornmeal. Dip in batter, allowing excess to drip off; place in skillet. Cook until golden brown, 2-4 minutes per side. Drain on paper towels. Serve in buns, topping with remaining ingredients if desired.

PER SERVING *1 sandwich: 476 cal., 15g fat (3g sat. fat), 42mg chol., 564mg sodium, 60g carb. (6g sugars, 5g fiber), 26g pro.*

BERNIE'S PORK CHOP SANDWICHES

ZESTY GRILLED CHOPS

ZESTY GRILLED CHOPS

These pork chops make a quick dish for company. Our family enjoys them on the grill, as the summer weather in our part of the country is hot and muggy. In the wintertime, they're just as wonderful prepared in the broiler.

—**BLANCHE BABINSKI** MINOT, ND

PREP: 10 MIN. + MARINATING
GRILL: 10 MIN. • **MAKES:** 6 SERVINGS

- **¾ cup soy sauce**
- **¼ cup lemon juice**
- **1 tablespoon chili sauce**
- **1 tablespoon brown sugar**
- **1 garlic clove, minced**
- **6 bone-in pork loin or rib chops (about 1½ inches thick)**

1. In a large resealable plastic bag, combine first five ingredients; reserve 1/3 cup mixture for brushing over chops. Add pork chops to bag; seal bag and turn to coat. Refrigerate overnight.

2. Drain pork, discarding marinade. Grill chops, covered, over medium heat or broil 4 in. from the heat until thermometer reads 145°, 6-8 minutes per side. Brush occasionally with reserved soy mixture during the last 5 minutes. Let stand 5 minutes before serving.

PER SERVING *1 pork chop: 246 cal., 11g fat (4g sat. fat), 82mg chol., 598mg sodium, 1g carb. (1g sugars, 0 fiber), 34g pro.* ***Diabetic Exchanges:*** *5 lean meat.*

FARMERS MARKET PASTA

When we moved into our house, little did we know that we had a wild asparagus patch. Twenty years later, that little patch still gives us plenty of asparagus. This recipe can be used almost any time of year with almost any assortment of vegetables the season has to offer. By cooking without butter or oil, you can cut fat and calories, but the flavors are still there.

—**WENDY BALL** BATTLE CREEK, MI

PREP: 20 MIN. • **COOK:** 20 MIN.
MAKES: 6 SERVINGS

- **9 ounces uncooked whole wheat linguine**
- **1 pound fresh asparagus, trimmed and cut into 2-inch pieces**
- **2 medium carrots, thinly sliceed**
- **1 small red onion, chopped**
- **2 medium zucchini or yellow summer squash, thinly sliced**
- **½ pound sliced fresh mushrooms**
- **2 garlic cloves, minced**
- **1 cup half-and-half cream**
- **⅔ cup reduced-sodium chicken broth**
- **1 cup frozen petite peas**
- **2 cups cubed fully cooked ham**
- **2 tablespoons julienned fresh basil**
- **¼ teaspoon pepper**
- **½ cup grated Parmesan cheese**
- **Additonal fresh basil and Parmesan cheese**

1. In a 6-qt. stockpot, cook linguine according to the package directions, adding asparagus and carrots during the last 3-5 minutes of cooking. Drain; return to pot.

2. Place a large skillet coated with cooking spray over medium heat. Add onion; cook and stir 3 minutes. Add squash, mushrooms, and garlic; cook and stir until crisp-tender, 4-5 minutes.

3. Add cream and broth; bring to a boil, stirring to loosen browned bits from pan. Reduce heat; simmer, uncovered, until sauce is thickened slightly, about 5 minutes. Stir in peas, ham, 2 tablespoons basil and pepper; heat through.

4. Add to linguine mixture; stir in 1/2 cup cheese. If desired, top with additional basil and cheese.

PER SERVING *2 cups: 338 cal., 9g fat (4g sat. fat), 53mg chol., 817mg sodium, 46g carb. (8g sugars, 8g fiber), 23g pro.* ***Diabetic Exchanges:*** *2½ starch, 2 lean meat, 1 vegetable, ½ fat.*

FARMERS MARKET PASTA

ITALIAN PORK STEW

ITALIAN PORK STEW C

Don't skip the anchovy paste in this stew! It gives a savory, salty flavor but doesn't taste fishy at all. Add a salad and artisan bread for a wholesome meal.

—LYNNE GERMAN WOODLAND HILLS, CA

PREP: 30 MIN. • **COOK:** 2¼ HOURS
MAKES: 8 SERVINGS (2 QUARTS)

- **⅔ cup all-purpose flour**
- **2 pounds boneless pork loin, cut into 1-inch pieces**
- **4 tablespoons olive oil, divided**
- **1 large onion, chopped**
- **5 garlic cloves, crushed**
- **1 can (28 ounces) diced tomatoes, undrained**
- **1 cup dry red wine or beef broth**
- **3 bay leaves**
- **1 cinnamon stick (3 inches)**
- **1 tablespoon tomato paste**
- **1 tablespoon red wine vinegar**
- **1 teaspoon anchovy paste**
- **1 teaspoon each dried oregano, basil and sage leaves**
- **½ teaspoon salt**
- **½ teaspoon crushed red pepper flakes**
- **¼ teaspoon pepper**
- **¼ cup minced fresh parsley**
- **Hot cooked bow tie pasta**
- **Grated Parmesan cheese**

1. Place flour in a large resealable plastic bag. Add pork, a few pieces at a time, and shake to coat. In a Dutch oven, brown pork in 3 tablespoons oil in batches. Remove and keep warm.

2. In the same pan, saute onion in remaining oil until crisp-tender. Add garlic; cook 1 minute longer. Stir in the tomatoes, wine, bay leaves, cinnamon, tomato paste, vinegar, anchovy paste, herbs, salt, pepper flakes, pepper and pork; bring to a boil.

3. Reduce heat; cover and simmer for 1½ hours, stirring occasionally. Stir in parsley. Cover and cook 30-40 minutes longer or until meat is tender. Skim fat; discard bay leaves and cinnamon.

4. Serve with pasta; sprinkle with cheese.

FREEZE OPTION *Place individual portions of cooled stew in freezer containers and freeze. To use, partially thaw in refrigerator overnight. Heat through in a saucepan, stirring occasionally and adding a little water if necessary.*

PER SERVING *1 cup: 256 cal., 12g fat (3g sat. fat), 59mg chol., 349mg sodium, 12g carb. (4g sugars, 2g fiber), 24g pro.* ***Diabetic Exchanges:*** *3 lean meat, 1 vegetable, 1 fat.*

TENDER SWEET 'N' SOUR PORK CHOPS

C FAST FIX

Years ago, my best friend gave me the recipe for these delightful pork chops. It's become one of my family's favorites, and I prepare the meat often for us.

—GINA YOUNG LAMAR, CO

START TO FINISH: 25 MIN. • **MAKES:** 6 SERVINGS

- **6 boneless pork loin chops (4 ounces each)**
- **¾ teaspoon pepper**
- **½ cup water**
- **⅓ cup cider vinegar**
- **¼ cup packed brown sugar**
- **2 tablespoons reduced-sodium soy sauce**
- **1 tablespoon Worcestershire sauce**
- **1 tablespoon cornstarch**
- **2 tablespoons cold water**

1. Sprinkle pork chops with pepper. In a large nonstick skillet coated with cooking spray, cook pork over medium heat for 4-6 minutes on each side or until lightly browned. Remove and keep warm.

2. Add the water, vinegar, brown sugar, soy sauce and Worcestershire sauce to skillet; stir to loosen browned bits. Bring to a boil. Combine cornstarch and cold water until smooth; stir into skillet. Bring to a boil; cook and stir for 2 minutes or until thickened.

3. Return chops to the pan. Reduce heat; cover and simmer for 4-5 minutes or until meat is tender.

PER SERVING *1 pork chop with 3 tablespoons sauce: 198 cal., 6g fat (2g sat. fat), 55mg chol., 265mg sodium, 12g carb. (10g sugars, 0 fiber), 22g pro.* ***Diabetic Exchanges:*** *3 lean meat, 1 starch.*

BLACKENED PORK CAESAR SALAD

C FAST FIX

START TO FINISH: 30 MIN. • **MAKES:** 2 SERVINGS

- **2 tablespoons mayonnaise**
- **1 tablespoon olive oil**
- **1 tablespoon lemon juice**
- **1 garlic clove, minced**
- **⅛ teaspoon seasoned salt**
- **⅛ teaspoon pepper**

SALAD

- **¾ pound pork tenderloin, cut into 1-inch cubes**
- **1 tablespoon blackened seasoning**
- **1 tablespoon canola oil**
- **6 cups torn romaine**
- **Salad croutons and shredded Parmesan cheese, optional**

1. For dressing, in a small bowl, mix the first six ingredients until blended.

2. Toss pork with blackened seasoning. In a large skillet, heat oil over medium-high heat. Add pork; cook and stir 5-7 minutes or until tender.

3. To serve, place romaine in a large bowl; add dressing and toss to coat. Top with pork, and, if desired, croutons and cheese.

PER SERVING *2½ cups: 458 cal., 31g fat (5g sat. fat), 100mg chol., 464mg sodium, 8g carb. (2g sugars, 3g fiber), 36g pro.*

HEALTH TIP *Switch to a baby kale salad blend for more fiber, vitamin C, calcium and iron.*

When I cook, my goal is to have enough leftovers for lunch the next day. This Caesar with pork has fantastic flavor even when the meat is chilled.

—**PENNY HEDGES** DEWDNEY, BC

BLACKENED PORK CAESAR SALAD

PORK ROAST WITH HERB RUB

PORK ROAST WITH HERB RUB C

Herbs and spices like sage and celery seed give pork loin roast a mild, subtly spiced flavor. Everyone flocks to the table for this tender roast.

—**CAROLYN POPE** MASON CITY, IA

PREP: 5 MIN. + CHILLING • **BAKE:** 1¼ HOURS + STANDING
MAKES: 12 SERVINGS

- **2 tablespoons sugar**
- **2 teaspoons dried marjoram**
- **2 teaspoons rubbed sage**
- **1 teaspoon salt**
- **½ teaspoon celery seed**
- **½ teaspoon ground mustard**
- **⅛ teaspoon pepper**
- **1 boneless pork loin roast (4 pounds)**

1. Mix first seven ingredients; rub over roast. Refrigerate at least 4 hours.

2. Preheat oven to 350°. Place roast on a rack in a roasting pan, fat side up. Roast until a thermometer reads 145°, 1¼ to 1¾ hours.

3. Remove roast from oven; tent with foil. Let stand for 15 minutes before slicing.

PER SERVING *4 ounces cooked pork: 198 cal., 7g fat (3g sat. fat), 75mg chol., 240mg sodium, 2g carb. (2g sugars, 0 fiber), 29g pro.* ***Diabetic Exchanges:*** *4 lean meat.*

APPLE-CHERRY PORK MEDALLIONS

APPLE-CHERRY PORK MEDALLIONS FAST FIX

If you're too busy to cook, my pork medallions with tangy apple-cherry sauce, fresh rosemary and thyme deliver the goods in a hurry.

—**GLORIA BRADLEY** NAPERVILLE, IL

START TO FINISH: 30 MIN.
MAKES: 4 SERVINGS

- **1 pork tenderloin (1 pound)**
- **1 teaspoon minced fresh rosemary or ¼ teaspoon dried rosemary, crushed**
- **1 teaspoon minced fresh thyme or ¼ teaspoon dried thyme**
- **½ teaspoon celery salt**
- **1 tablespoon olive oil**
- **1 large apple, sliced**
- **⅔ cup unsweetened apple juice**
- **3 tablespoons dried tart cherries**
- **1 tablespoon honey**
- **1 tablespoon cider vinegar**
- **1 package (8.8 ounces) ready-to-serve brown rice**

1. Cut tenderloin crosswise into 12 slices; sprinkle with rosemary, thyme and celery salt. In a large nonstick skillet, heat the oil over medium-high heat. Brown pork on both sides; remove from pan.

2. In same skillet, combine the apple, apple juice, cherries, honey and the vinegar. Bring to a boil, stirring to loosen browned bits from pan. Reduce heat; simmer, uncovered, 3-4 minutes or just until apple is tender.

3. Return pork to pan, turning to coat with sauce; cook, covered, 3-4 minutes or until pork is tender. Meanwhile, prepare rice according to package directions; serve with pork mixture.

PER SERVING *3 ounces cooked pork with 1/3 cup rice and 1/4 cup apple mixture: 349 cal., 9g fat (2g sat. fat), 64mg chol., 179mg sodium, 37g carb. (16g sugars, 4g fiber), 25g pro.* ***Diabetic Exchanges:*** *3 lean meat, 2½ starch.*

TEMPTING PORK TENDERLOIN BURGERS

FAST FIX

Pork tenderloin is a family favorite at my house. I'm always looking for new ways to cook it, so I came up with this burger recipe for a simple weeknight dinner. Chopped prunes, dried figs or dried blueberries can be substituted for the dried cranberries with great success!

—**DEBORAH BIGGS** OMAHA, NE

START TO FINISH: 30 MIN.
MAKES: 4 SERVINGS

- **1 large egg white, lightly beaten**
- **⅓ cup panko (Japanese) bread crumbs**
- **3 tablespoons dried cranberries, chopped**
- **½ teaspoon poultry seasoning**
- **1 pork tenderloin (1 pound), cubed**
- **3 tablespoons Dijon mustard**
- **3 tablespoons mayonnaise**
- **1½ teaspoons maple syrup**
- **4 whole wheat hamburger buns, split and lightly toasted**
- **Arugula or baby spinach**

1. In a large bowl, mix the first four ingredients. In a food processor, pulse pork until finely chopped. Add to egg white mixture; mix lightly but thoroughly. Shape into four ½-in.-thick patties. Mix the mustard, mayonnaise and syrup.

2. Place the patties on an oiled grill rack; grill, covered, over medium heat until a thermometer reads 160°, 4-6 minutes per side. Serve in buns with arugula and mustard mixture.

PER SERVING *1 burger: 378 cal., 14g fat (3g sat. fat), 64mg chol., 620mg sodium, 33g carb. (11g sugars, 4g fiber), 28g pro.* ***Diabetic Exchanges:*** *3 lean meat, 2 starch, 1 fat.*

TEMPTING PORK TENDERLOIN BURGERS

CARIBBEAN ROAST PORK LOIN S C

Here's an easy, different treatment for a boneless pork loin roast. Simply combine the oil and seasonings, rub it over the roast and bake. The meat turns out tender and serves a big group.

—**DENISE ALBERS** FREEBURG, IL

PREP: 5 MIN.
BAKE: 1¼ HOURS + STANDING
MAKES: 12 SERVINGS

- **2 teaspoons olive oil**
- **1 teaspoon pepper**
- **¾ teaspoon ground cinnamon**
- **¾ teaspoon ground nutmeg**
- **1 boneless rolled pork loin roast (3½ pounds)**

1. Preheat oven to 350°. Mix first four ingredients; rub over roast. Place on a rack in a roasting pan. Roast until a thermometer reads 145°, 1¼ to 1½ hours.

2. Remove roast from oven; tent with foil. Let stand for 15 minutes before slicing.

PER SERVING *3 ounces cooked pork: 172 cal., 7g fat (2g sat. fat), 66mg chol., 38mg sodium, 0 carb. (0 sugars, 0 fiber), 26g pro.*

GRILLED PORK CHOPS WITH SMOKIN' SAUCE

GRILLED PORK CHOPS WITH SMOKIN' SAUCE

C FAST FIX

Growing up, my husband always had pork chops that were were pan-fried or baked, but he knew they could be better. So he combined his love of grilling with the desire to create his own signature sauce, and the result was this recipe.

—**VICKY DRNEK** ROME, GA

START TO FINISH: 25 MIN.
MAKES: 4 SERVINGS

- **¼ cup water**
- **¼ cup ketchup**
- **1 tablespoon Dijon mustard**
- **1 tablespoon molasses**
- **1½ teaspoons packed brown sugar**
- **1 teaspoon Worcestershire sauce**
- **¼ teaspoon kosher salt**
- **¼ teaspoon chipotle hot pepper sauce**
- **⅛ teaspoon pepper**

PORK CHOPS

- **1¼ teaspoons mustard seed**
- **1¼ teaspoons smoked paprika**
- **1¼ teaspoons whole peppercorns**
- **1 teaspoon onion powder**
- **1 teaspoon garlic powder**
- **½ teaspoon kosher salt**
- **¼ teaspoon cayenne pepper**
- **1½ teaspoons brown sugar**
- **4 bone-in pork loin chops (7 ounces each)**

1. In a small saucepan, mix the first nine ingredients; bring to a boil over medium heat. Reduce heat; simmer, uncovered, until slightly thickened, about 10 minutes, stirring occasionally. Reserve ¼ cup sauce for serving.

2. Using a mortar and pestle or spice grinder, crush seasonings with brown sugar. Rub mixture over chops.

3. Place chops on an oiled grill over medium heat. Grill, covered, until thermometer reads 145°, 5-6 minutes per side, brushing top with the remaining sauce after turning. Let the pork chops stand 5 minutes before serving. Serve with reserved sauce.

PER SERVING *1 pork chop with 1 tablespoon sauce: 263 cal., 9g fat (3g sat. fat), 86mg chol., 721mg sodium, 14g carb. (11g sugars, 1g fiber), 31g pro.* ***Diabetic Exchanges:*** *4 lean meat, 1 starch.*

DID YOU KNOW?

Molasses is a byproduct of refining cane or beets into sugar. Light and dark molasses are made from the first and second cooking procedures, respectively. Blackstrap, made from the third procedure, is strongest, darkest and most intensely flavored. Dark molasses will work well in most recipes.

182

181

171

Fish & Seafood

“I headed straight for the kitchen when I decided to pick up a more healthy lifestyle. This salmon with veggies proves that smart choices can be both simple and satisfying.”

—MATTHEW TEIXEIRA MILTON, ON
about his recipe, Salmon and Spud Salad, on page 169

CAJUN BAKED CATFISH FAST FIX

This well-seasoned fish gets many compliments from family and friends whenever I serve it. It's moist and flaky, and the coating is crispy, crunchy and flecked with paprika.

—**JIM GALES** MILWAUKEE, WI

START TO FINISH: 25 MIN.
MAKES: 2 SERVINGS

- **2 tablespoons yellow cornmeal**
- **2 teaspoons Cajun or blackened seasoning**
- **½ teaspoon dried thyme**
- **½ teaspoon dried basil**
- **¼ teaspoon garlic powder**
- **¼ teaspoon lemon-pepper seasoning**
- **2 catfish or tilapia fillets (6 ounces each)**
- **¼ teaspoon paprika**

1. Preheat oven to 400°. In a shallow bowl, mix the first six ingredients.
2. Dip fillets in cornmeal mixture to coat both sides. Place on a baking sheet coated with cooking spray. Sprinkle with paprika.
3. Bake 20-25 minutes or until fish just begins to flake easily with a fork.

PER SERVING *1 fillet: 242 cal., 10g fat (2g sat. fat), 94mg chol., 748mg sodium, 8g carb. (0 sugars, 1g fiber), 27g pro.* ***Diabetic Exchanges:*** *4 lean meat, ½ starch.*

My father made up this sweet, flavorful recipe for my mother when he would cook for the night. We serve it with whole wheat pasta or brown rice.

—**ANN MARIE EBERHART** GIG HARBOR, WA

COD WITH HEARTY TOMATO SAUCE

CAJUN BAKED CATFISH

COD WITH HEARTY TOMATO SAUCE FAST FIX

START TO FINISH: 30 MIN.
MAKES: 4 SERVINGS

- **2 cans (14½ ounces each) diced tomatoes with basil, oregano and garlic, undrained**
- **4 cod fillets (6 ounces each)**
- **2 tablespoons olive oil, divided**
- **2 medium onions, halved and thinly sliced (about 1½ cups)**
- **½ teaspoon dried oregano**
- **¼ teaspoon pepper**
- **¼ teaspoon crushed red pepper flakes**
- **Hot cooked whole wheat pasta**
- **Minced fresh parsley, optional**

1. Place tomatoes in a blender. Cover and process until pureed.
2. Pat fish dry with paper towels. In a large skillet, heat 1 tablespoon oil over medium-high heat. Add cod fillets; cook 2-4 minutes on each side or until surface of fish begins to color. Remove from pan.
3. In same skillet, heat remaining oil over medium-high heat. Add onions; cook and stir 2-4 minutes or until tender. Stir in seasonings and pureed tomatoes; bring to a boil. Add cod; return just to a boil, spooning sauce over tops. Reduce heat; simmer, uncovered, 5-7 minutes or until fish just begins to flake easily with a fork. Serve with pasta. If desired, sprinkle with parsley.

PER SERVING *1 fillet with ¾ cup sauce: 271 cal., 8g fat (1g sat. fat), 65mg chol., 746mg sodium, 17g carb. (9g sugars, 4g fiber), 29g pro.* ***Diabetic Exchanges:*** *3 lean meat, 2 vegetable, 1½ fat.*

SALMON AND SPUD SALAD FAST FIX (PICTURED ON P. 166)

I headed straight for the kitchen when I decided to pick up a more healthy lifestyle. This salmon with veggies proves that smart choices can be both simple and satisfying.

—**MATTHEW TEIXEIRA** MILTON, ON

START TO FINISH: 30 MIN.
MAKES: 4 SERVINGS

- **1 pound fingerling potatoes**
- **½ pound fresh green beans**
- **½ pound fresh asparagus**
- **4 salmon fillets (6 ounces each)**
- **1 tablespoon plus ⅓ cup red wine vinaigrette, divided**
- **¼ teaspoon salt**
- **¼ teaspoon pepper**
- **4 cups fresh arugula or baby spinach**
- **2 cups cherry tomatoes, halved**
- **1 tablespoon minced fresh chives**

1. Cut potatoes lengthwise in half. Trim and cut the green beans and asparagus into 2-in. pieces. Place the potatoes in a 6-qt. stockpot; add water to cover. Bring to a boil. Reduce heat; cook, uncovered, 10-15 minutes or until tender, adding green beans and asparagus during the last 4 minutes of cooking. Drain.

2. Meanwhile, brush salmon with 1 tablespoon vinaigrette; sprinkle with salt and pepper. Place fish on oiled grill rack, skin side down. Grill, covered, over medium-high heat or broil 4 in. from heat 6-8 minutes or until fish just begins to flake easily with a fork.

3. In a large bowl, combine potato mixture, arugula, tomatoes and chives. Drizzle with remaining vinaigrette; toss to coat. Serve with salmon.

PER SERVING *1 salmon fillet with 2 cups salad: 480 cal., 23g fat (4g sat. fat), 85mg chol., 642mg sodium, 33g carb. (8g sugars, 6g fiber), 34g pro.* ***Diabetic Exchanges:*** *5 lean meat, 2 vegetable, 1½ starch, 1½ fat.*

SKEWERED SHRIMP & VEGETABLES C

Serve these flavorful and colorful kabobs as an appetizer or as the main dish—either way, guests will love them!

—**SHARON WILSON** AFTON, VA

PREP: 20 MIN. + MARINATING
GRILL: 5 MIN.
MAKES: 4 SERVINGS

- **¾ cup olive oil**
- **⅓ cup lemon juice**
- **1½ teaspoons coarsely ground pepper**
- **2 garlic cloves, minced**
- **½ teaspoon salt**
- **½ teaspoon sugar**
- **½ teaspoon crushed red pepper flakes**
- **½ teaspoon grated lemon peel**
- **16 uncooked shrimp (26-30 per pound), peeled and deveined**
- **1 medium red onion, cut into eight wedges**
- **8 large fresh mushrooms, halved**
- **8 grape tomatoes**
- **Hot cooked rice, optional**
- **¼ cup grated Parmesan cheese**

1. In a large bowl, combine the first eight ingredients. Pour ⅔ cup into a large resealable plastic bag; add the shrimp. Seal the bag and turn to coat; refrigerate for 30 minutes. Cover and refrigerate remaining marinade.

2. Drain and discard the marinade. On eight metal or soaked wooden skewers, alternately thread the shrimp and vegetables. Grill, covered, over medium heat for 2-3 minutes on each side or until shrimp turn pink, turning once and basting frequently with the reserved marinade. Serve with rice if desired; sprinkle with cheese.

PER SERVING *2 skewers: 221 cal., 15g fat (3g sat. fat), 84mg chol., 249mg sodium, 8g carb. (2g sugars, 2g fiber), 15g pro.* ***Diabetic Exchanges:*** *2½ fat, 2 lean meat, 1 vegetable.*

SKEWERED SHRIMP & VEGETABLES

CURRIED SHRIMP-STACKED TOMATOES

CURRIED SHRIMP-STACKED TOMATOES

C FAST FIX

In Florida we're known for tomatoes and Gulf shrimp, so I use both in this tasty lunch. These stack up fast and keep the kitchen cool.

—**JUDY BATSON** TAMPA, FL

START TO FINISH: 20 MIN.
MAKES: 4 SERVINGS

- **4 large heirloom tomatoes**
- **6 tablespoons reduced-fat mayonnaise**
- **1 teaspoon curry powder**
- **¼ teaspoon salt**
- **¼ teaspoon ground ginger**
- **¾ pound peeled and deveined cooked shrimp (61-70 per pound)**
- **1 celery rib, chopped**
- **½ cup finely chopped cucumber**
- **1 small navel orange, peeled and finely chopped**
- **2 green onions, thinly sliced**

1. Trim and cut each tomato into three thick slices; drain on paper towels.

2. In a large bowl, mix mayonnaise and seasonings; stir in remaining ingredients. For each serving, stack three slices tomatoes, layering with shrimp mixture.

PER SERVING *217 cal., 9g fat (1g sat. fat), 137mg chol., 435mg sodium, 14g carb. (9g sugars, 3g fiber), 20g pro.* ***Diabetic Exchanges:*** *3 lean meat, 2 vegetable, 1 fat.*

LEMON-PEPPER TILAPIA WITH MUSHROOMS

C FAST FIX

My husband and I are trying to add more fish and healthier entrees to our diet, and this one makes it easy. It comes together in less than 30 minutes, so it's perfect for hectic weeknights.

—**DONNA MCDONALD** LAKE ELSINORE, CA

START TO FINISH: 25 MIN.
MAKES: 4 SERVINGS

- **2 tablespoons butter**
- **½ pound sliced fresh mushrooms**
- **¾ teaspoon lemon-pepper seasoning, divided**
- **3 garlic cloves, minced**
- **4 tilapia fillets (6 ounces each)**
- **¼ teaspoon paprika**
- **⅛ teaspoon cayenne pepper**
- **1 medium tomato, chopped**
- **3 green onions, thinly sliced**

1. In a 12-in. skillet, heat butter over medium heat. Add mushrooms and 1/4 teaspoon lemon pepper; cook and stir 3-5 minutes or until tender. Add garlic; cook 30 seconds longer.

2. Place fillets over mushrooms; sprinkle with paprika, cayenne and the remaining lemon pepper. Cook, covered, 5-7 minutes or until fish just begins to flake easily with a fork. Top with tomato and green onions.

PER SERVING *1 fillet: 216 cal., 8g fat (4g sat. fat), 98mg chol., 173mg sodium, 5g carb. (2g sugars, 1g fiber), 34g pro.* ***Diabetic Exchanges:*** *4 lean meat, 1½ fat.*

LEMON-PEPPER TILAPIA WITH MUSHROOMS

CHICKPEA CRAB SALAD WITH CITRUS VINAIGRETTE FAST FIX

(PICTURED ON P. 167)

Crab lovers will get a kick out of this salad that's just as eye-appealing as it is appetizing. I like to add a little crumbled feta cheese, and sometimes I substitute chicken or turkey for the crab.

—**SALLY SIBTHORPE** SHELBY TOWNSHIP, MI

START TO FINISH: 20 MIN.
MAKES: 2 SERVINGS

- **3 tablespoons orange juice**
- **3 tablespoons olive oil**
- **4½ teaspoons lime juice**
- **1 small garlic clove, minced**
- **¼ to ½ teaspoon ground cumin**
- **⅛ to ¼ teaspoon salt**
- **⅛ teaspoon cayenne pepper**
- **¾ cup canned garbanzo beans or chickpeas, rinsed and drained**
- **3 radishes, thinly sliced**
- **2 green onions, thinly sliced**
- **⅓ cup shredded carrot**
- **⅓ cup minced fresh parsley**
- **2 tablespoons pistachios, chopped**
- **1 can (6 ounces) lump crabmeat, drained**
- **3 cups spring mix salad greens**

In a bowl, whisk together first seven ingredients. Stir in beans, radishes, green onions, carrot, parsley and pistachios. Gently stir in crab. Serve over greens.

PER SERVING *446 cal., 27g fat (4g sat. fat), 76mg chol., 635mg sodium, 27g carb. (7g sugars, 8g fiber), 25g pro.*

CRUNCHY SALMON CAKES WITH GREEK YOGURT SAUCE

CRUNCHY SALMON CAKES WITH GREEK YOGURT SAUCE

Whether you use fresh or leftover salmon, you can serve these cakes with sauce as a main dish, appetizer or put them on a salad.

—**CINDY FAN** SAN GABRIEL, CA

PREP: 30 MIN. + CHILLING • **BAKE:** 15 MIN.
MAKES: 4 SERVINGS

- **1¼ pounds salmon fillet**
- **⅛ teaspoon plus ¼ teaspoon pepper, divided**
- **1 teaspoon olive oil**
- **1 small onion, finely chopped**
- **2 tablespoons minced fresh parsley**
- **1½ cups panko (Japanese) bread crumbs, divided**
- **½ cup reduced-fat mayonnaise**
- **1 tablespoon lemon juice**
- **¼ teaspoon salt**
- **1 teaspoon hot pepper sauce, optional**
- **2 large egg whites, lightly beaten**
- **Cooking spray**

SAUCE

- **¼ cup reduced-fat plain Greek yogurt**
- **1 teaspoon snipped fresh dill**
- **¾ teaspoon lemon juice**
- **¼ teaspoon capers, drained and chopped**

1. Place salmon on a baking sheet coated with cooking spray; sprinkle with 1/8 teaspoon pepper. Bake, uncovered, at 350° for 14-17 minutes or until fish flakes easily with a fork. Cool slightly; remove the skin, if necessary. Transfer the salmon to a shallow dish; refrigerate, covered, for 2 hours or until chilled.

2. In a large skillet, heat oil over medium-high heat. Add onion; cook and stir until tender. Stir in parsley.

3. In a large bowl, combine 1/2 cup bread crumbs, mayonnaise, lemon juice, salt, remaining pepper and the onion mixture; if desired, add pepper sauce. Flake salmon; add to bread crumb mixture, mixing lightly. Shape into eight 2 1/2-in. patties.

4. Place egg whites and remaining bread crumbs in separate shallow bowls. Dip salmon patties in egg whites, then roll in crumbs to coat. Place on a baking sheet coated with cooking spray. Spritz tops with cooking spray. Bake, uncovered, at 425° for 14-17 minutes or until golden brown.

5. In a small bowl, mix the sauce ingredients; serve with salmon cakes.

PER SERVING *2 salmon cakes with 1 tablespoon sauce: 422 cal., 25g fat (4g sat. fat), 82mg chol., 541mg sodium, 17g carb. (3g sugars, 1g fiber), 29g pro.*

FISH & SEAFOOD

TROPICAL TILAPIA F S FAST FIX

Take a walk on the wild side and venture into the tropics with this one-skillet dish. Cool mint balances the sweet heat from the jelly.

—ROXANNE CHAN ALBANY, CA

START TO FINISH: 25 MIN. • **MAKES:** 4 SERVINGS

4 tilapia fillets (4 ounces each)
1 teaspoon Caribbean jerk seasoning
1 can (15 ounces) mixed tropical fruit, undrained
¼ cup dried tropical fruit
2 green onions, chopped
¼ cup red jalapeno pepper jelly
2 tablespoons sliced almonds
2 tablespoons minced fresh mint
1 tablespoon lime juice
Hot cooked rice

1. Season fillets with jerk seasoning. In a large nonstick skillet coated with cooking spray, cook fillets over medium-high heat for 3-5 minutes or until fish flakes easily with a fork, turning once. Transfer fillets to a serving platter and keep warm.
2. In the same skillet, combine the fruit, onions, jelly and almonds; heat through. Stir in mint and lime juice. Serve with fish and rice.

PER SERVING *1 fillet with ½ cup salsa: 283 cal., 3g fat (1g sat. fat), 55mg chol., 128mg sodium, 45g carb. (15g sugars, 3g fiber), 22g pro.*

TROPICAL TILAPIA

SHRIMP & NECTARINE SALAD

SHRIMP & NECTARINE SALAD FAST FIX

For a cool salad on a hot summer day, I combine shrimp, corn, tomatoes and nectarines with a drizzle of tarragon dressing. We love it chilled, but it's great warm, too.

—MARY ANN LEE CLIFTON PARK, NY

START TO FINISH: 30 MIN. • **MAKES:** 4 SERVINGS

⅓ cup orange juice
3 tablespoons cider vinegar
1½ teaspoons Dijon mustard
1½ teaspoons honey
1 tablespoon minced fresh tarragon

SALAD

4 teaspoons canola oil, divided
1 cup fresh or frozen corn
1 pound uncooked shrimp (26-30 per pound), peeled and deveined
½ teaspoon lemon-pepper seasoning
¼ teaspoon salt
8 cups torn mixed salad greens
2 medium nectarines, cut into 1-inch pieces
1 cup grape tomatoes, halved
½ cup finely chopped red onion

1. In a small bowl, whisk orange juice, vinegar, mustard and honey until blended. Stir in tarragon.
2. In a large skillet, heat 1 teaspoon oil over medium-high heat. Add corn; cook and stir 1-2 minutes or until crisp-tender. Remove from pan.
3. Sprinkle shrimp with lemon pepper and salt. In same skillet, heat remaining oil over medium-high heat. Add shrimp; cook and stir 3-4 minutes or until shrimp turn pink. Stir in corn.
4. In a large bowl, combine remaining ingredients. Drizzle with ⅓ cup dressing and toss to coat. Divide mixture among four plates. Top with shrimp mixture; drizzle with the remaining dressing. Serve immediately.

PER SERVING *252 cal., 7g fat (1g sat. fat), 138mg chol., 448mg sodium, 27g carb. (14g sugars, 5g fiber), 23g pro.*
Diabetic Exchanges: *3 lean meat, 2 vegetable, 1 fat, ½ starch, ½ fruit.*

GINGER SALMON WITH BROWN RICE FAST FIX

What fun it is to prepare a heavenly salmon with only five ingredients! My dressing serves as a glaze and a flavor-booster for the rice.

—**NAYLET LAROCHELLE** MIAMI, FL

START TO FINISH: 25 MIN. • **MAKES:** 4 SERVINGS

- **4 salmon fillets (6 ounces each)**
- **5 tablespoons reduced-fat sesame ginger salad dressing, divided**

RICE

- **⅓ cup shredded carrot**
- **4 green onions, chopped, divided**
- **1½ cups instant brown rice**
- **1½ cups water**
- **⅓ cup reduced-fat sesame ginger salad dressing**

1. Preheat oven to 400°. Place fillets on a foil-lined baking sheet; brush with 3 tablespoons salad dressing. Bake, uncovered, 10-12 minutes or until fish just begins to flake easily with a fork. Brush with remaining salad dressing.

2. Meanwhile, place a large saucepan coated with cooking spray over medium heat. Add carrot and half of the green onion; cook and stir 2-3 minutes or until crisp-tender. Add rice and water; bring to a boil. Reduce heat; simmer, covered, 5 minutes.

3. Remove from heat; stir in salad dressing. Let stand, covered, 5 minutes or until liquid is absorbed and rice is tender. Fluff with a fork; serve with salmon. Sprinkle with remaining green onions.

PER SERVING *1 fillet with ½ cup rice mixture: 446 cal., 19g fat (3g sat. fat), 85mg chol., 605mg sodium, 34g carb. (6g sugars, 2g fiber), 32g pro.* ***Diabetic Exchanges:*** *5 lean meat, 2 starch, 2 fat.*

LEMON-PARSLEY BAKED COD C FAST FIX

This is the first fish recipe that got two thumbs up from my picky "meat-only" eaters. The tangy lemon gives the cod some oomph.

—**TRISHA KRUSE** EAGLE, ID

START TO FINISH: 30 MIN. • **MAKES:** 4 SERVINGS

- **3 tablespoons lemon juice**
- **3 tablespoons butter, melted**
- **¼ cup all-purpose flour**
- **½ teaspoon salt**
- **¼ teaspoon paprika**
- **¼ teaspoon lemon-pepper seasoning**
- **4 cod fillets (6 ounces each)**
- **2 tablespoons minced fresh parsley**
- **2 teaspoons grated lemon peel**

1. Preheat oven to 400°. In a shallow bowl, mix lemon juice and butter. In a separate shallow bowl, mix the flour and seasonings. Dip fillets in lemon juice mixture, then in flour mixture to coat both sides; shake off excess.

2. Place in a 13x9-in. baking dish coated with cooking spray. Drizzle with remaining lemon juice mixture. Bake 12-15 minutes or until fish just begins to flake easily with a fork. Mix parsley and lemon peel; sprinkle over fish.

PER SERVING *1 fillet: 232 cal., 10g fat (6g sat. fat), 87mg chol., 477mg sodium, 7g carb. (0 sugars, 0 fiber), 28g pro.* ***Diabetic Exchanges:*** *4 lean meat, 2 fat, ½ starch.*

PARMESAN FISH STICKS FAST FIX

I wanted a healthier approach to fish sticks and developed a baked tilapia with a slightly peppery bite. My husband and sons love the crispy coating.

—**CANDY SUMMERHILL** ALEXANDER, AR

START TO FINISH: 25 MIN.
MAKES: 4 SERVINGS

- **⅓ cup all-purpose flour**
- **½ teaspoon salt**
- **⅛ to ¼ teaspoon pepper**
- **2 large eggs**
- **1 cup panko (Japanese) bread crumbs**
- **⅓ cup grated Parmesan cheese**
- **2 tablespoons garlic-herb seasoning blend**
- **1 pound tilapia fillets**
- **Cooking spray**

1. Preheat oven to 450°. In a shallow bowl, mix flour, salt and pepper. In another bowl, whisk eggs. In a third bowl, toss bread crumbs with cheese and seasoning blend.

2. Cut fillets into 1-in.-wide strips. Dip fish in flour mixture to coat both sides; shake off excess. Dip in eggs, then in crumb mixture, patting to help the coating adhere.

3. Place on a foil-lined baking sheet coated with cooking spray. Spritz tops with cooking spray until the crumbs appear moistened. Bake 10-12 minutes or until golden brown and fish just begins to flake easily with a fork.

PER SERVING *281 cal., 11g fat (3g sat. fat), 154mg chol., 641mg sodium, 16g carb. (1g sugars, 1g fiber), 28g pro.* ***Diabetic Exchanges:*** *3 lean meat, 1 starch, 1 fat.*

TOP TIP

Tilapia, catfish, haddock, cod and other lean types of fish may be frozen for up to six months. Oily fish, such as mackerel, salmon and grouper, shouldn't be frozen for more than three months.

SPICY SHRIMP-SLAW PITAS

SPICY SHRIMP-SLAW PITAS

My mother brought me peach salsa from Georgia, inspiring this recipe for shrimp pitas. Edamame gives them awesome texture, or swap in some baby lima beans.

—**ANGELA MCCLURE** CARY, NC

PREP: 30 MIN. • **BROIL:** 5 MIN.
MAKES: 6 SERVINGS

- **1½ pounds uncooked shrimp (31-40 per pound), peeled, deveined and coarsely chopped**
- **1 tablespoon olive oil**
- **1 teaspoon paprika**

SLAW

- **⅓ cup reduced-fat plain Greek yogurt**
- **⅓ cup peach salsa or salsa of your choice**
- **1 tablespoon honey**
- **½ teaspoon salt**
- **½ teaspoon pepper**
- **1 package (12 ounces) broccoli coleslaw mix**
- **2 cups fresh baby spinach**
- **¼ cup shredded carrots**
- **¼ cup frozen shelled edamame, thawed**
- **12 whole wheat pita pocket halves**

1. Preheat broiler. In a small bowl, toss shrimp with oil and paprika. Transfer to a foil-lined 15x10x1-in. baking pan. Broil 4-5 in. from heat 3-4 minutes or until the shrimp turn pink, stirring once.

2. In a small bowl, whisk yogurt, salsa, honey, salt and pepper. Add coleslaw mix, spinach, carrots, edamame and shrimp; toss to coat.

3. Place pita pockets on a baking sheet. Broil 4-5 in. from heat for 1-2 minutes on each side or until lightly toasted. Fill each pita half with ½ cup shrimp mixture.

PER SERVING *2 filled pita halves: 322 cal., 6g fat (1g sat. fat), 139mg chol., 641mg sodium, 41g carb. (7g sugars, 7g fiber), 28g pro.* ***Diabetic Exchanges:*** *3 lean meat, 2 starch, 1 vegetable, ½ fat.*

SALMON WITH MANGO-CITRUS SALSA FAST FIX

My mother would make this for us on weeknights in summer—this was the only way we would eat fish. You can make the salsa a day ahead of time. Just keep it in the refrigerator covered with plastic wrap.

—**NAJMUSSAHAR AHMED** ANN ARBOR, MI

START TO FINISH: 30 MIN.
MAKES: 4 SERVINGS (2 CUPS SALSA)

- **1 large navel orange**
- **1 medium lemon**
- **2 tablespoons olive oil**
- **1 tablespoon capers, drained and coarsely chopped**
- **1½ teaspoons minced fresh mint**
- **1½ teaspoons minced fresh parsley**
- **¼ teaspoon crushed red pepper flakes**
- **⅛ teaspoon plus ½ teaspoon salt, divided**
- **⅛ teaspoon plus ¼ teaspoon pepper, divided**
- **1 medium mango, peeled and chopped**
- **1 green onion, thinly sliced**
- **4 salmon fillets (6 ounces each)**
- **1 tablespoon canola oil**

1. For salsa, finely grate enough peel from orange to measure 2 teaspoons; finely grate enough peel from lemon to measure ½ teaspoon. Place the citrus peels in a small bowl. Cut lemon crosswise in half; squeeze lemon to add 2 tablespoons of juice to bowl.

2. Cut a thin slice from top and bottom of orange; stand orange upright on a cutting board. Use a knife to cut off peel and outer membrane from orange. Cut along the membrane of each segment to remove fruit.

3. Add olive oil, capers, mint, parsley, pepper flakes and ⅛ teaspoon each salt and pepper to the lemon juice mixture. Gently stir in mango, green onion and orange sections.

4. Sprinkle salmon with remaining salt and pepper. In a large skillet, heat canola oil over medium heat. Add the salmon; cook 5-6 minutes on each side or until fish just begins to flake easily with a fork. Serve with salsa.

PER SERVING *1 fillet with ½ cup salsa: 433 cal., 26g fat (4g sat. fat), 85mg chol., 516mg sodium, 19g carb. (16g sugars, 3g fiber), 30g pro.* ***Diabetic Exchanges:*** *5 lean meat, 1½ fat, 1 fruit.*

SALMON WITH MANGO-CITRUS SALSA

SPECIAL SCALLOP SALAD

SPECIAL SCALLOP SALAD C FAST FIX

What an easy way to fix a special and delicious meal. The balsamic, tarragon and honey blend beautifully in the warm dressing.

—**MARY RELYEA** CANASTOTA, NY

START TO FINISH: 20 MIN.
MAKES: 4 SERVINGS

- **12 sea scallops (about 1½ pounds)**
- **¼ teaspoon salt**
- **⅛ teaspoon pepper**
- **3 tablespoons olive oil, divided**
- **1 tablespoon fresh minced chives**
- **1 tablespoon balsamic vinegar**
- **2 garlic cloves, minced**
- **2 teaspoons minced fresh tarragon**
- **2 teaspoons honey**
- **1 teaspoon Dijon mustard**
- **1 package (5 ounces) spring mix salad greens**
- **1 cup shredded carrots**
- **½ cup chopped tomato**

1. Pat scallops dry with paper towels; sprinkle with salt and pepper. In a large skillet, heat 2 tablespoons oil over medium-high heat. Add scallops; sear 1-2 minutes on each side or until golden brown and firm. Remove from pan; keep warm.

2. In same pan, combine chives, vinegar, garlic, tarragon, honey, mustard and remaining oil. Bring to a boil; cook and stir until slightly thickened, about 30 seconds.

3. Divide salad greens, carrots and tomato among four plates; top with scallops. Drizzle with the dressing; serve immediately.

PER SERVING *247 cal., 11g fat (2g sat. fat), 41mg chol., 821mg sodium, 15g carb. (6g sugars, 2g fiber), 22g pro.* ***Diabetic Exchanges:*** *3 lean meat, 2 fat, 1 vegetable, ½ starch.*

SHRIMP AVOCADO SALAD

SHRIMP AVOCADO SALAD C

This salad can be served as a cool and satisfying dinner or lunch. The delicious taste of avocados mixed with the crisp shrimp salad is heavenly.

—**TERI RASEY** CADILLAC, MI

PREP: 25 MIN. + CHILLING
MAKES: 6 SERVINGS

- **1 pound peeled and deveined cooked shrimp, coarsely chopped**
- **2 plum tomatoes, seeded and chopped**
- **2 green onions, chopped**
- **¼ cup finely chopped red onion**
- **1 jalapeno pepper, seeded and minced**
- **1 serrano pepper, seeded and minced**
- **2 tablespoons minced fresh cilantro**
- **2 tablespoons lime juice**
- **2 tablespoons seasoned rice vinegar**
- **2 tablespoons olive oil**
- **1 teaspoon adobo seasoning**
- **3 medium ripe avocados, peeled and cubed**
- **Bibb lettuce leaves**
- **Lime wedges**

1. Place first seven ingredients in a large bowl. Mix lime juice, vinegar, oil and adobo seasoning; stir into shrimp mixture. Refrigerate, covered, to allow flavors to blend, about 1 hour.

2. To serve, gently stir in avocados. Serve over lettuce. Serve with lime wedges.

NOTE *Wear disposable gloves when cutting hot peppers; the oils can burn skin. Avoid touching your face.*

PER SERVING *¾ cup of avocado mixture: 252 cal., 16g fat (2g sat. fat), 115mg chol., 523mg sodium, 11g carb. (3g sugars, 5g fiber), 17g pro.* ***Diabetic Exchanges:*** *3 fat, 2 lean meat, ½ starch.*

COD WITH BACON & BALSAMIC TOMATOES

C FAST FIX

START TO FINISH: 30 MIN.
MAKES: 4 SERVINGS

- **4 center-cut bacon strips, chopped**
- **4 cod fillets (5 ounces each)**
- **½ teaspoon salt**
- **¼ teaspoon pepper**
- **2 cups grape tomatoes, halved**
- **2 tablespoons balsamic vinegar**

1. In a large skillet, cook bacon over medium heat until crisp, stirring occasionally. Remove with a slotted spoon; drain on paper towels.

2. Sprinkle fillets with salt and pepper. Add fillets to bacon drippings; cook over medium-high heat 4-6 minutes on each side or until fish just begins to flake easily with a fork. Remove and keep warm.

3. Add tomatoes to skillet; cook and stir 2-4 minutes or until tomatoes are softened. Stir in vinegar; reduce heat to medium-low. Cook 1-2 minutes longer or until sauce is thickened. Serve cod with tomato mixture and bacon.

PER SERVING *1 fillet with ¼ cup tomato mixture and 1 tablespoon bacon: 178 cal., 6g fat (2g sat. fat), 64mg chol., 485mg sodium, 5g carb. (4g sugars, 1g fiber), 26g pro.* ***Diabetic Exchanges:*** *4 lean meat, 1 vegetable.*

Let's face it: Everything really is better with bacon. I fry it up, add cod fillets to the pan and finish with a big, tomato-y pop.

—**MAUREEN MCCLANAHAN** SAINT LOUIS, MO

COD WITH BACON & BALSAMIC TOMATOES

FISH & SEAFOOD

CRUNCHY TUNA WRAPS FAST FIX

We love tuna salad wraps loaded with lots of crunchy veggies like celery, red pepper and water chestnuts. It's a great way to shake up standard tuna salad.

—**EDIE FARM** FARMINGTON, NM

START TO FINISH: 10 MIN.
MAKES: 2 SERVINGS

- **1 pouch (6.4 ounces) light tuna in water**
- **¼ cup finely chopped celery**
- **¼ cup chopped green onions**
- **¼ cup sliced water chestnuts, chopped**
- **3 tablespoons chopped sweet red pepper**
- **2 tablespoons reduced-fat mayonnaise**
- **2 teaspoons prepared mustard**
- **2 spinach tortillas (8 inches), room temperature**
- **1 cup shredded lettuce**

In a small bowl, mix the first seven ingredients until blended. Spread over tortillas; sprinkle with lettuce. Roll up tightly jelly-roll style.

PER SERVING *1 wrap: 312 cal., 10g fat (2g sat. fat), 38mg chol., 628mg sodium, 34g carb. (2g sugars, 3g fiber), 23g pro.* ***Diabetic Exchanges:*** *3 lean meat, 2 starch, ½ fat.*

HOISIN-PINEAPPLE SALMON

CRUNCHY TUNA WRAPS

HOISIN-PINEAPPLE SALMON FAST FIX

My mouth waters when I think of this sweet and tangy flavor. The pairing of sweet orange and slightly acidic pineapple makes for a delicious contrast with the hoisin-glazed salmon. A sprinkle of cilantro adds some freshness!

—**NAYLET LAROCHELLE** MIAMI, FL

START TO FINISH: 20 MIN.
MAKES: 4 SERVINGS

- **4 salmon fillets (6 ounces each)**
- **2 tablespoons hoisin sauce**
- **¼ teaspoon pepper**
- **½ cup unsweetened crushed pineapple**
- **¼ cup orange marmalade**
- **2 tablespoons chopped fresh cilantro**

1. Preheat oven to 400°. Spread the salmon with hoisin sauce; sprinkle with pepper. Place fish on a greased foil-lined baking sheet, skin side down. Bake 12-15 minutes or until fish begins to flake easily with a fork.

2. Meanwhile, in a small saucepan, combine pineapple and marmalade. Bring to a boil, stirring occasionally; cook and stir 4-6 minutes or until slightly thickened. Spoon over salmon; sprinkle with cilantro.

PER SERVING *1 salmon fillet with 2 tablespoons sauce: 349 cal., 16g fat (3g sat. fat), 86mg chol., 226mg sodium, 21g carb. (18g sugars, 1g fiber), 29g pro.* ***Diabetic Exchanges:*** *4 lean meat, 1½ starch.*

TOP TIP

Hoisin sauce is a thick, sweet and somewhat spicy condiment popular in Chinese cooking. It's often made with fermented soybeans (miso), garlic, spices and sweet ingredients such as plums or sweet potatoes.

SHRIMP & VEGETABLE BOIL F

When my children were small, they liked picking out the ingredients for making this supper. When there's no shrimp on hand, we use crab or chicken.

—**JOYCE GUTH** MOHNTON, PA

PREP: 20 MIN. • **COOK:** 30 MIN.
MAKES: 6 SERVINGS

- **4 cups water**
- **4 cups chicken broth**
- **2 teaspoons salt**
- **2 teaspoons ground nutmeg**
- **½ teaspoon sugar**
- **2 pounds red potatoes (about 8 medium), cut into wedges**
- **1 medium head cauliflower, broken into florets**
- **2 large onions, quartered**
- **3 medium carrots, sliced**
- **1 pound fresh peas, shelled (about 1 cup)**
- **2 pounds uncooked shell-on shrimp (26-30 per pound), deveined**
- **6 ounces fresh baby spinach (about 8 cups)**
- **1 tablespoon minced fresh parsley**
- **Salt and pepper to taste**

1. In a stockpot, combine the first five ingredients; add potatoes, cauliflower, onions, carrots and peas. Bring to a boil. Reduce heat; simmer, uncovered, 12-15 minutes or until vegetables are tender.

2. Stir in shrimp and spinach; cook 3-5 minutes longer or until shrimp turn pink. Drain; transfer to a large serving bowl. Sprinkle with parsley; season with salt and pepper.

PER SERVING *2⅔ cups: 367 cal., 3g fat (1g sat. fat), 185mg chol., 721mg sodium, 50g carb. (12g sugars, 11g fiber), 35g pro.* ***Diabetic Exchanges:*** *4 lean meat, 3 starch.*

SHRIMP & VEGETABLE BOIL

MAHI MAHI & VEGGIE SKILLET

MAHI MAHI & VEGGIE SKILLET C FAST FIX

Cooking mahi mahi and ratatouille may seem complex, but I've developed a skillet recipe to bring out the wow factor without the worry.

—**SOLOMON WANG** ARLINGTON, TX

START TO FINISH: 30 MIN.
MAKES: 4 SERVINGS

- **3 tablespoons olive oil, divided**
- **4 mahi mahi or salmon fillets (6 ounces each)**
- **3 medium sweet red peppers, cut into thick strips**
- **½ pound sliced baby portobello mushrooms**
- **1 large sweet onion, cut into thick rings and separated**
- **⅓ cup lemon juice**
- **¾ teaspoon salt, divided**
- **½ teaspoon pepper**
- **¼ cup minced fresh chives**
- **⅓ cup pine nuts, optional**

1. In a large skillet, heat 2 tablespoons oil over medium-high heat. Add fillets; cook 4-5 minutes on each side or until fish just begins to flake easily with a fork. Remove from pan.

2. Add the remaining oil, peppers, mushrooms, onion, lemon juice and 1/4 teaspoon salt. Cook, covered, over medium heat for 6-8 minutes or until the vegetables are tender, stirring occasionally.

3. Place fish over the vegetables; sprinkle with pepper and remaining salt. Cook, covered, 2 minutes longer or until heated through. Sprinkle with minced chives and, if desired, pine nuts before serving.

PER SERVING *307 cal., 12g fat (2g sat. fat), 124mg chol., 606mg sodium, 15g carb. (9g sugars, 3g fiber), 35g pro.* ***Diabetic Exchanges:*** *4 lean meat, 3 vegetable, 2 fat.*

CEDAR PLANK SCALLOPS F C

I got this idea from the fishmonger at our farmers market and a kitchen store that had cedar cooking planks on sale. I made the first batch for my wife and me, made some adjustments and tried the recipe again with friends. Now all of my friends who tried them have gone out and bought cedar planks for cooking.

—**ROBERT HALPERT** NEWBURYPORT, MA

PREP: 10 MIN. + SOAKING • **GRILL:** 15 MIN. • **MAKES:** 4 SERVINGS

- **2 cedar grilling planks**
- **¼ cup dry white wine**
- **2 tablespoons olive oil**
- **2 teaspoons minced fresh basil**
- **1 teaspoon minced fresh thyme**
- **1 teaspoon lime juice**
- **12 sea scallops (about 1½ pounds)**

1. Soak planks in water at least 1 hour. In a large bowl, whisk wine, oil, basil, thyme and lime juice. Add scallops; gently toss to coat. Let stand 15 minutes.

2. Place the planks on grill rack over direct medium heat. Cover and heat 4-5 minutes or until light to medium smoke comes from the plank and the wood begins to crackle. (This indicates the plank is ready.) Turn plank over and place on indirect heat. Drain scallops, discarding marinade. Place scallops on plank. Grill, covered, over indirect medium heat 10-12 minutes or until firm and opaque.

PER SERVING *3 scallops: 142 cal., 3g fat (1g sat. fat), 41mg chol., 667mg sodium, 6g carb. (0 sugars, 0 fiber), 21g pro.* ***Diabetic Exchanges:*** *3 lean meat, ½ starch, ½ fat.*

CEDAR PLANK SCALLOPS

TOMATO-POACHED HALIBUT

TOMATO-POACHED HALIBUT FAST FIX

My simple halibut with a burst of lemon comes together in one pan. Try it with polenta, angel hair pasta or crusty bread.

—**DANNA ROGERS** WESTPORT, CT

START TO FINISH: 30 MIN. • **MAKES:** 4 SERVINGS

- **1 tablespoon olive oil**
- **2 poblano peppers, finely chopped**
- **1 small onion, finely chopped**
- **1 can (14½ ounces) fire-roasted diced tomatoes, undrained**
- **1 can (14½ ounces) no-salt-added diced tomatoes, undrained**
- **¼ cup chopped pitted green olives**
- **3 garlic cloves, minced**
- **¼ teaspoon pepper**
- **⅛ teaspoon salt**
- **4 halibut fillets (4 ounces each)**
- **⅓ cup chopped fresh cilantro**
- **4 lemon wedges**
- **Crusty whole grain bread, optional**

1. In a large nonstick skillet, heat oil over medium-high heat. Add poblano peppers and onion; cook and stir for 4-6 minutes or until tender.

2. Stir in tomatoes, olives, garlic, pepper and salt. Bring to a boil. Adjust heat to maintain a gentle simmer. Add fillets. Cook, covered, 8-10 minutes or until fish just begins to flake easily with a fork. Sprinkle with cilantro. Serve with lemon wedges and, if desired, bread.

PER SERVING *1 fillet with 1 cup sauce: 224 cal., 7g fat (1g sat. fat), 56mg chol., 651mg sodium, 17g carb. (8g sugars, 4g fiber), 24g pro.* ***Diabetic Exchanges:*** *3 lean meat, 1 starch, ½ fat.*

SPICY COCONUT SHRIMP WITH QUINOA

PREP: 20 MIN. • **COOK:** 20 MIN. • **MAKES:** 4 SERVINGS

- **1 cup quinoa, rinsed**
- **2 cups water**
- **¼ teaspoon salt**

SHRIMP

- **1 teaspoon olive oil**
- **1 medium onion, chopped**
- **1 tablespoon minced fresh gingerroot**
- **½ teaspoon curry powder**
- **½ teaspoon ground cumin**
- **¼ teaspoon salt**
- **¼ teaspoon cayenne pepper**
- **1 pound uncooked shrimp (26-30 per pound), peeled and deveined**
- **2 cups fresh snow peas (about 7 ounces), trimmed**
- **3 tablespoons light coconut milk**
- **1 tablespoon orange juice**
- **¼ cup flaked coconut, toasted**
- **¼ cup minced fresh cilantro**

> Help yourself to a plateful—generous servings are still low in calories and big on protein. If you have company, you can add a salad and call it a day.
> —**KERI WHITNEY** CASTRO VALLEY, CA

SPICY COCONUT SHRIMP WITH QUINOA

1. In a large saucepan, combine the quinoa, water and salt; bring to a boil. Reduce the heat; simmer, covered, for 12-15 minutes or until liquid is absorbed. Remove from heat; fluff with a fork.
2. Meanwhile, in a large nonstick skillet, heat the oil over medium heat. Add onion; cook and stir 4-6 minutes or until tender. Stir in the ginger, curry powder, cumin, salt and cayenne; cook 1 minute longer.
3. Add shrimp and snow peas to skillet; cook and stir 3-4 minutes or until shrimp turn pink and snow peas are crisp-tender. Stir in coconut milk and orange juice; heat through. Serve with quinoa; top each serving with coconut and cilantro.

NOTE *To toast coconut, bake in a shallow pan in a 350° oven for 5-10 minutes or cook in a skillet over low heat until golden brown, stirring occasionally.*

PER SERVING *1 cup shrimp mixture with ¾ cup quinoa: 330 cal., 8g fat (3g sat. fat), 138mg chol., 451mg sodium, 37g carb. (6g sugars, 5g fiber), 26g pro.* ***Diabetic Exchanges:*** *3 lean meat, 2 starch, 1 vegetable, ½ fat.*

HEALTH TIP *Quinoa is a good source of trace minerals—specifically manganese and copper—that are important in turning carbohydrates into energy.*

CRUNCHY OVEN-BAKED TILAPIA

F C FAST FIX (PICTURED ON P. 167)

This baked tilapia is perfectly crunchy. Dip it in the fresh lime mayo to send it over the top.
—**LESLIE PALMER** SWAMPSCOTT, MA

START TO FINISH: 25 MIN. • **MAKES:** 4 SERVINGS

- **4 tilapia fillets (6 ounces each)**
- **1 tablespoon reduced-fat mayonnaise**
- **1 tablespoon lime juice**
- **¼ teaspoon grated lime peel**
- **½ teaspoon salt**
- **¼ teaspoon onion powder**
- **¼ teaspoon pepper**
- **½ cup panko (Japanese) bread crumbs**
- **Cooking spray**
- **2 tablespoons minced fresh cilantro or parsley**

1. Preheat oven to 425°. Place the fillets on a baking sheet coated with cooking spray. In a small bowl, mix the mayonnaise, lime juice and peel, salt, onion powder and pepper. Spread mayonnaise mixture over fish. Sprinkle with bread crumbs; spritz with cooking spray.
2. Bake 15-20 minutes or until fish just begins to flake easily with a fork. Sprinkle with cilantro.

PER SERVING *1 fillet: 186 cal., 3g fat (1g sat. fat), 84mg chol., 401mg sodium, 6g carb. (0 sugars, 0 fiber), 33g pro.* ***Diabetic Exchanges:*** *5 lean meat, ½ starch.*

HEALTH TIP *Look for U.S. or Canadian tilapia that's been farmed in closed tanks for the least impact on the environment.*

FANTASTIC FISH TACOS FAST FIX

Searching for a lighter substitute to traditional fried fish tacos, I came up with this entree. It's been a hit with friends and family. These fillets are so mild that even those who don't like fish are pleasantly surprised.

—JENNIFER PALMER
RANCHO CUCAMONGA, CA

START TO FINISH: 30 MIN.
MAKES: 4 SERVINGS

- **½ cup fat-free mayonnaise**
- **1 tablespoon lime juice**
- **2 teaspoons fat-free milk**
- **1 large egg**
- **1 teaspoon water**
- **⅓ cup dry bread crumbs**
- **2 tablespoons salt-free lemon-pepper seasoning**
- **1 pound mahi mahi or cod fillets, cut into 1-inch strips**
- **4 corn tortillas (6 inches), warmed**

TOPPINGS

- **1 cup coleslaw mix**
- **2 medium tomatoes, chopped**
- **1 cup shredded reduced-fat Mexican cheese blend**
- **1 tablespoon minced fresh cilantro**

1. For sauce, in a small bowl, mix mayonnaise, lime juice and milk; refrigerate until serving.
2. In a shallow bowl, whisk together egg and water. In another bowl, toss bread crumbs with lemon pepper. Dip fish in the egg mixture, then in the crumb mixture, patting to help coating adhere.
3. Place a large nonstick skillet coated with cooking spray over medium-high heat. Add fish; cook 2-4 minutes per side or until golden brown and fish just begins to flake easily with a fork. Serve in tortillas with toppings and sauce.

PER SERVING *1 taco: 321 cal., 10g fat (5g sat. fat), 148mg chol., 632mg sodium, 29g carb. (5g sugars, 4g fiber), 34g pro.* ***Diabetic Exchanges:*** *4 lean meat, 2 starch.*

FANTASTIC FISH TACOS

GARLIC TILAPIA WITH SPICY KALE FAST FIX

(PICTURED ON P. 167)

We make this main dish and side together, and adjust the heat from the red pepper flakes depending on who's at the table.

—TARA CRUZ KERSEY, CO

START TO FINISH: 30 MIN.
MAKES: 4 SERVINGS

- **3 tablespoons olive oil, divided**
- **2 garlic cloves, minced**
- **1 teaspoon fennel seed**
- **½ teaspoon crushed red pepper flakes**
- **1 bunch kale, trimmed and coarsely chopped (about 16 cups)**
- **⅔ cup water**
- **4 tilapia fillets (6 ounces each)**
- **¾ teaspoon pepper, divided**
- **½ teaspoon garlic salt**
- **1 can (15 ounces) cannellini beans, rinsed and drained**
- **½ teaspoon salt**

1. In 6-qt. stockpot, heat a tablespoon of oil over medium heat. Add garlic, fennel and pepper flakes; cook and stir 1 minute. Add kale and water; bring to a boil. Reduce heat; simmer, covered, 10-12 minutes or until kale is tender.
2. Meanwhile, sprinkle tilapia with 1/2 teaspoon pepper and garlic salt. In a large skillet, heat the remaining oil over medium heat. Add tilapia; cook 3-4 minutes on each side or until fish just begins to flake easily with a fork.
3. Add beans, salt and remaining pepper to kale; heat through, stirring occasionally. Serve with tilapia.

PER SERVING *1 fillet with 1 cup kale mixture: 359 cal., 13g fat (2g sat. fat), 83mg chol., 645mg sodium, 24g carb. (0 sugars, 6g fiber), 39g pro.* ***Diabetic Exchanges:*** *5 lean meat, 2 fat, 1½ starch.*

HEALTH TIP *Nearly half of Americans don't get enough vitamin A. One serving gives you three times the daily recommendation for this immune-boosting vitamin.*

ARTICHOKE COD WITH SUN-DRIED TOMATOES

ARTICHOKE COD WITH SUN-DRIED TOMATOES

C FAST FIX

Cod is a great break from really rich dishes around the holidays. I like to serve it over a bed of greens, pasta or quinoa. A squeeze of lemon gives it another layer of freshness.

—**HIROKO MILES** EL DORADO HILLS, CA

START TO FINISH: 30 MIN.
MAKES: 6 SERVINGS

- **1 can (14 ounces) quartered water-packed artichoke hearts, drained**
- **½ cup julienned soft sun-dried tomatoes (not packed in oil)**
- **2 green onions, chopped**
- **3 tablespoons olive oil**
- **1 garlic clove, minced**
- **6 cod fillets (6 ounces each)**
- **1 teaspoon salt**
- **½ teaspoon pepper**
- **Salad greens and lemon wedges, optional**

1. Preheat oven to 400°. In a small bowl, combine first five ingredients; toss to combine.
2. Sprinkle both sides of cod with salt and pepper; place in a 13x9-in. baking dish coated with cooking spray. Top with artichoke mixture.
3. Bake, uncovered, 15-20 minutes or until fish just begins to flake easily with a fork. If desired, serve over greens with lemon wedges.

NOTE *This recipe was tested with sun-dried tomatoes that can be used without soaking. When using sun-dried tomatoes that are not oil-packed, cover with boiling water and let stand until soft. Drain before using.*

PER SERVING *1 fillet with ⅓ cup artichoke mixture: 231 cal., 8g fat (1g sat. fat), 65mg chol., 665mg sodium, 9g carb. (3g sugars, 2g fiber), 29g pro.* ***Diabetic Exchanges:*** *4 lean meat, 1½ fat, 1 vegetable.*

SALMON VEGGIE PACKETS

C FAST FIX

I feel the spirit of Julia Child when I make lemon-pepper salmon en papillote—(in paper). This healthy technique seals in vitamins and flavor.

—**RENEE GREENE** SMITHTOWN, NY

START TO FINISH: 30 MIN.
MAKES: 4 SERVINGS

- **2 tablespoons white wine**
- **1 tablespoon olive oil**
- **¼ teaspoon salt**
- **¼ teaspoon pepper**
- **2 medium sweet yellow peppers, julienned**
- **2 cups fresh sugar snap peas, trimmed**

SALMON

- **2 tablespoons white wine**
- **1 tablespoon olive oil**
- **1 tablespoon grated lemon peel**
- **½ teaspoon salt**
- **¼ teaspoon pepper**
- **4 salmon fillets (6 ounces each)**
- **1 medium lemon, halved**

1. Preheat oven to 400°. Cut four 18x15-in. pieces of parchment paper or heavy-duty foil; fold each crosswise in half, forming a crease. In a large bowl, mix wine, oil, salt and pepper. Add vegetables and toss to coat.
2. In a small bowl, mix the first five salmon ingredients. To assemble, lay open one piece of parchment paper; place a salmon fillet on one side. Drizzle with 2 teaspoons wine mixture; top with one-fourth of the vegetables.
3. Fold paper over fish and vegetables; fold the open ends two times to seal. Repeat with remaining packets. Place on baking sheets.
4. Bake 12-16 minutes or until the fish just begins to flake easily with a fork, opening packets carefully to allow steam to escape.
5. To serve, squeeze lemon juice over vegetables.

PER SERVING *400 cal., 23g fat (4g sat. fat), 85mg chol., 535mg sodium, 13g carb. (3g sugars, 3g fiber), 32g pro.* ***Diabetic Exchanges:*** *5 lean meat, 1½ fat, 1 vegetable.*

SALMON VEGGIE PACKETS

188

197

199

Meatless Mains

"My husband has to watch his cholesterol. This is a dish I found that's healthy for him and yummy for our five children."

—**MICHELLE THOMAS** BANGOR, ME
about her recipe, Tasty Lentil Tacos, on page 197

FETA GARBANZO BEAN SALAD M FAST FIX

This super-quick garbanzo bean salad is a hit with my crowd. If there are any leftovers, which will be unlikely, stuff them into a pita for lunch.

—**JUDY DOEPEL** CHARLTON, NY

START TO FINISH: 15 MIN.
MAKES: 4 SERVINGS

- **1 can (15 ounces) garbanzo beans or chickpeas, rinsed and drained**
- **1½ cups coarsely chopped English cucumber (about ½ medium)**
- **1 can (2¼ ounces) sliced ripe olives, drained**
- **1 medium tomato, seeded and chopped**
- **¼ cup thinly sliced red onion**
- **¼ cup chopped fresh parsley**
- **3 tablespoons olive oil**
- **1 tablespoon lemon juice**
- **¼ teaspoon salt**
- **⅛ teaspoon pepper**
- **5 cups torn mixed salad greens**
- **½ cup crumbled feta cheese**

Place the first 11 ingredients in a large bowl; toss to combine. Sprinkle with feta cheese.

PER SERVING *2 cups: 268 cal., 16g fat (3g sat. fat), 8mg chol., 586mg sodium, 24g carb. (4g sugars, 7g fiber), 9g pro.* ***Diabetic Exchanges:*** *3 fat, 1 starch, 1 vegetable, 1 lean meat.*

FETA GARBANZO BEAN SALAD

CRISPY RICE PATTIES WITH VEGETABLES & EGGS

CRISPY RICE PATTIES WITH VEGETABLES & EGGS M FAST FIX

Serve these patties at any time of day. The recipe features protein, grains and vegetables all in one dish. It's also a great way to use leftover rice.

—**MEGUMI GARCIA** MILWAUKEE, WI

START TO FINISH: 30 MIN.
MAKES: 4 SERVINGS

- **2 packages (7.4 ounces each) ready-to-serve white sticky rice**
- **1 tablespoon plus 2 teaspoons canola oil, divided**
- **1 teaspoon reduced-sodium soy sauce**
- **2 cups thinly sliced Brussels sprouts**
- **1 cup julienned carrots**
- **1 medium sweet red pepper, julienned**
- **½ teaspoon sesame oil**
- **½ teaspoon salt**
- **⅛ teaspoon freshly ground pepper**
- **1 tablespoon water**
- **4 large eggs**
- **Minced fresh chives**
- **Additional pepper**

1. Cook rice according to package directions; cool slightly. Press a fourth of the rice into a ½-cup measuring cup that has been moistened lightly with water; invert onto a large sheet of plastic wrap. Fold plastic around rice; shape rice into a ½-in.-thick patty. Repeat three times.

2. In a large nonstick skillet, heat 1 tablespoon canola oil over medium-high heat. Cook patties until crisp, 3-5 minutes per side; brush tops with soy sauce after turning. Remove from pan; keep warm.

3. In same pan, cook and stir vegetables over medium-high heat until lightly browned. Stir in sesame oil, salt and pepper. Add the water; reduce heat to medium. Cook, covered, until vegetables are crisp-tender, 1-2 minutes. Remove from pan; keep warm.

4. In same pan, heat remaining canola oil over medium heat. Break eggs, one at a time, into pan; immediately reduce heat to low. Cook, uncovered, until whites are completely set and yolks just begin to thicken, about 5 minutes. To serve, top rice patties with vegetables and eggs. Sprinkle with chives and additional pepper.

PER SERVING *1 patty: 320 cal., 11g fat (2g sat. fat), 186mg chol., 447mg sodium, 43g carb. (4g sugars, 3g fiber), 11g pro.* ***Diabetic Exchanges:*** *3 starch, 1 medium-fat meat, 1 fat.*

HEALTH TIP *The protein in eggs helps power up muscles, and their B vitamins are essential for energy metabolism.*

GREEK SALAD PITAS M FAST FIX

This healthy meal-in-a-pocket combines fresh Greek salad with a zesty chickpea spread. You can also serve the spread with crackers or use it as a dip with cut fresh vegetables.

—**NICOLE FILIZETTI** STEVENS POINT, WI

START TO FINISH: 20 MIN.
MAKES: 2 SERVINGS

- **¾ cup canned chickpeas, rinsed and drained**
- **2 tablespoons lemon juice**
- **1 tablespoon sliced green olives with pimientos**
- **1 teaspoon olive oil**
- **1 garlic clove, minced**
- **1 cup fresh baby spinach**
- **¼ cup chopped seeded peeled cucumber**
- **¼ cup crumbled feta cheese**
- **2 tablespoons chopped marinated quartered artichoke hearts**
- **2 tablespoons sliced Greek olives**
- **¼ teaspoon dried oregano**
- **2 whole wheat pita pocket halves**

1. Place the first five ingredients in a food processor; cover and process until smooth. Set aside.
2. In a small bowl, combine spinach, cucumber, cheese, artichokes, olives and oregano.
3. Spread bean mixture into pita halves; add salad. Serve immediately.

PER SERVING *1 filled pita half: 292 cal., 12g fat (3g sat. fat), 8mg chol., 687mg sodium, 38g carb. (3g sugars, 7g fiber), 10g pro.* ***Diabetic Exchanges:*** *2 starch, 1 lean meat, 1 fat.*

CHEESY SPINACH-STUFFED SHELLS F M

I'm very proud of this personal recipe because I am still a beginner cook and it was the first dish I created. You can adjust it to your liking by adding more spinach or some meat to it.

—**LACI HOOTEN** MCKINNEY, TX

PREP: 45 MIN. • **BAKE:** 45 MIN.
MAKES: 12 SERVINGS

- **1 package (12 ounces) jumbo pasta shells**
- **1 tablespoon butter**
- **1 cup sliced mushrooms**
- **1 small onion, finely chopped**
- **4 garlic cloves, minced**
- **2 large eggs, lightly beaten**
- **1 carton (15 ounces) part-skim ricotta cheese**
- **1 package (10 ounces) frozen chopped spinach, thawed and squeezed dry**
- **2 tablespoons minced fresh basil or 2 teaspoons dried basil**
- **¼ teaspoon pepper**
- **1 can (4¼ ounces) chopped ripe olives**
- **1½ cups shredded Italian cheese blend, divided**
- **1½ cups shredded part-skim mozzarella cheese, divided**
- **1 jar (24 ounces) marinara sauce**
- **Additional minced fresh basil, optional**

1. Preheat oven to 375°. Cook the pasta shells according to package directions for al dente. Drain; rinse with cold water.
2. Meanwhile, in a small skillet, heat butter over medium-high heat. Add mushrooms and onion; cook and stir 4-6 minutes or until the vegetables are tender. Add garlic; cook 1 minute longer. Remove from the heat; cool mixture slightly.
3. In a large bowl, mix eggs, ricotta cheese, spinach, basil and pepper. Stir in olives, mushroom mixture and ¾ cup each cheese blend and mozzarella cheese.
4. Spread 1 cup sauce into a 13x9-in. baking dish coated with cooking spray. Fill pasta shells with cheese mixture; place in baking dish, overlapping ends slightly. Spoon remaining sauce over top.
5. Bake, covered, 40-45 minutes or until heated through. Uncover; sprinkle with remaining cheeses. Bake 5 minutes longer or until cheese is melted. Let stand 5 minutes before serving. If desired, sprinkle with additional basil.

PER SERVING *3 stuffed shells: 313 cal., 13g fat (7g sat. fat), 65mg chol., 642mg sodium, 32g carb. (5g sugars, 3g fiber), 18g pro.* ***Diabetic Exchanges:*** *2 starch, 2 medium-fat meat, ½ fat.*

CHEESY SPINACH-STUFFED SHELLS

NO-FRY BLACK BEAN CHIMICHANGAS M FAST FIX

START TO FINISH: 25 MIN.
MAKES: 6 SERVINGS

- **2 cans (15 ounces each) black beans, rinsed and drained**
- **1 package (8.8 ounces) ready-to-serve brown rice**
- **⅔ cup frozen corn**
- **⅔ cup minced fresh cilantro**
- **⅔ cup chopped green onions**
- **½ teaspoon salt**
- **6 whole wheat tortillas (8 inches), warmed if necessary**
- **4 teaspoons olive oil, divided**
- **Guacamole and salsa, optional**

1. Preheat broiler. In a large microwave-safe bowl, mix beans, rice and corn; microwave, covered, 4-5 minutes or until heated through, stirring halfway. Stir in cilantro, green onions and salt.

2. To assemble, spoon ¾ cup bean mixture across center of each tortilla. Fold bottom and sides of tortilla over filling and roll up. Place on a greased baking sheet, seam side down.

3. Brush tops with 2 teaspoons oil. Broil 3-4 inches from heat 45-60 seconds or until golden brown. Turn over; brush tops with remaining oil. Broil 45-60 seconds longer or until golden brown. If desired, serve with guacamole and salsa.

PER SERVING *1 chimichanga: 337 cal., 5g fat (0 sat. fat), 0 chol., 602mg sodium, 58g carb. (2g sugars, 10g fiber), 13g pro.*

NO-FRY BLACK BEAN CHIMICHANGAS

CHARD & WHITE BEAN PASTA M (PICTURED ON P. 185)

I love to prepare gluten-free and dairy-free dishes, and this recipe meets the criteria when you use gluten-free pasta. This dish shows you can use delicious, healthy products to create a crowd-pleasing meal. It's also soy-free, nut-free and vegetarian.
—AMIE VALPONE NEW YORK, NY

PREP: 20 MIN. • **COOK:** 20 MIN.
MAKES: 8 SERVINGS

- **1 package (12 ounces) uncooked whole wheat or brown rice penne pasta**
- **2 tablespoons olive oil**
- **4 cups sliced leeks (white portion only)**
- **1 cup sliced sweet onion**
- **4 garlic cloves, sliced**
- **1 tablespoon minced fresh sage or 1 teaspoon rubbed sage**
- **1 large sweet potato, peeled and cut into ½-inch cubes**
- **1 medium bunch Swiss chard (about 1 pound), cut into 1-inch slices**
- **1 can (15½ ounces) great northern beans, rinsed and drained**
- **¾ teaspoon salt**
- **¼ teaspoon chili powder**
- **¼ teaspoon crushed red pepper flakes**
- **⅛ teaspoon ground nutmeg**
- **⅛ teaspoon pepper**
- **⅓ cup finely chopped fresh basil**
- **1 tablespoon balsamic vinegar**
- **2 cups marinara sauce, warmed**

1. Cook pasta according to package directions. Drain, reserving ¾ cup pasta water.

2. In a 6-qt. stockpot, heat oil over medium heat; saute leeks and onion until tender, 5-7 minutes. Add garlic and sage; cook and stir 2 minutes.

3. Add the sweet potato and chard; cook, covered, over medium-low heat 5 minutes. Stir in beans, seasonings and the reserved pasta water; cook, covered, until potato and chard are tender, about 5 minutes.

4. Add pasta, basil and vinegar; toss and heat through. Serve with sauce.

PER SERVING *1⅓ cups pasta mixture with ½ cup sauce: 369 cal., 6g fat (1g sat. fat), 1mg chol., 801mg sodium, 67g carb. (13g sugars, 13g fiber), 14g pro.*

BUTTERNUT & PORTOBELLO LASAGNA

BUTTERNUT & PORTOBELLO LASAGNA M

Lasagna gets fresh flavor and color when you make it with roasted butternut squash, portobello mushrooms, basil and spinach. We feast on this.

—EDWARD AND DANIELLE WALKER TRAVERSE CITY, MI

PREP: 1 HOUR • **BAKE:** 45 MIN. + STANDING
MAKES: 12 SERVINGS

- **1 package (10 ounces) frozen cubed butternut squash, thawed**
- **2 teaspoons olive oil**
- **1 teaspoon brown sugar**
- **¼ teaspoon salt**
- **⅛ teaspoon pepper**

MUSHROOMS

- **4 large portobello mushrooms, coarsely chopped**
- **2 teaspoons balsamic vinegar**
- **2 teaspoons olive oil**
- **¼ teaspoon salt**
- **⅛ teaspoon pepper**

SAUCE

- **2 cans (28 ounces each) whole tomatoes, undrained**
- **2 teaspoons olive oil**
- **2 garlic cloves, minced**
- **1 teaspoon crushed red pepper flakes**
- **½ cup fresh basil leaves, thinly sliced**
- **¼ teaspoon salt**
- **⅛ teaspoon pepper**

LASAGNA

- **9 no-cook lasagna noodles**
- **4 ounces fresh baby spinach (about 5 cups)**
- **3 cups part-skim ricotta cheese**
- **1½ cups shredded part-skim mozzarella cheese**

1. Preheat oven to 350°. In a large bowl, combine first five ingredients. In another bowl, combine ingredients for mushrooms. Transfer vegetables to separate foil-lined 15x10x1-in. baking pans. Roast 14-16 minutes or until tender, stirring occasionally.

2. Meanwhile, for the sauce, drain tomatoes, reserving juices; coarsely chop tomatoes. In a large saucepan, heat oil over medium heat. Add garlic and pepper flakes; cook 1 minute longer. Stir in chopped tomatoes, reserved tomato juices, basil, salt and pepper; bring to a boil. Reduce heat; simmer, uncovered, 35-45 minutes or until thickened, stirring occasionally.

3. Spread 1 cup sauce into a greased 13x9-in. baking dish. Layer with three noodles, 1 cup sauce, spinach and mushrooms. Continue layering with three noodles, 1 cup sauce, ricotta cheese and roasted squash. Top with remaining noodles and sauce. Sprinkle with mozzarella cheese.

4. Bake, covered, 30 minutes. Bake, uncovered, 15-20 minutes longer or until bubbly. Let stand 15 minutes before serving.

PER SERVING *1 piece: 252 cal., 10g fat (5g sat. fat), 27mg chol., 508mg sodium, 25g carb. (5g sugars, 4g fiber), 15g pro.* ***Diabetic Exchanges:*** *2 starch, 1 medium-fat meat, ½ fat.*

ZESTY VEGGIE PITAS

M FAST FIX

Cilantro adds oomph wherever it goes. That's why I use it with ingredients from the fridge for a zesty, refreshing sandwich combo.

—KRISTA FRANK RHODODENDRON, OR

START TO FINISH: 20 MIN.
MAKES: 4 SERVINGS

- **½ cup hummus**
- **4 whole pocketless pita breads or flatbreads, warmed**
- **4 slices pepper jack cheese**
- **1 cup thinly sliced cucumber**
- **1 large tomato, cut into wedges**
- **¼ cup sliced pepperoncini**
- **¼ cup sliced ripe olives**
- **¼ cup fresh cilantro leaves**

Spread hummus over pita breads. Top with remaining ingredients; fold pitas to serve.

PER SERVING *1 sandwich: 323 cal., 11g fat (4g sat. fat), 23mg chol., 758mg sodium, 42g carb. (2g sugars, 4g fiber), 14g pro.* ***Diabetic Exchanges:*** *3 starch, 1 medium-fat meat.*

BLACK BEAN QUINOA BOWLS M

Did you know that quinoa is a seed? This recipe tastes so good, you'd never guess it was the healthy main-dish equivalent of eating straight spinach!

—**LAURA LEWIS** BOULDER, CO

PREP: 15 MIN. • **COOK:** 30 MIN. • **MAKES:** 4 SERVINGS

- 1 tablespoon olive oil
- 2 cups sliced baby portobello mushrooms
- 1 medium onion, chopped
- 3 garlic cloves, minced
- ¾ cup quinoa, rinsed
- 1 teaspoon ground cumin
- ⅛ teaspoon cayenne pepper
- ⅛ teaspoon pepper
- 1½ cups vegetable broth
- 1 medium zucchini, halved and thinly sliced
- 1 can (15 ounces) black beans, rinsed and drained
- 1 cup frozen corn (about 5 ounces)
- ½ cup crumbled feta cheese
- Minced fresh cilantro

1. In a large saucepan, heat oil over medium-high heat; saute mushrooms and onion until tender and lightly browned, 4-6 minutes. Add garlic; cook and stir 1 minute. Stir in quinoa, seasonings and broth; bring to a boil. Reduce heat; simmer, covered, 15 minutes. Stir in zucchini; cook, covered, until crisp-tender, about 5 minutes.

2. Stir in beans and corn; heat through. Top with cheese and cilantro.

PER SERVING *1½ cups: 333 cal., 8g fat (2g sat. fat), 8mg chol., 699mg sodium, 50g carb. (5g sugars, 9g fiber), 15g pro.* ***Diabetic Exchanges:*** *3 starch, 1 lean meat, 1 fat.*

BLACK BEAN QUINOA BOWLS

ITALIAN HERB-LENTIL PATTIES WITH MOZZARELLA

ITALIAN HERB-LENTIL PATTIES WITH MOZZARELLA M

My family has requested this meatless recipe over and over again. It is simple to prepare and even meat lovers enjoy it.

—**GERALDINE LUCAS** OLDSMAR, FL

PREP: 50 MIN. • **COOK:** 10 MIN./BATCH • **MAKES:** 10 SERVINGS

- 3 cups dried lentils, rinsed
- 3 large eggs, lightly beaten
- 1 tablespoon dried minced onion
- 1 tablespoon dried parsley flakes
- 1 teaspoon dried basil
- 1 teaspoon salt
- ½ teaspoon dried thyme
- ¼ teaspoon pepper
- 8 packets plain instant oatmeal (about 2 cups)
- 2 tablespoons canola oil
- 10 slices part-skim mozzarella cheese or provolone cheese
- Marinara sauce, warmed, optional

1. Cook lentils according to package directions; drain and cool slightly.

2. In a large bowl, combine eggs and seasonings; stir in cooked lentils and oatmeal. Shape into ten ¾-in.-thick patties.

3. In a large nonstick skillet, heat 1 tablespoon oil over medium heat. Cook patties in batches 4-6 minutes on each side or until golden brown and a thermometer reads 160°, adding additional oil as needed. Top with cheese; cook 1-2 minutes longer or until cheese is melted. If desired, serve with marinara sauce.

PER SERVING *1 patty: 416 cal., 12g fat (4g sat. fat), 74mg chol., 517mg sodium, 54g carb. (2g sugars, 9g fiber), 26g pro.*

COCONUT LENTILS WITH RICE M

Years ago I made this recipe for my kids and they loved it. One of my daughter's friends would always request this dish when she came over to visit. I recommend using basmati rice.
—DIANE DONATO COLUMBUS, OH

PREP: 20 MIN. • **COOK:** 35 MIN. • **MAKES:** 6 SERVINGS

- **1 tablespoon canola oil**
- **6 green onions, chopped**
- **1 tablespoon minced fresh gingerroot**
- **2 garlic cloves, minced**
- **¼ teaspoon crushed red pepper flakes**
- **1½ cups dried lentils, rinsed**
- **1 teaspoon ground turmeric**
- **½ teaspoon salt**
- **5½ cups vegetable stock**
- **2 large tomatoes, chopped**
- **½ cup flaked coconut**
- **2 tablespoons minced fresh mint**
- **3 cups hot cooked rice**
- **⅓ cup plain Greek yogurt**

1. In a large saucepan, heat oil over medium heat; saute green onions, ginger, garlic and pepper flakes until onions are tender, 2-4 minutes. Stir in lentils, turmeric, salt and stock; bring to a boil. Reduce heat; simmer, covered, until lentils are tender, 25-30 minutes, stirring occasionally.
2. Stir in tomatoes, coconut and mint. Serve with rice; top with yogurt.

PER SERVING *374 cal., 7g fat (4g sat. fat), 3mg chol., 757mg sodium, 63g carb. (7g sugars, 7g fiber), 16g pro.*

HEALTH TIP *Cup for cup, lentils have twice as much protein and iron as quinoa.*

COCONUT LENTILS WITH RICE

LEMONY CHICKPEAS

LEMONY CHICKPEAS M FAST FIX

These saucy chickpeas add just a little heat to meatless Mondays. They're especially good over hot, fluffy brown rice.
—APRIL STREVELL RED BANK, NJ

START TO FINISH: 30 MIN. • **MAKES:** 4 SERVINGS

- **2 cups uncooked instant brown rice**
- **1 tablespoon olive oil**
- **1 medium onion, chopped**
- **2 cans (15 ounces each) chickpeas, rinsed and drained**
- **1 can (14 ounces) diced tomatoes, undrained**
- **1 cup vegetable broth**
- **¼ teaspoon crushed red pepper flakes**
- **¼ teaspoon pepper**
- **½ teaspoon grated lemon peel**
- **3 tablespoons lemon juice**

1. Cook rice according to package directions. Meanwhile, in a large skillet, heat oil over medium heat. Add onion; cook and stir 3-4 minutes or until tender.
2. Stir in chickpeas, tomatoes, broth, pepper flakes and pepper; bring to a boil. Reduce heat; simmer, covered, 10 minutes to allow flavors to blend. Uncover; simmer 4-5 minutes or until liquid is slightly reduced, stirring occasionally. Stir in lemon peel and lemon juice. Serve with rice.

FREEZE OPTION *Do not prepare rice until later. Freeze cooled chickpea mixture in freezer containers. To use, partially thaw in refrigerator overnight. Heat through in a saucepan, stirring occasionally and adding a little broth if necessary. Serve with rice.*

PER SERVING *1 cup chickpea mixture with 1 cup rice: 433 cal., 9g fat (0 sat. fat), 0 chol., 679mg sodium, 76g carb. (10g sugars, 12g fiber), 13g pro.*

MUSHROOM PENNE BAKE

MUSHROOM PENNE BAKE M

This is an easy, hearty and delicious meal for a chilly evening! Its cheesy goodness will have you going for seconds. Serve with salad and garlic bread.

—SUE ASCHEMEIER DEFIANCE, OH

PREP: 25 MIN. • **BAKE:** 25 MIN.
MAKES: 8 SERVINGS

- **1 package (12 ounces) whole wheat penne pasta**
- **1 tablespoon olive oil**
- **1 pound sliced baby portobello mushrooms**
- **2 garlic cloves, minced**
- **1 jar (24 ounces) marinara sauce**
- **1 teaspoon Italian seasoning**
- **½ teaspoon salt**
- **2 cups reduced-fat ricotta cheese**
- **1 cup shredded part-skim mozzarella cheese, divided**
- **½ cup grated Parmesan cheese**

1. Preheat oven to 350°. In a 6-qt. stockpot, cook pasta according to package directions. Drain and return to pot; cool slightly.
2. In a large skillet, heat oil over medium-high heat; saute mushrooms until tender, 4-6 minutes. Add garlic; cook 1 minute. Stir in marinara sauce and seasonings. Spread half of the mixture into a 13x9-in. baking dish coated with cooking spray.
3. Stir ricotta cheese and 1/2 cup of mozzarella cheese into pasta; spoon over mushroom mixture. Spread with remaining mushroom mixture.
4. Top with remaining mozzarella cheese and Parmesan cheese. Bake casserole, uncovered, until bubbly, 25-30 minutes.

PER SERVING *1 cup: 353 cal., 11g fat (4g sat. fat), 30mg chol., 748mg sodium, 44g carb. (10g sugars, 7g fiber), 20g pro.* ***Diabetic Exchanges:*** *3 starch, 2 lean meat, 1 fat.*

WARM RICE & PINTOS SALAD M FAST FIX

During my undergrad years, my roommate taught me how to cook vegetarian dishes like brown rice with pintos. It's so versatile; you can turn it into a wrap or casserole.

—NATALIE VAN APELDOORN VANCOUVER, BC

START TO FINISH: 30 MIN.
MAKES: 4 SERVINGS

- **1 tablespoon olive oil**
- **1 cup frozen corn**
- **1 small onion, chopped**
- **2 garlic cloves, minced**
- **1½ teaspoons chili powder**
- **1½ teaspoons ground cumin**
- **1 can (15 ounces) pinto beans, rinsed and drained**
- **1 package (8.8 ounces) ready-to-serve brown rice**
- **1 can (4 ounces) chopped green chilies**
- **½ cup salsa**
- **¼ cup chopped fresh cilantro**
- **1 bunch romaine, quartered lengthwise through the core**
- **¼ cup finely shredded cheddar cheese**

1. In a large skillet, heat oil over medium-high heat. Add corn and onion; cook and stir 4-5 minutes or until onion is tender. Stir in garlic, chili powder and cumin; cook and stir 1 minute longer.
2. Add the beans, rice, green chilies, salsa and cilantro; heat through, stirring occasionally.
3. Serve the mixture over romaine wedges. Sprinkle with cheese.

PER SERVING *331 cal., 8g fat (2g sat. fat), 7mg chol., 465mg sodium, 50g carb. (5g sugars, 9g fiber), 12g pro.* ***Diabetic Exchanges:*** *2 1/2 starch, 2 vegetable, 1 lean meat, 1/2 fat.*

WARM RICE & PINTOS SALAD

TOFU CHOW MEIN

KALE PESTO FLATBREAD

M FAST FIX

I'm always making different kinds of flatbreads. We love kale, so this recipe seemed perfect. Immediately it became our favorite flatbread pizza. We also top it with cooked shrimp before baking.

—**ADAM STRICKLAND** BROOKLYN, NY

START TO FINISH: 25 MIN.
MAKES: 4 SERVINGS

- **1 cup chopped fresh kale leaves**
- **3 tablespoons shredded Parmesan cheese**
- **1 tablespoon chopped walnuts**
- **1 tablespoon olive oil**
- **1 garlic clove, minced**
- **⅛ teaspoon pepper**
- **1½ cups reduced-fat ricotta cheese**
- **2 whole grain naan flatbreads**
- **1 package (8 ounces) frozen artichoke hearts**
- **3 pickled hot cherry peppers, chopped**
- **Thinly sliced fresh basil leaves**

1. Preheat oven to 450°. Place first six ingredients in a blender; process until smooth. Add ricotta cheese; pulse just until combined.
2. Place flatbreads on a baking sheet. Spread with kale mixture; top with artichoke hearts. Bake until crust is lightly browned, 10-12 minutes. Top with peppers and basil.

PER SERVING *1/2 flatbread with toppings: 363 cal., 15g fat (5g sat. fat), 30mg chol., 748mg sodium, 40g carb. (9g sugars, 7g fiber), 17g pro.* ***Diabetic Exchanges:*** *2 1/2 starch, 2 medium-fat meat, 1 fat.*

KALE PESTO FLATBREAD

TOFU CHOW MEIN

M

This is an easy recipe for a tofu beginner, as it teaches people how to use it. For best results, cut the tofu block in half and wrap well in a terry kitchen towel. Let it sit in the fridge for at least an hour to absorb excess water. For a complete meal, serve with Chinese soup and egg rolls!

—**AUTUMN SINCLAIRE** GOLD BEACH, OR

PREP: 15 MIN. + STANDING • **COOK:** 15 MIN.
MAKES: 4 SERVINGS

- **8 ounces uncooked whole wheat angel hair pasta**
- **3 tablespoons sesame oil, divided**
- **1 package (16 ounces) extra-firm tofu**
- **2 cups sliced fresh mushrooms**
- **1 medium sweet red pepper, julienned**
- **¼ cup reduced-sodium soy sauce**
- **3 green onions, thinly sliced**

1. Cook pasta according to package directions. Drain; rinse with cold water and drain again. Toss with 1 tablespoon oil; spread onto a baking sheet and let stand about 1 hour.
2. Meanwhile, cut tofu into ½-in. cubes and blot dry. Wrap in a clean kitchen towel; place on a plate and refrigerate until ready to cook.
3. In a large skillet, heat 1 tablespoon oil over medium heat. Add the pasta, spreading evenly; cook until bottom is lightly browned, about 5 minutes. Remove from pan.
4. In same skillet, heat remaining oil over medium-high heat; stir-fry mushrooms, pepper and tofu until mushrooms are tender, 3-4 minutes. Add pasta and soy sauce; toss and heat through. Sprinkle with green onions.

PER SERVING *1 1/2 cups: 417 cal., 17g fat (2g sat. fat), 0 chol., 588mg sodium, 48g carb. (3g sugars, 8g fiber), 21g pro.* ***Diabetic Exchanges:*** *3 fat, 2 1/2 starch, 2 lean meat, 1 vegetable.*

GRILLED CORN HUMMUS TOSTADAS

GRILLED CORN HUMMUS TOSTADAS M FAST FIX

This recipe is a combo of Mediterranean and Mexican cuisines, giving it a unique taste. Avocado and hummus may sound like a weird mix, but they really do complement each other.

—LAUREN KNOELKE MILWAUKEE, WI

START TO FINISH: 30 MIN.
MAKES: 4 SERVINGS

- **4 medium ears sweet corn, husks removed**
- **1 small red onion, cut crosswise into ½-inch slices**
- **2 tablespoons olive oil, divided**
- **8 corn tortillas (6 inches)**
- **1 container (8 ounces) hummus**
- **¼ teaspoon ground chipotle pepper**
- **1 cup cherry tomatoes, halved**
- **½ teaspoon salt**
- **1 medium ripe avocado, peeled and sliced**
- **½ cup crumbled feta cheese**
- **1 jalapeno pepper, thinly sliced**
- **Lime wedges, optional**
- **Fresh cilantro leaves, optional**
- **Mexican hot pepper sauce, optional**

1. Brush the corn and onion with 1 tablespoon oil. Grill corn and onion, covered, over medium-high heat until tender and lightly charred, 5-7 minutes, turning occasionally. Cool slightly.

2. Meanwhile, brush tortillas with the remaining oil. Grill, covered, until crisp and lightly browned, 2-3 minutes per side.

3. Cut corn from cobs. Process the hummus, chipotle pepper and 2 cups of the cut corn in a food processor until almost smooth. Coarsely chop grilled onion; toss with tomatoes, salt and any remaining corn.

4. Spread the hummus mixture over tortillas; top with the onion mixture, avocado, cheese and jalapeno. If desired, serve tostadas with limes, cilantro and pepper sauce.

NOTE *Wear disposable gloves when cutting hot peppers; the oils can burn skin. Avoid touching your face.*

PER SERVING *2 tostadas: 453 cal., 23g fat (5g sat. fat), 8mg chol., 692mg sodium, 55g carb. (9g sugars, 12g fiber), 14g pro.*

PORTOBELLO POLENTA BAKE M

PREP: 25 MIN. • **BAKE:** 25 MIN. + STANDING
MAKES: 6 SERVINGS

- **1 can (14½ ounces) reduced-sodium chicken broth**
- **1¼ cups water**
- **1 cup cornmeal**
- **2 teaspoons olive oil**
- **1 large onion, chopped**
- **½ pound sliced baby portobello mushrooms**
- **¼ cup julienned soft sun-dried tomatoes (not packed in oil)**
- **2 garlic cloves, minced**
- **2 large eggs, lightly beaten**
- **1 cup (4 ounces) shredded Gruyere or fontina cheese**
- **½ teaspoon salt**
- **1 cup part-skim ricotta cheese**
- **Minced fresh parsley**

1. Preheat oven to 350°. In a large heavy saucepan, bring broth and water to a boil. Reduce heat to a gentle boil; slowly whisk in cornmeal. Cook and stir until thickened and cornmeal is tender, 8-10 minutes.

2. Meanwhile, in a large nonstick skillet, heat oil over medium-high heat; saute onion and mushrooms until tender, 4-5 minutes. Stir in tomatoes and garlic; cook 1 minute.

3. Mix the eggs, Gruyere cheese and salt; stir into polenta. Spread half of the mixture into a greased 11x7-in. baking dish. Top with vegetable mixture. Drop ricotta cheese by tablespoonfuls over top. Spread with remaining polenta.

4. Bake, uncovered, until edges are lightly browned, 25-30 minutes. Let stand 10 minutes before serving. Sprinkle with parsley.

NOTE *This recipe was tested with sun-dried tomatoes that can be used without soaking. When using other sun-dried tomatoes that are not oil-packed, cover with boiling water, let stand until soft; drain before using.*

PER SERVING *304 cal., 13g fat (6g sat. fat), 96mg chol., 605mg sodium, 29g carb. (4g sugars, 3g fiber), 17g pro.* ***Diabetic Exchanges:*** *2 starch, 2 medium-fat meat, 1/2 fat.*

Any recipe with melted cheese in it is a favorite of mine. That's just one reason I love this polenta bake. It has a lot of protein for a meatless meal!
—**MARGEE BERRY** WHITE SALMON, WA

PORTOBELLO POLENTA BAKE

SWEET POTATO CURRY M

This is one of my favorite vegetarian dishes—it packs a lot of flavor and nutrition. Curry can be served over rice or on its own.
—**AUBREI WEIGAND** HARRISBURG, PA

PREP: 15 MIN. • **COOK:** 30 MIN. • **MAKES:** 6 SERVINGS

- 2 tablespoons olive oil
- 2 medium onions, chopped
- 4 celery ribs (including tops), chopped
- 2 large sweet potatoes (about 1½ pounds), cut into 1-inch cubes
- 3 garlic cloves, minced
- 3 teaspoons curry powder
- 1½ teaspoons chili powder
- ¾ teaspoon ground cumin
- ½ teaspoon salt
- ⅛ teaspoon crushed red pepper flakes
- 1 can (13.66 ounces) light coconut milk
- 1 cup vegetable broth
- 2 cups cut fresh green beans
- 1 can (15 ounces) chickpeas, rinsed and drained
- Hot cooked rice

1. In a 6-qt. stockpot, heat oil over medium-high heat; saute onions and celery until tender, 3-5 minutes. Stir in sweet potatoes, garlic, seasonings, coconut milk and broth; bring to a boil. Reduce heat; simmer, uncovered, just until sweet potatoes are tender, 15-20 minutes, stirring occasionally.
2. Stir in green beans and chickpeas; cook, uncovered, until green beans are tender, about 5 minutes, stirring occasionally. Serve with rice.
PER SERVING *1⅓ cups curry mixture: 314 cal., 11g fat (4g sat. fat), 0 chol., 502mg sodium, 48g carb. (18g sugars, 9g fiber), 6g pro.* ***Diabetic Exchanges:*** *3 starch, 2 fat, 1 lean meat.*

SWEET POTATO CURRY

QUINOA & BLACK BEAN-STUFFED PEPPERS

QUINOA & BLACK BEAN-STUFFED PEPPERS M FAST FIX

If you're thinking about a meatless meal, give these no-fuss peppers a try. They come together with a just few ingredients and put a tasty spin on a low-fat dinner!
—**CINDY REAMS** PHILIPSBURG, PA

START TO FINISH: 30 MIN. • **MAKES:** 4 SERVINGS

- 1½ cups water
- 1 cup quinoa, rinsed
- 4 large green peppers
- 1 jar (16 ounces) chunky salsa, divided
- 1 can (15 ounces) black beans, rinsed and drained
- ½ cup reduced-fat ricotta cheese
- ½ cup shredded Monterey Jack cheese, divided

1. Preheat oven to 400°. In a small saucepan, bring water to a boil. Add quinoa. Reduce heat; simmer, covered, for 10-12 minutes or until water is absorbed.
2. Meanwhile, cut and discard tops from peppers; remove seeds. Place in a greased 8-in. square baking dish, cut side down. Microwave, uncovered, on high 3-4 minutes or until crisp-tender. Turn peppers cut side up.
3. Reserve ⅓ cup salsa; add remaining salsa to quinoa. Stir in beans, ricotta cheese and ¼ cup Jack cheese. Spoon mixture into peppers; sprinkle with remaining cheese. Bake, uncovered, 10-15 minutes or until filling is heated through. Top with reserved salsa.
PER SERVING *1 stuffed pepper: 393 cal., 8g fat (4g sat. fat), 20mg chol., 774mg sodium, 59g carb. (10g sugars, 10g fiber), 18g pro.*

TASTY LENTIL TACOS M (PICTURED ON P. 184)

My husband has to watch his cholesterol. This is a dish I found that's healthy for him and yummy for our five children.
—**MICHELLE THOMAS** BANGOR, ME

PREP: 10 MIN. • **COOK:** 40 MIN. • **MAKES:** 6 SERVINGS

- **1 teaspoon canola oil**
- **1 medium onion, finely chopped**
- **1 garlic clove, minced**
- **1 cup dried lentils, rinsed**
- **1 tablespoon chili powder**
- **2 teaspoons ground cumin**
- **1 teaspoon dried oregano**
- **2½ cups vegetable or reduced-sodium chicken broth**
- **1 cup salsa**
- **12 taco shells**
- **1½ cups shredded lettuce**
- **1 cup chopped fresh tomatoes**
- **1½ cups shredded reduced-fat cheddar cheese**
- **6 tablespoons fat-free sour cream**

1. In a large nonstick skillet, heat oil over medium heat; saute onion and garlic until tender. Add lentils and seasonings; cook and stir 1 minute. Stir in broth; bring to a boil. Reduce heat; simmer, covered, until lentils are tender, 25-30 minutes.
2. Cook, uncovered, until mixture is thickened, 6-8 minutes, stirring occasionally. Mash lentils slightly; stir in salsa and heat through. Serve in taco shells. Top with remaining ingredients.
PER SERVING *2 tacos: 365 cal., 12g fat (5g sat. fat), 21mg chol., 777mg sodium, 44g carb. (5g sugars, 6g fiber), 19g pro.* ***Diabetic Exchanges:*** *2½ starch, 2 lean meat, 1 vegetable, 1 fat.*

VEGGIE BEAN BURGERS M

PREP: 45 MIN. • **BROIL:** 15 MIN. • **MAKES:** 8 SERVINGS

- **½ cup uncooked long grain brown rice**
- **1 cup water**
- **2 cans (15 ounces each) black beans, rinsed and drained**
- **2 large eggs, lightly beaten**
- **2 teaspoons hot pepper sauce**
- **3 teaspoons ground cumin**
- **3 teaspoons chili powder**
- **1½ teaspoons garlic powder**
- **¾ teaspoon salt**
- **1½ cups Fiber One bran cereal**
- **1 medium green pepper, coarsely chopped**
- **1 medium onion, quartered**
- **¾ cup sliced fresh mushrooms**
- **6 garlic cloves, minced**
- **¾ cup shredded part-skim mozzarella cheese**
- **8 whole wheat hamburger buns, split and warmed**
- **Lettuce leaves, optional**
- **Tomato slices, optional**
- **Sliced onion, optional**

1. Preheat broiler. In a small saucepan, combine rice and water; bring to a boil. Reduce heat; simmer, covered, until liquid is absorbed and rice is tender, 30-40 minutes.
2. In a large bowl, mash beans until almost smooth; stir in eggs, pepper sauce and seasonings. Pulse bran cereal in a food processor until finely ground; remove to a small bowl. Pulse vegetables and garlic in food processor until finely chopped; add to bean mixture. Add cheese and rice to food processor; pulse to blend, then add to bean mixture. Stir in ground cereal.
3. Shape mixture into eight ½-in.-thick patties; place on a greased foiled-lined baking sheet. Broil 4-6 in. from heat until browned, 6-8 minutes per side. Serve in buns. If desired, top with lettuce, tomato and onion.
NOTE *To bake the patties, preheat oven to 375°. Lightly oil a baking sheet; place patties on baking sheet and bake about 10 minutes on each side.*
PER SERVING *1 patty: 334 cal., 6g fat (2g sat. fat), 53mg chol., 814mg sodium, 60g carb. (6g sugars, 15g fiber), 16g pro.*

VEGGIE BEAN BURGERS

MEATLESS MAINS

AVOCADO & GARBANZO BEAN QUINOA SALAD M

This delicious and hearty salad is high in protein and holds well in the fridge for a few days. If you make it ahead, add the avocado and cherry tomatoes right before serving.

—ELIZABETH BENNETT SEATTLE, WA

PREP: 25 MIN. • **COOK:** 15 MIN.
MAKES: 6 SERVINGS

- **1 cup quinoa, rinsed**
- **1 can (15 ounces) garbanzo beans or chickpeas, rinsed and drained**
- **2 cups cherry tomatoes, halved**
- **1 cup (4 ounces) crumbled feta cheese**
- **½ medium ripe avocado, peeled and cubed**
- **4 green onions, chopped (about ½ cup)**

DRESSING

- **3 tablespoons white wine vinegar**
- **1 teaspoon Dijon mustard**
- **¼ teaspoon kosher salt**
- **¼ teaspoon garlic powder**
- **¼ teaspoon freshly ground pepper**
- **¼ cup olive oil**

1. Cook the quinoa according to package directions; transfer to a bowl and cool slightly.

2. Add the beans, tomatoes, cheese, avocado and green onions to quinoa; gently stir to combine.

3. In a small bowl, whisk first five dressing ingredients. Gradually whisk in oil until blended. Drizzle over salad; gently toss to coat.

NOTE *Look for quinoa in the cereal, rice or organic food aisle.*

PER SERVING *1⅓ cups: 328 cal., 17g fat (4g sat. fat), 10mg chol., 378mg sodium, 34g carb. (3g sugars, 7g fiber), 11g pro.* ***Diabetic Exchanges:*** *3 fat, 2 starch, 1 lean meat.*

TOP TIP

Feta is a salty, crumbly Greek-style cheese made traditionally with sheep's or goat's milk, but most American brands are made with cow's milk.

CRISPY TOFU WITH BLACK PEPPER SAUCE

CRISPY TOFU WITH BLACK PEPPER SAUCE

C M FAST FIX

Sometimes tofu can be boring and tasteless, but not in this recipe! The crispy vegetarian bean curd is so loaded with flavor, you'll never want to eat plain tofu again.

—NICK IVERSON MILWAUKEE, WI

START TO FINISH: 30 MIN.
MAKES: 4 SERVINGS

- **2 tablespoons reduced-sodium soy sauce**
- **2 tablespoons chili garlic sauce**
- **1 tablespoon packed brown sugar**
- **1 tablespoon rice vinegar**
- **4 green onions**
- **8 ounces extra-firm tofu, drained**
- **3 tablespoons cornstarch**
- **6 tablespoons canola oil, divided**
- **8 ounces fresh sugar snap peas (about 2 cups), thinly sliced**
- **1 teaspoon freshly ground pepper**
- **3 garlic cloves, minced**
- **2 teaspoons grated fresh gingerroot**

1. Mix first four ingredients. Mince white parts of green onions; thinly slice green parts.

2. Cut tofu into ½-in. cubes; pat dry with paper towels. Toss tofu with cornstarch. In a large skillet, heat 4 tablespoons oil over medium-high heat. Add tofu; cook until crisp and golden brown, 5-7 minutes, stirring occasionally. Remove from pan; drain on paper towels.

3. In same pan, heat 1 tablespoon oil over medium-high heat. Add peas; stir-fry until crisp-tender, 2-3 minutes. Remove from pan.

4. In same pan, heat remaining oil over medium-high heat. Add the pepper; cook 30 seconds. Add the garlic, ginger and minced green onions; stir-fry for 30-45 seconds.

5. Stir in the soy sauce mixture; cook and stir until slightly thickened. Remove from heat; stir in tofu and peas. Sprinkle with sliced green onions.

PER SERVING *1 cup: 316 cal., 24g fat (2g sat. fat), 0 chol., 583mg sodium, 20g carb. (8g sugars, 2g fiber), 7g pro.*

RUSTIC SUMMER VEGETABLE PASTA M

(PICTURED ON P. 185)

My pasta proves you can't have too much of a good thing. Change it up with whatever fresh veggies you find in the garden or at the farmers market.
—**BRYN NAMAVARI** CHICAGO, IL

PREP: 15 MIN. • **COOK:** 30 MIN.
MAKES: 8 SERVINGS

- **3 tablespoons olive oil, divided**
- **1 medium zucchini, cut into ¾-inch pieces**
- **1 medium yellow summer squash, cut into ¾-inch pieces**
- **1 medium onion, chopped**
- **1 medium eggplant, peeled and cut into ¾-inch pieces**
- **2 cups sliced fresh mushrooms**
- **2 garlic cloves, minced**
- **¾ teaspoon crushed red pepper flakes**
- **1 can (28 ounces) crushed tomatoes**
- **½ teaspoon salt**
- **½ teaspoon pepper**
- **1 tablespoon minced fresh oregano or 1 teaspoon dried oregano**
- **1 tablespoon minced fresh parsley**
- **3 tablespoons minced fresh basil or 1 tablespoon dried basil, divided**
- **1 package (14½ ounces) uncooked multigrain spaghetti**
- **½ cup shredded Parmesan cheese**

1. In a 6-qt. stockpot, heat 1 tablespoon oil over medium-high heat. Add zucchini and yellow squash; cook and stir until tender. Remove from the pot.
2. In same pot, heat 1 tablespoon oil over medium-high heat. Add onion, eggplant and mushrooms; cook and stir until tender. Add garlic and pepper flakes; cook 1 minute longer. Add the tomatoes, salt and pepper. Stir in the oregano, parsley and half of the basil; bring to a boil. Reduce the heat; simmer, uncovered, for 15 minutes, stirring occasionally.
3. Meanwhile, cook the spaghetti according to package directions. Drain; add spaghetti and squash to vegetable mixture. Drizzle with the remaining oil; toss to combine. Top with cheese and remaining basil.

PER SERVING *2 cups: 315 cal., 8g fat (2g sat. fat), 4mg chol., 445mg sodium, 50g carb. (9g sugars, 8g fiber), 15g pro.*

ROASTED SWEET POTATO & CHICKPEA PITAS M FAST FIX

Here's a hearty take on Mediterranean food, this time with sweet potatoes tucked inside. These pockets are delicious for lunch or dinner.
—**BETH JACOBSON** MILWAUKEE, WI

START TO FINISH: 30 MIN.
MAKES: 6 SERVINGS

- **2 medium sweet potatoes (about 1¼ pounds), peeled and cubed**
- **2 cans (15 ounces each) chickpeas, rinsed and drained**
- **1 medium red onion, chopped**
- **3 tablespoons canola oil, divided**
- **2 teaspoons garam masala**
- **½ teaspoon salt, divided**
- **2 garlic cloves, minced**
- **1 cup plain Greek yogurt**
- **1 tablespoon lemon juice**
- **1 teaspoon ground cumin**
- **2 cups arugula or baby spinach**
- **12 whole wheat pita pocket halves, warmed**
- **¼ cup minced fresh cilantro**

1. Preheat oven to 400°. Place potatoes in a large microwave-safe bowl; microwave, covered, on high 5 minutes. Stir in the chickpeas and onion; toss with 2 tablespoons oil, garam masala and 1/4 teaspoon salt.
2. Spread into a 15x10x1-in. pan. Roast until potatoes are tender, about 15 minutes. Cool slightly.
3. Place the garlic and remaining oil in a microwave-safe bowl; microwave on high until garlic is lightly browned, 1 to 1½ minutes. Stir in yogurt, lemon juice, cumin and remaining salt.
4. Toss potato mixture with arugula. Spoon into pitas; top with the sauce and cilantro.

NOTE *This recipe was tested in an 1,100-watt microwave.*

PER SERVING *2 filled pita halves: 462 cal., 15g fat (3g sat. fat), 10mg chol., 662mg sodium, 72g carb. (13g sugars, 12g fiber), 14g pro.*

ROASTED SWEET POTATO & CHICKPEA PITAS

209

210

207

The Bread Basket

“We love to add a healthy ingredient to all of our recipes. I like to see this as a challenge, and it’s something my family appreciates.”

—PEGGIE BROTT DAHLONEGA, GA
about her recipe, Veggie Corn Muffins, on page 202

THE BREAD BASKET

VEGGIE CORN MUFFINS

M FAST FIX (PICTURED ON P. 200)

We love to add a healthy ingredient to all of our recipes. I like to see this as a challenge, and it's something my family really appreciates.

—**PEGGIE BROTT** DAHLONEGA, GA

START TO FINISH: 30 MIN.
MAKES: 1 DOZEN

- **1 cup yellow cornmeal**
- **½ cup all-purpose flour**
- **½ cup whole wheat flour**
- **1 teaspoon baking powder**
- **¾ teaspoon salt**
- **1 large egg**
- **1 cup unsweetened almond milk**
- **¼ cup canola oil**
- **¼ cup honey**
- **½ cup finely shredded carrot**
- **½ cup finely chopped green pepper**

1. Preheat the oven to 400°. Coat 12 muffin cups with cooking spray.

2. Whisk together cornmeal, flours, baking powder and salt. In another bowl, whisk together egg, milk, oil and honey. Add to the cornmeal mixture; stir just until moistened. Fold in the vegetables. Fill prepared cups two-thirds full.

3. Bake until a toothpick inserted in center comes out clean, 12-15 minutes. Cool 5 minutes before removing from pan to a wire rack. Serve warm.

FREEZE OPTION *Freeze cooled muffins in resealable plastic freezer bags. To use, microwave each muffin on high until warmed, 30-45 seconds.*

PER SERVING *1 muffin: 159 cal., 6g fat (1g sat. fat), 16mg chol., 207mg sodium, 25g carb. (6g sugars, 2g fiber), 3g pro.* ***Diabetic Exchanges:*** *1½ starch, 1 fat.*

TOP TIP

For improved nutrition and a rustic texture, use stone-ground or water-ground cornmeal. This type contains more bran and germ than large commercial types, and up to 2½ times the fiber.

WHOLESOME BANANA BREAD

F S M

I cut a lot of fat out of my regular banana bread recipe. This bread always turns out moist and delicious.

—**SARAH BIALOCK** YUMA, AZ

PREP: 15 MIN. • **BAKE:** 30 MIN. + COOLING
MAKES: 2 MINI LOAVES (6 SLICES EACH)

- **2 tablespoons butter, softened**
- **⅓ cup packed brown sugar**
- **1 large egg**
- **½ cup mashed ripe banana**
- **2 tablespoons unsweetened applesauce**
- **½ teaspoon vanilla extract**
- **¾ cup all-purpose flour**
- **2 tablespoons whole wheat flour**
- **1½ teaspoons ground flaxseed**
- **1 teaspoon ground cinnamon**
- **½ teaspoon baking soda**
- **½ teaspoon ground nutmeg**
- **⅛ teaspoon salt**

1. In a large bowl, cream butter and brown sugar until light and fluffy. Add egg; beat well. Beat in the banana, applesauce and vanilla. Combine the remaining ingredients; add to creamed mixture.

2. Transfer to two 5¾x3x2-in. loaf pans coated with cooking spray. Bake at 350° for 25-30 minutes or until a toothpick inserted near the center comes out clean. Cool for 10 minutes before removing from pans to wire racks.

PER SERVING *1 slice: 91 cal., 3g fat (1g sat. fat), 23mg chol., 99mg sodium, 16g carb. (7g sugars, 1g fiber), 2g pro.* ***Diabetic Exchanges:*** *1 starch, ½ fat.*

WHOLESOME BANANA BREAD

CHAPATI BREADS

CHAPATI BREADS F M

My daughter and I make this Indian flatbread frequently. It's so fun and goes well with any spiced dish. We use the extras to make sandwich wraps.

—JOYCE MCCARTHY SUSSEX, WI

PREP: 20 MIN. • **COOK:** 5 MIN./BATCH
MAKES: 10 SERVINGS

- **1½ cups all-purpose flour**
- **½ cup whole wheat flour**
- **1 teaspoon salt**
- **¼ teaspoon garlic powder**
- **¾ cup hot water (140°)**
- **2 tablespoons olive oil**

1. In a large bowl, combine the flours, salt and garlic powder. Stir in the water and oil. Turn onto a floured surface; knead 10-12 times. Divide the dough into 10 portions. On a lightly floured surface, roll each into a 6-in. circle.

2. In a large nonstick skillet, cook breads over medium heat for 1 minute on each side or until lightly browned. Keep warm.

PER SERVING *113 cal., 3g fat (0 sat. fat), 0 chol., 237mg sodium, 19g carb. (0 sugars, 1g fiber), 3g pro.* ***Diabetic Exchanges:*** *1 starch, ½ fat.*

BLUEBERRY-BRAN MUFFINS F M

I created this recipe by trial and error. I've only had one outstanding bran muffin at a restaurant, and I wanted to come up with an awesome one to make myself. These are moist, healthy, not too sweet and so tasty! They're full of grains and fruits.

—NANCY RENS PRESCOTT, AZ

PREP: 25 MIN. • **BAKE:** 20 MIN.
MAKES: 1½ DOZEN

- **1½ cups bran flakes**
- **⅓ cup boiling water**
- **1 cup whole wheat flour**
- **1 cup all-purpose flour**
- **¾ cup packed brown sugar**
- **⅓ cup quick-cooking oats**
- **¾ teaspoon baking powder**
- **½ teaspoon baking soda**
- **½ teaspoon salt**
- **1 large egg**
- **1 cup buttermilk**
- **½ cup unsweetened applesauce**
- **2 tablespoons molasses**
- **¾ cup fresh or frozen blueberries**
- **¾ cup pitted dried plums, coarsely chopped**
- **¼ cup slivered almonds**
- **2 tablespoons honey**

1. Preheat oven to 375°. In a small bowl, combine bran flakes and boiling water; set aside.

2. Whisk together flours, brown sugar, oats, baking powder, baking soda and salt. In another bowl, whisk together the egg, buttermilk, applesauce and molasses; stir in bran mixture. Add to dry ingredients, stirring just until moistened. Fold in blueberries, plums and almonds.

3. Coat muffin cups with cooking spray; fill three-fourths full. Drizzle with honey. Bake until a toothpick inserted in center comes out clean, 18-20 minutes. Cool 5 minutes before removing from pans to wire racks. Serve warm.

NOTE *If using frozen blueberries, use without thawing to avoid discoloring the batter.*

PER SERVING *1 muffin: 155 cal., 2g fat (0 sat. fat), 12mg chol., 166mg sodium, 33g carb. (17g sugars, 2g fiber), 3g pro.* ***Diabetic Exchanges:*** *2 starch.*

BLUEBERRY-BRAN MUFFINS

HERB QUICK BREAD M

This simple loaf is especially good with soups and stews, but slices are also tasty alongside fresh green salads. The herbs make it a flavorful treat any time of the year.

—**DONNA ROBERTS** MANHATTAN, KS

PREP: 15 MIN. • **BAKE:** 40 MIN. + COOLING
MAKES: 1 LOAF (16 SLICES)

- **3 cups all-purpose flour**
- **3 tablespoons sugar**
- **1 tablespoon baking powder**
- **3 teaspoons caraway seeds**
- **½ teaspoon salt**
- **½ teaspoon ground nutmeg**
- **½ teaspoon dried thyme**
- **1 large egg**
- **1 cup fat-free milk**
- **⅓ cup canola oil**

1. Preheat the oven to 350°. In a large bowl, whisk together first seven ingredients. In another bowl, whisk together egg, milk and oil. Add to flour mixture; stir just until moistened.
2. Transfer to a 9x5-in. loaf pan coated with cooking spray. Bake until a toothpick inserted in center comes out clean, 40-50 minutes. Cool in pan 10 minutes before removing to a wire rack to cool.

PER SERVING *1 slice: 147 cal., 5g fat (1g sat. fat), 12mg chol., 160mg sodium, 21g carb. (3g sugars, 1g fiber), 3g pro.* ***Diabetic Exchanges:*** *1½ starch, 1 fat.*

HERB QUICK BREAD

TENDER WHOLE WHEAT MUFFINS

Simple whole wheat muffins are wonderful paired with soup or spread with a little jam for breakfast. You get the best of both worlds by eating a delicious bread that is lighter in calories.

—**KRISTINE CHAYES** SMITHTOWN, NY

TENDER WHOLE WHEAT MUFFINS

M FAST FIX

START TO FINISH: 30 MIN. • **MAKES:** 10 MUFFINS

- **1 cup all-purpose flour**
- **1 cup whole wheat flour**
- **2 tablespoons sugar**
- **2½ teaspoons baking powder**
- **1 teaspoon salt**
- **1 large egg**
- **1¼ cups milk**
- **3 tablespoons butter, melted**

1. Preheat oven to 400°. In a large bowl, whisk flours, sugar, baking powder and salt. In another bowl, whisk egg, milk and melted butter until blended. Add to flour mixture; stir just until moistened.
2. Fill greased muffin cups three-fourths full. Bake for 15-17 minutes or until a toothpick inserted in center comes out clean. Cool 5 minutes before removing from pan to a wire rack. Serve warm.

PER SERVING *1 muffin: 152 cal., 5g fat (3g sat. fat), 35mg chol., 393mg sodium, 22g carb. (4g sugars, 2g fiber), 5g pro.* ***Diabetic Exchanges:*** *1½ starch, 1 fat.*

CHOCOLATE CHOCOLATE CHIP MUFFINS F M

These extra chocolaty muffins feature nutritious ingredients such as whole wheat flour and applesauce to make a lighter muffin. Because they are so delicious and surprisingly healthy, we even serve these for breakfast at the school where I work.

—**THERESA HARRINGTON** SHERIDAN, WY

PREP: 20 MIN. • **BAKE:** 20 MIN./BATCH • **MAKES:** 32 MUFFINS

- **2½ cups all-purpose flour**
- **1¾ cups whole wheat flour**
- **1¾ cups packed brown sugar**
- **½ cup baking cocoa**
- **1¼ teaspoons salt**
- **1 teaspoon baking powder**
- **1 teaspoon baking soda**
- **2 large egg whites**
- **1 large egg**
- **2 cups unsweetened applesauce**
- **1¾ cups fat-free milk**
- **2 tablespoons canola oil**
- **2½ teaspoons vanilla extract**
- **1¼ cups semisweet chocolate chips**

1. Preheat oven to 350°. Whisk together first seven ingredients. In another bowl, whisk together egg whites, egg, applesauce, milk, oil and vanilla; add to dry ingredients, stirring just until moistened. Fold in the chocolate chips.
2. Coat muffin cups with cooking spray; fill three-fourths full with batter. Bake until a toothpick inserted in center comes out clean, 18-20 minutes. Cool 5 minutes before removing from pans to wire racks. Serve warm.

PER SERVING *1 muffin: 161 cal., 3g fat (1g sat. fat), 7mg chol., 150mg sodium, 31g carb. (18g sugars, 2g fiber), 3g pro.* ***Diabetic Exchanges:*** *2 starch, 1 fat.*

CHOCOLATE CHOCOLATE CHIP MUFFINS

BANANA WHEAT BREAD

BANANA WHEAT BREAD F M

A subtle banana flavor comes through in this bread-machine recipe. Flecked with poppy seeds, the sweet slices are wonderful warm or toasted and spread with butter.

—**LOUISE MYERS** POMEROY, OH

PREP: 15 MIN. • **BAKE:** 4 HOURS • **MAKES:** 1 LOAF (16 SLICES)

- **¾ cup water (70° to 80°)**
- **¼ cup honey**
- **1 large egg, lightly beaten**
- **4½ teaspoons canola oil**
- **½ teaspoon vanilla extract**
- **1 medium ripe banana, sliced**
- **2 teaspoons poppy seeds**
- **1 teaspoon salt**
- **1¾ cups bread flour**
- **1½ cups whole wheat flour**
- **2¼ teaspoons active dry yeast**

In bread machine pan, place all the ingredients in order suggested by manufacturer. Select basic bread setting. Choose crust color and loaf size if available. Bake according to bread machine directions (check dough after 5 minutes of mixing; add 1 to 2 tablespoons of water or flour if needed).

FREEZE OPTION *Freeze sliced loaf in resealable plastic freezer bag. To use, thaw at room temperature.*

NOTE *We recommend you do not use a bread machine's time-delay feature for this recipe.*

PER SERVING *1 slice: 125 cal., 2g fat (0 sat. fat), 13mg chol., 153mg sodium, 24g carb. (6g sugars, 2g fiber), 4g pro.* ***Diabetic Exchanges:*** *1½ starch, ½ fat.*

YOGURT YEAST ROLLS

YOGURT YEAST ROLLS F M

People will snap up these fluffy golden rolls in a hurry whenever you take them to a potluck. It's a nice contribution because rolls are easy to transport and one batch goes a long way.

—**CAROL FORCUM** MARION, IL

PREP: 30 MIN. + RISING • **BAKE:** 15 MIN.
MAKES: 2 DOZEN

- **1½ cups whole wheat flour**
- **3¼ cups all-purpose flour, divided**
- **2 packages (¼ ounce each) active dry yeast**
- **2 teaspoons salt**
- **½ teaspoon baking soda**
- **1½ cups (12 ounces) plain yogurt**
- **½ cup water**
- **3 tablespoons butter**
- **2 tablespoons honey**
- **Additional melted butter, optional**

1. In a large bowl, combine whole wheat flour, 1/2 cup all-purpose flour, yeast, salt and the baking soda. In a saucepan over low heat, heat yogurt, water, butter and honey to 120°-130°. Pour over dry ingredients; blend well. Beat on medium speed for 3 minutes. Add enough remaining all-purpose flour to form a soft dough.
2. Turn onto a floured surface; knead the dough until smooth and elastic, about 6-8 minutes. Place in a greased bowl, turning once to grease top. Cover and let rise in a warm place until doubled, about 1 hour.
3. Punch dough down. Turn onto a lightly floured surface; divide into 24 portions. Roll each into a 10-in. rope. Shape rope into an "S", then coil each end until it touches the center. Place 3 in. apart on greased baking sheets. Cover and let rise until doubled, about 30 minutes. Preheat oven to 400°.
4. Bake until golden brown, about 15 minutes. If desired, brush tops with additional butter while warm. Remove from pans to wire racks to cool.

PER SERVING *1 roll: 115 cal., 2g fat (1g sat. fat), 6mg chol., 245mg sodium, 21g carb. (3g sugars, 1g fiber), 3g pro.* ***Diabetic Exchanges:*** *1½ starch, ½ fat.*

APPLE-ALMOND MUFFINS M

I like to snack on apple slices slathered with almond butter, which is the flavor combo that inspired these muffins. Add a dash of almond extract to boost the nuttiness in every bite.

—**KELLY ALESSO** CHICAGO, IL

PREP: 15 MIN. • **BAKE:** 20 MIN.
MAKES: 15 MUFFINS

- **1 cup all-purpose flour**
- **¾ cup whole wheat flour**
- **¼ cup sugar**
- **¼ cup packed brown sugar**
- **3 teaspoons baking powder**
- **¾ teaspoon ground cinnamon**
- **½ teaspoon salt**
- **1 large egg**
- **1¼ cups 2% milk**
- **⅓ cup creamy almond butter**
- **2 tablespoons canola oil**
- **1 teaspoon vanilla extract**
- **1 medium apple, peeled and finely chopped**
- **½ cup slivered almonds, divided**

1. Preheat oven to 400°. In a large bowl, whisk the first seven ingredients. In another bowl, whisk egg, milk, almond butter, oil and vanilla until blended. Add to flour mixture; stir just until moistened. Fold in apple and 1/4 cup almonds.
2. Fill 15 greased or paper-lined muffin cups three-fourths full. Sprinkle with remaining almonds.
3. Bake 18-20 minutes or until a toothpick inserted in center comes out clean. Cool 5 minutes before removing from pans to wire racks. Serve warm.

FREEZE OPTION *Freeze cooled muffins in resealable plastic freezer bags. To use, thaw at room temperature or, if desired, microwave each muffin on high setting for 20-30 seconds or until heated through.*

PER SERVING *1 muffin: 168 cal., 8g fat (1g sat. fat), 16mg chol., 189mg sodium, 22g carb. (9g sugars, 2g fiber), 5g pro.* ***Diabetic Exchanges:*** *1½ starch, 1 fat.*

HEALTH TIP *Per ounce, almonds contain more fiber and protein than any other tree nut.*

APPLE-ALMOND MUFFINS

ONION-GARLIC HERB ROSETTES F S C M

Flood your kitchen with the heavenly aroma of these special rolls baking in the oven. I initially created the recipe for a traditional loaf pan, but people really enjoy the individual rosettes.

—RYAN GARDNER RICHMOND, VA

PREP: 1 HOUR + RISING
BAKE: 10 MIN./BATCH • **MAKES:** 4 DOZEN

- **1 package (¼ ounce) active dry yeast**
- **2 cups warm water (110° to 115°)**
- **1 cup old-fashioned oats**
- **¼ cup canola oil**
- **6 garlic cloves, minced**
- **2 tablespoons minced fresh parsley**
- **2 tablespoons minced fresh rosemary**
- **1 tablespoon sugar**
- **2 teaspoons salt**
- **2 cups whole wheat flour**
- **2½ to 3 cups all-purpose flour**
- **2 cups shredded cheddar cheese**
- **1 large onion, chopped**

EGG WASH

- **1 large egg**
- **1 tablespoon water**

1. In a large bowl, dissolve yeast in warm water. Add the oats, oil, garlic, parsley, rosemary, sugar, salt and whole wheat flour. Beat on medium speed for 3 minutes or until smooth. Stir in enough all-purpose flour to form a firm dough. Stir in the cheese and onion.

2. Turn onto a floured surface; knead dough until smooth and elastic, about 6-8 minutes. Place in a greased bowl, turning once to grease the top. Cover with plastic wrap and let rise in a warm place until doubled, about 1 hour.

3. Punch dough down. Divide dough into 48 balls. Roll each into a 12-in. rope; tie into a loose knot. Bring the bottom end up and tuck into center of roll; wrap top end around and tuck under roll. Place 2 in. apart on greased baking sheets. Cover and let rise in a warm place until doubled, about 30 minutes.

4. In a small bowl, combine egg and water. Brush over rolls. Bake at 350° for 10-15 minutes or until golden brown. Remove from pans to wire racks to cool.

PER SERVING *1 roll: 81 cal., 3g fat (1g sat. fat), 9mg chol., 129mg sodium, 11g carb. (1g sugars, 1g fiber), 3g pro.* ***Diabetic Exchanges:*** *1 starch.*

OVERNIGHT HONEY-WHEAT ROLLS F S M

PREP: 30 MIN. + CHILLING • **BAKE:** 10 MIN.
MAKES: 1½ DOZEN

- **1 package (¼ ounce) active dry yeast**
- **1¼ cups warm water (110° to 115°), divided**
- **2 large egg whites**
- **⅓ cup honey**
- **¼ cup canola oil**
- **1 teaspoon salt**
- **1½ cups whole wheat flour**
- **2½ cups all-purpose flour**
- **Melted butter, optional**

1. In a small bowl, dissolve yeast in 1/4 cup warm water. In a large bowl, beat egg whites until foamy. Add the yeast mixture, honey, oil, salt, whole wheat flour and remaining water. Beat on medium speed for 3 minutes. Beat until smooth. Stir in enough all-purpose flour to form a soft dough (dough will be sticky). Cover and refrigerate overnight.

2. Punch dough down. Turn onto a floured surface; divide in half. Shape each portion into nine balls. To form knots, roll each ball into a 10-in. rope; tie into a knot. Tuck ends under.

3. Place rolls 2 in. apart on greased baking sheets. Cover and let rise until doubled, about 50 minutes.

4. Bake at 375° for 10-12 minutes or until golden brown. Brush with melted butter if desired.

PER SERVING *1 roll: 147 cal., 3g fat (0 sat. fat), 0 chol., 139mg sodium, 26g carb. (6g sugars, 2g fiber), 4g pro.* ***Diabetic Exchanges:*** *1½ starch, ½ fat.*

These yeast rolls don't require kneading, and the make-ahead dough saves you time on the day of your meal. But the best part is the hint of honey flavor.

—LISA VARNER EL PASO, TX

OVERNIGHT HONEY-WHEAT ROLLS

CHERRY-CHIP OAT SCONES M (PICTURED ON P. 201)

My family loves scones and anything with oatmeal. I started with my basic scone recipe and added oat flour to increase the oat flavor and texture. I also included ingredients that are harmonious with the mellow taste of oats. I have learned that everyone loves them most when I add special ingredients you can find in each bite.
—**AMY BRNGER** PORTSMOUTH, NH

PREP: 15 MIN. • **BAKE:** 20 MIN.
MAKES: 10 SERVINGS

- **1½ cups all-purpose flour**
- **½ cup oat flour**
- **½ cup old-fashioned oats**
- **3 tablespoons brown sugar**
- **1 teaspoon baking soda**
- **1 teaspoon cream of tartar**
- **½ teaspoon salt**
- **3 tablespoons cold butter, cubed**
- **1 cup buttermilk**
- **⅓ cup dried cherries, chopped**
- **⅓ cup miniature semisweet chocolate chips**
- **¼ cup finely chopped pecans, toasted**

TOPPING

- **1 tablespoon coarse sugar**
- **1 tablespoon old-fashioned oats**

1. Preheat the oven to 400°. Whisk together first seven ingredients; cut in butter until mixture resembles coarse crumbs. Add buttermilk, stirring just until moistened. Stir in the cherries, chocolate chips and pecans.
2. Transfer to a parchment paper-lined baking sheet; pat into a 6-in. circle. Cut into 10 wedges, but do not separate. Sprinkle with coarse sugar and oats.
3. Bake until brown, 20-25 minutes. Serve warm.

FREEZE OPTION *Freeze cooled scones in resealable plastic freezer bags. To use, thaw at room temperature or, if desired, microwave each scone on high until heated through, 20-30 seconds.*

PER SERVING *1 scone: 229 cal., 8g fat (4g sat. fat), 10mg chol., 321mg sodium, 36g carb. (13g sugars, 2g fiber), 5g pro.*

OATMEAL MINI LOAVES

OATMEAL MINI LOAVES F M

I first came across this recipe in an old cookbook. As I became more brave with bread baking, I decided to redo the recipe, changing and adding ingredients to enhance flavor and nutrition.
—**DORIS KOSMICKI** PINCKNEY, MI

PREP: 25 MIN. + RISING • **BAKE:** 30 MIN.
MAKES: 5 MINI LOAVES (5 SLICES EACH)

- **1½ cups old-fashioned oats**
- **¾ cup whole wheat flour**
- **½ cup packed brown sugar**
- **¼ cup toasted wheat germ**
- **3 teaspoons salt**
- **1 package (¼ ounce) active dry yeast**
- **2½ cups water**
- **2 tablespoons butter**
- **5½ to 6 cups all-purpose flour**
- **Melted butter, optional**
- **Additional old-fashioned oats, optional**

1. In a large bowl, combine the oats, whole wheat flour, brown sugar, wheat germ, salt and yeast. In a small saucepan, heat water and butter to 120°-130°. Add to dry ingredients just until moistened. Add 3 cups all-purpose flour; beat until smooth. Stir in enough remaining all-purpose flour to form a soft dough.
2. Turn onto a floured surface; knead until smooth and elastic, about 6-8 minutes. Place in a greased bowl, turning once to grease top. Cover and let rise in a warm place until doubled, about 1 hour.
3. Punch the dough down. Turn onto a lightly floured surface; divide into five portions. Shape each into a loaf. Place in five greased 5x3x2-in. loaf pans. Cover and let rise until doubled, about 30 minutes.
4. Bake at 350° for 30-35 minutes or until golden brown. Remove from pans to wire racks. Brush with melted butter; sprinkle with additional oats if desired. Cool.

NOTE *Two greased 9x5x3-in. loaf pans may be used; bake for 35-40 minutes.*

PER SERVING *1 slice: 159 cal., 2g fat (1g sat. fat), 2mg chol., 295mg sodium, 32g carb. (5g sugars, 2g fiber), 5g pro.* ***Diabetic Exchanges:** 2 starch, ½ fat.*

TOP TIP

Wheat germ, the embryo of the wheat plant, is a concentrated nutrient source. Each tablespoon adds 2 grams protein and 1 gram fiber to dishes. So go ahead and shake some over your cereal, add to granola recipes or blend it into smoothies.

WHOLE WHEAT POTATO ROLLS

WHOLE WHEAT POTATO ROLLS M

My cousin gave me this recipe for classic potato rolls with a twist. If you have leftovers, go ahead and freeze them for later. They'll be just as tasty!
—DEVON VICKERS GODDARD, KS

PREP: 30 MIN.+ RISING • **BAKE:** 10 MIN.
MAKES: 24 ROLLS

- **1 package (¼ ounce) active dry yeast**
- **2 cups warm water (110° to 115°)**
- **½ cup sugar**
- **½ cup canola oil**
- **2 large eggs**
- **⅓ cup mashed potato flakes**
- **1½ teaspoons salt**
- **2 cups all-purpose flour**
- **4 to 4¾ cups whole wheat flour**
- **2 tablespoons butter, melted**
- **Quick-cooking oats, optional**

1. In a small bowl, dissolve yeast in warm water. In a large bowl, combine the sugar, oil, eggs, potato flakes, salt, yeast mixture, all-purpose flour and 2½ cups whole wheat flour. Beat until smooth. Stir in enough remaining whole wheat flour to form a soft dough (dough will be sticky).

2. Turn onto a floured surface; knead until smooth and elastic, about 6-8 minutes. Place in a greased bowl, turning once to grease the top. Cover with plastic wrap and let rise in a warm place until doubled, about 1½ hours.

3. Punch down dough. Turn onto a lightly floured surface; divide and shape into 24 balls. Place 2 in. apart on greased baking sheets. Cover with kitchen towels; let rise in a warm place until doubled, about 30 minutes.

4. Preheat oven to 375°. Brush tops with melted butter; if desired, sprinkle with oats. Bake 9-11 minutes or until lightly browned. Serve warm.

PER SERVING *1 roll: 182 cal., 7g fat (1g sat. fat), 20mg chol., 163mg sodium, 28g carb. (4g sugars, 3g fiber), 5g pro.* ***Diabetic Exchanges:*** *2 starch, 1 fat.*

SPICY APPLESAUCE FRUIT BREAD F M

PREP: 20 MIN. • **BAKE:** 30 MIN. + COOLING
MAKES: 2 LOAVES (12 SLICES EACH)

- **2 cups plus 2 tablespoons all-purpose flour, divided**
- **2 teaspoons baking powder**
- **1 teaspoon salt**
- **1 teaspoon ground cinnamon**
- **1 teaspoon ground nutmeg**
- **½ teaspoon ground allspice**
- **½ teaspoon ground cloves**
- **½ teaspoon baking soda**
- **2 large eggs**
- **1¼ cups unsweetened applesauce**
- **¾ cup sugar**
- **¼ cup packed brown sugar**
- **¼ cup butter, melted**
- **1 tablespoon grated orange peel**
- **½ cup dried cranberries or raisins**
- **½ cup chopped candied citron**

1. Preheat oven to 350°. In a large bowl, whisk 2 cups flour, the baking powder, salt, spices and baking soda. In another bowl, whisk eggs, applesauce, sugars, melted butter and orange peel until blended. Add to flour mixture; stir just until moistened. In a small bowl, toss cranberries and candied citron with remaining flour; fold into batter.

2. Transfer to two greased 8x4-in. loaf pans. Bake 30-35 minutes or until a toothpick inserted in center comes out clean. Cool in pans 10 minutes before removing to wire racks to cool.

PER SERVING *1 slice: 126 cal., 3g fat (1g sat. fat), 21mg chol., 194mg sodium, 25g carb. (15g sugars, 1g fiber), 2g pro.* ***Diabetic Exchanges:*** *1½ starch, ½ fat.*

I've had this fruity loaf in my recipe collection since 1975. I tweak it with spices and candied fruit, depending on the season.
—DAWN E. LOWENSTEIN HUNTINGDON VALLEY, PA

SPICY APPLESAUCE FRUIT BREAD

WHOLE WHEAT BLUEBERRY-NUT BREAD M

This bread-machine loaf owes its healthy heartiness to a combination of flaxseeds and whole wheat flour. Moist and flavorful, it has a nutty texture that's great for sandwiches or toast.

—**AMY BLOM** MARIETTA, GA

PREP: 1¼ HOURS + RISING • **BAKE:** 45 MIN.
MAKES: 1 LOAF (16 SLICES)

- **1⅓ cups water (70° to 80°)**
- **¼ cup olive oil**
- **¼ cup honey or maple syrup**
- **1¼ teaspoons salt**
- **¾ cup ground flaxseed**
- **¼ cup nonfat dry milk powder**
- **3½ cups white whole wheat flour**
- **½ cup old-fashioned oats**
- **¼ cup vital wheat gluten**
- **2½ teaspoons active dry yeast**
- **½ cup dried blueberries or cranberries**
- **⅓ cup chopped walnuts, toasted**
- **Additional olive oil**

1. In bread machine pan, place all the ingredients in order suggested by manufacturer. Select dough setting.
2. Check dough after 5 minutes of mixing; add 1 to 2 tablespoons water or flour if needed. Just before the final kneading (your machine may audibly signal this), add berries and walnuts.
3. When the cycle is completed, turn dough onto a lightly floured surface. Punch down; shape into a loaf. Place in a greased 9x5-in. loaf pan. Cover and let rise until doubled, about 45 minutes.
4. Bake at 350° for 45-50 minutes or until golden brown, tent with foil after 30 minutes. Remove from pan to wire rack to cool. Brush top with oil.

PER SERVING *1 slice: 226 cal., 8g fat (1g sat. fat), 0 chol., 194mg sodium, 35g carb. (7g sugars, 6g fiber), 8g pro.*

DID YOU KNOW?

Vital wheat gluten is almost pure protein. It's a great addition to whole-grain breads because it makes the dough more elastic.

FLAXSEED BREAD

FLAXSEED BREAD M

This hearty, whole grain bread is among my all-time favorites. The flaxseed adds a nutty texture that everyone seems to enjoy. Every slice is so satisfying. Give it a try and see for yourself.

—**JENNIFER NIEMI** KINGSTON, NS

PREP: 40 MIN. + RISING
BAKE: 35 MIN. + COOLING
MAKES: 1 LOAF (16 SLICES)

- **1½ cups whole wheat flour**
- **1½ to 2 cups all-purpose flour**
- **1 package (¼ ounce) active dry yeast**
- **1 teaspoon salt**
- **1½ cups fat-free milk**
- **¼ cup packed brown sugar**
- **2 tablespoons honey**
- **2 tablespoons plus 1½ teaspoons butter, divided**
- **½ cup ground flaxseed**
- **½ cup whole flaxseed**

1. In a large bowl, combine the whole wheat flour, 1 cup all-purpose flour, yeast and salt. In a large saucepan, heat the milk, brown sugar, honey and 2 tablespoons butter to 120°-130°. Add to dry ingredients; beat until smooth. Stir in ground and whole flaxseed until blended. Stir in enough of the remaining all-purpose flour to form a firm dough.
2. Turn onto a lightly floured surface; knead until smooth and elastic, about 6-8 minutes. Place in a large bowl coated with cooking spray, turning once to coat top. Cover and let rise in a warm place until doubled, about 1 hour.
3. Punch dough down. Turn onto a lightly floured surface. Shape into a loaf; place in a 9x5-in. loaf pan coated with cooking spray. Cover and let rise until doubled, about 30 minutes.
4. Bake at 375° for 35-40 minutes or until golden brown. Remove from pan to a wire rack. Melt remaining butter; brush over bread. Cool.

PER SERVING *1 slice: 169 cal., 5g fat (2g sat. fat), 5mg chol., 183mg sodium, 27g carb. (7g sugars, 4g fiber), 6g pro.*
***Diabetic Exchanges:** 2 starch, 1 fat.*

223

218

224

Cakes & Pies

"This is the first dessert I think of when that blushed golden fruit finally arrives at fruit stands. What a delightful way to celebrate the arrival of peaches. It's just plain perfection. You can make this tart with other varieties of fruit, too."

—LORRAINE CALAND SHUNIAH, ON
about her recipe, Pretty Peach Tart, on page 225

RUSTIC CHOCOLATE RASPBERRY TART

RUSTIC CHOCOLATE RASPBERRY TART S M

Here's a delectable dessert that all ages will enjoy. From raspberries to a Nutella-covered homemade pastry crust, you won't be able to get enough of this.
—**CHRISTINA SEREMETIS** ROCKLAND, MA

PREP: 20 MIN. + CHILLING • **BAKE:** 45 MIN.
MAKES: 16 SERVINGS

- **5 ounces cream cheese, softened**
- **6 tablespoons butter, softened**
- **1½ cups all-purpose flour**

FILLING

- **2 cups fresh raspberries**
- **2 tablespoons sugar**
- **1 teaspoon cornstarch**
- **⅓ cup Nutella**

1. Process cream cheese and butter in a food processor until blended. Add flour; process just until a dough forms. Shape into a disk; wrap in plastic. Refrigerate 1 hour or overnight.
2. Preheat oven to 350°. In a small bowl, toss raspberries, sugar and cornstarch with a fork, mashing some of the berries slightly.
3. On a lightly floured surface, roll the dough into a 14x8-in. rectangle. Transfer to a parchment paper-lined baking sheet. Spread with Nutella to within 1 in. of edges. Top with the raspberry mixture. Fold pastry edge toward center of tart, pleating and pinching as needed.
4. Bake until crust is golden brown, 45-50 minutes. Transfer tart to a wire rack to cool.

PER SERVING *1 piece: 157 cal., 9g fat (5g sat. fat), 20mg chol., 65mg sodium, 17g carb. (6g sugars, 2g fiber), 2g pro.*

MAKEOVER LEMON POUND CAKE M

For this lovely cake, I use fat-free yogurt to trim the calories. It's great for days when it's warm enough to dine outside.
—**LAUREN GILMORE** PENNINGTON, NJ

PREP: 20 MIN. • **BAKE:** 50 MIN. + COOLING
MAKES: 1 LOAF (16 SERVINGS)

- **¼ cup butter, softened**
- **¾ cup sugar**
- **3 large eggs**
- **2 tablespoons canola oil**
- **2 tablespoons lemon juice**
- **2 teaspoons grated lemon peel**
- **1 teaspoon vanilla extract**
- **2 tablespoons poppy seeds, optional**
- **1½ cups all-purpose flour**
- **2½ teaspoons baking powder**
- **¾ teaspoon salt**
- **1 cup fat-free vanilla Greek yogurt**
- **Candied lemon slices, optional**

1. Preheat oven to 350°. Coat a 9x5-in. loaf pan with cooking spray. In a large bowl, beat butter and sugar until crumbly. Add the eggs, one at a time, beating well after each addition. Beat in oil, lemon juice, peel, vanilla and, if desired, poppy seeds. In another bowl, whisk flour, baking powder and salt; add to creamed mixture alternately with yogurt, beating after each addition just until combined.
2. Transfer to prepared pan. Bake 50-60 minutes or until a toothpick inserted in center comes out clean. Cool in pan 10 minutes before removing to a wire rack to cool completely. If desired, top with candied lemon slices.

CANDIED LEMON SLICES *Bring ¾ cup sugar and ¾ cup water to a boil; stir until sugar is dissolved, about 3 minutes. Add 1 thinly sliced lemon and simmer 5-7 minutes or until tender. Drain and cool slices completely on a wire rack.*

PER SERVING *145 cal., 6g fat (2g sat. fat), 43mg chol., 253mg sodium, 20g carb. (11g sugars, 0 fiber), 4g pro.*
***Diabetic Exchanges:** 1 starch, 1 fat.*

MAKEOVER LEMON POUND CAKE

PUMPKIN TARTLETS M

Refrigerated pie pastry and a muffin tin make it easy to create these little pumpkin tarts. And I love that they're just 200 calories apiece.

—**JESSIE OLESON** SANTA FE, NM

PREP: 20 MIN. • **BAKE:** 40 MIN. + COOLING
MAKES: 16 TARTLETS

- **1 package (15 ounces) refrigerated pie pastry**
- **1 can (15 ounces) solid-pack pumpkin**
- **1 can (12 ounces) evaporated milk**
- **¾ cup sugar**
- **2 large eggs**
- **½ teaspoon salt**
- **1 teaspoon ground cinnamon**
- **½ teaspoon ground ginger**
- **¼ teaspoon ground cloves**
- **Miniature marshmallows, optional**

1. Preheat oven to 425°. On a lightly floured surface, unroll each pastry sheet; roll to ⅛-in. thickness. Using a floured 4-in. round cutter, cut out 16 circles, rerolling scraps if necessary. Press circles into muffin pans coated with cooking spray.
2. In a large bowl, whisk pumpkin, milk, sugar, eggs, salt and spices until blended. Pour into pastry cups. Bake 15 minutes. Reduce oven setting to 350°.
3. Bake 25-30 minutes or until a knife inserted near center comes out clean. If desired, top with marshmallows and bake 2-3 minutes longer or until marshmallows are lightly browned. Cool 5 minutes.
4. Carefully run a knife around sides to loosen tarts. Cool in pans on wire racks before removing. Serve or refrigerate within 2 hours.

NOTE *For 9-in. Pumpkin Pie: Preheat oven to 425°. Unroll 1 refrigerated pie pastry sheet into a 9-in. pie plate; flute edge. Prepare filling as directed; pour into pastry shell. Bake 15 minutes. Reduce oven setting to 350°; bake 35-45 minutes longer, covering edge loosely with foil during last 10 minutes if needed to prevent overbrowning.*

PER SERVING *1 tartlet: 200 cal., 9g fat (4g sat. fat), 38mg chol., 203mg sodium, 27g carb. (13g sugars, 1g fiber), 3g pro.*

APPLE-WALNUT CAKE WITH ORANGE GLAZE

APPLE-WALNUT CAKE WITH ORANGE GLAZE M

I tinkered with a plain apple cake recipe to create this moist, delicious winner. The result: old-fashioned goodness with a heavenly aroma! This cake is the perfect fall treat or holiday dessert, but it also works well as a special breakfast or brunch item.

—**LISA SPEER** PALM BEACH, FL

PREP: 25 MIN. • **BAKE:** 65 MIN. + COOLING
MAKES: 16 SERVINGS

- **¾ cup sugar**
- **¾ cup packed brown sugar**
- **½ cup unsweetened applesauce**
- **¼ cup canola oil**
- **3 large eggs**
- **1 tablespoon vanilla extract**
- **3 cups all-purpose flour**
- **1¾ teaspoons apple pie spice**
- **1 teaspoon baking soda**
- **½ teaspoon salt**
- **3 medium apples, peeled and finely chopped**
- **1 cup chopped walnuts, toasted**

GLAZE

- **1½ cups confectioners' sugar**
- **1 teaspoon grated orange peel**
- **2 to 3 tablespoons orange juice**

1. Preheat oven to 325°. Coat a 10-in. fluted tube pan with cooking spray; dust with flour, tapping out extra.
2. Beat the first six ingredients until well blended. In another bowl, whisk together flour, pie spice, baking soda and salt; gradually beat into sugar mixture. Fold in apples and walnuts. Transfer to prepared pan.
3. Bake 65-75 minutes or until a toothpick inserted in center comes out clean. Cool in pan 10 minutes before removing to a wire rack; cool slightly.
4. Mix the confectioners' sugar, orange peel and enough juice to to reach a drizzling consistency. Spoon over warm cake.

NOTE *To toast nuts, bake in a shallow pan in a 350° oven for 5-10 minutes or cook in a skillet over low heat until lightly browned, stirring occasionally.*

PER SERVING *1 slice: 316 cal., 9g fat (1g sat. fat), 35mg chol., 170mg sodium, 54g carb. (34g sugars, 2g fiber), 5g pro.*

PINEAPPLE BREEZE TORTE

constantly; cook and stir until thickened, 1-2 minutes. Cool completely.

4. Spread topping gently over torte. Refrigerate, covered, until set, at least 4 hours. Remove rim from pan.

PER SERVING *1 slice: 243 cal., 7g fat (5g sat. fat), 87mg chol., 156mg sodium, 39g carb. (27g sugars, 1g fiber), 6g pro.* ***Diabetic Exchanges:*** *2 starch, 1½ fat, ½ fruit.*

BLUEBERRY CUSTARD MERINGUE PIE M

This mouthwatering pie is the result of combining two favorite recipes with fresh blueberries. Because it's so delicious, no one believes me when I tell them it's light!

—**DONNA HESS** CHAMBERSBURG, PA

PREP: 40 MIN. • **BAKE:** 20 MIN. + CHILLING • **MAKES:** 8 SERVINGS

- **10 whole reduced-fat graham crackers, quartered**
- **3 tablespoons butter, melted**
- **1 large egg white**

FILLING

- **½ cup sugar**
- **¼ cup cornstarch**
- **¼ teaspoon salt**
- **2 cups fat-free milk**
- **2 large egg yolks**
- **1 cup fresh blueberries**
- **½ teaspoon vanilla extract**

MERINGUE

- **3 large egg whites**
- **¼ teaspoon cream of tartar**
- **6 tablespoons sugar**

1. Preheat oven to 350°. Pulse crackers in a food processor until fine crumbs form. Add melted butter and egg white; pulse until blended. Press mixture onto bottom and up sides of a 9-in. pie plate coated with cooking spray. Bake 7-9 minutes or until set. Cool on a wire rack.

2. In a small heavy saucepan, mix sugar, cornstarch and salt. Whisk in milk. Cook and stir over medium heat until thickened and bubbly. Reduce heat to low; cook and stir 2 minutes longer. Remove from heat.

3. In a small bowl, whisk a small amount of hot mixture into egg yolks; return all to pan, whisking constantly. Bring to a gentle boil; cook and stir 2 minutes. Remove from heat; stir in blueberries and vanilla.

4. For meringue, in a bowl, beat egg whites with cream of tartar on medium speed until foamy. Gradually add sugar, 1 tablespoon at a time, beating on high after each addition until sugar is dissolved. Continue beating until soft glossy peaks form.

5. Transfer the hot filling to the crust. Spread meringue evenly over top, sealing to edge of crust. Bake at 350° for 16-20 minutes or until meringue is golden brown. Cool 1 hour on a wire. Refrigerate 1-2 hours before serving. Refrigerate the leftovers.

PER SERVING *1 piece: 212 cal., 6g fat (3g sat. fat), 66mg chol., 211mg sodium, 35g carb. (28g sugars, 1g fiber), 5g pro.* ***Diabetic Exchanges:*** *2 starch, 1 fat.*

PINEAPPLE BREEZE TORTE M

This lovely torte features ladyfingers, a creamy filling and a crushed pineapple topping. It's a special treat for my large family and a must at Christmas.

—**BARBARA JOYNER** FRANKLIN, VA

PREP: 25 MIN. + CHILLING • **COOK:** 5 MIN. + COOLING
MAKES: 12 SERVINGS

- **3 packages (3 ounces each) soft ladyfingers, split**

FILLING

- **1 package (8 ounces) fat-free cream cheese**
- **3 ounces cream cheese, softened**
- **⅓ cup sugar**
- **2 teaspoons vanilla extract**
- **1 carton (8 ounces) frozen reduced-fat whipped topping, thawed**

TOPPING

- **⅓ cup sugar**
- **3 tablespoons cornstarch**
- **1 can (20 ounces) unsweetened crushed pineapple, undrained**

1. Line bottom and sides of an ungreased 9-in. springform pan with ladyfinger halves; reserve remaining ladyfingers for layering.

2. Beat cream cheeses, sugar and vanilla until smooth; fold in whipped topping. Spread half of the mixture over bottom ladyfingers. Layer with remaining ladyfingers, overlapping as needed. Spread with the remaining filling. Refrigerate, covered, while preparing topping.

3. In a small saucepan, mix sugar and cornstarch; stir in the pineapple. Bring to a boil over medium heat, stirring

HOT FUDGE CAKE M

What better way to top off a great meal than with a rich, chocolaty cake? Mom served this dessert with a scoop of ice cream or with cream poured over—and no matter what, I'd always have room for it.

—VERA REID LARAMIE, WY

PREP: 20 MIN. • **BAKE:** 35 MIN. • **MAKES:** 9 SERVINGS

- **1 cup all-purpose flour**
- **¾ cup sugar**
- **6 tablespoons baking cocoa, divided**
- **2 teaspoons baking powder**
- **¼ teaspoon salt**
- **½ cup 2% milk**
- **2 tablespoons canola oil**
- **1 teaspoon vanilla extract**
- **1 cup packed brown sugar**
- **1¾ cups hot water**
- **Ice cream or whipped cream, optional**

1. Preheat oven to 350°. In a large bowl, whisk flour, sugar, 2 tablespoons cocoa, baking powder and salt. In another bowl, whisk milk, oil and vanilla until blended. Add to flour mixture; stir just until moistened.

2. Transfer to an ungreased 9-in. square baking pan. In a small bowl, mix brown sugar and remaining cocoa; sprinkle over batter. Pour hot water over all; do not stir.

3. Bake 35-40 minutes. Serve warm. If desired, top with ice cream.

PER SERVING *1 piece: 253 cal., 4g fat (1g sat. fat), 2mg chol., 171mg sodium, 54g carb. (41g sugars, 1g fiber), 3g pro.*

HOT FUDGE CAKE

APPLE-CINNAMON MINI PIES

APPLE-CINNAMON MINI PIES S C M

I came up with the idea for these little pies while snacking on applesauce one night and thought it would make a quick and delicious pie filling. What's better than an apple pie you can actually hold in your hand to eat?

—KANDY BINGHAM GREEN RIVER, WY

PREP: 20 MIN. • **BAKE:** 15 MIN. • **MAKES:** 1 DOZEN

- **1 package (14.1 ounces) refrigerated pie pastry**
- **½ cup chunky applesauce**
- **3 teaspoons cinnamon sugar, divided**
- **2 tablespoons butter, cut into 12 pieces**
- **1 tablespoon 2% milk, divided**

1. Preheat oven to 350°. On a lightly floured surface, unroll pastry sheets. Using a floured 3½-in. round cookie cutter, cut six circles from each sheet.

2. In a small bowl, mix applesauce with 1½ teaspoons cinnamon sugar. Place 2 teaspoons applesauce mixture on one half of each circle; dot with butter. Moisten pastry edges with some of the milk. Fold pastry over filling; press edges with a fork to seal.

3. Transfer to ungreased baking sheets. Brush tops with remaining milk; sprinkle with remaining cinnamon sugar. Bake 12-15 minutes or until golden brown. Remove from pans to wire racks. Serve warm or at room temperature.

PER SERVING *1 mini pie: 104 cal., 6g fat (3g sat. fat), 8mg chol., 77mg sodium, 11g carb. (3g sugars, 0 fiber), 1g pro.*

REESE'S CHOCOLATE SNACK CAKE M

My family constantly requests this easy cake. Its yellow and orange toppings make it the perfect dessert for a Halloween party.

—EILEEN TRAVIS UKIAH, CA

PREP: 15 MIN. • **BAKE:** 30 MIN. + COOLING
MAKES: 20 SERVINGS

- **3⅓ cups all-purpose flour**
- **⅔ cup sugar**
- **⅔ cup packed brown sugar**
- **½ cup baking cocoa**
- **2 teaspoons baking soda**
- **1 teaspoon salt**
- **2 cups water**
- **⅓ cup canola oil**
- **⅓ cup unsweetened applesauce**
- **2 teaspoons white vinegar**
- **1 teaspoon vanilla extract**
- **1 cup Reese's pieces**
- **½ cup coarsely chopped salted peanuts**

1. Preheat the oven to 350°. Coat a 13x9-in. pan with cooking spray.
2. Whisk together first six ingredients. In another bowl, whisk together water, oil, applesauce, vinegar and vanilla. Add to flour mixture, stirring just until blended. Transfer batter to prepared pan. Sprinkle with the Reese's pieces and peanuts.
3. Bake for 30-35 minutes or until a toothpick inserted in center comes out clean. Cool on a wire rack.

PER SERVING *1 piece: 240 cal., 8g fat (2g sat. fat), 0 chol., 280mg sodium, 38g carb. (19g sugars, 2g fiber), 5g pro.*

REESE'S CHOCOLATE SNACK CAKE

RASPBERRY RUMBLE

RASPBERRY RUMBLE M

My guy is a raspberry fan, so that's what I use in this cake with a classic fluffy frosting. Freeze the berries so they don't stain the batter.

—LORRAINE CALAND SHUNIAH, ON

PREP: 40 MIN. • **BAKE:** 25 MIN. + COOLING
MAKES: 12 SERVINGS

- **2 cups fresh raspberries**
- **¼ cup butter, softened**
- **¾ cup sugar**
- **2 large eggs**
- **2¼ cups all-purpose flour**
- **2 teaspoons baking powder**
- **1 teaspoon salt**
- **¾ cup 2% milk**

TOPPING

- **3 large egg whites**
- **1 cup sugar**
- **⅛ teaspoon cream of tartar**
- **¼ to ½ cup boiling water, optional**
- **¼ teaspoon almond extract**
- **Sliced almonds**

1. Place raspberries on a baking sheet; freeze until firm. Preheat oven to 350°.
2. In a large bowl, cream butter and sugar until light and fluffy; beat in eggs. In another bowl, whisk together the flour, baking powder and salt; add to creamed mixture alternately with milk, beating well. Fold in frozen raspberries. Spread into a greased 13x9-in. baking pan.
3. Bake 25-30 minutes or until a toothpick inserted in center comes out clean. Cool completely in pan on a wire rack.
4. For topping, whisk together egg whites, sugar and cream of tartar in a large heatproof bowl. Place over simmering water in a large saucepan over medium heat; whisking constantly, heat mixture until a thermometer reads 160°. Remove from heat.
5. Beat on high speed until stiff glossy peaks form, about 5 minutes. If desired, thin frosting with water by slowly beating in enough boiling water until desired consistency is reached. Fold in extract. Spread over cake. Sprinkle with almonds. Refrigerate the leftovers.

PER SERVING *1 piece: 266 cal., 5g fat (3g sat. fat), 42mg chol., 323mg sodium, 51g carb. (31g sugars, 2g fiber), 5g pro.*

TOP TIP

Raspberries, a cooler-weather crop, are generally best in late spring and early fall. For a pretty look, bake the rumble with a mix of golden, black and red raspberries.

GINGERED STRAWBERRY TART M

When I came across this strawberry dessert recipe years ago, I knew I had to try it. I love to bake new things, and I especially like the elegance of this pretty tart.

—MARIE RIZZIO INTERLOCHEN, MI

PREP: 40 MIN. + CHILLING
BAKE: 10 MIN. + COOLING
MAKES: 8 SERVINGS

- **24 gingersnap cookies (about 6 ounces)**
- **2 tablespoons plus ⅓ cup sugar, divided**
- **¼ cup butter, melted**
- **2 tablespoons cornstarch**
- **3 cups chopped fresh strawberries**
- **¼ cup water**
- **1 teaspoon finely chopped crystallized ginger, optional**

TOPPING

- **2 cups sliced fresh strawberries**
- **5 tablespoons seedless strawberry jam**

1. Preheat oven to 350°. Pulse cookies in a food processor until finely ground. Add 2 tablespoons sugar and melted butter; pulse until blended. Press onto bottom and up sides of a 9-in. fluted tart pan with a removable bottom. Place on a baking sheet; bake until lightly browned, 8-10 minutes. Cool completely.

2. In a large saucepan, mix cornstarch and remaining sugar until smooth. Add chopped strawberries, water and, if desired, ginger. Bring to a boil, stirring occasionally; cook and stir 2 minutes. Reduce the heat; simmer, uncovered, about 4-6 minutes until thickened. Cool 30 minutes. Pour into crust. Refrigerate, covered, until set, about 2 hours.

3. Arrange sliced strawberries over top. In a microwave, warm jam until melted; brush over berries.

PER SERVING *1 piece: 252 cal., 8g fat (4g sat. fat), 15mg chol., 196mg sodium, 45g carb. (31g sugars, 3g fiber), 2g pro.*

CHUNKY MONKEY CUPCAKES M

Peanut butter is a favorite of ours, and it brings a fun element to these cupcakes. They're good with or without garnishes.

—HOLLY JONES KENNESAW, GA

PREP: 30 MIN. • **BAKE:** 20 MIN. + COOLING
MAKES: 2 DOZEN

- **2 cups mashed ripe bananas (about 5 medium)**
- **1½ cups sugar**
- **3 large eggs**
- **½ cup unsweetened applesauce**
- **¼ cup canola oil**
- **3 cups all-purpose flour**
- **1 teaspoon baking soda**
- **½ teaspoon baking powder**
- **½ teaspoon salt**
- **1 cup semisweet chocolate chunks**

FROSTING

- **4 ounces reduced-fat cream cheese**
- **¼ cup creamy peanut butter**
- **3 tablespoons butter, softened**
- **1 to 1¼ cups confectioners' sugar**
- **Chopped salted peanuts, optional**

1. Preheat the oven to 350°. Line 24 muffin cups with paper liners.

2. Beat first five ingredients until well blended. In another bowl, whisk together flour, baking soda, baking powder and salt; gradually beat into banana mixture. Fold in chocolate chunks.

3. Fill prepared cups three-fourths full. Bake 20-25 minutes or until a toothpick inserted in center comes out clean. Cool in pans 10 minutes before removing to wire racks to cool completely.

4. For frosting, beat cream cheese, peanut butter and the butter until smooth. Gradually beat in enough confectioners' sugar to reach desired consistency. Spread over cupcakes. If desired, sprinkle with peanuts. Refrigerate leftovers.

PER SERVING *1 cupcake: 250 cal., 9g fat (4g sat. fat), 30mg chol., 165mg sodium, 40g carb. (25g sugars, 2g fiber), 4g pro.*

CHUNKY MONKEY CUPCAKES

APRICOT UPSIDE-DOWN CAKE

APRICOT UPSIDE-DOWN CAKE M

My Aunt Anne, who is a great cook, gave me a taste of this golden cake. I couldn't believe how delicious it was. Apricots give the classic cake a rare and attractive twist.
—**RUTH ANN STELFOX** RAYMOND, AB

PREP: 30 MIN. • **BAKE:** 35 MIN. + COOLING
MAKES: 9 SERVINGS

- **2 large eggs, separated**
- **2 cans (15 ounces each) apricot halves**
- **¼ cup butter, cubed**
- **½ cup packed brown sugar**
- **⅔ cup cake flour**
- **¾ teaspoon baking powder**
- **¼ teaspoon salt**
- **⅔ cup sugar**

1. Place egg whites in a bowl; let stand at room temperature for 30 minutes. Preheat oven to 350°. Drain apricots, reserving 3 tablespoons syrup (discard remaining syrup); set aside.

2. Place butter in a 9-in. square baking dish. Place in oven 3-4 minutes or until butter is melted; swirl carefully to coat evenly. Sprinkle with the brown sugar. Arrange apricot halves in a single layer over brown sugar, cut side up.

3. In a small bowl, whisk flour, baking powder and salt. In a large bowl, beat egg yolks until slightly thickened. Gradually add sugar, beating on high speed until thick and lemon-colored. Beat in reserved apricot syrup. Fold in flour mixture.

4. With clean beaters, beat egg whites on medium speed until stiff peaks form. Fold into batter. Spoon over apricots. Bake 35-40 minutes or until a toothpick inserted in center comes out clean. Cool 10 minutes before inverting onto a serving plate. Serve warm.

PER SERVING *1 piece: 272 cal., 6g fat (4g sat. fat), 55mg chol., 162mg sodium, 53g carb. (44g sugars, 1g fiber), 3g pro.*

NANA'S CHOCOLATE CUPCAKES WITH MINT FROSTING M

These cupcakes remind me of when Nana used to make them at Christmas. Even though she's no longer with us, baking them brings me joy because it gives the cakes special meaning.
—**CHEKOTA HUNTER** CASSVILLE, MO

PREP: 25 MIN. • **BAKE:** 15 MIN. + COOLING
MAKES: 1 DOZEN

- **½ cup baking cocoa**
- **1 cup boiling water**
- **¼ cup butter, softened**
- **1 cup sugar**
- **2 large eggs**
- **1⅓ cups all-purpose flour**
- **2 teaspoons baking powder**
- **¼ teaspoon salt**
- **¼ cup unsweetened applesauce**

FROSTING

- **1 cup confectioners' sugar**
- **3 tablespoons butter, softened**
- **4 teaspoons heavy whipping cream**
- **Dash peppermint extract**
- **1 drop green food coloring, optional**
- **2 tablespoons miniature semisweet chocolate chips**
- **Mint Andes candies, optional**

1. Preheat the oven to 375°. Line 12 muffin cups with paper or foil liners. Mix cocoa and boiling water until smooth; cool completely.

2. Beat butter and sugar until blended. Beat in eggs, one at a time. In another bowl, whisk together flour, baking powder and salt; add to butter mixture, alternately with applesauce, beating well after each addition. Beat in cocoa mixture.

3. Fill prepared muffin cups three-fourths full. Bake until a toothpick inserted in center comes out clean, 15-18 minutes. Cool 10 minutes before removing to a wire rack to cool completely.

4. Beat confectioners' sugar, butter, cream and extract until smooth. If desired, tint frosting green with food coloring. Stir in chocolate chips. Frost cupcakes. If desired, top with candies.

PER SERVING *1 cupcake: 253 cal., 9g fat (5g sat. fat), 51mg chol., 196mg sodium, 41g carb. (28g sugars, 1g fiber), 3g pro.*

DID YOU KNOW?

Dutch process cocoa is treated with an alkaline solution when it's made. It has a smoother, richer flavor and darker color than regular cocoa. Baked goods made with Dutch process cocoa are a more intense chocolate brown color than those made with regular cocoa.

NANA'S CHOCOLATE CUPCAKES
WITH MINT FROSTING

SPICED CARROT CAKE

SPICED CARROT CAKE M

My mom made this carrot cake once for my birthday because carrot cake is her favorite. Turns out, it's my favorite, too! Now when I make it, I love it with lots of spice. The pumpkin pie spice is a shortcut, but you could use a custom blend of cinnamon, ginger, nutmeg and cloves.

—**JARIS DYKAS** KNOXVILLE, TN

PREP: 30 MIN. • **BAKE:** 20 MIN. + COOLING
MAKES: 16 SERVINGS

- **3 large eggs**
- **1 cup packed brown sugar**
- **¾ cup fat-free plain yogurt**
- **¼ cup canola oil**
- **2 teaspoons vanilla extract**
- **2½ cups all-purpose flour**
- **3 teaspoons pumpkin pie spice**
- **2 teaspoons baking soda**
- **1 teaspoon salt**
- **3 cups shredded carrots (about 6 medium)**

FROSTING

- **½ cup heavy whipping cream**
- **4 ounces reduced-fat cream cheese**
- **½ cup confectioners' sugar**

1. Preheat oven to 350°. Line bottoms of two greased 9-in. round baking pans with parchment paper; grease paper.

2. Beat first five ingredients until well blended. In another bowl, whisk together flour, pie spice, baking soda and salt; stir into egg mixture. Fold in carrots.

3. Transfer to prepared pans. Bake until a toothpick inserted in center comes out clean, 20-25 minutes. Cool in pans 10 minutes before removing to wire racks; remove paper. Cool completely.

4. For frosting, beat cream until soft peaks form. In another bowl, beat cream cheese and confectioners' sugar until smooth; gradually fold in whipped cream.

5. If cakes are domed, trim tops with a serrated knife. Spread frosting between layers and over top of cake. Refrigerate leftovers.

PER SERVING *1 slice: 241 cal., 9g fat (3g sat. fat), 49mg chol., 375mg sodium, 36g carb. (19g sugars, 1g fiber), 5g pro.*

RUSTIC CRANBERRY TARTS M

PREP: 15 MIN. • **BAKE:** 20 MIN./BATCH
MAKES: 2 TARTS (6 SERVINGS EACH)

- **1 cup orange marmalade**
- **¼ cup sugar**
- **¼ cup all-purpose flour**
- **4 cups fresh or frozen cranberries, thawed**
- **1 package (14.1 ounces) refrigerated pie pastry**
- **1 large egg white, lightly beaten**
- **1 tablespoon coarse sugar**

1. Preheat oven to 425°. In a large bowl, mix marmalade, sugar and flour; stir in cranberries.

2. Unroll one pastry sheet onto a parchment paper-lined baking sheet. Spoon half of the cranberry mixture over pastry to within 2 in. of edge. Fold pastry edge over filling, pleating as you go and leaving a 5-in. opening in the center. Brush folded pastry with egg white and sprinkle with half of the coarse sugar.

3. Bake 18-22 minutes or until crust is golden and filling is bubbly. Repeat with remaining ingredients. Transfer tarts to wire racks to cool.

PER SERVING *1 piece: 260 cal., 9g fat (4g sat. fat), 6mg chol., 144mg sodium, 45g carb. (24g sugars, 2g fiber), 2g pro.*

Bright red cranberries with a kiss of orange marmalade are always perfect for the holidays. I bundle them up in store-bought pastry sheets for easy, gorgeous rustic tarts. —**HOLLY BAUER** WEST BEND, WI

RUSTIC CRANBERRY TARTS

ROSEMARY & THYME LEMON PUDDING CAKES S M (PICTURED ON P. 213)

These simple little cakes are absolutely divine and are perfect with hot tea. Think English tea party! Your guests will love them.

—**CRYSTAL JO BRUNS** ILIFF, CO

PREP: 30 MIN. • **BAKE:** 20 MIN.
MAKES: 6 SERVINGS

- **3 large eggs**
- **2 tablespoons butter, melted, divided**
- **7 tablespoons sugar, divided**
- **1 cup unsweetened vanilla almond milk**
- **2 teaspoons dried rosemary, crushed**
- **2 teaspoons dried thyme**
- **¼ cup all-purpose flour**
- **3 teaspoons grated lemon peel**
- **¼ cup lemon juice**
- **1 tablespoon coarse sugar**

1. Separate eggs; let stand at room temperature 30 minutes. Lightly brush the inside of six 6-oz. ramekins or custard cups with 1 tablespoon melted butter. Dust each with ½ teaspoon sugar.
2. Preheat oven to 350°. In a small saucepan, combine milk and herbs; bring just to a boil. Immediately remove from the heat; let stand 10 minutes. Strain milk through a fine-mesh strainer; discard herbs.
3. Place flour and 2 tablespoons sugar in a large bowl; whisk in yolks, lemon peel, lemon juice, remaining melted butter and strained milk. In a separate bowl, beat the egg whites on medium speed until foamy. Gradually add the remaining 4 tablespoons sugar, 1 tablespoon at a time, beating on high after each addition until sugar is dissolved. Continue beating until stiff glossy peaks form; fold gently into flour mixture. Divide among ramekins.
4. Bake until tops spring back when lightly touched, 17-20 minutes. (Cakes will fall slightly.) Sprinkle with coarse sugar; cool 5 minutes on a wire rack. Serve warm.

PER SERVING *1 serving: 165 cal., 7g fat (3g sat. fat), 103mg chol., 97mg sodium, 23g carb. (17g sugars, 1g fiber), 4g pro.* ***Diabetic Exchanges:*** *1½ starch, 1½ fat.*

PERFECT PLUM & PEACH PIE

PERFECT PLUM & PEACH PIE S M

I created this recipe to fit with in-season summer fruit. The plums give the pie a splash of color as well as flavor, and the cinnamon crumb topping is both easy and excellent!

—**RACHEL JOHNSON** SHIPPENSBURG, PA

PREP: 25 MIN. • **BAKE:** 40 MIN. + COOLING
MAKES: 8 SERVINGS

- **1 sheet refrigerated pie pastry**

FILLING

- **6 medium peaches, peeled and sliced**
- **6 medium black plums, sliced**
- **½ cup all-purpose flour**
- **½ cup confectioners' sugar**
- **½ teaspoon ground cinnamon**
- **½ teaspoon ground nutmeg**

TOPPING

- **¼ cup all-purpose flour**
- **¼ cup packed brown sugar**
- **2 tablespoons butter, softened**
- **¼ teaspoon ground cinnamon**

1. Preheat oven to 375°. Unroll pastry sheet onto a lightly floured surface; roll to a 12-in. circle. Transfer to a 9-in. deep-dish pie plate; trim and flute edge. Refrigerate while preparing the filling.
2. Toss peaches and plums with flour, sugar and spices; transfer to crust. Using a fork, mix topping ingredients until crumbly; sprinkle over fruit.
3. Bake on a lower oven rack until golden brown and bubbly, 40-50 minutes. Cool on a wire rack.

PER SERVING *1 piece: 311 cal., 10g fat (5g sat. fat), 13mg chol., 125mg sodium, 53g carb. (29g sugars, 3g fiber), 4g pro.*

HEALTH TIP *Using a crumb topping instead of a top pastry crust is an easy way to lighten up your favorite fruit pie. Here it saves more than 50 calories and 5 grams of fat.*

SHERBET-FILLED ANGEL FOOD CAKE

SHERBET-FILLED ANGEL FOOD CAKE F S M

Here's a cool way to treat angel food cake—fill it with sherbet or ice cream! We finish this cake with a tart and sweet lime glaze.

—**LEAH REKAU** MILWAUKEE, WI

PREP: 50 MIN. + FREEZING
BAKE: 45 MIN. + COOLING
MAKES: 16 SERVINGS

- **12 large egg whites (about 1⅔ cups)**
- **1 cup cake flour**
- **1½ cups sugar, divided**
- **1 vanilla bean or 1 teaspoon vanilla extract**
- **½ teaspoon cream of tartar**
- **¼ teaspoon salt**
- **2½ to 3 cups raspberry sherbet or ice cream of your choice**

GLAZE

- **2 cups confectioners' sugar**
- **1 teaspoon grated lime peel**
- **3 to 4 tablespoons lime juice**

1. Place egg whites in a large bowl; let stand at room temperature 30 minutes.

2. Preheat oven to 325°. In a small bowl, mix the flour and ¾ cup sugar until blended.

3. Add seeds from the vanilla bean (or extract if using), cream of tartar and salt to the egg whites. Beat on medium speed until soft peaks form. Gradually add remaining ¾ cup sugar, 1 tablespoon at a time, beating on high after each addition until the sugar is dissolved. Continue beating until soft glossy peaks form. Gradually fold in flour mixture, about ½ cup at a time.

4. Gently transfer the batter to an ungreased 10-in. tube pan. Cut through batter with a knife to remove air pockets. Bake on lowest oven rack 45-55 minutes or until top springs back when touched. Immediately invert pan; cool completely in pan, about 1½ hours.

5. Run a knife around sides and center tube of pan. Remove cake to a serving plate. Using a serrated knife, cut a 1-in. slice off top of cake. Hollow out the remaining cake, leaving a 1-in.-thick shell (save removed cake for another use). Fill the tunnel with sherbet, mounding slightly; replace cake top. Wrap cake securely in plastic wrap; freeze overnight.

6. To serve, in a small bowl, mix confectioners' sugar, lime peel and enough lime juice to reach desired consistency. Unwrap cake; spread glaze over top, allowing some to drip down sides. Freeze until serving.

NOTE *To remove the seeds from a vanilla bean, cut bean lengthwise in half with a sharp knife; scrape out the dark, pulpy seeds.*

PER SERVING *1 slice: 193 cal., 1g fat (0 sat. fat), 0 chol., 78mg sodium, 44g carb. (37g sugars, 0 fiber), 3g pro.*

LEMON CUPCAKES WITH STRAWBERRY FROSTING M

I call these my Triple Lemon Whammy Cupcakes because they take full advantage of vibrant citrus flavor. Fresh strawberries really nudge this dessert over the top and make it a summery treat!

—**EMMA SISK** PLYMOUTH, MN

PREP: 20 MIN. • **BAKE:** 25 MIN. + COOLING
MAKES: 2 DOZEN

- **1 package white cake mix (regular size)**
- **¼ cup lemon curd**
- **3 tablespoons lemon juice**
- **3 teaspoons grated lemon peel**
- **½ cup butter, softened**
- **3½ cups confectioners' sugar**
- **¼ cup seedless strawberry jam**
- **2 tablespoons 2% milk**
- **1 cup sliced fresh strawberries**

1. Line 24 muffin cups with paper liners. Prepare cake mix batter according to package directions, decreasing water by 1 tablespoon and adding lemon curd, lemon juice and lemon peel before mixing batter. Fill prepared cups about two-thirds full. Bake and cool cupcakes as package directs.

2. In a large bowl, beat the butter, confectioners' sugar, jam and milk until smooth. Frost the cooled cupcakes; top with strawberries. Refrigerate leftovers.

PER SERVING *1 cupcake: 219 cal., 7g fat (3g sat. fat), 13mg chol., 171mg sodium, 23g carb. (29g sugars, 0 fiber), 1g pro.* ***Diabetic Exchanges:*** *1½ starch, 1½ fat.*

LEMON CUPCAKES WITH STRAWBERRY FROSTING

TRIPLE PEAR PIE

PRETTY PEACH TART S M

(PICTURED ON P. 212)

This is the first dessert I think of when that blushed golden fruit finally arrives at fruit stands. What a delightful way to celebrate the arrival of peaches. It's just plain perfection. You can make this tart with other varieties of fruit, too.

—**LORRAINE CALAND** SHUNIAH, ON

PREP: 30 MIN. • **BAKE:** 40 MIN. + COOLING
MAKES: 8 SERVINGS

- **¼ cup butter, softened**
- **3 tablespoons sugar**
- **¼ teaspoon ground nutmeg**
- **1 cup all-purpose flour**

FILLING

- **2 pounds peaches (about 7 medium), peeled and sliced**
- **⅓ cup sugar**
- **2 tablespoons all-purpose flour**
- **¼ teaspoon ground cinnamon**
- **⅛ teaspoon almond extract**
- **¼ cup sliced almonds**
- **Whipped cream, optional**

1. Preheat oven to 375°. Cream butter, sugar and nutmeg until light and fluffy. Beat in flour until blended (mixture will be dry). Press firmly onto bottom and up sides of an ungreased 9-in. fluted tart pan with removable bottom.

2. Place on a baking sheet. Bake on a middle oven rack until lightly browned, 10-12 minutes. Cool on a wire rack.

3. In a large bowl, toss peaches with sugar, flour, cinnamon and extract; add to crust. Sprinkle with almonds.

4. Bake tart on a lower oven rack until crust is golden brown and peaches are tender, 40-45 minutes. Cool on a wire rack. If desired, serve with whipped cream.

PER SERVING *1 piece: 222 cal., 8g fat (4g sat. fat), 15mg chol., 46mg sodium, 36g carb. (21g sugars, 3g fiber), 4g pro.*

HEALTH TIP *To dollop or not to dollop? Calories per ¼ cup: whipped topping, 50; light ice cream, 50; ice cream, 70; sweetened whipped cream, 114.*

TRIPLE PEAR PIE S M

I won a giveaway one year and received three different kinds of pears. After sharing a few with family, I decided to use the rest to prepare a pie for our dessert at Easter that year. Put this together with some vanilla ice cream and it's the perfect pairing!

—**JENN TIDWELL** FAIR OAKS, CA

PREP: 30 MIN. + CHILLING
BAKE: 50 MIN. + COOLING
MAKES: 10 SERVINGS

- **2 tablespoons fat-free milk**
- **1 teaspoon lemon juice**
- **¾ cup all-purpose flour**
- **½ cup whole wheat flour**
- **2 tablespoons sugar**
- **⅛ teaspoon salt**
- **⅓ cup cold butter, cubed**
- **1 to 3 tablespoons ice water**

FILLING

- **½ cup sugar**
- **⅓ cup all-purpose flour**
- **½ teaspoon ground cinnamon**
- **⅛ teaspoon salt**
- **2 medium ripe Anjou pears**
- **2 medium ripe Bartlett pears**
- **2 medium Bosc pears**
- **3 tablespoons lemon juice**

STREUSEL

- **¼ cup all-purpose flour**
- **¼ cup packed brown sugar**
- **2 tablespoons butter, softened**

1. Mix milk and lemon juice; let stand 5 minutes. Place the flours, sugar and salt in a food processor; pulse until blended. Add butter; pulse until butter is the size of peas. While pulsing, add milk mixture and just enough ice water to form moist crumbs. Shape dough into a disk; wrap in plastic wrap. Refrigerate 1 hour or overnight.

2. Preheat oven to 375°. On a lightly floured surface, roll the dough to a ⅛-in.-thick circle; transfer to a 9-in. deep dish pie plate. Trim pastry to ½ in. beyond rim of plate; flute edge.

3. Mix sugar, flour, cinnamon and salt. Peel and thinly slice pears; toss with flour mixture and lemon juice. Place in crust.

4. Using a fork, mix streusel ingredients until crumbly; sprinkle over filling. Bake on a lower oven rack until golden brown and filling is bubbly, 50-60 minutes. Cool on a wire rack.

PER SERVING *1 piece: 288 cal., 9g fat (5g sat. fat), 22mg chol., 130mg sodium, 52g carb. (29g sugars, 4g fiber), 3g pro.*

GINGER PLUM TART

GINGER PLUM TART S M

Sweet cravings, begone: This free-form plum tart is done in only 35 minutes. Plus, it's awesome when served warm.

—*TASTE OF HOME* TEST KITCHEN

PREP: 15 MIN. • **BAKE:** 20 MIN. + COOLING
MAKE: 8 SERVINGS

- **1 sheet refrigerated pie pastry**
- **3½ cups sliced fresh plums (about 10 medium)**
- **3 tablespoons plus 1 teaspoon coarse sugar, divided**
- **1 tablespoon cornstarch**
- **2 teaspoons finely chopped crystallized ginger**
- **1 large egg white**
- **1 tablespoon water**

1. Preheat oven to 400°. On a work surface, unroll pastry sheet. Roll to a 12-in. circle. Transfer to a parchment paper-lined baking sheet.

2. In a large bowl, toss plums with 3 tablespoons sugar and cornstarch. Arrange plums on pastry to within 2 in. of edges; sprinkle with ginger. Fold pastry edge over plums, pleating as you go.

3. In a small bowl, whisk egg white and water; brush over folded pastry. Sprinkle with remaining sugar.

4. Bake 20-25 minutes or until crust is golden brown. Cool on pan on a wire rack. Serve warm or at room temperature.

PER SERVING *1 piece: 190 calories, 7g fat (3g saturated fat), 5mg cholesterol, 108mg sodium, 30g carbohydrate (14g sugars, 1g fiber), 2g protein.* ***Diabetic Exchanges:*** *1-1/2 starch, 1 fat, 1/2 fruit.*

PINEAPPLE UPSIDE-DOWN MUFFIN CAKES M

PREP: 25 MIN. • **BAKE:** 15 MIN.
MAKES: 1 DOZEN

- **⅓ cup packed brown sugar or 3 tablespoons brown sugar substitute blend**
- **2 tablespoons butter, melted**
- **3 canned pineapple slices**

CAKES

- **⅓ cup butter, softened**
- **½ cup sugar**
- **1 large egg**
- **½ teaspoon vanilla extract**
- **1 cup all-purpose flour**
- **1 teaspoon baking powder**
- **¼ teaspoon baking soda**
- **¼ teaspoon salt**
- **½ cup fat-free lemon or vanilla Greek yogurt**
- **¼ cup fat-free milk**

1. Preheat the oven to 350°. Coat 12 muffin cups with cooking spray. Mix brown sugar and melted butter; divide among prepared cups. Quarter each pineapple slice; place one piece in each cup.

2. For cakes, cream butter and sugar until light and fluffy; beat in the egg and vanilla. In another bowl, whisk together flour, baking powder, baking soda and salt; add to creamed mixture alternately with yogurt and milk, beating well after each addition.

3. Fill prepared cups two-thirds full. Bake until a toothpick inserted in the center comes out clean, 12-15 minutes. Cool in pan 5 minutes; invert onto a serving plate. Serve warm or at room temperature.

PER SERVING *1 muffin cake: 177 cal., 8g fat (5g sat. fat), 34mg chol., 178mg sodium, 25g carb. (17g sugars, 0 fiber), 3g pro.* ***Diabetic Exchanges:*** *1½ starch, 1½ fat.*

A friend submitted this recipe to a cookbook our school district was compiling. The first time I made them, the whole family declared them a winner. Delicious and healthy to boot, they remain favorites to this day. —**JOAN HALLFORD** NORTH RICHLAND HILLS, TX

PINEAPPLE UPSIDE-DOWN MUFFIN CAKES

BUTTERNUT HARVEST PIES

BUTTERNUT HARVEST PIES M

This egg- and dairy-free pie is a great alternative to standard pumpkin pie. We love to make the pies with squash from our garden. Feel free to spice up this pie even more by adding more of your favorite spices. You'll be glad the recipe makes two.

—**JULIANA THETFORD** ELLWOOD CITY, PA

PREP: 65 MIN. • **BAKE:** 40 MIN. + CHILLING
MAKES: 2 PIES (6 SERVINGS EACH)

- **1 large butternut squash (about 4 pounds)**
- **1 package (10½ ounces) silken firm tofu**
- **1 cup sugar**
- **⅓ cup cornstarch**
- **2 tablespoons honey**
- **2 teaspoons ground cinnamon**
- **1 teaspoon ground ginger**
- **1 teaspoon ground nutmeg or ground mace**
- **Two 9-inch graham cracker crusts (about 6 ounces each)**
- **Sweetened whipped cream, optional**

1. Preheat oven to 400°. Halve squash lengthwise; discard seeds. Place squash on a baking sheet, cut side down. Roast until tender, 45-55 minutes. Cool the squash slightly. Scoop out pulp and mash (you should have about 4 cups).

2. Place tofu, sugar, cornstarch, honey and spices in a food processor; process until smooth. Add squash; pulse just until blended. Divide between crusts.

3. Bake at 400° until a knife inserted near the center comes out clean, 40-50 minutes. Cool 1 hour on a wire rack. Refrigerate, covered, until cold. If desired, serve with whipped cream.

PER SERVING *1 piece: 281 cal., 8g fat (2g sat. fat), 0 chol., 174mg sodium, 51g carb. (35g sugars, 3g fiber), 4g pro.*

CHOCOLATE ESPRESSO CAKE M

You can have your cake and eat it too with this lower-calorie treat. The rich chocolate cake is draped with a sweet cherry-port sauce.

—**JACYN SIEBERT** SAN FRANCISCO, CA

PREP: 30 MIN. • **BAKE:** 15 MIN. + COOLING
MAKES: 12 SERVINGS

- **2 large eggs**
- **2 large egg whites**
- **½ cup buttermilk**
- **⅓ cup strong brewed coffee**
- **3 tablespoons canola oil**
- **1 teaspoon vanilla extract**
- **1 cup all-purpose flour**
- **⅔ cup baking cocoa**
- **½ cup packed brown sugar**
- **1½ teaspoons baking powder**
- **¼ teaspoon baking soda**
- **¼ teaspoon salt**

TOPPING

- **½ cup cherry juice blend**
- **½ cup port wine or additional cherry juice**
- **⅔ cup dried tart cherries**
- **2 tablespoons honey**
- **Dash salt**
- **1 package (12 ounces) frozen pitted dark sweet cherries, thawed and halved**
- **1 tablespoon cornstarch**
- **2 tablespoons cold water**
- **½ teaspoon almond extract**
- **1 cup sweetened whipped cream**

1. Preheat oven to 350°. Coat a 9-in. round baking pan with cooking spray; dust with cocoa, tapping out extra.

2. In a large bowl, beat eggs, egg whites, buttermilk, coffee, oil and vanilla until well blended. In another bowl, whisk together flour, cocoa, brown sugar, baking powder, baking soda and salt; gradually beat into egg mixture. Transfer to prepared pan.

3. Bake until a toothpick inserted in center comes out clean, 15-20 minutes. Cool 10 minutes before removing from pan to a wire rack. Cool completely.

4. In a large saucepan, combine cherry juice, wine, dried cherries, honey and salt; bring to a boil. Reduce heat; simmer, uncovered, until liquid is reduced by half, about 10 minutes. Stir in halved cherries; cook 2 minutes.

5. Mix cornstarch and water until smooth; stir into cherry mixture. Bring to a boil, stirring constantly; cook and stir mixture until thickened, 1-2 minutes. Remove from heat; stir in extract. Cool. Serve cake with cherry sauce and whipped cream.

PER SERVING *1 slice: 255 cal., 9g fat (3g sat. fat), 43mg chol., 306mg sodium, 39g carb. (24g sugars, 2g fiber), 5g pro.*

TOP TIP

No buttermilk? Then place 1½ teaspoons of white vinegar or lemon juice in a measuring cup and add enough milk to measure ½ cup. Stir, then let stand for 5 minutes.

235

232

243

Treat Yourself

"My husband enjoys when I make dessert. Fruit crisps are easy and quick to prepare, so I make them often! This fall-flavored grilled version features fresh pears and items that I had on hand. My husband and I loved it."

—RONNA FARLEY ROCKVILLE, MD
about her recipe, Grilled Cranberry Pear Crumble, on page 240

BUTTERMILK PEACH ICE CREAM

BUTTERMILK PEACH ICE CREAM S M

My mother's family owned peach orchards in Missouri, and I live in Tennessee, a top consumer of buttermilk. This summery ice cream combines my past and present.

—**KIM HIGGINBOTHAM** KNOXVILLE, TN

PREP: 15 MIN. + CHILLING
PROCESS: 30 MIN./BATCH + FREEZING
MAKES: 2 QUARTS

- **2 pounds ripe peaches (about 7 medium), peeled and quartered**
- **½ cup sugar**
- **½ cup packed brown sugar**
- **1 tablespoon lemon juice**
- **1 teaspoon vanilla extract**
- **Pinch salt**
- **2 cups buttermilk**
- **1 cup heavy whipping cream**

1. Place peaches in a food processor; process until smooth. Add sugars, lemon juice, vanilla and salt; process until blended.

2. In a large bowl, mix buttermilk and cream. Stir in peach mixture. Refrigerate, covered, for 1 hour or until cold.

3. Fill cylinder of ice cream maker no more than two-thirds full. Freeze according to the manufacturer's directions, refrigerating any remaining mixture to process later. Transfer the ice cream to freezer containers, allowing headspace for expansion. Freeze 2-4 hours or until firm. Let ice cream stand at room temperature 10 minutes before serving.

PER SERVING *½ cup: 137 cal., 6g fat (4g sat. fat), 22mg chol., 75mg sodium, 20g carb. (19g sugars, 1g fiber), 2g pro.* ***Diabetic Exchanges:*** *1 starch, 1 fat.*

FRUITY DESSERT TACOS M

Here's a dessert you can feel good about eating! Fresh fruit and zippy jalapenos make a tasty filling for sweetened tortillas. Fruit-flavored yogurt or honey can be drizzled over the tortillas if desired.

—**DIANE HALFERTY** CORPUS CHRISTI, TX

START TO FINISH: 15 MIN.
MAKES: 2 SERVINGS

- **3 teaspoons sugar, divided**
- **½ teaspoon ground cinnamon**
- **½ cup cubed fresh pineapple**
- **½ cup sliced peeled kiwifruit**
- **½ cup sliced fresh strawberries**
- **1 teaspoon chopped seeded jalapeno pepper, optional**
- **2 whole wheat tortillas (8 inches), room temperature**
- **Butter-flavored cooking spray**

1. Mix 2 teaspoons sugar and cinnamon. In another bowl, toss fruit with remaining sugar and, if desired, jalapeno.

2. Coat both sides of tortillas with cooking spray. In a large skillet, cook tortillas until golden brown, 45-60 seconds per side.

3. Remove from pan and dust immediately with sugar mixture. Top with fruit mixture; fold to serve.

NOTE *Wear disposable gloves when cutting hot peppers; the oils can burn skin. Avoid touching your face.*

PER SERVING *1 taco: 227 cal., 4g fat (0 sat. fat), 0 chol., 172mg sodium, 43g carb. (17g sugars, 5g fiber), 5g pro.*

FRUITY DESSERT TACOS

My family loves cookie bars, like this luscious dessert with a buttery crust, raspberry jam, chocolate and meringue. Bake it for a buffet, party or household treat.

—**NANCY HEISHMAN** LAS VEGAS, NV

RASPBERRY-CHOCOLATE MERINGUE SQUARES

RASPBERRY-CHOCOLATE MERINGUE SQUARES S M

PREP: 15 MIN. • **BAKE:** 20 MIN. + COOLING
MAKES: 9 SERVINGS

- **3 large egg whites, divided**
- **¼ cup butter, softened**
- **¼ cup confectioners' sugar**
- **1 cup all-purpose flour**
- **¼ cup sugar**
- **½ cup seedless raspberry jam**
- **3 tablespoons miniature semisweet chocolate chips**

1. Preheat oven to 350°. Place two egg whites in a small bowl; let stand at room temperature 30 minutes. Meanwhile, in a large bowl, cream butter and confectioners' sugar until light and fluffy. Beat in remaining egg white; gradually add flour to creamed mixture, mixing well.

2. Press into a greased 8-in. square baking pan. Bake 9-11 minutes or until lightly browned. Increase oven setting to 400°.

3. With clean beaters, beat reserved egg whites on medium speed until foamy. Gradually add the sugar, 1 tablespoon at a time, beating on high after each addition until sugar is dissolved. Continue beating until stiff glossy peaks form. Spread jam over crust; sprinkle with chocolate chips. Spread meringue over top.

4. Bake for 8-10 minutes or until meringue is lightly browned. Cool completely in pan on a wire rack.

PER SERVING *1 bar: 198 cal., 6g fat (4g sat. fat), 14mg chol., 60mg sodium, 33g carb. (22g sugars, 1g fiber), 3g pro.* ***Diabetic Exchanges:*** *2 starch, 1 fat.*

STRAWBERRY SCHAUM TORTE S M

This low-fat recipe was handed down from my German grandma. She took great pride in serving this delicate dessert. Whenever I make it, I'm filled with warm memories of my childhood.

—**DIANE KRISMAN** HALES CORNERS, WI

PREP: 15 MIN. • **BAKE:** 50 MIN. + COOLING
MAKES: 12 SERVINGS

- **8 large egg whites**
- **1 tablespoon white vinegar**
- **1 teaspoon vanilla extract**
- **¼ teaspoon salt**
- **2 cups sugar**
- **3 cups sliced fresh strawberries**
- **1½ cups whipped cream**

1. Place egg whites in a large bowl and let stand at room temperature for 30 minutes.

2. Preheat oven to 300°. Add vinegar, vanilla and salt to egg whites; beat on medium speed until soft peaks form. Gradually beat in the sugar, about 2 tablespoons at a time, on high until stiff glossy peaks form and sugar is dissolved.

3. Spread into a greased 10-in. springform pan. Bake 50-60 minutes or until lightly browned. Remove to a wire rack to cool (meringue will fall).

4. Serve with strawberries and whipped cream. Store leftovers in the refrigerator.

PER SERVING *1 piece: 206 cal., 6g fat (3g sat. fat), 20mg chol., 92mg sodium, 37g carb. (36g sugars, 1g fiber), 3g pro.*

DID YOU KNOW?

Schaum torte is a classic Austrian dessert consisting of a meringue shell, fresh fruit (usually strawberries) and whipped cream. Ice cream is used sometimes, too.

MERINGUE SHELLS WITH LEMON CURD F S M

We love a dazzling dessert of meringue shells filled with lemon curd. It's sweet and tart, crunchy and fluffy. Top it with whipped cream and berries.

—**KRIS BRILL** MILWAUKEE, WI

PREP: 25 MIN. + CHILLING
BAKE: 45 MIN. + STANDING
MAKES: 12 SERVINGS

- **6 large egg whites**
- **1 teaspoon white vinegar**
- **1 teaspoon vanilla extract**
- **¼ teaspoon salt**
- **¼ teaspoon cream of tartar**
- **1½ cups sugar**

LEMON CURD

- **½ cup sugar**
- **2 tablespoons potato starch**
- **1 cup water**
- **½ cup plus 1 tablespoon lemon juice, divided**
- **3 large eggs, beaten**
- **2 teaspoons grated lemon peel**
- **Whipped topping and fresh berries, optional**

1. Place egg whites in a large bowl; let stand at room temperature 30 minutes.
2. Preheat oven to 225°. Add vinegar, vanilla, salt and cream of tartar to egg whites; beat on medium speed until foamy. Gradually add sugar, 1 tablespoon at a time, beating on high after each addition until sugar is dissolved. Continue beating until stiff glossy peaks form.
3. Cut a small hole in tip of a pastry bag or in a corner of a food-safe plastic bag; insert a large star tip. Transfer meringue to bag. On a parchment paper-lined baking sheet, pipe meringue into twelve 3-in. round disks, building up the sides with meringue to form shells. Bake 45-50 minutes or until set and dry. Turn off oven (do not open door); leave meringues in oven 1 hour. Remove from oven; cool completely on baking sheet.
4. Meanwhile, in a small heavy saucepan, mix sugar and potato starch. Whisk in water and 1/2 cup lemon juice until smooth. Cook and stir over medium-high heat until thickened and bubbly. Reduce heat to low; cook and stir 2 minutes longer.
5. Remove from heat. Stir a small amount of hot mixture into eggs; return all to pan, stirring constantly. Bring to a gentle boil; cook and stir 2 minutes. Remove from heat. Gently stir in lemon peel and remaining lemon juice. Transfer to a small bowl; cool without stirring. Refrigerate, covered, until cold.
6. Spoon lemon curd into meringue shells. If desired, top with whipped topping and berries.

HEALTH TIP *At a little more than 100 calories each, these meringue shells make a light, special treat. Try them filled with a scoop of sorbet, fresh fruit or chocolate pudding.*

PER SERVING *1 meringue shell with 2 tablespoons curd: 146 cal., 0 fat (0 sat. fat), 0 chol., 77mg sodium, 36g carb. (34g sugars, 0 fiber), 2g pro.*

MERINGUE SHELLS WITH LEMON CURD

POACHED PEARS WITH CHOCOLATE SAUCE

POACHED PEARS WITH CHOCOLATE SAUCE F S M

Poached pears are always an elegant dessert, especially when they're drizzled with a homemade chocolate sauce.
—**PATTI HAGGARD** PAYSON, AZ

PREP: 15 MIN. • **COOK:** 35 MIN.
MAKES: 2 SERVINGS

- **2 medium firm pears**
- **2 cups water**
- **¾ teaspoon clear vanilla extract**
- **1 cinnamon stick (2 inches)**
- **¼ teaspoon ground nutmeg**
- **2 tablespoons sugar**
- **1 tablespoon baking cocoa**
- **1 teaspoon cornstarch**
- **⅛ teaspoon ground cinnamon**
- **6 tablespoons 2% milk**

1. Core pears from bottom, leaving stems intact. Peel pears. Cut 1/4 in. from bottom to level if necessary.
2. Place the pears in a large saucepan; add the water, vanilla, cinnamon stick and nutmeg. Bring to a boil. Reduce heat; cover and simmer pears for 35-40 minutes or until they are almost tender.
3. Meanwhile, in a small saucepan, combine the sugar, cocoa, cornstarch and cinnamon. Gradually whisk in milk until smooth. Bring to a boil over medium-high heat; cook and stir for 1-2 minutes or until thickened and bubbly. Cool.
4. Drain pears; place on dessert plates. Drizzle with chocolate sauce.
PER SERVING *187 cal., 2g fat (1g sat. fat), 3mg chol., 23mg sodium, 43g carb. (32g sugars, 5g fiber), 3g pro.*

FRUIT 'N' CAKE KABOBS

M FAST FIX

A neighbor served these kabobs at a family picnic and brought some over for us to sample. I was pleasantly surprised at the tasty toasted cake and juicy grilled fruit.
—**MARY ANN DELL** PHOENIXVILLE, PA

START TO FINISH: 25 MIN.
MAKES: 8 SERVINGS

- **½ cup apricot preserves**
- **1 tablespoon water**
- **1 tablespoon butter**
- **⅛ teaspoon ground cinnamon**
- **⅛ teaspoon ground nutmeg**
- **3 medium nectarines, quartered**
- **3 medium peaches, quartered**
- **3 medium plums, quartered**
- **1 loaf (10¾ ounces) frozen pound cake, thawed and cut into 1½-inch cubes**

1. In a small saucepan, combine the first five ingredients; cook and stir over medium heat until blended. Remove from heat.
2. On eight metal or soaked wooden skewers, alternately thread fruit and pound cake. Place on a greased rack over medium heat. Grill, uncovered, until lightly browned and fruit is tender, brushing occasionally with apricot mixture.
PER SERVING *1 kabob: 259 cal., 8g fat (4g sat. fat), 58mg chol., 161mg sodium, 46g carb. (33g sugars, 3g fiber), 4g pro.*

FRUIT 'N' CAKE KABOBS

RASPBERRY-BANANA SOFT SERVE F S M

PREP: 10 MIN. + FREEZING • **MAKES:** 2½ CUPS

- **4 medium ripe bananas**
- **½ cup fat-free plain yogurt**
- **1 to 2 tablespoons maple syrup**
- **½ cup frozen unsweetened raspberries**
- **Fresh raspberries, optional**

1. Thinly slice bananas; transfer to a large resealable plastic freezer bag. Arrange slices in a single layer; freeze overnight.
2. Pulse bananas in a food processor until finely chopped. Add yogurt, maple syrup and raspberries. Process just until smooth, scraping the sides as needed. Serve immediately, adding fresh berries if desired.

PER SERVING *½ cup: 104 cal., 0 fat (0 sat. fat), 1mg chol., 15mg sodium, 26g carb. (15g sugars, 2g fiber), 2g pro.* ***Diabetic Exchanges:*** *1 fruit, ½ starch.*

CHOCOLATE-PEANUT BUTTER SOFT SERVE
Substitute 2 tablespoons each creamy peanut butter and baking cocoa for the raspberries; proceed as directed.

When I make this ice cream, I mix and match bananas for their ripeness. Very ripe ones add more banana flavor, and less ripe ones lend a fluffier texture.
—**MELISSA HANSEN** MILWAUKEE, WI

RASPBERRY-BANANA SOFT SERVE

FROZEN WATERMELON LEMON CREAM TARTS

FROZEN WATERMELON LEMON CREAM TARTS F S C M

These fruit tarts are so refreshing on a hot summer day! They are extremely healthy and convenient, and just a few ingredients means they're easy to make.
—**BETHANY DICARLO** HARLEYSVILLE, PA

PREP: 20 MIN. + FREEZING • **MAKES:** 8 SERVINGS

- **2 cups cubed seedless watermelon**
- **1 cup fat-free plain Greek yogurt**
- **2 tablespoons honey**
- **1½ teaspoons grated lemon peel**
- **1 tablespoon lemon juice**
- **2 tablespoons sliced almonds, toasted**
- **Halved lemon slices, optional**

1. Line eight muffin cups with paper liners. Puree the watermelon in a food processor; divide among prepared cups. Freeze 1 hour.
2. Mix yogurt, honey, lemon peel and lemon juice; spoon over watermelon layer. Sprinkle with almonds. Freeze until firm, about 1 hour. If desired, top tarts with lemon slices before serving.

NOTE *To toast nuts, cook in a skillet over low heat until lightly browned, stirring occasionally.*

PER SERVING *1 tart: 55 cal., 1g fat (0 sat. fat), 0 chol., 17mg sodium, 10g carb. (9g sugars, 0 fiber), 4g pro.* ***Diabetic Exchanges:*** *½ starch.*

MINT TWIST MERINGUES F S C M

Meringues flavored with peppermint are a yuletide tradition, but I also use extracts like almond and vanilla to make these crispy delights year-round.

—**CHERYL PERRY** HERTFORD, NC

PREP: 30 MIN. • **BAKE:** 40 MIN. + STANDING • **MAKES:** 2 DOZEN

- **2 large egg whites**
- **½ teaspoon cream of tartar**
- **¼ teaspoon peppermint extract**
- **½ cup sugar**
- **¼ cup crushed red and green mint candies**

1. Place egg whites in a small bowl; let stand at room temperature 30 minutes.

2. Preheat oven to 250°. Add cream of tartar and extract to egg whites; beat on medium speed until foamy. Gradually add sugar, 1 tablespoon at a time, beating on high after each addition until sugar is dissolved. Continue beating until stiff glossy peaks form. Cut a small hole in the tip of a pastry bag or in a corner of a food-safe plastic bag; insert a small star tip. Transfer meringue to bag. Pipe 1½-in.-diameter cookies 2 in. apart onto parchment paper-lined baking sheets. Sprinkle with candies.

3. Bake 40-45 minutes or until firm to the touch. Turn oven off; leave meringues in oven 1 hour. Remove from pans to a wire rack. Store in an airtight container.

PER SERVING *1 cookie: 17 cal., 0 fat (0 sat. fat), 0 chol., 5mg sodium, 4g carb. (3g sugars, 0 fiber), 0 pro.*

MINT TWIST MERINGUES

STRAWBERRY POT STICKERS F S C M

(PICTURED ON P. 229)

My wife and daughter love this unusual dessert. I combined my favorite fruit—strawberries with chocolate and cinnamon—with my favorite dim sum dish to create this surprise combo.

—**RICK BROWNE** RIDGEFIELD, WA

PREP: 30 MIN. + COOLING • **COOK:** 10 MIN./BATCH
MAKES: 32 POT STICKERS (⅔ CUP SAUCE)

- **3 ounces milk chocolate, chopped**
- **¼ cup half-and-half cream**
- **1 teaspoon butter**
- **1 teaspoon vanilla extract**
- **¼ teaspoon ground cinnamon**

POT STICKERS

- **2 cups chopped fresh strawberries**
- **3 ounces milk chocolate, chopped**
- **1 tablespoon brown sugar**
- **¼ teaspoon ground cinnamon**
- **32 pot sticker or gyoza wrappers**
- **1 large egg, lightly beaten**
- **2 tablespoons canola oil, divided**
- **½ cup water, divided**

1. Place chocolate in a small bowl. In a small saucepan, bring cream and butter just to a boil. Pour over chocolate; whisk until smooth. Stir in vanilla and cinnamon. Cool to room temperature, stirring occasionally.

2. For pot stickers, in a small bowl, toss strawberries and chopped chocolate with brown sugar and cinnamon. Place 1 tablespoon mixture in the center of each gyoza wrapper. (Cover remaining wrappers with a damp paper towel until ready to use.)

3. Moisten wrapper edges with egg. Fold wrapper over filling; seal edges, pleating the front side several times to form a pleated pouch. Stand pot stickers on a work surface to flatten bottoms; curve slightly to form crescent shapes, if desired.

4. In a large skillet, heat 1 tablespoon oil over medium-high heat. Arrange half of the pot stickers, flat side down, in concentric circles in pan; cook 1-2 minutes or until bottoms are golden brown. Add ¼ cup water; bring to a simmer. Cook, covered, 3-5 minutes or until water is almost absorbed and wrappers are tender.

5. Cook, uncovered, 1 minute or until bottoms are crisp and water is completely evaporated. Repeat with remaining pot stickers. Serve with sauce.

PER SERVING *1 pot sticker with 1 teaspoon sauce: 58 cal., 3g fat (1g sat. fat), 6mg chol., 18mg sodium, 8g carb. (4g sugars, 0 fiber), 1g pro.* ***Diabetic Exchanges:*** *½ starch, ½ fat.*

CITRUS GINGERBREAD COOKIES

CITRUS GINGERBREAD COOKIES F S C M

Orange and lemon zest give gingerbread cutouts a refreshing twist. Brushing a honey glaze over the top adds a subtle shine and extra touch of sweetness.

—**MONIQUE HOOKER** DESOTO, WI

PREP: 40 MIN. + CHILLING
BAKE: 10 MIN./BATCH + COOLING
MAKES: 6 DOZEN

- **¾ cup sugar**
- **½ cup honey**
- **½ cup molasses**
- **½ cup unsalted butter, cubed**
- **1 large egg**
- **3½ cups all-purpose flour**
- **¼ cup ground almonds**
- **2 teaspoons baking powder**
- **2 teaspoons grated lemon peel**
- **2 teaspoons grated orange peel**
- **1 teaspoon each ground cardamom, ginger, nutmeg, cinnamon and cloves**

GLAZE

- **½ cup honey**
- **2 tablespoons water**

1. In a large saucepan, combine sugar, honey and molasses. Bring to a boil; remove from heat. Let stand 20 minutes. Stir in butter; let stand 20 minutes longer.

2. Beat in egg. In another bowl, whisk flour, almonds, baking powder, lemon peel, orange peel and spices; gradually beat into sugar mixture. Refrigerate, covered, 8 hours or overnight.

3. Preheat oven to 375°. On a lightly floured surface, divide dough into three portions. Roll each portion to ¼-in. thickness. Cut with a floured 2-in. tree-shaped cookie cutter. Place 2 in. apart on baking sheets coated with cooking spray.

4. Bake 7-8 minutes or until lightly browned. Cool on pans 1 minute. Remove to wire racks to cool completely. In a small bowl, mix glaze ingredients; brush over cookies. Let stand until set.

TO MAKE AHEAD *Dough can be made 2 days in advance. Wrap in plastic wrap and place in a resealable bag. Store in the refrigerator.*

FREEZE OPTION *Freeze undecorated cookies in freezer containers. To use, thaw in covered containers and decorate as directed.*

PER SERVING *1 cookie: 66 cal., 2g fat (1g sat. fat), 6mg chol., 13mg sodium, 12g carb. (7g sugars, 0 fiber), 1g pro.* ***Diabetic Exchanges:*** *1 starch, ½ fat.*

TWO-BERRY PAVLOVA S M

Here's a light and airy dessert that I first tried in Ireland. When I got home, I made it for my kids, who loved to build their own with their favorite fruits. The whipped cream makes for icing on the cake!

—**NORMA STEVENSON** EAGAN, MN

PREP: 20 MIN. + STANDING
BAKE: 45 MIN. + COOLING
MAKES: 12 SERVINGS

- **4 large egg whites**
- **½ teaspoon cream of tartar**
- **1 cup sugar**
- **1 tablespoon cornstarch**
- **1 teaspoon lemon juice**

TOPPINGS

- **2 cups fresh blackberries**
- **2 cups sliced fresh strawberries**
- **¼ cup plus 3 tablespoons sugar, divided**
- **1¼ cups heavy whipping cream**

1. Place the egg whites in a large bowl; let stand at room temperature 30 minutes. Meanwhile, line a baking sheet with parchment paper; draw a 10-in. circle on paper. Invert paper.

2. Preheat oven to 300°. Add cream of tartar to egg whites; beat on medium speed until soft peaks form. Gradually add sugar, 1 tablespoon at a time, beating on high after each addition until sugar is dissolved. Continue beating until stiff glossy peaks form. Fold in cornstarch and lemon juice.

3. Spoon meringue onto prepared pan; with the back of a spoon, shape into a 10-in. circle, forming a shallow well in the center. Bake 45-55 minutes or until meringue is set and dry. Turn off oven (do not open oven door); leave meringue in oven 1 hour. Remove from oven; cool completely on baking sheet.

4. To serve, toss berries with ¼ cup sugar in a small bowl; let stand 10 minutes. Meanwhile, in a large bowl, beat cream until it begins to thicken. Add the remaining sugar; beat until soft peaks form.

5. Remove meringue from parchment paper; place on a serving plate. Spoon whipped cream over top, forming a slight well in the center. Top with berries.

PER SERVING *1 piece: 208 cal., 9g fat (6g sat. fat), 34mg chol., 29mg sodium, 30g carb. (27g sugars, 2g fiber), 2g pro.* ***Diabetic Exchanges:*** *2 starch, 2 fat.*

HEALTH TIP *Anthocyanins are a group of compounds that give berries their vibrant red-violet color. They may help protect against cardiovascular disease and cancer.*

TWO-BERRY PAVLOVA

FIESTA FRUIT CUPS

FIESTA FRUIT CUPS M

FAST FIX

Two types of melon and other fresh fruit combine with peach preserves in this best-of-summer fruit dish. These colorful fruit bowls are great to serve for dessert, brunch or as a snack.

—KAREN ANN BLAND GOVE CITY, KS

START TO FINISH: 25 MIN.
MAKES: 6 SERVINGS

- **6 flour tortillas (6 inches)**
- **3 tablespoons butter, melted**
- **3 tablespoons cinnamon sugar**
- **2 cups halved fresh strawberries**
- **1 cup cubed cantaloupe**
- **1 cup cubed honeydew**
- **1 large navel orange, peeled and sectioned**
- **½ cup peach preserves**
- **Whipped topping, optional**

1. Preheat the oven to 350°. Brush tops of tortillas with melted butter; sprinkle with cinnamon sugar. Cut each tortilla into six wedges; transfer to ungreased baking sheets. Bake tortilla chips until lightly browned, 12-15 minutes. Cool completely.

2. Meanwhile, place strawberries, cantaloupe and honeydew in a large bowl. Cut a thin slice from top and bottom of orange; stand orange upright on a cutting board. With a knife, cut off peel and the outer membrane. Cut along the membrane of each segment to remove fruit and add to bowl. Gently stir in preserves.

3. Divide the fruit among six dessert dishes. Serve with chips and, if desired, whipped topping.

PER SERVING *280 cal., 9g fat (4g sat. fat), 15mg chol., 288mg sodium, 49g carb. (32g sugars, 2g fiber), 4g pro.*

HUMBLE BUMBLE CRUMBLE BARS S M

While developing a treat for my bingo group, I asked my husband for ideas. He suggested a fruity bar. This berry bar is lightly sweet and so easy to make.

—NANCY PHILLIPS PORTLAND, ME

PREP: 30 MIN. • **BAKE:** 45 MIN. + COOLING
MAKES: 15 SERVINGS

- **½ cup butter, softened**
- **¾ cup sugar**
- **1 large egg**
- **2½ cups all-purpose flour**
- **½ teaspoon baking powder**
- **¼ teaspoon salt**
- **¼ cup packed brown sugar**
- **1 teaspoon ground cinnamon**

FILLING

- **2 cups chunky applesauce**
- **½ teaspoon ground cinnamon**
- **⅛ teaspoon ground nutmeg**
- **2 cups fresh blackberries**
- **2 cups fresh raspberries**

1. Preheat oven to 350°. In a large bowl, cream butter and sugar until light and fluffy. Beat in egg. In another bowl, whisk flour, baking powder and salt; gradually beat into the creamed mixture. Reserve ½ cup crumb mixture for topping. Press remaining mixture onto bottom of a greased 13x9-in. baking pan. Bake 12-15 minutes or until lightly browned. Cool on a wire rack.

2. Stir brown sugar and cinnamon into reserved topping; set aside. In a large bowl, combine applesauce, cinnamon and nutmeg until blended. Spread over crust; top with berries and reserved topping. Bake 30-35 minutes or until golden brown. Cool in pan on a wire rack. Cut into bars.

PER SERVING *1 piece: 228 cal., 7g fat (4g sat. fat), 29mg chol., 109mg sodium, 39g carb. (20g sugars, 3g fiber), 3g pro.*

HUMBLE BUMBLE CRUMBLE BARS

HOT QUICK BANANA BOATS

HOT QUICK BANANA BOATS S M FAST FIX

These delicious warm bananas are great on campouts or in the backyard. You can eat them right out of the foil bowl, which makes cleanup easy.

—SHEILA PARKER RENO, NV

START TO FINISH: 20 MIN.
MAKES: 4 SERVINGS

- **4 large unpeeled bananas**
- **8 teaspoons semisweet chocolate chips**
- **8 teaspoons trail mix**
- **¼ cup miniature marshmallows**

1. Place each banana on a 12-in. square of foil; crimp and shape foil around bananas so they sit flat.
2. Cut each banana lengthwise about ½ in. deep, leaving ½ in. uncut at both ends. Gently pull each banana peel open, forming a pocket. Fill pockets with chocolate chips, trail mix and marshmallows.
3. Grill the bananas, covered, over medium heat for 4-5 minutes or until marshmallows are melted and golden brown.

PER SERVING *196 cal., 5g fat (2g sat. fat), 0 chol., 7mg sodium, 41g carb. (24g sugars, 4g fiber), 2g pro.*

READER RAVE

I made these the other night, without the trail mix, and with dark chocolate syrup drizzle after cooking. They were awesome! I think I'll cut them into bite-size pieces before filling & cooking from now on.

— JROSEB TASTEOFHOME.COM

PARMESAN CRISP BAKED APPLES M FAST FIX

A dear friend and I wanted to make an easy apple crisp. We made a Parmesan filling, stuffed the apples and baked them whole. It's pure genius.

—SUSAN STETZEL GAINESVILLE, NY

START TO FINISH: 25 MIN.
MAKES: 2 SERVINGS

- **2 small Braeburn or Gala apples**
- **¼ cup grated Parmesan cheese**
- **3 tablespoons quick-cooking oats**
- **2 tablespoons all-purpose flour**
- **2 tablespoons brown sugar**
- **Dash ground nutmeg**
- **1 tablespoon butter, melted**
- **Honey, optional**

1. Preheat oven to 350°. Cut a ¼-in. slice off top of each apple. Core the apples, leaving bottoms intact; place in a microwave-safe 8-in. square baking dish. Microwave, covered, 3-4 minutes or until tender.
2. In a small bowl, mix cheese, oats, flour, brown sugar and nutmeg; stir in melted butter until crumbly. Carefully fill apples with oat mixture. Bake, uncovered, 12-15 minutes or until topping is golden brown. If desired, drizzle with honey.

NOTE *This recipe was tested in a 1,100-watt microwave.*

PER SERVING *1 stuffed apple: 255 cal., 9g fat (6g sat. fat), 24mg chol., 204mg sodium, 39g carb. (24g sugars, 3g fiber), 6g pro.*

PARMESAN CRISP BAKED APPLES

GRILLED CRANBERRY PEAR CRUMBLE S M FAST FIX

My husband enjoys when I make dessert. Fruit crisps are easy and quick to prepare, so I make them often! This fall-flavored grilled version features fresh pears and items that I had on hand. My husband and I loved it.

—**RONNA FARLEY** ROCKVILLE, MD

START TO FINISH: 30 MIN. • **MAKES:** 6 SERVINGS

- **3 medium ripe pears, sliced**
- **½ cup dried cranberries**
- **¼ cup sugar**
- **2 tablespoons all-purpose flour**
- **¼ teaspoon ground cinnamon**
- **1 tablespoon butter**

TOPPING

- **2 tablespoons butter, melted**
- **¼ teaspoon ground cinnamon**
- **1 cup granola without raisins**

1. Toss the pears and cranberries with sugar, flour and cinnamon. Place 1 tablespoon butter in a 9-in. cast-iron skillet. Place on grill rack over medium heat until butter is melted. Stir in fruit; grill, covered, until pears are tender, 15-20 minutes, stirring occasionally.

2. For topping, mix melted butter and cinnamon; toss with granola. Sprinkle over pears. Grill, covered, 5 minutes. Serve warm.

PER SERVING *258 cal., 9g fat (4g sat. fat), 15mg chol., 54mg sodium, 47g carb. (29g sugars, 7g fiber), 4g pro.*

GRILLED CRANBERRY PEAR CRUMBLE

SUPER SPUD BROWNIES

SUPER SPUD BROWNIES S M

These moist and cake-like brownies came from my mom's old cookbook. Mashed potatoes may seem like an unusual ingredient, but this recipe took first place at a local festival.

—**MARLENE GERER** DENTON, MT

PREP: 15 MIN. • **BAKE:** 25 MIN. • **MAKES:** 16 SERVINGS

- **¾ cup mashed potatoes**
- **½ cup sugar**
- **½ cup packed brown sugar**
- **½ cup canola oil**
- **2 large eggs, lightly beaten**
- **1 teaspoon vanilla extract**
- **½ cup all-purpose flour**
- **⅓ cup cocoa powder**
- **½ teaspoon baking powder**
- **⅛ teaspoon salt**
- **½ cup chopped pecans, optional**
- **Confectioners' sugar**

1. In a large bowl, combine the mashed potatoes, sugars, oil, eggs and vanilla. Combine the flour, cocoa, baking powder and salt; gradually add to potato mixture. Fold in pecans if desired. Transfer to a greased 9-in. square baking pan.

2. Bake at 350° for 23-27 minutes or until a toothpick inserted near the center comes out clean. Cool on a wire rack. Dust with confectioners' sugar. Cut into bars.

PER SERVING *1 brownie: 150 cal., 8g fat (1g sat. fat), 27mg chol., 68mg sodium, 19g carb. (13g sugars, 0 fiber), 2g pro.* ***Diabetic Exchanges:*** *1½ fat, 1 starch.*

BERRIES WITH VANILLA CUSTARD S M

PREP: 20 MIN. + CHILLING • **MAKES:** 4 SERVINGS

- **1 cup half-and-half cream**
- **2 large egg yolks**
- **2 tablespoons sugar**
- **2 teaspoons vanilla extract**
- **2 cups fresh raspberries**

1. In a small heavy saucepan, mix cream, egg yolks and sugar. Cook and stir over low heat until mixture is just thick enough to coat a metal spoon and a thermometer reads at least 160°. Do not allow to boil.
2. Transfer to a bowl; stir in vanilla. Refrigerate, covered, until cold. Serve over raspberries.
PER SERVING *1/2 cup berries with 1/4 cup sauce: 166 cal., 9g fat (5g sat. fat), 132mg chol., 34mg sodium, 16g carb. (11g sugars, 4g fiber), 4g pro.* ***Diabetic Exchanges:*** *1 1/2 fat, 1/2 starch, 1/2 fruit.*

What a delectable way to enjoy fresh raspberries! This recipe also tastes good with other fruit, such as strawberries or peaches.
—SARAH VASQUES MILFORD, NH

BERRIES WITH VANILLA CUSTARD

HEALTHY APPLE CRISP

HEALTHY APPLE CRISP S M FAST FIX

This is the perfect ending to a meal. It's as quick as a boxed cake mix but is a healthier dessert choice. It's ideal in fall when it seems like everyone has a bag of fresh apples to give away!
—TERRI WETZEL ROSEBURG, OR

START TO FINISH: 20 MIN. • **MAKES:** 6 SERVINGS

- **4 medium tart apples, peeled and thinly sliced**
- **¼ cup sugar**
- **1 tablespoon all-purpose flour**
- **2 teaspoons lemon juice**
- **¼ teaspoon ground cinnamon**

TOPPING

- **⅔ cup old-fashioned oats**
- **½ cup packed brown sugar**
- **¼ cup all-purpose flour**
- **½ teaspoon ground cinnamon**
- **3 tablespoons cold butter**
- **Vanilla ice cream, optional**

1. Toss the apples with sugar, flour, lemon juice and cinnamon. Transfer to a greased microwave-safe 9-in. deep-dish pie plate.
2. Mix first four topping ingredients. Cut in butter until crumbly; sprinkle over filling.
3. Cover with waxed paper. Microwave on high until apples are tender, 5-7 minutes. If desired, serve with ice cream.
NOTE *This recipe was tested in a 1,100-watt microwave.*
PER SERVING *1 cup: 252 cal., 7g fat (4g sat. fat), 15mg chol., 66mg sodium, 49g carb. (35g sugars, 3g fiber), 2g pro.*

LOW-FAT VANILLA ICE CREAM F S M

This is my recipe for yummy light ice cream. It's smooth and creamy with wonderful vanilla flavor.

—REBECCA BAIRD SALT LAKE CITY, UT

PREP: 20 MIN. + CHILLING
PROCESS: 20 MIN. + FREEZING
MAKES: 1 QUART

- **¾ cup sugar**
- **3 tablespoons cornstarch**
- **⅛ teaspoon salt**
- **4 cups fat-free half-and-half**
- **2 large egg yolks**
- **3 teaspoons vanilla extract**

1. In a large saucepan, combine sugar, cornstarch and salt. Gradually add half-and-half; stir until smooth. Bring to a boil over medium heat; cook and stir 2 minutes or until thickened. Remove from heat.

2. In a small bowl, whisk a small amount of hot mixture into egg yolks; return all to pan, whisking constantly. Bring to a gentle boil; cook and stir 2 minutes. Remove from heat. Stir in vanilla.

3. Quickly transfer to a bowl; place bowl in a pan of ice water. Stir gently and occasionally for 2 minutes. Press plastic wrap onto surface of custard. Refrigerate several hours or overnight.

4. Fill cylinder of ice cream maker; freeze according to manufacturer's directions. Transfer ice cream to freezer containers, allowing headspace for expansion. Freeze 2-4 hours or until firm.

PER SERVING *½ cup: 182 cal., 1g fat (0 sat. fat), 53mg chol., 139mg sodium, 34g carb. (26g sugars, 0 fiber), 5g pro.* ***Diabetic Exchanges:*** *2 starch.*

TOP TIP

Most vanilla comes from Madagascar and Reunion Island—formerly known as the Bourbon Islands—off the southeast coast of Africa. Bourbon vanilla has a strong, clear vanilla flavor and creamy finish.

BERRY ICE MILK POPS

BERRY ICE MILK POPS F S C M

Kids and adults alike will love these ice pops speckled with colorful mixed berries. They make a healthy and refreshing treat.

—SHARON GUINTA STAMFORD, CT

PREP: 10 MIN. + FREEZING • **MAKES:** 10 POPS

- **1¾ cups whole milk, divided**
- **1 to 2 tablespoons honey**
- **¼ teaspoon vanilla extract**
- **1½ cups fresh raspberries**
- **1 cup fresh blueberries**
- **10 freezer pop molds or 10 paper cups (3 ounces each) and wooden pop sticks**

1. In a microwave, warm ¼ cup milk; stir in honey until blended. Stir in remaining 1½ cups milk and vanilla.

2. Divide berries among molds; cover with milk mixture. Top molds with holders. If using cups, top with foil and insert sticks through foil. Freeze until firm.

PER SERVING *1 pop: 51 cal., 2g fat (1g sat. fat), 4mg chol., 19mg sodium, 8g carb. (6g sugars, 2g fiber), 2g pro.* ***Diabetic Exchanges:*** *½ starch.*

FRESH FRUIT SAUCE F S M FAST FIX

I used to peel the fruits when making this sauce, but not anymore. The skins help hold the juicy summer fruit together when they are left on.

—KATIE KOZIOLEK HARTLAND, MN

START TO FINISH: 10 MIN.
MAKES: 2¼ CUPS

- **1 tablespoon cornstarch**
- **1 cup orange juice**
- **⅓ cup honey**
- **1 cup sliced fresh peaches**
- **1 cup sliced fresh plums**
- **Vanilla ice cream**

1. In a small saucepan, mix cornstarch and orange juice until smooth; stir in honey. Bring to a boil over medium heat; cook and stir until thickened, about 1 minute.

2. Remove from heat; stir in fruit. Serve warm over ice cream.

PER SERVING *¼ cup sauce: 71 cal., 0 fat (0 sat. fat), 0 chol., 1mg sodium, 18g carb. (16g sugars, 1g fiber), 0 pro.* ***Diabetic Exchanges:*** *1 starch.*

FROZEN CHOCOLATE MONKEY TREATS S C M

Everyone needs a fun, friendly way for kids to play with food. These bites are nutty and yummy when you coat bananas in chocolate and dip them into peanuts, sprinkles or coconut.

—SUSAN HEIN BURLINGTON, WI

PREP: 20 MIN. + FREEZING
MAKES: 1½ DOZEN

- **3 medium bananas**
- **1 cup (6 ounces) dark chocolate chips**
- **2 teaspoons shortening**
- **Toppings: chopped peanuts, toasted flaked coconut and/or colored jimmies**

1. Cut each banana into six pieces (about 1 in.). Insert a toothpick into each piece; transfer to a waxed paper-lined baking sheet. Freeze until completely firm, about 1 hour.

2. In a microwave, melt chocolate and shortening; stir until smooth. Dip banana pieces in chocolate mixture; allow excess to drip off. Dip in toppings as desired; return to baking sheet. Freeze at least 30 minutes before serving.

NOTE *To toast coconut, bake in a shallow pan in a 350° oven for 5-10 minutes or cook in a skillet over low heat until golden brown, stirring occasionally.*

PER SERVING *1 treat: 72 cal., 4g fat (2g sat. fat), 0 chol., 0 sodium, 10g carb. (7g sugars, 1g fiber), 1g pro.* ***Diabetic Exchanges:*** *1 fat, ½ starch.*

FROZEN CHOCOLATE MONKEY TREATS

WATERMELON CHOCOLATE CHIP SORBET

WATERMELON CHOCOLATE CHIP SORBET F S M

This pretty sorbet is good even without the mini chocolate chips, but they're fun to include because they look like the dark seeds inside a pink melon.

—RACHEL LEWIS DANVILLE, VA

PREP: 15 MIN. + CHILLING
PROCESS: 30 MIN. + FREEZING
MAKES: 1 QUART

- **1 cup sugar**
- **½ cup water**
- **3 cups chopped seedless watermelon**
- **1 cup orange juice**
- **2 tablespoons lime juice**
- **½ cup miniature semisweet chocolate chips, optional**

1. In a small saucepan, bring sugar and water to a boil. Reduce heat; simmer, uncovered, 5 minutes, stirring occasionally to dissolve sugar. Cool slightly.

2. Place watermelon in a food processor; process until pureed. Add orange juice, lime juice and cooled syrup; process until blended. Transfer to a large bowl; refrigerate, covered, 3 hours or until cold.

3. Pour mixture into cylinder of ice cream freezer. Freeze according to manufacturer's directions; if desired, add chocolate chips during the last 10 minutes of processing. Transfer sorbet to freezer containers, allowing headspace for expansion. Freeze 2-4 hours or until firm.

PER SERVING *½ cup: 129 cal., 0 fat (0 sat. fat), 0 chol., 1mg sodium, 33g carb. (32g sugars, 0 fiber), 1g pro.*

General Recipe Index

• *Table-ready in 30 minutes or less.*

CHICKEN & CHICKEN SAUSAGE

CHOCOLATE & COCOA

COCONUT & COCONUT MILK

COOKIES, BROWNIES & BARS

CORN

CORNMEAL & POLENTA

CRANBERRIES

CREAM CHEESE

CUCUMBERS

DESSERTS *(ALSO SEE CAKES & CUPCAKES; COOKIES, BROWNIES & BARS; PIES & TARTS)*

EGGS

HERBS *(CONTINUED)*

HONEY

HOT PEPPERS

HUMMUS

JAM, JELLY, MARMALADE & PRESERVES

KALE

LAMB

LEMON

LENTILS

LETTUCE *(ALSO SEE ARUGULA)*

INDEX

POTATOES

PUMPKIN

QUINOA

RAISINS

RASPBERRIES

RICE

SALADS

Main Dishes

Side Dishes

SALSA

SANDWICHES & WRAPS

SAUSAGE

SEAFOOD (ALSO SEE FISH)

SIDE DISHES

SLOW COOKER RECIPES

SOUPS, STEWS & CHILI

SPINACH

SQUASH (SEE WINTER SQUASH; ZUCCHINI & SUMMER SQUASH)

STRAWBERRIES

SUN-DRIED TOMATOES

SWEET POTATOES

SWISS CHARD

Alphabetical Index

• *Table-ready in 30 minutes or less.*

INDEX